Human Resource Accounting

Advances in Concepts, Methods, and Applications

Eric G. Flamholtz

Human Resource Accounting

Second Edition, Revised and Expanded

Jossey-Bass Publishers
San Francisco • London • 1985

HUMAN RESOURCE ACCOUNTING
Advances in Concepts, Methods, and Applications
by Eric G. Flamholtz

Library of Congress Cataloging-in-Publication Data

Flamholtz, Eric.
Human resource accounting.

(The Jossey-Bass management series)
Bibliography: p. 356
Includes index.
1. Human capital—Accounting. I. Title. II. Series.
HF5681.H8F55 1985 658.3 85-45053
ISBN 0-87589-657-X (alk. paper)

Manufactured in the United States of America

The paper in this book meets the guidelines for permanence and durability of the Committee on Production Guidelines for Book Longevity of the Council on Library Resources.

JACKET DESIGN BY WILLI BAUM

SECOND EDITION, REVISED AND EXPANDED

Code 8529

The Jossey-Bass
Management Series

To my parents,
Pearl and Alexander Flamholtz, and
to my wife, Diana Troik Flamholtz

Preface

The United States is currently undergoing a fundamental transformation from an industrial to a service-based economy.[1] This transformation, which began around the end of World War II, has led to changes in the composition of the labor force, affecting the sectors in which people are employed and also the types and levels of skills that are needed.

At present, ours is rapidly becoming a knowledge-based economy, requiring "high-technology services" from people who are highly trained and educated as well as experienced in their fields. Engineers, computer programmers, software developers, medical technicians, lawyers, and university professors are all high-tech service personnel. Thus, the economy is increasingly composed of white collar, technical, professional personnel.

Growing Recognition of the Importance of Human Assets

The distinctive feature of the emerging economy is an increasing emphasis on human capital—the knowledge, skills, and experience of people—rather than on physical capital. A related attribute is the costliness of developing human capital; significant investments are required by individuals and the organizations that employ them.

Organizations spend money to recruit, select, hire, and train employees, and this money represents an investment in people. Organizations often spend more on investments in people than on investments in equipment. For example, if an organization purchases a microcomputer to use in word processing, it may spend \$3,000 to \$5,000. If the organization wishes to hire a senior vice-president for manufacturing, it may have to initiate a nationwide search for the individual, advertise the position in newspapers, incur the expense of bringing possible candidates to visit its facilities and be interviewed, and even pay an executive search firm 30 percent of the manager's first year's compensation. The investment in this executive can amount to \$20,000 to \$50,000 or more. Yet under present accounting conventions, the microcomputer would be treated as an asset while the investment made in acquiring the executive would be treated as an expense and charged against the current period's revenues. This is clearly a distortion of income measurement because no firm would make such substantial investments in a person unless he or she represented "human capital"—an asset with expected future benefits.

Impetus for Development of Human Resource Accounting

Since the 1960s a growing body of research, experiment, and theory has attempted to develop methods of accounting for an organization's human assets. This research is the outgrowth of recognition that human assets and human capital play a greater role in our economy today than in the past.

Under agricultural and industrial economic structures where the extent of human capital was significantly less than it is today, the theories and methods of accounting did not treat either people or investments in people as assets (with the exception of slaves, who were viewed as property). However, with the increasing importance of human capital to the economy as a whole, as well as to individual firms, a great deal of research has been designed to develop concepts and methods of accounting for people as assets. This field, described below, has come to be known as *human resource accounting*.

Human resource accounting (HRA) has been defined by the American Accounting Association's Committee on Human Resource Accounting as "the process of identifying and measuring data about human resources and communicating this information to interested parties."[2] It involves measuring the costs incurred by business firms and other organizations to recruit, select, hire, train, and develop human assets. It also involves measuring the economic value of people to organizations. In brief, it involves accounting for people as organizational resources, for managerial as well as financial accounting purposes.

HRA is, at least in part, a recognition that the skills, experience, and knowledge that people possess are assets that can be termed "human capital." This concept is the basis of the economic theory of human capital. Theodore Schultz, who received a Nobel Prize for his work on this theory, stated that "laborers have become capitalists not from a diffusion of the ownership of corporation stocks as folklore would have it, but from the acquisition of knowledge and skill that have economic value."[3] In a review of the history of the development of the economic theory of human capital, Kiker indicated that early economists who recognized that human capital exists included Petty, Say, Senior, List, Von Thunon, Roscher, Walras, Fischer, and Adam Smith.[4] The two methods used by economists to measure human capital were based on cost-of-production and capitalized-earnings procedures.

Human resource accounting has also developed from a parallel tradition in personnel management known as the "human resources school," which is based on the premise that people are valuable organizational resources and, therefore, ought to be managed as such. Personnel theorists such as Odiorne and organizational psychologists such as Likert have treated people as valuable organizational resources in their work.[5] For example, in his book *The Human Organization: Its Management and Value,* the late noted organizational theorist Rensis Likert stated that "every aspect of a firm's activities is determined by the competence, motivation and general effectiveness of its human organization."[6]

There is also support among some of the early accounting theorists for treating people as assets and accounting for their value, even before the nature of our economic structure changed and human capital increased in importance. For example, D. R. Scott noted that "a trained force of technical operatives is always a valuable asset."[7] Similarly, W. A. Paton stated that "in a business enterprise a well-organized and loyal personnel may be a much more important asset than a stock of merchandise."[8]

In addition to academic theorists, practicing managers have also recognized the importance of human assets for quite some time. For example, the 1966 annual report of Uniroyal stated that "our prime resource is people. [We are] essentially a collection of skills—the varied expertise of our 68,000 employees. . . . Uniroyal has plants and has capital, but most of all, it has people."[9]

Taken together, these various streams of thought all lead to the conclusion that organizations possess valuable assets in the people who are in their employ—that the people themselves are a form of capital, human capital. During the 1960s, this recognition led to academic research and business development of concepts and methods of measuring the cost and value of people as organizational assets, to the development of the field known as human resource accounting.

The foundation for this new field was laid between 1967 and the early 1970s. In 1974, I published the first book dealing with this emerging area, *Human Resource Accounting*. It was intended to present the state of the art of the field. The existence of that book as well as the research on which it was based evidenced the growing recognition of the importance of human resources, and, in turn, the need to develop methods of human resource accounting.

Extent of Change in This Edition

The present edition, which is a descendant of the 1974 edition, has been substantially revised and updated to reflect the current state of development of the field. The following paragraphs highlight major changes:

1. Four chapters in the present volume—Chapters Five, Ten, Twelve, and Thirteen—present research conducted since the 1974 edition was published. These chapters describe significant new applications of HRA. Specifically, Chapter Five reports the application of HRA in a major bank, listed on the New York Stock Exchange, which at the time of the study had more than $20 billion in assets. The research at this bank was one of the earliest analyses involving the application of HRA in a major U.S. organization. Chapter Five also presents a study sponsored by the Manpower Committee of the U.S. Office of Naval Research which involved measuring the replacement cost of civilian engineers. Chapter Ten reports a major study involving the application of human resource accounting to corporate income tax accounting for the acquisition of human assets from an organizational purchase. This research, which was conducted for a large U.S. financial institution listed on the New York Stock Exchange, has the potential of having a significant impact on corporate merger and acquisition decisions. It also has the potential for a widespread, significant impact on corporate financial reporting

because of the possibility of amortizing the human assets acquired for income tax purposes. Chapter Twelve describes three major examples of how human resource accounting can be used in making management decisions. One example is based on a study that I performed for one of the largest U.S. aerospace corporations. Chapter Thirteen reports the results of a pilot research study involving the application of human resource accounting at a major international Big Eight CPA firm. It involves the development of a human resource planning and decision analysis support system supported by HRA information. This previously unpublished research represents the first reported attempt at an integrated system of accounting for human resource cost and value by any major firm. A more detailed description of this material is presented in the overview of the contents in the next section.

2. A preface and an introduction have been added to this volume. These provide perspective on the changes that have occurred in the environment in which human resource professionals operate, explain the nature of HRA and the original impetus for its development, and trace the history of the field since its inception. A selected annotated bibliography of research and other literature on HRA has also been added.

3. All of the remaining chapters have been revised to incorporate the most recent work on concepts and applications relevant to HRA. The overall organization of the book has also been changed to reflect a reorientation of the book toward the needs of human resource professionals, line managers, and others, rather than toward accounting or procedural methods. All of the relevant measurement and procedural material is included; however, the emphasis is on HRA as a set of organizational tools rather than merely on its measurement aspects. Chapter One has been substantially rewritten to focus on HRA from the perspective of human resource professionals and senior managers. Chapter Two, which combines materials from some chapters of the prior edition, has been reorganized. Chapter Seven has undergone a major revision of its underlying framework and content. Other chapters have been less extensively rewritten. I have also deleted the tenth chapter of the former edition as well as certain research summaries and technical appendixes. The purpose of these changes has been to emphasize the usefulness of HRA, especially for human resource professionals, and to improve the overall structure and presentation of the entire book.

Purpose of This Book and Overview of the Contents

This book presents the current state of the art of human resource accounting. Its goals are (1) to examine the concepts and methods of accounting for people as human resources; (2) to explain the present and potential uses of HRA as a tool for human resource professionals, line managers, and investors; (3) to describe the research, experiments, and applications of human resource accounting in organizations; (4) to consider the steps involved in developing a human resource accounting system; and (5) to identify some of the remaining aspects of HRA that require future research.

Part One provides an introduction and overview of human resource accounting for professionals in the field, managers, and external users. Chapter One examines ways human resource professionals as well as line managers can use HRA. It includes an example that illustrates how a human resource accounting system can work for human resource professionals and line managers. The chapter examines the dual role of HRA as a paradigm to guide thinking about human resource management as well as a technology for measuring human resource cost and value so that they can be used as components in decisions to acquire, develop, allocate, conserve, and utilize people as organizational resources.

Chapter Two deals with the uses of human resource accounting by external users—stakeholders who are not members of an organization. For example, it examines the role of human resource accounting for investors in publicly held corporations. The chapter addresses the fundamental issues involved in accounting for human assets in corporate financial reports, including the limitations of conventional financial statements that do not include human assets, and how human assets can be reported in financial reports.

Part Two deals with accounting for human resource costs. Chapter Three presents the concepts and methods for measuring human resource costs and examines the foundation of human resource cost accounting. It explains the basic accounting concepts of costs and introduces the human resource accounting concept of human resource costs. It presents models for measuring the original and replacement cost of human resources.

Chapters Four and Five examine the actual systems of measuring and accounting for human resource costs that have been developed by organizations. Chapter Four presents the first generation of human resource cost accounting systems, which were developed prior to 1974, including systems by a professional athletic organization, a manufacturing company, a CPA firm, and an insurance company. Chapter Five presents the second generation of systems of accounting for human resource costs, including applications by one of the ten largest U.S. banks and the U.S. Navy.

In Part Three, we deal with accounting for human resource value. Chapter Six explains the economic concept of human resource value and presents methods of accounting for it. It presents models to explain the nature and determinants of an individual's as well as a group's value to an economic organization.

Chapter Seven deals with the measurement of the economic value of human resources in monetary terms. It presents a model for the measurement of human resource value and explains what is required for the application of that model in actual organizations. It also considers the conditions under which this model cannot be applied and the alternative models that can be used in such circumstances. It deals with the methods of measuring the value of individuals, groups, and the total human organization.

Chapter Eight presents methods for measuring the economic value of people as organizational resources in nonmonetary terms. It deals with circumstances under which nonmonetary measurement of human resource value is appropriate as well as the methods that can be used in such measurement.

The next two chapters in Part Three, Chapters Nine and Ten, present the first and second generations of systems that have been developed to account for human resource value. Chapter Nine describes the first published attempt to develop a system of accounting for the value of people as organizational resources. It examines the reasons for the organization's interest in developing a system of human resource valuation, the nature of the system developed, and how it was used. Chapter Ten presents a research study to measure the value of human resources acquired in an acquisition of one company by another. It examines the need to measure the value of people as organizational assets for purposes of calculating corporate income taxes, and presents the model developed. It also illustrates how the model was actually applied. This study is potentially of widespread significance because it has implications for corporate income taxation for corporations engaged in the acquisition of companies whose assets consist to a great extent of human capital.

Part Four of the book deals with the design and application of human resource accounting. Chapter Eleven examines different types of HRA systems as well as the steps involved in developing a system. Chapter Twelve examines three major examples of the application of human resource accounting in management decisions. The first involves the use of HRA in cost/benefit analyses. In particular, it focuses on the use of measurements of the value of executive time in deciding whether to acquire corporate aircraft rather than use commercial transportation. The second involves the use of HRA cost information in making personnel layoff decisions. The third application deals with the use of human resource accounting to evaluate the return on investment from management development programs.

Chapter Thirteen presents a case study of the development of an integrated HRA system by one of the leading certified public accounting firms in the United States, Touche Ross & Company. I am working with the firm to develop the system on an experimental basis. It represents the first reported attempt by any major organization to devise and implement a system for measuring human resource cost and value.

Intended Audience

This book provides a comprehensive review of the state of the art of human resource accounting. It is intended for a variety of different groups that possess a present or potential interest in HRA.

Human resource professionals, such as personnel managers and directors of human resource management, are the primary audience for this book. Given the emerging role of human resource professionals as advisers to senior line management with respect to human resource issues, this book is designed to provide a powerful analytical tool to assist in making decisions about personnel management. It also provides a technology for measuring human resource cost and value that will assist professionals in the field in translating management decisions into monetary terms.

Another major audience for whom this book is intended are CPAs and lawyers who are taxation specialists, corporate acquisition specialists, and chief financial officers of corporations. This group will be especially interested in the tax aspects of human resource accounting. This book will be particularly useful for those who are concerned with acquisitions of firms that largely comprise human assets. It will also serve as a handbook for developing potential services for clients.

This book is also intended for senior managers of all organizations, especially ones that are progressive in their concern for people as organizational resources. For such companies, human resource accounting represents the next logical step in developing concepts and tools to assist in the effective management of the organization's most valuable asset—its people.

In addition, professors of human resource management and accounting will find the book of interest in terms of its applications for theory, research, and teaching. Cases have been appended to each chapter that may be used to illustrate concepts and methods and in connection with assignments to students.

I hope this book will make a contribution to the field of human resource accounting and prove a practical tool for human resource professionals, senior managers, accountants, investors, organizational psychologists, corporate acquisition specialists, and others who are interested in improving the management of our most valuable resource—people.

Acknowledgments

My interest in human resource accounting began when I was a doctoral student at the University of Michigan, where I studied in the Graduate School of Business Administration and was employed as a researcher in the Institute for Social Research (ISR). I am especially indebted to R. Lee Brummet (now Ross Graham Walker Professor at the University of North Carolina), who first interested me in this area and later served as a member of my dissertation committee. I am also very much indebted to the late Rensis Likert, who was director of ISR during my years at Michigan. Rensis Likert was one of the earliest advocates for the development of human resource accounting, and research support for my doctoral studies came from his discretionary funds as director of ISR. I am also indebted to Lee Danielson, who served as chairman of my dissertation committee, and to George Odiorne, Edward Miller, and Meyer Ryder, who were also members of that committee.

After leaving Michigan I joined the faculty of the University of California, Los Angeles, where I have found a very supportive environment for research in human resource accounting under four outstanding deans: George Robbins, Harold Williams, John Buckley, and Clay La Force. The first edition of this book was written while I was on the accounting faculty of the Graduate School of Business at Columbia University. My colleagues at Columbia, including Gordon Schillinglaw, Carl Nelson, Sandy Burton, and Rashad Abdel-Khalik, were very supportive during that period.

Throughout the development of the research leading to this book, as well as during the preparation of the manuscript itself, I have benefited from the assistance of many individuals and organizations. In addition to the contributions previously acknowledged in the first edition, I wish to express my gratitude for the direct or indirect assistance of several individuals and organizations with the second edition. Richard A. Kaumeyer, Jr., has been an invaluable colleague. He has been fully supportive of human resource accounting; he was a coresearcher for the study concerning the bank in Chapter Five; and he took time from a busy schedule to read and comment on the book. Bennett Dolin was one of the earliest to perceive the role of human resource accounting in human resource management and sponsored the research project involving the bank in Chapter Five. The U.S. Office of Naval Research (ONR) has provided financial support for two human resource accounting research projects under my direction at the Center for Human Resource Management of the Institute of Industrial Relations, University of California, Los Angeles. Their support came, as described in the introduction, at a critical point in the development of human resource accounting. Special acknowledgment is appropriate for Wallace Sinaiko, who first introduced me and my research to the Manpower Committee of the Office of Naval Research; Glenn Bryan, a man of considerable vision, who supported the idea of ONR sponsorship of research in human resource accounting; Neal Glassman, who has served as contracting officer on the projects; and James Colvard of Naval Material Command (NAVMAT) and James W. Tweedale of Navy Personnel Research and Development Center, who agreed to have NAVMAT participate in the project as a research site. I am also indebted to the industrial engineering personnel in the navy installations at Seal Beach and Coronado, California, who assisted in the study, especially Donald Owen. I would like to acknowledge the role and assistance of George Geis in the ONR project as well. I am also indebted to D. Gerald Searfoss of Touche Ross & Company, who was the catalyst for the human resource accounting project described in Chapter Thirteen. Special acknowledgment is made to Russell Coff and Yvonne Randle, both doctoral students in the Graduate School of Management, University of California, Los Angeles, who assisted with the preparation of Chapter Twelve. Russell

Coff also assisted in the preparation of Chapters Ten and Thirteen. In addition, George Geis, Richard Perle, and Diana Ho were part of the research team that assisted me in the original research that underlies Chapter Ten. I am also indebted to the company that served as a site for the study reported in Chapter Ten, though its identity must remain confidential.

The word processing and preparation of the manuscript for this book were done primarily by the operations support staff of Management Systems Consulting Corporation, including Robbie Amodio (operations coordinator), Karen Nitao, Jana Lubert, and Joanne Cotter. Their thoroughness and care in preparing the final manuscript are appreciated very much.

I am indebted to the staff of Jossey-Bass Publishers for the highly professional and competent way in which this project was handled. Although company policy prohibits mentioning individuals by name, I wish to acknowledge my appreciation and respect for the individuals involved. It has been a genuine pleasure to work with them.

Diana Troik Flamholtz, associate professor of accounting at Loyola Marymount University, has always been my most constructive critic. She has contributed ideas to the book's structure and content.

Portions of this manuscript were used in my various courses at the Graduate School of Management, University of California, Los Angeles, including courses on human resource management for the MBA and executive MBA programs and a seminar on human resource accounting in the winter of 1985. Participants in these classes provided constructive feedback to me.

I am also grateful to Yvonne Randle for assistance in revising the manuscript from the first edition. She assisted with several aspects of its preparation.

Although I acknowledge with gratitude the contributions of all the people cited above, I remain responsible for the book and its remaining imperfections.

Los Angeles, California Eric G. Flamholtz
September 1985

Contents

The Author

Eric G. Flamholtz is professor of accounting-information systems and human resource management at the Graduate School of Management, University of California at Los Angeles, and assistant director of the Institute of Industrial Relations, University of California at Los Angeles, where he heads the Center for Research on Human Resource Management. He has also served as vice-chairman of the Graduate School of Management and director of the Accounting-Information Systems Research Program. Flamholtz teaches courses in a variety of areas including accounting-information systems, human resource management, planning and control systems, managerial decision making, and entrepreneurial management. He is also the president of Management Systems Consulting Corporation, which he founded in 1978.

Flamholtz received his Ph.D. degree from the University of Michigan, where he served on the staff of the Institute for Social Research under the direction of Rensis Likert. His doctoral dissertation, "The Theory and Measurement of an Individual's Value to an Organization," was cowinner of the McKinsey Foundation for Management Research Dissertation Award.

Flamholtz has also served on the faculties at Columbia University and the University of Michigan and has been a faculty fellow at Price Waterhouse & Co. He has broad interests in management and has done research on a variety of management topics, ranging from accounting and human resource management to organizational development and strategic planning. Flamholtz has conducted research projects for the National Science Foundation, the National Association of Accountants, and the U.S. Office of Naval Research.

The author of more than fifty articles and chapters on a variety of management topics, Flamholtz published the first edition of this book, which is considered the standard for the field, in 1974. Three other books are forthcoming: *Human Resource Management, Organizational Control,* and *Financial Accounting* (coauthored). He is in the process of completing two additional books: *Principles of Accounting* (coauthored) and *How to Make the Transition from an Entrepreneurship to a Professionally Managed Firm.*

As a consultant, Flamholtz has extensive experience with firms ranging from entrepreneurships to members of the New York Stock Exchange and the *Fortune* 500. He has also presented seminars and management development programs for organizations in Belgium, France, West Germany, Greece, Mexico, and the People's Republic of China as well as throughout the United States.

Human Resource Accounting

Advances in Concepts, Methods, and Applications

Introduction: The Development and State of the Art of Human Resource Accounting

Although human resource accounting (HRA) is a relatively new field, its development has already passed through several discernible stages. The first stage of development, from 1960 to 1966, was marked by interest in HRA and the derivation of basic HRA concepts from related bodies of theory. The initial impetus for the development of HRA came from a variety of sources, including the economic theory of human capital, organizational psychologists' concern for leadership effectiveness, the new human resource perspective, and a concern for human assets as components of corporate goodwill.

The second stage of the development of HRA was a period of basic academic research to develop and assess the validity of models for the measurement of human resource cost (both historical and replacement cost) and value (both monetary and nonmonetary). It was also a time of research designed to formulate the present and potential uses of HRA as a tool for human resource professionals, line managers, and external users of corporate financial information. This stage, which occurred from 1966 to 1971, also included a few exploratory experimental applications of HRA in actual organizations.

One of the earliest studies in human resource accounting during the second stage was conducted by Roger Hermanson, who was at that time a Ph.D. candidate at Michigan State University. Hermanson dealt with the problem of how to measure the value of human assets as an element of goodwill when they have not been purchased. His pioneering study is described in Chapter Seven. A great deal of the research done during the second stage of the development of HRA was done at the University of Michigan. In addition, beginning in 1967, a research team that included the late Rensis Likert, R. Lee Brummet, William C. Pyle, and myself carried out a series of projects designed to develop concepts and methods of accounting for human resources. Under the direction of William Pyle, then a Ph.D. candidate, research was conducted on the measurement of the historical cost of human resources at the R. G. Barry Corporation, a relatively small soft goods manufacturer headquartered in Columbus, Ohio. The system developed at R. G. Barry is described in Chapter Four.

The third stage of development of HRA, which dated from 1971 to 1976, was a period of rapid growth of interest in human resource accounting. It involved a great deal of academic research throughout the Western world and in Australia and Japan. It was a time of increasing attempts to apply HRA in business organizations. Most of these applications were conducted by relatively small entrepreneurial organizations, such as R. G. Barry Corporation (see Chapter Four) and Lester Witte & Company (see Chapter Nine).

The research at R. G. Barry Corporation during HRA's second stage of development involved one of the first attempts to develop a system of accounting for the historical cost of human resources. During the third stage, the R. G. Barry experiment received considerable recognition because, at least for a few years, the company published pro forma financial statements that included human assets. This, in turn, stimulated increasing interest in HRA. Unfortunately, the publication of those financial statements also had a negative side effect; they led to the widespread erroneous impression that human resource accounting was concerned only with treating people as "financial objects." Although preparing financial statements that included human resources was undoubtedly a part of human resource accounting, it was not by far the most significant part. Yet precisely because it was dramatic and innovative, "putting people on the balance sheet" became the dominant image of HRA for many people.

The research during stage three also involved assessments of the potential impact of HRA information on decisions by human resource professionals, line managers, and investors. It also involved the continued development of concepts and models for measuring and accounting for human resource cost and value. This stage was characterized by a considerable amount of published research dealing with HRA as well as a great deal of seminar activity. Many of the studies conducted during this stage are included in the annotated bibliography section of this book.

During the third stage, the American Accounting Association established committees on human resource accounting in 1971-1972 and 1972-1973. These committees published reports on the development of HRA. Also during this stage (in 1974) the first edition of this book was published, presenting the state of the art of HRA.

The fourth stage in the evolution of HRA, from 1976 to 1980, was a period of declining interest both in academia and in the corporate world. One of the reasons for the reduced interest was that most of the relatively easy preliminary research had been accomplished; the remaining research required to develop HRA was complex, could only be accomplished by a relatively few scholars, and required the cooperation of organizations willing to serve as research sites for applied research studies. Since relatively few individuals had either the skills required to do such research or the qualifications required to obtain the necessary corporate participation, few major studies were performed. During this period, corporate interest was diverted to other, more pressing issues. Furthermore, the required research involved the application of HRA in organizations, and the cost of subsidizing such research was significant while the benefits were either uncertain or would accrue to the field as a whole and not necessarily to the sponsoring firm. It was at this point that HRA seemed to have been an idea that was promising but that would not be developed much further. However, significant megatrends in the environment changed all that in just a few years.

Stage five, the current stage of development of HRA, which can be dated from 1980 to the present, has involved the beginnings of a resurgence of interest in the theory and practice of human resource accounting. Although interest in HRA had clearly waned during the period from 1976 to 1980, it never completely died. The first sparks of renewal occurred during 1980, and since that time there have been an increasing number of significant new research studies dealing with the development and application of HRA as well as an increasing (albeit relatively small) number of attempts to apply human resource accounting by major organizations.

One of the most significant events that served as a catalyst to the renewal of interest in HRA was a decision by the U.S. Office of Naval Research (ONR) to sponsor a research project dealing with the feasibility of the application of HRA to naval human resource management issues. The resulting study, which I conducted, is described in Chapter Five. In undertaking the study, the manpower committee of ONR indicated that they viewed part of their mission as supporting areas of promising research that might be too costly for individual companies in the private sector to undertake. This was the first project of significant scope by a major institution in either the public or private sector.

At about this time, several other things happened that also began to accelerate interest in HRA. First, there began to be a growing concern throughout the United States for increased productivity, and especially for the potential contribution of human resources to such increased productivity. Human resource professionals and line managers as well as academics began to investigate a variety of potential tools to increase employee productivity, including human resource accounting. Another major influence upon the renewal of interest in HRA was the growing concern with the Japanese as major world-class competitors and the related awareness that Japanese organizations were managing their people differently from their U.S. counterparts. Specifically, Japanese organizations such as Nippon Steel and Mitsubishi followed practices of lifetime employment without layoffs and viewed their employees as fixed assets, while their counterparts at U.S. Steel and General Motors frequently invoked layoffs and viewed their people as "expenses." The knowledge that human resource accounting was based on the idea that people are resources and not expenses and that Japanese organizations employing that philosophy seemed to have a work force with greater motivation and corporate loyalty convinced some human resource professionals as well as line managers to investigate HRA. The third, and perhaps decisive, factor in the renewal of interest in HRA was the recognition that the U.S. economy had undergone a fundamental metamorphosis from an industrial to a high-tech service economy in which human capital is the critical resource.

Taken together, all of these factors have resulted in a growing number of organizational applications of HRA concepts and models as well as renewed academic research. Some examples of these applications and research include:

- A U.S. bank with more than $20 billion in assets that applied HRA to measure the replacement cost of tellers and management trainees to resolve an internal debate over their true cost. This study is described in Chapter Five.
- Two studies by the U.S. Office of Naval Research to investigate the application of HRA to Naval human resource management, including the replacement cost of civilian industrial engineers. One of these studies is described in Chapter Five.
- A major U.S. financial institution that sponsored a project to measure the value of human assets acquired in a corporate purchase in order to determine the amortization of human capital for corporate income tax purposes. This study is described in Chapter Ten.
- A major U.S. aerospace firm that sponsored a study using HRA to measure the value of executive time saved when corporate aircraft was used in place of commercial aircraft. This application is described in Chapter Twelve.
- A $450 million industrial components distributor that was experiencing a high rate of personnel turnover but could not get the CEO's attention until HRA methods were used to quantify the cost of turnover.
- A major Europe-based business equipment manufacturer that investigated the replacement cost of its personnel.
- A major Canadian industrial company that has established a project to account for human resources in order to assess cost and benefits of layoff decisions in terms of their impact on human resource replacement cost as well as short-term payroll savings. An application analogous to this one is described in Chapter Twelve.
- A major U.S. pharmaceutical company that has attempted to measure the value of its human assets in order to assess its return on investment in human resource development.
- One of the so-called Big Eight international certified public accounting firms that has initiated a project to develop an operational system of accounting for the cost and value of its human resources. This study is described in Chapter Thirteen.

From the examples cited above, it is clear that there has been a significant resurgence of interest in HRA, and that the field has developed sufficiently since the first edition of this book was published in 1974 to warrant a revision updating the state of the art. These applications are of special significance to the development of the field because they indicate that major institutions have chosen to develop and/or apply HRA. This is in contrast to the initial periods of development of HRA when the major studies involved relatively small entrepreneurial organizations. Several of the applications cited above will be examined in depth in this book.

Future Directions of HRA

It is my judgment that human resource accounting has entered a period of rapid growth in its applications. Even as this book is going to press, new projects involving the application of HRA are beginning. Human resource accounting is being developed and used in a wide variety of ways by accountants, lawyers, corporate acquisition specialists, human resource professionals, and senior managers. Many of these applications are described throughout this book. However, the most exciting aspect of human resource accounting, for me at least, is people increasingly discovering new uses for its measurement technology and conceptual framework.

I believe that human resource accounting has the potential to lead to a profound reconceptualization of the management of people in organizations. Specifically, it can contribute to an organizational culture in which the belief that people are valuable organizational resources is manifested in decisions and actions rather than merely being given lip service. I believe that the tax aspect of human resource valuation (described in Chapter Ten) can also lead to a major shift in accounting and financial reporting practices and principles.

In brief, it is my opinion that we are at the leading edge of what is still a relatively new paradigm and measurement technology that will have profound effects on the way in which people are managed in organizations. The accuracy of these views is left to the reader and the future to decide. In the interim, I hope that readers will find this book interesting and that it will make a contribution to the development of the field of human resource accounting.

ONE

Uses for Managers and Human Resource Professionals

One of the primary purposes of a human resource accounting system is to help management plan and control the use of human resources effectively and efficiently. This chapter examines the role of human resource accounting in the process of managing people in organizations and presents a model depicting how human resource accounting provides the information needed to acquire, develop, allocate, conserve, utilize, evaluate, and reward human resources. As will be seen in this chapter, human resource accounting is intended as a framework and a set of tools both for human resource professionals and for senior management.

The Emerging Role of the Human Resource Professional

The increasing importance of human capital throughout the economy has profound implications for the role of the human resource professional in organizations. In brief, the primary role of the human resource professional in the contemporary environment is to serve as the human resource adviser to senior management. The traditional role of the "personnel specialist" was to serve as a technician responsible for certain specialties such as employment, training, compensation design and administration, and employee relations. Today, however, the role of the human resource professional is in the process of rapid evolution, if not revolution, to a broader, more conceptual, and strategic set of responsibilities. One aspect of the emerging role is to advise senior management on a wide variety of human resource issues—how to design a corporate culture for optimal use of human resources, whether the firm should hire people from the outside only at the entry level and then advance them gradually to higher levels, whether a company should lay off personnel during a recession or retain them to protect its human assets, and how much to invest in human resource development.

The most sophisticated and successful U.S. corporations, such as IBM, Motorola, Eli Lilly, and Pepsico, as well as many others, have already reconceptualized the role of the human resource professional from personnel specialist to adviser. In many of these companies, the senior human resource professional has an important voice in line management decisions and is responsible for assessing the human resource implications of business strategies.

Human resource accounting is the next logical step for progressive companies that have already adopted the human resource perspective in contrast to the traditional personnel specialist approach. Human resource accounting represents both a paradigm (a way of looking at human resource decisions and issues) and a set of measures for quantifying the effects of human resource management strategies upon the cost and value of people as organizational resources. These functions of human resource accounting are shown schematically in Figure 1-1.

To appreciate how human resource accounting provides a perspective on management decisions in terms of their effects on the cost and value of people as organizational resources, consider the example of a layoff decision. Most companies faced with a recessionary environment begin to lay off people. The immediate result of a layoff is a reduction in payroll costs and, in turn, an improvement in the firm's net income or so-called bottom line. However, the layoff strategy has more subtle costs that are not quantified by conventional accounting practices. Specifically, some of the people who are laid off may accept employment elsewhere and will not return to the company when business expands. This means that the firm must invest in training new people. Thus there is a hidden replacement cost attributable to the layoff that the firm may have to incur at a subsequent date, and it ought to be factored into management's decision. Moreover, layoffs have attitudinal and motivational effects. Although some people may work harder because they fear being laid off, many others will respond by taking actions to protect their jobs, including stretching out work. The net effect is that the layoff policy may cause people to feel that the company will only exploit them and, therefore, they need to protect themselves against their own employer.

Figure 1-1

THE FUNCTIONS OF HUMAN RESOURCE ACCOUNTING

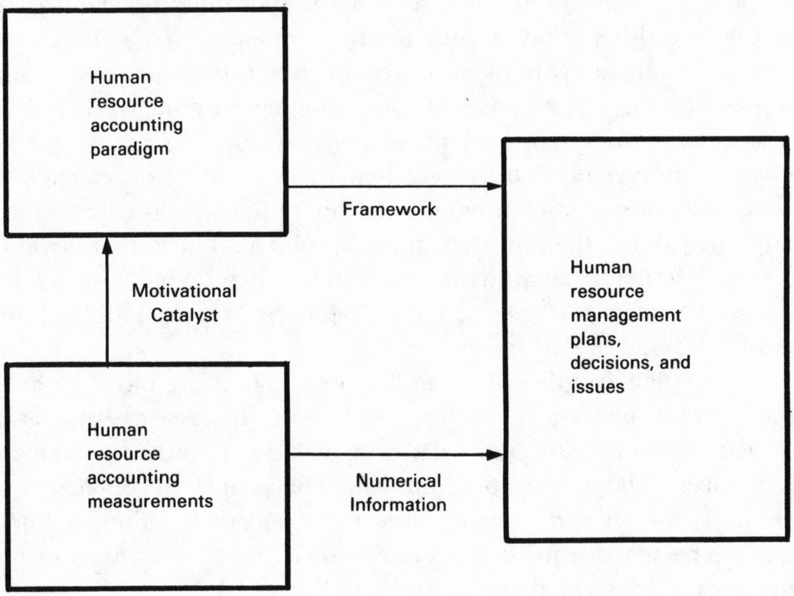

The role of the human resource professional is to help senior management understand the implications of their business decisions. Human resource accounting provides a perspective for analyzing the effects of decisions (such as a layoff) on the human organization and for explaining the consequences to management. Thus the human resource professional can help management to appreciate the long-range consequences and hidden costs of certain business decisions.

The other major dimension of human resource accounting involves its use as a measure of the costs and value of human resources. Continuing the example of the layoff decision, human resource professionals can use their expertise to quantify the costs of the layoff (including the estimated replacement cost that will be incurred because of the need to replace lost work force). The central point here is not that companies should adopt a policy of no layoffs but, rather, that management ought to consider all the costs and benefits of such practices. Thus one role of the measurement aspect of human resource accounting is to provide numerical information as an input to management decisions.

There is, however, another effect of the measurement dimension of human resource accounting—in brief, the very act of monitoring and quantifying the costs and value of people from a human resource perspective. According to the traditional way of thinking about people in organizations, they represent an "expense." In conventional accounting, all funds required to recruit, select, train, and compensate people are treated as expenses in computing net income, while much of those expenditures represent investments in building assets that will provide future value to the enterprise. Accordingly, management either consciously or unconsciously tends to think of people as expenses to be minimized rather than as assets to be optimized. Thus one function of human resource accounting is to motivate management to adopt a human resource perspective, either explicitly or implicitly, in their decisions.

In summary, then, human resource accounting has three major functions for the human resource professional: It serves as a framework to facilitate human resource decision making; it provides numerical information about the cost and value of people as organizational resources; and it can motivate line management to adopt a human resource perspective in their decisions involving people. Each of these functions is represented schematically in Figure 1-1.

Specific Uses of Human Resource Accounting

Thus far we have discussed the broad functions of human resource accounting. In this section we shall examine some of the specific uses of human resource accounting information in the context of a model of the human resource management process. This model provides a framework for analyzing management issues from a human resource accounting perspective. The model of human resource management shown schematically in Figure 1-2 is based on a systems approach. It indicates an organization's human resource management functions, which, in turn, imply certain information needs that can be satisfied by human resource accounting.

The model shown in Figure 1-2 indicates that human resource management is a system designed to transform inputs (human resources) into outputs (human services). The *inputs* are people: individuals, groups, and the total "human organization." The *transformation processes* are managerial subsystems for acquiring, developing, allocating, conserving, utilizing, evaluating, and rewarding people. The

Figure 1-2

AN INPUT-OUTPUT MODEL OF THE HUMAN RESOURCE MANAGEMENT SYSTEM

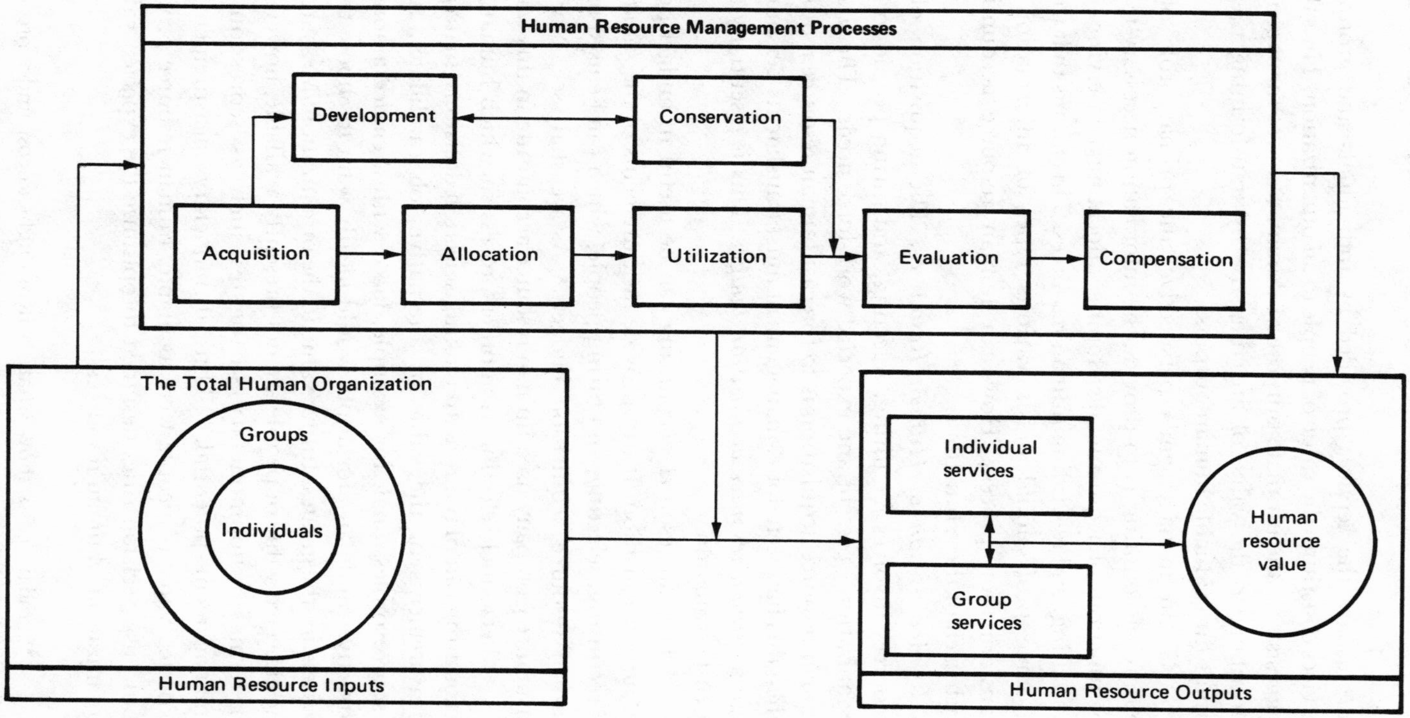

outputs are the services provided by individuals and groups. These services constitute the value of people to an organization. Thus the model suggests that the ultimate purpose of human resource management is to contribute to the value of an enterprise by transforming raw human inputs into valuable human outputs.

From management's perspective, the primary role of human resource accounting is to provide the information necessary to perform the functions of acquiring, developing, allocating, conserving, utilizing, evaluating, and rewarding human resources. This means that the human resource professional needs various types of information for the transformation process. How can human resource accounting help with each of these functions?

Acquisition of Human Resources. The acquisition of human resources involves recruiting, selecting, and hiring people to meet the organization's present and expected work-force needs.[1] The first step in human resource acquisition is to forecast human resource requirements; when this has been done, management must translate its personnel needs into a *human resource acquisition budget.* This is essentially a process of cost estimation.

Human resource accounting can be useful in budgeting human resource acquisition. It can provide measurements of the *standard costs* of recruiting, selecting, and hiring people, which can be used to prepare human resource acquisition budgets.* As we shall see, Northeastern Insurance Company used human resource accounting in this way.

Personnel selection is another process in which human resource accounting can play a role. In making selection decisions, managers need measurements of the value of alternative job candidates. A human resource professional, for example, faced with a choice among several attractive candidates for a job, would ideally want to choose the person possessing the greatest future value to the organization. Measurements of the expected value of people are not presently available, however, except in terms of nonmonetary surrogates such as scores on tests of "management potential." Thus if monetary measurements of the expected value of people were available, human resource professionals could use decision rules designed to optimize the expected value of an organization's human resources.

*Standard costs show what an item ought to cost under predetermined operating conditions.

Development of Human Resources. The development of human resources involves various forms of training designed to enhance people's technical, administrative, and interpersonal skills. These skills, in turn, increase their value to an organization. Development may occur through formal programs or on-the-job learning.

Human resource professionals face two problems in budgeting human resource development: assessing the value of a proposed investment in human resource development and then estimating the cost of the proposed expenditure. The first is a question of resource allocation (human capital budgeting); the second is a problem of cost estimation.

Human resource accounting can facilitate decisions involving the allocation of resources to human resource development by measuring the expected rate of return on proposed investments. As discussed in the next section, at the Largetown Branch of Northeastern Insurance Company such a measurement helped the human resource manager decide to invest in a course in business law for claims investigators. Similarly, suppose that Southwestern Telephone Company is building a new plant to manufacture cable and components. Such facilities typically achieve standard productivity within two or three years. Management, however, may wish to accelerate the start-up process and may therefore consider an investment in organizational development. The plant's personnel, for example, may participate in a "team-building" program in order to develop an effectively functioning human organization more rapidly. Although most investments in such programs are based on faith in their benefits, a more rational decision might be based on an assessment of the expected return on the proposed human capital investment. The data for such an analysis would be provided by human resource accounting.

Acquisition and Development Policy. Human resource accounting can also be useful to management in formulating policy for human resource acquisition and development. Consider, for example, the problem facing the human resource planning committee of the E. R. McLean Electric Company. The tasks of this committee are to formulate policies for acquiring and developing people at McLean Electric and to review and make recommendations with respect to budgetary requests sought by the personnel function.

In 19X2, the company was faced with a need for 200 additional employees, including production and maintenance workers, supervisors, draftspeople, engineers, and engineering managers. The question facing the committee was this: Should McLean train currently employed personnel for the new positions and recruit only at the entry level, or should it recruit experienced personnel from the outside? Although certain noneconomic factors were involved in this decision, the committee believed that the economics of the situation ought to be a major criterion in its final recommendation.

By providing estimates of the historical and current costs to acquire and develop people for the various positions, human resource accounting can help management assess the trade-offs between the costs of recruitment from outside and development from within. Thus it can provide the economic information management needs to assist in formulating personnel acquisition and development policy. This decision is analogous to a "make or buy" decision in manufacturing.

Allocation of Human Resources. The allocation of human resources is the process of assigning people to various organizational roles and tasks. There are several (sometimes conflicting) objectives involved in allocation decisions. First, the task to be performed should be completed in the most efficient way. This may mean that management will allocate the "most qualified" person to a particular job. In addition, however, an organization's human resources must be developed, and management may wish to provide people with the opportunity to develop their skills through on-the-job learning—which suggests that the "most qualified" (experienced) person will not be assigned to a task. Furthermore, management wants to allocate people to jobs that satisfy their needs. Thus, ideally, management allocates people to jobs in a way that will optimize these three variables: job productivity, human resource development, and individual satisfaction.

Human resource accounting can be useful to management in making such allocation decisions. It can help quantify the variables involved in the allocation decision and express them in the common denominator of monetary units. This perspective will help management understand the trade-offs involved in allocation decisions and thus enable executives to select the optimal course of action. If these variables can be quantified, management will be able to apply linear programming to determine an optimal solution to the work-force allocation problem.*

*Linear programming is a set of mathematical procedures by which management can maximize or minimize a performance measure (effectiveness criterion) subject to various constraints. See, for example, M. Alexis and C. Wilson, *Organizational Decision Making* (Englewood Cliffs, N.J.: Prentice-Hall, 1967), chap. 4.

Incorrect allocation decisions can be costly to individuals and to society as a whole as well as to organizations. Organizations can actually deplete the value of their human assets by failing to assign people to jobs in which they can develop their skills. For example, an engineer in the aerospace industry may be assigned to work on the design and development of a single wing of an aircraft for several years. Once the project is phased out, the engineer may be technologically obsolete.

Although, in principle, allocation decisions ought to be made to optimize (jointly maximize) the three variables described above, in practice this is not usually done. In a laboratory experiment involving personnel allocation decisions made by partners in a Big Eight CPA firm, the author found that when the decisions were made without human resource accounting information, the major variable considered was job productivity. When human resource accounting information was introduced, the partners of the international CPA firm made different decisions and used different criteria such as the effect of the job assignment upon the future value of the people involved.[2]

Conservation of Human Resources. An organization's human resources may take several forms, such as the technical capabilities of individuals or those of an effectively functioning management team (a human organization). Conservation of human resources is the process of maintaining the capabilities of people as individuals and the effectiveness of the human system developed by an organization. Unless systematically monitored and maintained, the capabilities of human resources may deteriorate, as in the case of the aerospace engineer just mentioned. As a result, an organization will have to incur either retraining costs or replacement costs to rebuild its human capabilities. Similarly, management must monitor the effectiveness of the human organization to assess the extent to which it is being maintained or depleted.

Failure to measure the extent to which human resources are being conserved in a division, plant, or department can be costly to an organization. In the short run, a divisional manager can put pressure on people temporarily to increase their productivity or reduce costs, with the effects upon employee motivation, attitudes, and labor relations going unnoticed. As a result, highly trained and skilled employees become dissatisfied and leave an organization. The cost of replacing them may be substantial.

Management must account for an organization's human assets in order to prevent their depletion. Currently, an organization's conservation of its human resources typically is measured in terms of turnover rates. Measures of turnover, however, are inadequate indicators of human resource conservation for two reasons. First, they are historical and therefore unavailable to management until *after* turnover has occurred. Thus they cannot be used as an early warning signal to suggest the need for special efforts at conservation. Second, turnover rates do not fully represent the economic impact of turnover, which is more realistically demonstrated by monetary measures.

To illustrate the impact of human resource accounting on the conservation process, consider the situation of a medium-sized electronic components distributor we shall call Rapid Growth Electronics. The firm, which had grown rapidly during the past few years, was experiencing turnover rates of up to 70 percent in certain job classifications. When the vice-president of human resources, Harold Williams, could not get the attention of the firm's president, Warren Hawkins, with these numbers, he decided to measure what the turnover was costing the firm on an annual basis. Using the model for measuring replacement costs described in Chapter Three, he determined that it was costing Rapid Growth Electronics an amount equal to one year's net income. That number got the president's attention, and an outside consultant was engaged to study the causes of turnover and recommend ways of reducing it.

Human resource accounting can also assist management in conserving its human organization by providing an early warning system. It can measure and report certain (social-psychological) indicators of the condition of the human organization, and management can assess trends in these variables prior to the actual occurrence of turnover.

Utilization of Human Resources. Human resource utilization is the process of using human services to achieve organizational objectives. Human resource accounting can help managers use human resources effectively and efficiently by providing a paradigm or conceptual framework.

At present, the management of human resources in organizations is less effective than it might be because it lacks a unifying framework to guide it. Managers have neither a valid criterion to guide decisions affecting people nor a methodology for assessing the anticipated or actual consequences of such decisions. Clearly the criteria of productivity and satisfaction, which frequently underlie strategies of human resource management, have not been entirely helpful in coping with the problems of managing people. Similarly, since it is exceedingly difficult to measure productivity and satisfaction—or to assess the trade-offs a manager should be willing to make to increase one by decreasing the other—it is frequently impossible to predict the economic consequences of alternative actions with respect to people.

The notion of *human resource value* provides one possible solution to these problems. It can serve as the raison d'être of human resource management; it can simultaneously provide the goals and the criterion for the management of human resources. More specifically, the aim of human resource management can be viewed as the need to contribute to the value of the organization as a whole by optimizing the value of its human assets; the effectiveness criterion can be the measured change in the value of the organization's human resources.

If the aim of human resource management is seen as the optimization of human resource value, then task design, selection, role assignment, development, performance appraisal, and compensation are not merely a set of service functions to be performed; rather, they are a set of strategies that can be adopted to change the value of human assets and, in turn, the value of the organization as a whole.

Thus managers do have a theoretical framework to guide their decisions in regard to people. This framework posits that the ultimate guide to decision making involving people is the extent to which human resource value is optimized. It also means that managers will receive measurements of the extent to which their ultimate objective is being achieved—that is, the degree to which the value of people to the organization is being optimized.

In summary, then, human resource accounting can provide a framework to help managers utilize human resources effectively and efficiently. This paradigm involves thinking of human resource acquisition, development, allocation, and conservation as strategies designed to influence the value of people. We shall develop this theoretical framework further throughout the book, especially in Chapter Six.

Evaluation and Reward of Human Resources. Human resource evaluation is the process of assessing the value of people to an organization. It involves measuring the productivity (performance) and promotability of people.

At present, human resources are typically evaluated by nonmonetary methods (discussed in Chapter Eight). These methods, however, cannot be used in most of the human resource acquisition, development, allocation, and conservation decisions cited above; monetary methods of human resource evaluation are needed instead.

Human resource accounting can be useful in the evaluation process by developing reliable methods of measuring the value of people to an organization. These methods include both monetary and nonmonetary measurements. They permit human resource management decisions to be made on a cost-value basis.

Human resource accounting will also have an impact on the administration of reward systems. These systems are intended to motivate and reinforce the optimal performance of people in achieving organizational objectives. *Rewards* include compensation, promotion, and symbolic recompense such as performance appraisals. Human resource evaluation permits rewards to be administered in relation to a person's value to an organization. It enables management, for example, to base compensation decisions on the value of people to the firm.

Human resource accounting can also be used to evaluate the efficiency of personnel management per se. It can help establish standard costs of acquiring and developing people, and these standards can be compared with the actual costs the personnel department incurs in performing its acquisition and development functions. Deviations from the standards may be analyzed to identify inefficiencies in the acquisition and development of the work force.

Overall Function of Human Resource Accounting. From an overall perspective, human resource accounting has a dual purpose. It is a way of thinking about the management of an organization's human resources. The paradigm is based on the notion that people are valuable organizational resources. It proposes that management (both senior management and human resource professionals) base its human resource decisions on a cost-value calculus—that is, on an assessment of the cost and the value involved in a decision. But human resource accounting is also a system of providing management with the information needed to manage human resources effectively and efficiently. It furnishes information about the cost and value of people to an organization; the organization's specific needs determine the types of information required.

Example of a Human Resource Accounting System

In the preceding sections, we have examined the functions and uses of human resource accounting for human resource professionals, and, in turn, senior line management, from a conceptual perspective. Another useful way to appreciate the role of human resource accounting is to examine how it would be used in the context of an actual business enterprise. This section explains how a real business might apply some aspects of human resource accounting in its operations and illustrates the uses of this approach in human resource management.

Description of the Company. The Northeastern Insurance Company (NIC) is a medium-sized insurance company with about $1 billion in assets that has offices throughout the United States. The company has approximately 5,000 employees, and 25 percent are salespeople. It is organized on a regional basis with the home office providing a variety of support services. Each region comprises several branches. The branch is the basic unit for sales and handling claims; the home office handles investments.

Human Resource Problems. In April 19X5, home office management held a meeting to review company-wide operations. One area of particular concern was human resource planning and utilization. The general consensus was that NIC faced a variety of personnel problems.

One immediate problem was an apparently high turnover among salespeople. Although no turnover data were available, it was the general impression that "quits" had been unusually high since the beginning of the year. Was this a random event or a trend? No one could be certain. The corporate controller pointed out that administrative costs were increasing in almost all of the firm's branches, and he thought that personnel costs such as recruiting and training probably accounted for the lion's share of the increases. He was unable to provide precise data, however, because the company's accounting system did not classify personnel costs separately.

Another problem was that some branch managers did not pay enough attention to human resource development. The company was relying on a few branches for a substantial proportion of its promotion to executive positions. The other branches were simply not doing a good job of training people. Someone remarked that many employees wanted transfers to the branches with high promotion rates and that such transfers were costly to the firm. Moreover, the apparent lack of opportunity in certain branches might be contributing to the recent turnover.

One fact that clearly emerged from this meeting was the obvious lack of information about the firm's human resources. The firm did not have a corporate human resource professional to whom these problems could be addressed. As a result, the decision was made to engage an outside consultant to study the situation.

The Consultant's Recommendations. The consultant examined the company for two months and then made his report. The firm was badly in need of coordination of human resource activities, he reported. Moreover, he found that many human resource activities carried on in the branches were often insufficient and at times contrary to the best interests of the firm as a whole. Furthermore, the firm's personnel and accounting records were too fragmentary to reveal either the extent or the causes of the problems or to serve as a basis for remedial action. And, finally, there was little systematic effort to plan for human resource requirements or the development of human resources beyond one year in the branches and no means of doing so for the organization as a whole.

The consultant recommended that the firm coordinate human resource activities under a director of human resource planning and utilization and develop a human resource accounting system. Acting on these recommendations, the firm hired the former director of human resources of a large manufacturing company. The director believed that his most urgent need was to develop an information system for human resource planning and control.

Developing the Human Resource Accounting System. The starting point was to identify the kinds of information needed to manage the firm's human resources effectively. The director presumed that different information would be required at different levels of the organization, and he asked regional managers, branch managers, and human resource specialists at the branch level to identify the types of decisions that were made regarding personnel problems, the frequency of those decisions, the data that were actually required to make such decisions, and the data that were typically available. The director also identified his own information needs. Moreover, each member of the board of directors was requested to indicate the information that ought to be available to the board; they were also asked to specify the information that should be furnished to outside investors.

After collecting data, the director and his assistant analyzed it for patterns of information needs. They were able to summarize their basic information needs at all levels of the organization.

Information for Human Resource Planning. From this survey of management's human resource information needs it became clear that a great deal of information was required to facilitate human resource planning. Working with the accounting staff to revise the system of accounts, branch personnel departments were able for the first time to get information about the actual cost of recruitment and selection. Several weeks spent in tracing costs for these activities for the past two years provided a reasonable basis for projecting expenses for the coming year. An illustration of the data for the Largetown Branch is shown in Table 1-1.

Table 1-1

NORTHEASTERN INSURANCE COMPANY – LARGETOWN BRANCH

Budgeted Acquisition Costs for Human Resources

Costs	*Salesman*	*Claims*	*Total*
Recruitment	$ 25,000	$ 5,000	$ 30,000
Selection	60,000	15,000	75,000
Hiring	80,000	20,000	100,000
Total expenses	$165,000	$40,000	$205,000

Each branch was requested to prepare a tentative budget for investments in training and development. Training investments were to be classified in two forms: (1) "required training," or training that is a prerequisite for normal performance on the job, and (2) "discretionary training," or training undertaken to develop new or improved skills. The budget for the coming year for the Largetown Branch is shown in Table 1-2.

The branches were also requested to estimate rates of return to support their requests for discretionary investments in training. One discretionary training proposal involved sending claims investigators to Largetown University for an evening course in business law. It was estimated that this knowledge would reduce the likelihood of costly claims procedure errors by investigators. Savings per investigator for the

Table 1-2

NORTHEASTERN INSURANCE COMPANY – LARGETOWN BRANCH

Budgeted Training Investments

19X5

Classes of Investment	*Sales*	*Claims*	*Total*
Required training	$150,000	$50,000	$200,000
Discretionary training	60,000	25,000	85,000
Total investments	$210,000	$75,000	$285,000

first year were estimated at $2,000. (For simplicity, no returns are expected to be derived from the investment in future years.) The branch manager considered this estimate to be conservative. The cost of the training (tuition, books, evening meals, transportation, and so on) was expected to total $500 for the one-year course. Moreover, an opportunity cost of lost productivity during the year spent in training was estimated at $500. The projected rate of return was calculated as follows:

$$\text{Projected return on investment} = \frac{\text{net savings}}{\text{investment}} = \frac{\$1,000}{\$1,000} = 100\%$$

Even after allowance for some error in these estimates, management concluded that the proposed training was a sound investment and it was budgeted for ten claims investigators.

Information for Control of Human Resource Costs. The survey of managers' information needs also indicated that the firm required information for controlling personnel costs. There was no means of evaluating the performance of management in controlling personnel costs. To overcome this problem, management decided to establish a system of standard costs for personnel recruitment, selection, and training.

Because there was no analytical means of determining a cost formula for such activities, various human resource professionals at the branch level participated with the controller's staff in setting standards. It was understood that these standards would serve as cost targets and that some variations might reasonably be expected. Actual costs would be reported to human resource professionals as incurred, and it was hoped that this information would assist them in controlling costs. The

Table 1-3

NORTHEASTERN INSURANCE COMPANY – LARGETOWN BRANCH

Standard Personnel Costs – Claims Personnel
19X5

Positions	*Acquisition*	*Training*	*Total*
Claims investigator	$ 600	$4,000	$4,600
Claims adjuster	600	4,000	4,600
Office adjuster	5,600	1,100	6,700
Claims examiner	7,100	1,000	8,100

standards established for selected claims personnel are shown in Table 1-3.

Information for Control of Turnover Cost. Another aspect of the cost control problem facing the company involved turnover. Under the new system, both turnover rates and costs were to be reported. A primary reason for this practice was to increase management's awareness of the cost of turnover. The director of human resource planning and utilization recommended that the cost of turnover be measured in terms of three constructs: the investment lost, the replacement cost, and the loss of human resource value. He also proposed that the total cost of turnover for each branch be reported to the regional general manager. An illustration of the turnover cost control report is shown in Table 1-4.

The first report was prepared in July 19X5. This report was accompanied by supporting schedules showing the cost of turnover for each group of personnel—sales and claims. Because the cost of turnover was quite significant, the director of human resource planning and utilization recommended steps to control it. The first step was to develop methods of forecasting expected turnover. To do this, the firm developed an attitude questionnaire that focused on employee satisfaction with pay, supervisors, job, and other variables thought to relate to turnover. The intention was to test the power of the measure to predict the probability of turnover. The second step in the control program was to identify means of increasing satisfaction with the organization, which would, in turn, increase the probability that sales and claims personnel would remain in the company. The third step was to evaluate these proposals

Table 1-4

NORTHEASTERN INSURANCE COMPANY – EASTERN REGION

Turnover Cost Control Report for the Period
January 1 - June 30, 19X5

Branches	*Unamortized Investment*	*Replacement Cost*	*Economic Value*
Largetown	$160,000	$200,000	$ 500,000
Liberty-Bell Town	80,000	100,000	320,000
Beantown	100,000	140,000	420,000
Steeltown	65,000	90,000	240,000
Total for Region	$405,000	$530,000	$1,480,000

on a cost-value basis. Thus the company was using both monetary and nonmonetary measures to help control turnover costs.

Information for Evaluation of Management Effectiveness. The survey of information needs had also shown that management's effectiveness in developing and utilizing people would have to be measured. Thus each branch and, in turn, each region was required to report the changes in the value of human assets during each year. Written explanations were also requested. This information was reported to the home office.

Information for the Board and Stockholders. Under the new system, the board of directors was to receive information about the change in the company's *human resource investment* and its *human resource value*. Each of these measures was intended to indicate different aspects of management's attention to building and maintaining human resources.

Moreover, the board decided to report the information on the company's investment in human assets to investors. These data were to be included in the president's letter in the corporate annual report (Table 1-5). It was to be explicitly pointed out that the data were unaudited.

Conclusion. The system described above has illustrated some aspects of how human resource accounting can be used by the human resource professional in making personnel decisions and as an adviser to line management. In brief, we have seen that human resource accounting can provide information to facilitate aspects of human resource planning, including human resource costs for budgeting personnel

Table 1-5

NORTHEASTERN INSURANCE COMPANY

Capital Investments in Human Resources
Actual for the Year 19X5 and Budgeted for 19X6

Investments in Human Resources	*Actual 19X1*	*Budgeted 19X2*
New Investments:		
(1) Acquisition	$ 600,000	$ 700,000
(2) Development	1,500,000	2,000,000
Total invested	$2,100,000	$2,700,000
Disinvestments:		
(1) Turnover	1,000,000	800,000
Net change	$1,100,000	$1,900,000

acquisition and development. Similarly, we have seen how human resource accounting can be used in evaluating proposed investments in training and developing people, so that such investments can be based upon an economic assessment of their costs and benefits rather than on blind faith. The example has also shown that human resource accounting can provide information for the control of personnel costs and can help management to appreciate the magnitude of turnover costs. Finally, the example has suggested how information about changes in human resource value can facilitate the assessment of the human resource aspect of management's effectiveness. Not all of the potential uses of human resource accounting were illustrated in the Northeastern Insurance Company example; nevertheless, it provides a scenario for how a human resource accounting system can help the human resource professional manage a company's human assets more effectively.

Summary

A major purpose of human resource accounting is to help human resource professionals and senior managers to use an organization's human resources effectively and efficiently. Human resource accounting is intended to provide these users with information needed to acquire, develop, allocate, conserve, utilize, evaluate, and reward human resources. Human resource accounting develops measures of the cost and value of people to an organization for use in a variety of management decisions. Not only does it provide a framework for thinking about the management of people in organizations, but it also motivates management to appreciate the effects of business decisions on human assets.

This chapter has described the potential role of human resource accounting for management and human resource professionals. The following chapter examines the uses of human resource accounting for investors.

Case 1-1: R. G. Barry (A)

R. G. Barry Corporation has established five basic areas as the responsibility of all members of management. Three of these areas of management are common to all businesses: profit responsibility, solvency responsibility, and physical resource responsibility. The other two—customer resource responsibility and organizational resource responsibility—are recognized as necessary by other businesses but frequently are not afforded equal status with the preceding three.

Total Resource Measurement. Conventional accounting provides adequate measures of profit, solvency, and physical assets such as plant, equipment, and inventory. Measurement of the two human resources has not been addressed in normal accounting practice.

Value of Human Resources. There is, however, recognition of the dollar value of the human resources of a business under conventional accounting practice when one business acquires another. The amount by which the sale price exceeds the net worth really represents, first, the value of customers who are loyal to the company and can be expected to continue to purchase the products or services and, second, the value of the human organization that knows how to make and sell products or services at a profit. This is generally termed "goodwill" by the accountant.

These external and internal human resources are as distinctly assets to the company as the cash, brick and mortar, equipment, and inventory that are accounted for in considerable detail under established accounting procedure. Consequently, the R. G. Barry manager's job is to contribute to the profitability of the company while maintaining the

Note: The statements in this case present a slightly modified version of quotations from the 1968 annual report of R. G. Barry Corporation, Columbus, Ohio. The case is included as a historical illustration of one of the earliest experiments in developing human resource accounting.

solvency of the firm and preserving, if not enhancing, the physical, organizational, and customer resources entrusted to his care.

Developing a System. It is obvious that a manager can liquidate a physical asset and generate cash that is reflected as improved profit. This kind of mismanagement would be evident in a conventional accounting system. A manager can likewise depreciate a customer asset and improve profit in the short run by, for example, cutting back on quality. Or a manager can destroy organizational assets and improve profit in the short run through the simple expedient of withholding merit increases or driving employees harder.

If managers are to understand what is happening to all resources entrusted to their care, they must have information about the status of organizational and customer resources. It is to this need that our efforts to develop a system of accounting for human resources are addressed.

The basic objectives in developing a human resource accounting system are:

1. To provide Barry managers with specific information on their performance in managing the organizational resources and customer loyalty resources entrusted to their care so that they can make proper adjustments to their pattern of operations to correct adverse trends or further improve the condition of these resources
2. To provide Barry managers with additional information pertaining to human resources to assist in their decision making
3. To provide the organization with a more accurate accounting of its return on total resources employed, rather than just the physical resources, and to enable management to analyze how changes in the status of resources affect the achievement of corporate objectives

R. G. Barry, working with Rensis Likert and the Institute for Social Research of the University of Michigan, began work in 1967 on a system to account for the human resources represented by the people within the Barry organization. This was done by accounting for cash outlays made to obtain, maintain, and develop the organization's human resources. In 1968 the system covered only managerial personnel. Outlay costs for recruiting, training, familiarizing, and developing management personnel were accumulated and capitalized for management people. In 1969 this cash outlay accounting approach was extended to nonmanagement personnel at one manufacturing location.

The human resource capital accounts are used for internal information only and are not reflected, of course, in the financial data presented in the company's annual report. It is conceivable that in the years ahead conventional accounting will come to recognize the impact of human resources on the long-term economic health of the enterprise and place these figures on the balance sheet. From the standpoint of the investor, as well as from the perspective of top management, knowledge of the change in the status of all the resources of a business is necessary for proper decision making and planning long-range growth.

First Pioneering Step. The organizational resource outlay cost system at R. G. Barry at this point lacks refinement. It is but a first pioneering step toward the goal of a sophisticated human resource accounting system. Even in its present experimental state, however, it has provided considerable information about investments made in acquiring and developing people—one of our most important resources.

Question

R. G. Barry Corporation, listed on the American Stock Exchange, was one of the first companies to do exploratory work in developing human resource accounting. Do you agree with R. G. Barry's decision to undertake research to develop a system of accounting for its human resources? Explain.

Case 1-2: The University of Michigan (A)

During the spring of 1971, the University of Michigan was, like most institutions of higher education, faced with budgetary problems. Specifically, the university was confronting a gap between its budgeted needs and the funds that the state of Michigan appeared willing to provide.

Writing in *The University of Michigan Today,* President R. W. Fleming argued that the budget proposed by the state would pose a dilemma for the university. Referring to the budget gap, Fleming stated: "For all practical purposes, no matter what label is applied to the methods of covering this gap, the difference must be made up by increasing the work load [of faculty], dropping programs and people, and diluting the quality of our work."[3]

In the same issue, an unsigned article stated that "salary improvements had the top priority in the 1971–72 budget request sent to the State by U-M." It also said that the increases in faculty salaries were "aimed at catching up to the increasing costs of living and return U-M to a more competitive salary level with comparable institutions. . . . U-M's average salary position has slipped when compared to the nation's institutions of higher education and salary increases at U-M over the last five years have lagged below those of comparable universities."[4]

Question

Are there any potentially undesirable consequences of the state's budget for the university? Explain.

Case 1-3: Northeastern Insurance Company

This chapter has presented a detailed example of the development of a human resource accounting system at the Northeastern Insurance Company. Suppose you are a consultant engaged to evaluate the system developed by the company.

Questions

1. Did Northeastern Insurance Company need a human resource accounting system? Explain.
2. Do you believe that the new system will be useful to the company? Explain.
3. For what specific groups of users will the system be most useful? For what users will it be least useful?
4. How could this system be made more useful to management?

TWO

Uses in Corporate Financial Reporting

In Chapter One, we examined the uses of human resource accounting as a tool for human resource professionals and senior management in a company. But human resource accounting also has significant uses for investors and other external users of accounting information. This chapter examines the role of human resource accounting as a tool for users of corporate financial reports. First, it discusses the problems of reporting on human assets to investors and financial analysts; then it explores the role of human resource accounting in "social accounting."

Human Resource Accounting for Investors

Present and potential stockholders of a company have long been interested in obtaining information about an organization's human assets, as suggested in a poem by Sir Matthew Webster Jenkinson:

Though your balance-sheet's a model of
  what balance-sheets should be,
Typed and ruled with great precision
  in a type that all can see;
Though the grouping of the assets is
  commendable and clear,
And the details which are given more
  than usually appear;

> Though investments have been valued at
> the sale price of the day,
> And the auditor's certificate shows
> everything O.K.;
> One asset is omitted—and its worth
> I want to know,
> The asset is the value of the men who
> run the show.[1]

Investors' Human Resource Information Needs. As Jenkinson's poem implies, investors would like to know the value of a firm's human assets. Moreover, they want to know about an organization's investment in human resources. This information would assist them in making decisions to acquire, retain, or dispose of stock.

Unfortunately, such information is not available to investors. At present, financial statements prepared in accordance with "generally accepted accounting principles" do not indicate the value of any of an organization's assets; they report the depreciated *cost* of assets as a surrogate for value. Furthermore, financial statements do not inform investors of an organization's investment in human assets; conventional accounting treats investments in human resources as expenses rather than as assets.

Given the importance of these problems to present and potential investors, this section examines the basic issues involved in accounting for human assets in corporate financial reports: What are the limitations of financial statements without human assets? Are people assets? How can investments in human assets be presented in corporate financial reports? What are the accounting problems of reporting human assets in financial statements?

Limitations of Financial Statements Without Human Assets. The practice of accounting for investments in human resources as expenses rather than as assets results in distorted income statements and balance sheets. In the income statement, the figure designated "net income" is distorted because accountants treat all expenditures made to acquire or develop human resources as expenses during the period incurred, rather than capitalizing and amortizing them over their expected service life. The balance sheet is distorted because the figure labeled "total assets" does not include the organization's human assets. There is, therefore, no indication of the organization's actual investment in its human assets.

The distortion of net income caused by present accounting practice for investments in people is illustrated in Table 2-1. This table shows how the income statement of Southwestern Electronics Company would be calculated both under currently accepted accounting conventions and under human resource accounting.

Table 2-1

SOUTHWESTERN ELECTRONICS COMPANY

Income Statements
For the Year Ending December 31, 19X5

	Conventional Accounting	*Human Resource Accounting*
Sales	$10,000,000	$10,000,000
Expenses:		
Expenses, excluding depreciation and amortization	7,500,000	7,000,000
Depreciation	1,000,000	1,000,000
Amortization	N.A.	50,000
Income Before Taxes	$ 1,500,000	$ 1,950,000

Note: Investments in Human Resources have been amortized on a straight-line basis over an expected service life of ten years.

Southwestern Electronics Company anticipates substantial growth during the next decade, and therefore it has incurred investments this year in recruiting, selecting, and training 100 technical personnel. The cost of recruitment and selection totaled $150,000 and the cost of training totaled $350,000. These costs are expected to have a useful life of approximately ten years. As Table 2-1 shows, conventional accounting practice treats these investments as expenses of the current year. The implicit assumption is that the expenditures are not expected to provide benefits beyond the current accounting period. Human resource accounting, on the other hand, capitalizes and amortizes expenditures for human resources over their expected useful life. Under this system, Southwestern Electronics Company's balance sheet would appear as shown in Table 2-2. This statement shows investments in human assets, net of amortization, amounting to $450,000. Amortization was calculated on a straight-line basis for the expected life of ten years. The difference between the company's assets as measured under conventional and

Table 2-2

SOUTHWESTERN ELECTRONICS COMPANY

Partial Balance Sheets
as of December 31, 19X5

	Conventional Accounting	Human Resource Accounting
Current Assets	$ 4,000,000	$ 4,000,000
Long-lived Assets:		
Plant and equipment, net*	15,000,000	15,000,000
Patents, net*	1,000,000	1,000,000
Human resource investments, net *	N.A.	450,000
Total Assets	$20,000,000	$20,450,000

*The long-lived assets are shown net of depreciation and/or amortization.

human resource accounting is equivalent to the firm's unamortized investments in people.

Conventional accounting thus treats every dollar spent by management to build human assets as an expense in the year incurred, even though the expenditures are made with the intention of providing benefits beyond the current period. Management, by investing in human resources to protect or enhance the future earning power of a business, will actually produce relatively lower reported current earnings. Management therefore may appear to be doing poorly when it is in fact doing well. As a consequence, there may be conflict between the long-run interests of the organization and the short-run interests of management.

In periods of a profit squeeze or when management wants to bolster reported current earnings, it may simply avoid or postpone needed investments in human resources. This strategy is analogous to postponing preventive maintenance or research and development, and the results are similar. Thus conventional accounting for human resources can lead management to make myopic decisions regarding investments in people.

From the viewpoint of both management and investors, current accounting practice for human assets causes another problem: It distorts the measurement of return on investment. The concept of rate of return on investment is a crucial variable in management and investor decisions. As Alfred P. Sloan, former chairman of the board of General Motors, observed: "No other financial principle with which I am acquainted serves better than rate of return as an objective aid to business judgment."[2]

Since rate of return is the ratio of net income to total assets, it becomes distorted because of distortions in its components. Investors who wish to base their decisions on an organization's rate of return must attempt to adjust for investments in human assets.

There is theoretical support for the human resource accounting approach to this problem. The report of an American Accounting Association committee states:

> A conversion is a recombination of asset services reflecting the production of new utility. Expenditures and other costs devoted to such activities as research and development, personnel recruitment and training, and marketing campaigns often involve an element of future usefulness and are examples of conversions that would be recognized if quantifiable and verifiable.[3]

This statement suggests that the principal constraint upon treating personnel costs as assets is the measurement problem, which is an empirical question of feasibility. The committee's report also recognized the distorting effects of the conventional treatment:

> Present practice recognizes such costs as assets . . . only when a physical product or such a legal privilege as a patent results. When practice refuses to recognize the conversion to asset status by assigning a zero value to the asset it assigns all the expenditure to the expense category, thus presenting an expense that is equally unverifiable as deserving expense status. This is somewhat curious in view of a popular emphasis upon the income statement but understandable in terms of the tendency to conservatism in asset valuation.[4]

Thus if it is possible to develop valid and reliable measurement techniques for human resource costs, they should be treated as assets to avoid distortion of net income.

People as "Assets." The preceding discussion suggests that the fundamental issue involved in accounting for human resources in corporate financial reports is: Are people assets? Stated differently, the question is: Should people be reported as assets in financial statements? Questions of this type have been raised principally by critics of the idea of accounting for human assets in financial statements.[5] Viewed broadly, such questions are legitimate and deserve an answer; but the question as it stands is poorly framed.

The essential issue is not whether people per se should be treated as assets in financial statements. People are not assets; the *services* people are expected to provide to an organization comprise the asset. To treat people as an asset is to confuse the agent that provides services with the asset itself (the expected services). Thus the real issue is: Should investments in people be treated as assets? This question turns on the nature of assets and the extent to which investments in people satisfy the criteria established for treating an object as an asset.

Historically, the term *asset* has been defined in many ways, and no single definition of the concept has ever become generally accepted. Nevertheless, certain criteria must be met before something can be treated as an asset for purposes of corporate financial reporting.

The main criteria for an asset are these: It must possess future service potential; it must be measurable in monetary terms; and it must be subject to the ownership or control of the accounting entity. The primary criterion is future service potential; if the object is not expected to render future services, it cannot be an asset.

A second criterion is that it must be measurable in monetary terms, the common denominator of corporate financial reporting. Thus an object may possess expected future service potential, but unless its future services can be measured in monetary terms, we cannot treat it as an asset. Indeed, this was the argument made by W. A. Paton in 1922, in his classic book *Accounting Theory,* when he stated that personnel could not be treated as assets:

> In the business enterprise, a well-organized and loyal personnel may be a more important "asset" than a stock of merchandise. . . . At present there seems to be no way of measuring such factors in terms of the dollar; hence, they cannot be recognized as specific economic assets. But let us, accordingly, admit the serious limitation of the conventional balance sheet as a statement of financial condition.[6]

If something possesses future service potential but its services cannot be measured in monetary terms, we may wish to view it as a "resource" but not as an asset.

The third criterion is that the object must be subject either to the ownership or control of the accounting entity. The key element of this criterion is the notion of control. Drawing upon Irving Fisher, the accounting entity must have the right to the *chance* of attaining some or all of the future services of the object.[7] Commonly the right to the chance of obtaining the future services is based on ownership; that is, the firm owns the objects and possesses a legal right to use them. However, there are examples of things treated as assets even though they are not owned in the conventional sense. For example, long-term leases under sale and lease-back agreements are commonly treated as assets. (That is, the expected future rental payments are capitalized.) Similarly, intercorporate investments in subsidiaries are consolidated in financial statements and treated as assets even if the subsidiaries are not wholly owned. The rationale is that they are subject to substantial *control* of the parent corporation.

Anything that satisfies all three criteria is an asset. It should be noted that the first and third criteria can be applied as tests for an asset only on a probabilistic basis. There is virtually always uncertainty about an object's expected future service potential, and even if it is owned there is still uncertainty about the likelihood that an object's future services will be realized. If investments in people satisfy these criteria, they may be treated as assets. If these investments are expected to possess future service potential, if they are measurable in monetary terms, and if they are subject to the control of the organization (at least on a probabilistic basis), then they are assets.

Some accounting theorists may disagree with these conclusions about the criteria for assets and the validity of treating investments in people as assets. Some would probably argue that ownership, not control, is the key to the third criterion—and because people cannot be owned, they cannot be assets. Others might argue that there is too much uncertainty surrounding the realization of human services—after all, people are free to leave an organization. They might add that accounting must be "conservative"—and therefore investments in people, while logically assets, should not be treated as such in practice. Still others might argue that the timing of benefits to be derived is uncertain—and therefore capitalizing investments in people will give management more latitude to manipulate earnings.

All these objections to treating investments in people as assets have some validity. However, there are counterarguments for each. The basic argument against ownership as a rigid criterion for an asset is that it is an arbitrary prerequisite. The most essential criterion for determining whether a cost is an asset or an expense relates to the notion of future service potential; this is the *sine qua non* of all assets. Moreover, there are, as we have observed, assets such as long-term leases that do not satisfy the ownership criterion. The argument that there is significant uncertainty in the potential for realizing the services of people is well taken. However, it does not follow that we must be conservative and treat investments in people as expenses in the period incurred; we have seen that this practice is undesirable because it distorts the income statements and balance sheet and may lead management to attempt to manipulate earnings numbers. Thus we should not sacrifice, in the name of conservatism, the fundamental aim of corporate financial reporting: the matching of revenues and expenses in the proper period. There are, as we shall see, other methods of dealing with the uncertainty of realizing the services of people.

Finally, we should recognize that the potential for manipulation of earnings exists not only if we capitalize investments in people, but also if we fail to capitalize them. As Arthur Andersen & Co., certified public accountants, stated in their book *Objectives of Financial Statements for Business Enterprises:* "Expenditures such as those made for human resources, for technical know-how, for customer attraction, and for obtaining competitive advantage for brand names may be very large. These expenditures may be increased or decreased almost at will in the short term, with consequent huge effects on earnings."[8]

In summary, then, there are two major reasons for treating investments in people as assets in corporate financial reports: First, present and potential investors need such information to help assess the value of a business enterprise, and, second, investments in people satisfy the criteria for treatment as an asset.

Methods of Reporting Investments in Human Assets. There are four possible methods of presenting investments in human assets in corporate annual reports. This information may be presented in the president's letter, in a statement of intangibles, in unaudited pro forma supplementary financial statements, or integrated into conventional financial statements.

The president's letter of corporate annual reports frequently includes information about expenditures in human resources that may be quite significant and may (especially in service industries) be relatively more important than expenditures for physical assets. As an interim measure toward full accounting for human assets, the president's letter may report expenditures made as investments in human assets during the current period. An airline, for example, might report its investment in pilot training. This information will help investors and financial analysts assess the extent to which management is paying attention to human resource development, a crucial factor in an organization's long-term profitability. Moreover, the president's letter should include information about employee turnover—its rate and cost. Perhaps the firm ought to report on turnover of key managers and technical specialists, who may join existing competitors or establish a new rival. This occurrence is not uncommon, especially in technologically oriented industries where research and development plays a crucial role. In 1968, an executive of Motorola resigned to join Fairchild Camera & Instrument Corp.; subsequently, other Motorola employees resigned and joined Fairchild. Motorola filed suit seeking damages from Fairchild Camera, and certain former executives and their wives, for "unfair competition." Clearly Motorola deemed the loss of these personnel significant. Thus significant losses of human assets might be reported in the president's letter.

A second approach is to present information about investments in human assets in a statement of intangibles. This approach was suggested by Arthur Andersen & Co. as a method of dealing with all so-called intangibles, including human assets.

The firm suggests that major expenditures for intangibles, including human resources, should be shown as separate classifications in the income statement. "In addition," they continue, "companies heavily engaged in expenditures for the creation of intangibles, particularly technologically oriented companies and service companies with large investments in personnel, plus companies growing by way of mergers and acquisitions and disbursing large amounts for goodwill of existing businesses, should present a statement of intangibles."[9] The statement would indicate the expenditures made for various classes of intangibles for the current period as well as for prior periods. Notes could be used to describe the nature of the expenditures, the status of projects, and other relevant information.

This proposal has appeal. It would provide investors with information about investments in human resources, while abiding the difficulties inherent in the problem of amortizing such assets. The major limitation of this proposal is that financial statements would still be distorted. The balance sheet would be distorted because the company's total assets (human as well as financial and physical) would be understated. The measurement of income would be distorted because all expenditures for human assets would be expensed in the period incurred. In turn, measurements of the firm's return on investments would still be distorted.

The third approach to this problem is to present information about investments in human resources in unaudited, pro forma financial statements. The company may prepare a set of financial statements showing investments in human assets under proposed human resource accounting conventions and include these statements as supplementary information in their annual report. The report would note that these statements should be considered separately from the conventional financial statements. It would also note that the supplementary statements were not prepared in accordance with currently accepted accounting standards, present management's rationale for the different accounting treatments, and note that the statements were not audited.

Steps toward this approach have been taken by a few organizations. For a few years in the 1970s, the R. G. Barry Corporation presented such statements in its annual report. (This practice is discussed in Chapter Four.) Readers of the company's financial report were cautioned that the information was provided only to illustrate the informational value of human resource accounting for more effective internal management of the business. They were also cautioned to use conventional accounting data to evaluate the firm's performance. Abt Associates is another organization that has presented supplementary financial statements reflecting investments in human assets (see Case 2-2). The firm's 1971 annual report includes both a "social balance sheet" and a "social income statement." The firm's social balance sheet includes a measure of its investment in training (net of amortization). However, Abt's social balance sheet and income statement are intended primarily as reports on the firm's progress in meeting its social responsibilities, rather than as information to investors per se.

The final, and perhaps the ultimate, method of presenting investments in human assets in corporate annual reports is to include them in conventional financial statements. This method involves capitalization of investments in human assets and amortization of such investments over their expected useful life. Although this treatment of investments in people is certainly not common, some corporations have followed this practice. For example, certain firms in human capital intensive industries (such as airlines, electronics, and professional sports) have accounted for investments in people in this way.

The Milwaukee Braves, Inc., capitalized expenditures for investments in "team development" from 1962 to 1965. In the president's letter of the corporation's 1963 annual report, John J. McHale stated that "we have continued to be a leader in the all-important area of future team development by investing in excess of $900,000 in 1963. Our expenditures for team development are comparable to other businesses and industries' expense for research and development. This department is the lifeline to the future."[10]

The company's income statement, shown in Exhibit 2-1, included $932,897 for "future team development and scouting." The balance sheet included an asset of $6,059,116 for "player contracts and development cost" (less accumulated amortization). From this information it appears that a portion of team development costs was capitalized and treated as a long-term asset. Although the available information is incomplete, apparently this asset was amortized over its expected useful life.

In 1965, the Milwaukee franchise was moved to Atlanta and the firm was renamed "Atlanta Braves, Inc." In the president's letter of the 1966 annual report, William C. Bartholomay noted that the corporation had changed its method of accounting for player contracts and development costs to conform with the accounting procedures of other major league teams. The company's income statement, shown in Exhibit 2-2, includes amounts of $1,902,170 and $1,758,300 for "team development and scouting" for 1966 and 1965, respectively. However, the balance sheet no longer includes "development cost" as an asset.

The Flying Tiger Line, Inc., is another corporation that has included investments in human assets in its financial statements. The company's 1967 balance sheet is shown in Exhibit 2-3. Under the label "other assets and deferred charges," it includes an item labeled "training costs applicable to aircraft, being amortized." This item amounted to $3,423,759 and $3,003,475 in 1966 and 1967, respectively. The firm's financial statements were audited by Arthur Andersen & Co. and the CPA firm issued an unqualified opinion (Exhibit 2-4).

Exhibit 2-1

MILWAUKEE BRAVES, INC.

Income Statement
From Inception (November 26, 1962) through October 31, 1963

Income		
Admissions, broadcast, concessions and other		$3,438,324
Operating Expense		
Team, park, games and concessions		$2,156,403
Future team development and scouting		932,897
General and administrative		266,631
		$3,355,931
Net Income from Operations		$ 82,393
Interest Expense		$ 125,771
Net income (loss) for the period		$ (43,378)

Balance Sheet—October 31, 1963

Assets		
Current (incl. $271,080 in cash and Treasury Bills)		$ 446,048
Player Contracts and Development Cost (less accumulated amortization)		6,059,116
Fixed Assets (less $155,434 accumulated depreciation)		20,854
League Membership at cost		50,000
		$6,576,018
Liabilities and Capital		
Current liabilities (incl. $73,600 due under Player Bonus Contracts)		$ 306,309
Advance ticket sales—1964 season		29,494
Player bonus liability due beyond one year		64,000
Long term debt (note 1)		3,000,000
Common stock $1.00 Par—500,000 authorized, 316,000 shares outstanding	316,000	
Capital surplus—paid in	2,903,593	
Net income (loss) for period	(43,378)	3,176,215
		$6,576,018

The accompanying notes to financial statements are an integral part of the above income statement and balance sheet.

SOURCE: *Milwaukee Braves, Inc. 1963 Annual Report.*

Exhibit 2-2

ATLANTA BRAVES, INC. AND SUBSIDIARIES

Consolidated Statements of Income
for the Years Ended October 31, 1966 and 1965

	1966	*1965*
Income:		
		(Note 1)
Admissions, broadcast, concessions, special events and other	$ 7,809,699	$ 2,147,188
Operating Expenses:		
Team, park and broadcasting	$ 3,799,190	$ 1,546,974
Team development and scouting (note 1)	1,902,170	1,758,300
Special stadium events	276,473	–
General and administrative	675,044	328,330
Interest	164,937	175,699
	$ 6,817,814	$ 3,809,303
Operating income (loss)	$ 991,885	$(1,662,115)
Special Items:		
Income from special Atlanta exhibition games, net	–	242,984
Franchise relocation costs, net	–	(97,930)
Income (loss) before provision for income taxes	$ 991,885	$(1,517,061)
Provision for Federal and State Income Taxes	500,000	–
Net Income (Loss) Before Special Credit	$ 491,885	$(1,517,061)
Special Credit, income tax reduction from prior years' operating losses (note 6)	500,000	–
Net Income (loss) Including Special Credit	$ 991,885	$(1,517,061)

Exhibit 2-2 (continued)

Consolidated Balance Sheet—October 31, 1966

Assets:		
Current (including $189,146 in cash)—(notes 3 and 5)		$ 1,116,437
Player contracts, less accumulated amortization (note 1)		3,310,794
Leasehold improvements and equipment, less $322,513 accumulated depreciation		782,368
Contribution receivable from stadium authority (note 3)		772,256
Deferred stadium rental, less $92,924 current (note 3)		475,556
League membership, at cost		50,000
		$ 6,507,411
Liabilities and Capital:		
Current (including $72,500 current maturities of long-term obligations)		$ 1,912,183
Long-term obligations (note 4)		3,427,778
Commitment and contingent matters (notes 2 and 3)		
Stockholders' investment (note 4)—		
Common stock, $1 par value, 500,000 shares authorized, 316,000 shares outstanding	$ 316,000	
Capital in excess of par value of common stock (no change during year)	2,903,593	
Retained earnings (deficit)	(2,052,143)	1,167,450
		$ 6,507,411

The accompanying notes are an integral part of these statements.

SOURCE: *Atlanta Braves, Inc. and Subsidiaries 1966 Annual Report.*

Exhibit 2-3

THE FLYING TIGER LINE, INC.

Balance Sheets for December 31, 1967 and 1966

Assets	*1967*	*1966*
Current Assets (including prepaid engine overhaul cost):		
Cash, including $11,500,000 and $10,800,000 of certificates of deposit at December 31, 1967 and 1966, respectively	$ 12,683,091	$ 15,416,088
Receivables, less reserves—		
Freight customers	4,433,736	5,102,779
Charters, service sales, etc.—		
United States Government	6,535,955	6,245,501
Other	4,071,079	2,920,173
Materials and supplies, at average cost	4,668,237	3,317,007
Aircraft acquired for sale	—	1,102,984
Prepaid insurance, rents, etc.	2,574,796	1,951,117
Prepaid engine overhaul cost	2,237,855	2,195,233
Total current assets	$ 37,204,749	$ 38,250,882
Temporary Cash Investments, Restricted to Disbursement for Equipment Acquisition	$ 46,630,000	$ —
Property and Equipment, at cost (notes 1 and 2):		
Aircraft, engines and other flight equipment	$ 89,501,268	$ 88,995,273
Other equipment	3,316,144	2,670,599
Land and buildings	6,387,706	6,146,697
	$ 99,205,118	$ 97,812,569
Less—reserves for depreciation	47,042,091	40,272,054
	$ 52,163,027	$ 57,540,515
Deposits on aircraft, engines, etc.	22,401,821	10,035,142
	$ 74,564,848	$ 67,575,657
Other Assets and Deferred Charges:		
Unamortized debt expense	$ 1,166,961	$ 110,852
Long-term lease deposits, receivables, etc.	1,218,026	1,028,797
Training costs applicable to aircraft, being amortized	3,003,475	3,423,759
	$ 5,383,462	$ 4,563,408
	$163,788,059	$110,389,947

Exhibit 2-4

AUDITOR'S OPINION ON THE FLYING TIGER LINE, INC.
1966 and 1967 Financial Statements

Arthur Andersen & Co.

1320 West Third Street
Los Angeles, California 90017

TO THE STOCKHOLDERS,
THE FLYING TIGER LINE INC.:

We have examined the balance sheets of THE FLYING TIGER LINE INC. (a Delaware corporation) as of December 31, 1967 and 1966, and the related statements of income, stockholders' equity, and funds for the years then ended. Our examinations were made in accordance with generally accepted auditing standards, and accordingly included such tests of the accounting records and such other auditing procedures as we considered necessary in the circumstances.

In our opinion, the financial statements referred to above present fairly the financial position of The Flying Tiger Line Inc. as of December 31, 1967 and 1966, and the results of its operations and the source and application of funds for the years then ended, in conformity with generally accepted accounting principles applied on a consistent basis during the periods.

Arthur Andersen & Co.

Los Angeles, California
February 9, 1968

SOURCE: *The Flying Tiger Line Inc. 1967 Annual Report.*

In 1969 the corporation changed its method of accounting for training costs and elected to expense them as incurred. This change was described in the Notes to Financial Statements in the report:

> The Financial Statements presented herein reflect a change in accounting treatments for initial training and preoperating costs relative to aircraft fleet acquisitions to charge off such costs when incurred. Previously, initial training and preoperating costs had been deferred and amortized over a five-year period. Years prior to 1969 have been retroactively restated to reflect this change in accounting method. The net effect of this change was to reduce net income $1,374,000 for 1969, $1,205,000 for 1968, and $1,345,000 for years prior to 1968. Initial training and preoperating costs included in depreciation and amortiza-

tion for 1969 and 1968 were $2,905,000 and $5,139,000, respectively, after restatement.[11]

Accounting Problems of Human Assets. Once the decision to report human assets in financial statements has been made, there are five major accounting questions to be resolved: What costs should be capitalized as assets? How should these costs be amortized? Under what circumstances should this asset be written off? How should investments in human assets be presented in financial statements? And how can we avoid the possibility that accounting for human assets will be simply another area in which management can manipulate earnings?

Capitalization of Human Resource Costs. The most basic question in accounting for human assets in financial statements is: What costs should be capitalized? This is essentially a question of classifying human resource costs into their expense and asset components.

The basic criterion for determining whether a cost is an asset or an expense is related to the notion of future service potential. Costs should be treated as expenses in the period in which their benefits are derived. If the expected benefits relate to a future time period, they should be treated as assets. For example, the 1970 annual report of Electronic Data Systems includes an item in the balance sheet for the cost of training systems engineers in the company's Systems Engineering Development Program. The item is included in the balance sheet as an asset because it is expected to have future service potential.

Amortization of Human Assets. Once human assets have been capitalized, the next accounting problem is the measurement of the portion of the asset's service life consumed during an accounting period. For physical assets such as machines, this process is known as depreciation; for so-called intangible assets, the process is known as amortization of capitalized costs. For human assets, we refer to amortization.

The principal objective of amortizing human assets is to match the consumption of an asset's services with the benefits derived. Conventionally, accounting calls this *matching expenses with revenues* (the "matching principle"). In amortizing human assets, the basic guideline is to amortize the asset over its expected service life (which must be estimated).

Some human assets may have a service life equivalent to a person's expected organizational tenure, while others may have a service life equivalent to the period a person is expected to occupy a certain position in the organization. The service life of still others may be a function of the expected state of technology. For example, the costs of acquiring people and bringing them into an organization may be anticipated to benefit the organization for the person's expected tenure. In contrast, investments in training a quality control engineer may not necessarily be useful if the person transfers to sales. Moreover, investments in training computer programmers in a particular programming language have a useful life equivalent to the expected life of the language.

It should be noted that group rather than individual amortization may be appropriate. An expected employee tenure of five years, for example, means that the average person will remain five years. Thus organizations may use both individual and group amortization—that is, group amortization for factory workers and clerical employees but individual amortization for managers.

Adjustment of Human Asset Accounts. Although the basic method of expensing human assets is amortization, there may be circumstances under which human asset accounts must be adjusted. For example, human assets may be written off as a result of turnover or changes in service life estimates. Turnover may occur either voluntarily or through layoffs, terminations, and so forth. In either case, the unamortized asset balance must be treated as a loss in the period it is incurred. A person's expected service life may change as a result of many factors. Deteriorating health, plans for early retirement, technological obsolescence—all may shorten an asset's future service life. When a material change in a person's expected service life has occurred, the asset should be adjusted. This write-down of human assets is analogous to a write-down of physical assets.

Presentation of Human Assets in Financial Statements. One aspect of human assets creating special reporting problems is the probability of turnover. Obviously people are not *owned* by organizations, although certain types of organizations do have employment contracts that limit the mobility of employees—professional athletic organizations like the Atlanta Braves have contracts with their personnel. In fact, such corporations presently have the right to buy, sell, and trade the contracts of personnel. In most cases however, people are relatively free to leave an organization. Thus there is a degree of uncertainty regarding the extent to which an employee's future service potential will actually be realized.

The basic accounting question here is: How can we take the degree of uncertainty of realizing human services into account in presenting investments in people in financial statements? This problem can be resolved by providing an allowance for expected turnover cost as an offset (contra account) to gross investment in human assets, as shown in Exhibit 2-5.

Exhibit 2-5

AEROSPACEX CORPORATION
PARTIAL BALANCE SHEET
1973

Assets	
Current assets	
Cash	$12,000,000
Receivables, net (note 1)	4,000,000
Materials and supplies	10,000,000
Property and equipment, net (note 2)	$26,000,000
	$60,000,000
Other assets	
Long-term lease deposits	$ 2,000,000
Investment in human assets, net (see note 3)	2,700,000
	$ 4,700,000
Total assets	$90,700,000

In the Notes to Financial Statements that would accompany Exhibit 2-5, note 3 might state: "Gross unamortized investment in human assets (principally investments in training) is $3,000,000. An allowance of $300,000 has been provided for unrealizable training investment due to expected turnover. Net investment in human assets is $2,700,000." Thus a contra account would be used to provide an allowance for unrealized investment in human assets attributable to expected turnover. The amount of this allowance would depend on the firm's experience with turnover. In firms where turnover is insignificant, the allowance might be unnecessary; where turnover is quite high, the allowance could be substantial.

The bookkeeping entry required to make such an allowance is:

Dr.	Turnover Expense	300,000	
	Cr. Allowance for Expected Turnover		300,000

This is an adjusting entry that would be made at the end of the accounting period.

The technique suggested for coping with the degree of uncertainty surrounding the realization of services from investments in human resources is analogous to methods of accounting for accounts receivable. If a firm's experience indicates that a certain percentage of accounts receivable will be uncollectible, it must provide for estimated future credit losses, and a contra account will be used to state accounts receivable at their amount expected to be realizable.

Manipulation of Earnings. The final issue involved in reporting human assets in financial statements concerns the possibility of earnings manipulation. Some accountants believe that so-called intangibles such as human assets should be expensed during the year they are incurred even though they are expected to provide future benefits, because there is too much uncertainty about the benefits that will be gained to capitalize such assets. There is some merit in this view, but the generalization is too sweeping. The decision to capitalize an investment in human assets depends on the degree of uncertainty *in the specific situation.* Under certain circumstances, it may not be useful to capitalize human assets because the future benefits may be too tenuous; however, such circumstances should be viewed as the exception and not as the general rule.

The question of earnings manipulation is not trivial, and future research must be designed to study this issue. Even so, the problem is not sufficient to override the necessity of accounting for human assets in external financial statements.

Human Resource Accounting in Social Accounting

As a result of a changing social ethos, business organizations are increasingly expected to meet culturally and governmentally defined standards of corporate responsibility with respect to the environment, consumerism, minority employment, women's rights, and employee satisfaction. If current trends persist, it is likely that business corporations increasingly will be held accountable for social as well as financial goals. They will be asked to demonstrate the extent of their social contribution. They may also come under the scrutiny of a social audit to assess the costs as well as the benefits of corporate activities.

The measurement methods of human resource accounting can facilitate corporate social accountability for employees. The techniques for measuring investments in human resources might be used to assess a corporation's contribution to socially valuable human capital. Many firms engage in hiring and developing the hard-core unemployed, for example, and one measure of a firm's social contribution might be its investment in building human resources among this group.

Human resource accounting measurement techniques may also be used to help control the liquidation and depletion of the economy's human capital. For example, there is a high risk of technological obsolescence in the aerospace industry. Engineers may become specialists on a single wing for a number of years, but once that wing is phased out the engineers may be obsolete. The firm may well find it less costly to recruit and hire recent college graduates than to invest in retraining its current engineers. As a result, highly trained and experienced people may find themselves unemployed. To meet its social responsibilities to its current employees, an aerospace company might invest in developing the *general* skills of its engineers in addition to investing in training for specific skills that are likely to become obsolete.

Human resource accounting measurements can also be used to assess the quality of the working life of employees. If present trends continue, the "Lordstown Syndrome" of rebellion against hard, monotonous, dehumanized work can be expected to spread. As a result of our changing social ethos, the ethic that hard work is a virtue and a duty is being abandoned. There is increasing concern for work to provide on-the-job satisfaction as well as a means to off-the-job satisfaction. Management therefore needs a way of measuring employees' satisfaction with aspects of work. The issue promises to appear increasingly in labor/management relations.

Steps toward corporate accountability for employees have already been taken by a few organizations. Abt Associates, Inc., includes a measure of the firm's social costs and benefits to its staff in a "social income statement." Abt's system is examined in Case 2-2. In the future, we can expect more and more corporations to report on their actions and programs involving employees. We may also anticipate that human resource accounting will serve as a tool to facilitate corporate social accountability for employees.

Summary

This chapter has examined the role of human resource accounting in corporate financial reporting; moreover, we have discussed the problems and methods of accounting for human assets for investors. Specifically, we have examined four basic issues involved in accounting for human assets in financial statements: What are the limitations of financial statements without human assets? Are people assets? How can investments in human assets be reported in corporate financial reports? And what are the accounting problems of reporting human assets in financial statements?

Current financial accounting practice treats all expenditures for investments in human resources as expenses rather than assets. This convention results in a distorted measure of an organization's return on investment. It therefore creates problems for investors who attempt to value an organization.

It is not the people themselves that are an organization's human assets, but rather *investments* in people. Since these investments satisfy the major criteria for classification as assets, they should be treated as such in corporate financial reports.

There are four possible methods of presenting investment in human assets in corporate financial reports: in the president's letter, in a statement of intangibles, in unaudited pro forma supplementary financial statements, and integrated into conventional financial statements.

The major accounting problems of reporting human assets in financial statements involve the capitalization, amortization, write-off, and presentation of human asset costs. Another problem concerns the potential for manipulation of corporate earnings through accounting for human resources.

This chapter has also examined the role of human resource accounting in corporate social accountability for employees. We have seen how human resource accounting can facilitate an organization's human resource accountability.

Case 2-1: McCormick & Company, Inc.

The consolidated balance sheet of McCormick & Company as of November 30, 1970 and 1971 (shown in Exhibit 2-6), includes an item labeled "Human Relations" as an asset. The amount of this asset is $1.

Exhibit 2-6

McCORMICK & COMPANY, INC., AND CONSOLIDATED SUBSIDIARIES

Balance Sheet

	November 30 1971	1970
Current Assets		
Cash	$ 2,186,703	$ 1,740,771
Receivables, less allowance for losses (1971 - $112,723, 1970 - $82,194)	17,481,018	18,005,029
Inventories, at lower of average cost or market	29,237,500	23,410,556
Expenses paid in advance	1,525,092	1,446,908
TOTAL CURRENT ASSETS	50,430,313	44,603,264
Investments		
Investments in and advances to unconsolidated subsidiary and 50%-owned companies (Note 1.)	8,092,688	6,734,732
Other	1,135,044	1,118,800
TOTAL INVESTMENTS	9,227,732	7,853,532
Property—At Cost		
Land	1,529,570	1,468,120
Buildings and improvements	10,383,577	6,519,158
Machinery and equipment	23,240,886	19,220,801
Construction in progress	705,932	1,030,742
	35,859,965	28,238,821
Less amount charged to expense to date (Note 9)	15,580,574	13,462,170
PROPERTY – NET	20,279,391	14,776,651
Excess Cost of Acquisition of Consolidated Subsidiaries (Note 1)	119,159	142,295
Patents and License Rights – At Amortized Cost	570,420	640,315
Goodwill, Trademarks, Formulae, Etc.	1	1
Human Relations	1	1
Other Assets		
Litigation claim – pending (Note 2)	2,452,000	2,752,000
Receivables from employees, etc. (group life insurance pledged as collateral)	210,200	223,000
Deferred income tax	291,568	308,553
Other	704,960	371,884
TOTAL OTHER ASSETS	3,658,728	3,655,437
TOTAL	$84,285,745	$71,671,496

Questions

1. What is McCormick & Company trying to indicate by including the item labeled "Human Relations" on its balance sheet?
2. Why does this item have a $1 valuation?

Case 2-2: Abt Associates, Inc.

Abt Associates, Inc., is a consulting firm founded in 1965. It specializes in the application of systems analysis and social science techniques to various social, economic, and technological problems. Its clients include industrial, governmental, and educational institutions.

The company is organized into six areas, including education, economic and regional development, human development, manpower and organizational development, social science research and development, and technology management. In 1971 the firm employed about 200 people. Its revenues totaled about $4.5 million.

The company's headquarters is located in Cambridge, Massachusetts, with branch offices in Washington, Atlanta, San Francisco, and Paris.

The Firm's Social Accounting System. In the president's letter of the 1971 annual report of Abt Associates, Inc., Clark C. Abt, president and treasurer, stated:

> This year we initiate an innovation in corporate reporting by presenting the qualified results of a Social Audit of Abt Associates Inc. Governments and industries have always invested in data collection and measurements promising the greatest utility to decision-making. This had led to a preference for "hard" or quantitative data. Until recently only the financial performance of an enterprise could be measured by quantitative units such as dollars. The social contribution of an enterprise, decisive as it might be for its own and societies' purposes, was put in qualitative terms whose accuracy was not subject to test. This made it difficult for managers to apply rational decision-making methods in allocating resources to the pursuit of objectives, and for investors to compare the

> qualities of their investments when they were interested in social as well as economic return. . . .
>
> Abt Associates Inc. has developed the Social Audit Method of estimating in quantitative, dollar-equivalent terms the social benefits and costs and the social assets and liabilities of organizations. . . . This method has been applied to our own company and the results are presented in detail on pp. 27-31 of this report.
>
> The basic concept used in the Social Audit to measure social benefits and costs to employees, communities, clients, and the general public is adopted from accounting practice. A thing is assumed to be worth what is paid for it, or what it costs, or the value received from it. This practice assumes all social impacts such as health, security, equality, environment, etc., can be expressed in terms of the money the people concerned have actually paid for the benefits or services, and what they have actually paid to avoid equivalent costs.
>
> It is our hope that many organizations, private and public, will soon adopt our procedure, so that measures of social contributions can be refined and standardized. . . .
>
> The Social Audit published here for the first time is not all that we would like it to be. As a first effort, it lacks completeness and precision. Some of its assumptions (to be found in the notes on p. 31) may be argued. Some of the data is only estimated, but no more so than the estimated worth of inventories or the depreciation of assets in financial statements. . . .

Social Accountability for Employees. The company's 1971 annual report included a social balance sheet (shown in Table 2-3), which lists "staff" as social assets available to the firm. It treats staff as consisting of two components: staff available to the firm per se and investments in staff (training).

The asset "staff available to the firm" is made up of two classes of staff: current staff assets (staff available within one year) and long-term staff assets (staff available after one year). In the Notes to the Social

Table 2-3

ABT ASSOCIATES, INC., SOCIAL BALANCE SHEET

Year Ended December 31, 1971, with Comparative Figures for 1970

Social Assets Available	*1971*	*1970*
Staff		
Available within one year (note I)	$ 2,594,390	$ 2,312,000
Available after one year (note J)	6,368,511	5,821,608
Training investment (note K)	507,405	305,889
	9,470,306	8,439,497
Less accumulated training obsolescence (note K)	136,995	60,523
Total staff assets	9,333,311	8,378,974
Organization		
Social capital investment (note L)	1,398,230	1,272,201
Retained earnings	219,136	–
Land	285,376	293,358
Buildings at cost	334,321	350,188
Equipment at cost	43,018	17,102
Total organization assets	2,280,081	1,932,849
Research		
Proposals (note M)	26,878	15,090
Child care research	6,629	–
Social audit	12,979	–
Total research	46,486	15,090
Public services consumed net of tax payments (note E)	152,847	243,399
Total social assets available	$11,812,725	$10,570,312

Table 2-3 (continued)

Social Commitments, Obligations, and Equity	*1971*	*1970*
Staff		
Committed to contracts within one year (note N)	$ 43,263	$ 81,296
Committed to contracts after one year (note O)	114,660	215,459
Committed to administration within one year (note N)	62,598	56,915
Committed to administration after one year (note O)	165,903	150,842
Total staff commitments	386,424	504,512
Organization		
Working capital requirements (note P)	60,000	58,500
Financial deficit	—	26,814
Facilities and equipment committed to contracts and administration (note N)	37,734	36,729
Total organization commitments	97,734	122,043
Environmental		
Government outlays for public services consumed, net of tax payment (note E)	152,847	243,399
Pollution from paper production (note Q)	1,770	770
Pollution from electric power production (note R)	2,200	1,080
Pollution from automobile commuting (note S)	10,493	4,333
Total environmental obligations	167,310	249,582
Total commitments and obligations	651,468	876,137
Society's Equity		
Contributed by staff (note T)	8,946,887	7,874,462
Contributed by stockholders (note U)	2,182,347	1,810,806
Generated by operations (note V)	32,023	8,907
Total equity	11,161,257	9,694,175
Total commitments, obligations and equity	$11,812,725	$10,570,312

SOURCE: *Abt Associates, Inc. 1971 Annual Report and Social Audit,* p. 28.

Balance Sheet and Income Statement, the firm states that current staff assets are calculated as the "annualized year-end staff payroll discounted to present value." The notes also state that the amount designated as "staff available after one year" is calculated: "total payroll of current staff after first year, discounted at average annual salary increase of 8.36 percent, based on mean staff tenure of 4.12 years. Long-term staff availability is total future payroll less unamortized training investment (note K)."

The other human asset shown in the social balance sheet is "training investment." This is the investment made by the firm in its staff. Note K describes this item: "Training investment is estimated at 25 percent of first-year salary for all current staff. This investment is depreciated on a straight-line basis over the mean staff tenure (note J)."

Questions

1. In discussing the company's social balance sheet and income statement, Clark Abt states: "The basic concept used in the Social Audit to measure social benefits and costs to employees, communities, clients, and the general public is adopted from accounting practice. A thing is assumed to be worth what is paid for it, or what it costs, or the value received from it." Do you agree? Explain.
2. In describing the company's system of social accounting, the president's letter states: "Some of the data is only estimated, but no more so than the estimated worth of inventories or the depreciation of assets in financial statements." Do you agree with these remarks? Explain.
3. The company's social balance sheet includes two different items of human assets: staff available and investments in training. In your opinion, is the company justified in treating each of these items as assets? Explain.
4. Is the method used to measure "staff availability within one year" reasonable? Explain.
5. In your own words, explain how the company measures staff assets available after one year.
6. Does the measure of long-term staff availability appear conceptually valid? Explain.

7. Is the method used to measure training investment reasonable? Explain.
8. Who might be interested in receiving the information about "staff assets" presented in Abt's 1971 annual report? How might this information be used by these audiences?

THREE

Measuring Human Resource Costs: Concept and Methods

This chapter presents the basic concepts and measurement techniques required to account for human resource costs. It provides the terminology and measurement models that are the building blocks of the actual systems of accounting for human resource costs described in the next chapter.

The chapter focuses on four questions: What is cost? What are human resource costs? What are the different types of human resource costs? And how can we measure human resource costs? These questions are basic to an understanding of how to account for human resource costs.

Accounting Concepts of Cost

Accounting uses the concept of cost in a variety of ways. References are made to historical cost, acquisition cost, outlay cost, replacement cost, current cost, direct and indirect cost, standard cost, incremental cost, sunk cost, fixed and variable cost, marginal costs, and opportunity cost, to cite some of the more common ways in which the term *cost* is used.

Definition of Cost. Formally defined, *cost* is a sacrifice incurred to obtain some anticipated benefit or service. A cost may be incurred to acquire tangible objects or intangible benefits.

Conceptually, all costs have "expense" and "asset" components. Conventionally defined, an *expense* is the portion of a cost that has been consumed during the current accounting period. An *asset* is the portion of a cost that is expected to provide benefits during future accounting periods. A fundamental accounting problem is, of course, measuring the expense and asset components of costs.

Original and Replacement Costs. Several accounting concepts of cost are of considerable importance to human resource accounting. Two of these concepts are original cost and replacement cost. *Original cost* refers to the sacrifice that was incurred to acquire or obtain a resource. This is typically termed *historical cost. Replacement cost* refers to the sacrifice that would have to be incurred to replace a resource presently owned or employed.

Outlay and Opportunity Costs. Outlay and opportunity costs are components of original and replacement costs. An *outlay cost* refers to the cash expenditure that must be incurred to acquire or replace a resource. As commonly defined, an *opportunity cost* refers to the income or revenue forgone or sacrificed in order to acquire or replace a resource. For example, if a salesperson devotes time to training or "breaking in" a sales trainee, the sales forgone during this period constitute an opportunity cost. Similarly, if a firm is out of merchandise when potential customers call in orders, an opportunity cost of lost sales is incurred. Thus an opportunity cost refers to the benefits that must be sacrificed in order to use a resource in an alternative way.

Direct and Indirect Costs. The terms *direct* and *indirect* are used to dichotomize the degree to which certain costs can be traced to an activity, a product, or a resource. *Direct costs* refer to the costs that can be traced directly to an activity, product, or resource. *Indirect costs* are costs that *cannot* be traced directly to a specific activity, product, or process, but which are incurred for general use in more than one activity. This class of costs may be assigned or allocated to specific products or activities on the basis of certain assumptions about the relation between the activity and the indirect costs. Of course, these allocations may be based upon rules of thumb and may be quite arbitrary.

Actual and Standard Costs. The terms *actual* and *standard* distinguish between what costs are and what they ought to be. *Standard costs* are the costs that ought to be incurred to attain some specified end under certain predefined conditions. Thus the standard cost concept is hypothetical—a target for what costs ought to be. *Actual costs* are the costs actually incurred to attain some specified end.

Thus we have defined some of the basic accounting concepts of cost. These concepts have their counterparts in human resource accounting.

Concepts of Human Resource Cost

The notion of "human resource cost" is derived from the general concept of cost. *Human resource costs* are costs incurred to acquire or replace people. Like other costs, they have expense and asset components; they may be composed of outlay and opportunity costs; and they may have both direct and indirect cost elements. In addition, it is possible to account for standard as well as actual human resource costs. Finally, the conventional accounting concepts of acquisition and replacement cost also have counterparts in human resource accounting.

Original Cost of Human Resources. The *original cost* of human resources refers to the sacrifice that was incurred to acquire and develop people. This notion is identical to the concept of original cost for other assets—for example, the original cost of plant and equipment is the cost incurred to acquire these resources.

The original cost of human resources typically includes costs of recruitment, selection, hiring, placement, orientation, and on-the-job training. Some of these items are direct costs while others are indirect costs. For example, the cost of a trainee's salary is a direct cost of training while the cost of a supervisor's time during training is an indirect cost.

The purpose of collecting these costs will influence their components. For managerial purposes, it is desirable to include opportunity costs incurred in the original cost of human resources. However, because there are often difficulties involved in measuring opportunity costs, it may not be feasible to obtain objective estimates. As a result, while it may be desirable to use opportunity costs for internal purposes, they may be too unreliable to be reported to external users of accounting data. For the purpose of external reporting, this convention would make accounting for human resource costs consistent with accounting for other costs.

Replacement Cost of Human Resources. The *replacement cost* of human resources refers to the sacrifice that would have to be incurred today to replace human resources presently employed. For example, if an individual were to leave an organization, costs would have to be incurred to recruit, select, and train a replacement.

The replacement cost of human resources typically includes the costs attributable to the turnover of a present employee as well as the costs of acquiring and developing a replacement. It includes both direct and indirect costs. Since replacement costs are intended for managerial use, they should include opportunity as well as outlay cost components.

In principle, the notion of human resource replacement cost can be extended to individuals, to groups of people, and to the human organization as a whole. At present, however, personnel managers typically think in terms of acquiring a substitute capable of rendering an equivalent set of services for a single specified position, rather than in terms of replacing an individual per se. In other words, they think in terms of replacing people in relation to specified roles rather than in terms of replacing the whole person.

This perspective suggests that there is a dual notion of replacement cost: positional and personal. In this context, *positional replacement cost* refers to the sacrifice that would have to be incurred today to replace a person presently employed in a specified position with a substitute capable of providing an equivalent set of services—in that given position. It refers to the cost of replacing the set of services required of any incumbent in a specified position. *Personal replacement cost* refers to the sacrifice that would have to be incurred today to replace a person presently employed with a substitute capable of rendering an equivalent set of services in *all* the positions the former might occupy. It is the cost of replacing a set of services provided by one person with an equivalent set to be provided by another.

These concepts of replacement cost can be extended to groups as well as to individuals. However, at present there has been virtually no research done on the replacement cost of groups. Instead, research has focused on individuals as the basic unit of analysis.

Measurement of Original Cost of Human Resources

We have defined the concept of the original cost of human resources as the sacrifice that was incurred to acquire and develop people. Our concern in this section will be with the measurement of the original cost of human resources.

Figure 3-1 presents a model for the measurement of original (historical) human resource costs. It identifies the two basic elements of original cost: acquisition costs and learning costs. Each of these elements has both direct and indirect cost components.

Figure 3-1

MODEL FOR MEASUREMENT OF ORIGINAL HUMAN RESOURCE COSTS

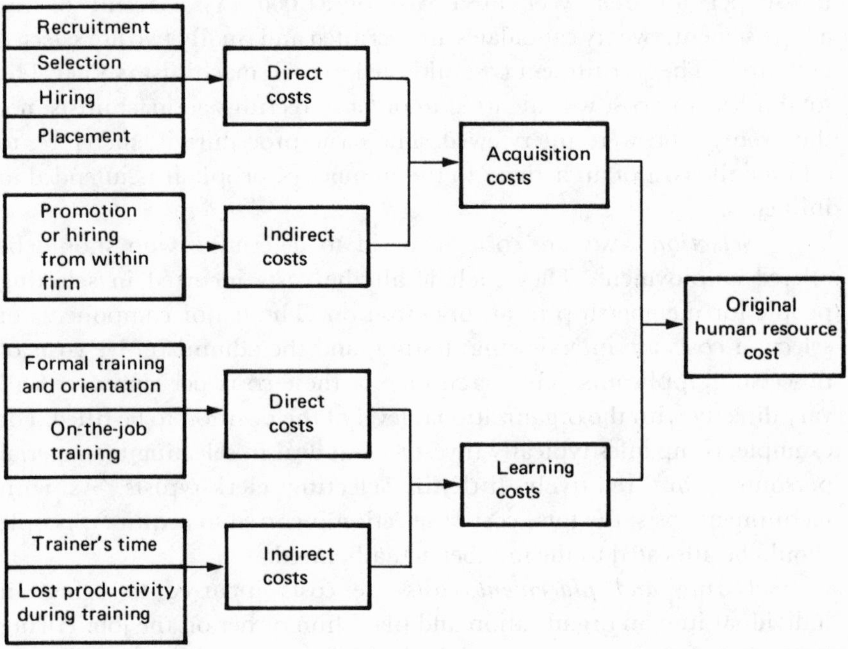

Acquisition Costs. These costs refer to the sacrifice that must be incurred to "acquire" a new position holder. They include all of the direct costs of recruitment, selection, hiring, and placement, as well as certain indirect costs.

Recruitment costs are costs incurred to identify sources of human resources, including those both inside and outside an organization. They are also incurred to attract possible future members of an organization. The major components of external recruitment costs are advertising, college recruiting, employment agency fees, entertainment, travel, and administrative expenses. Depending on the company, other costs may also be significant and worth classifying separately.

One important issue involved in accounting for recruitment costs is how to treat the costs attributable to people who are not hired. These costs should be treated as costs of recruiting the people actually hired;

that is, they should be allocated to the person hired. For example, the McLean Manufacturing Company has decided to hire two machinists. To recruit job candidates, it placed an advertisement in the local newspaper for one week at a cost of $1,000. As a result of the advertisement, twenty candidates are recruited and finally two are selected and hired. The recruitment cost allocated to each machinist is $500. The total recruiting cost was incurred in order to recruit *two* machinists, not the twenty who were interviewed. The basic procedure is, therefore, to allocate the cost of an activity to the number of people it is intended to influence.

Selection costs are costs incurred to determine who should be offered employment. They include all the costs incurred in selecting people for membership in an organization. The major components of selection costs are interviewing, testing, and the administrative costs of processing applicants. The magnitude of these costs per employee will vary directly with the organizational level of the position to be filled. For example, companies typically invest a great deal in selecting managerial personnel, but relatively little in selecting clerk-typists. As with recruitment costs, the total cost of selection incurred to acquire *n* people should be allocated to the number actually hired.

Hiring and placement costs are costs incurred to bring an individual into an organization and place him or her on the job. Hiring costs include moving and travel allowances and other related costs. Placement costs include a variety of administrative costs incurred to place an individual on the job. In practice, it may be desirable to treat these costs as a single classification—taken together, their purpose is to bring an individual into the organization and into a position. The magnitude of these costs will also vary in relation to position levels in the organization.

Learning Costs. These costs refer to the sacrifice that must be incurred to train a person and bring him or her to the level of performance normally expected from an individual in a given position. Learning costs are defined operationally as the differential cost incurred until an individual achieves the level of productivity normally expected in a given position.

Learning costs include both direct and indirect costs incurred in formal orientation and training as well as on-the-job training. The direct costs involve the expense of formal training programs, including trainer and trainee salaries. The indirect costs incurred during the learning period may include the opportunity cost of lost performance of others in addition to the trainee, which may result because the interaction of others with the trainee during his or her learning tends to decrease their productivity.

Formal training and orientation costs are associated with formal indoctrination and training. The orientation may involve becoming familiar with personnel policies, company products, facilities, and so on. Formal training may range from very simple instruction required to show a person how to do a repetitive job to highly specialized programs continuing over weeks, months, or perhaps years.

On-the-job training costs are incurred in training an individual on the job itself rather than in formal training programs. On-the-job training is used not only for production workers but also for professionals such as accountants and engineers. The major direct cost of such training is the cost of the trainee's salary for the period that he or she is unproductive.

Trainer's time is the cost of supervisory salaries during the period of training. The time supervisors spend in training should be treated as a cost of training.

Lost productivity during training is the cost of lost performance of people other than the trainee during the training period. Until an individual achieves the normal level of productivity expected of someone in his or her position, others may be affected. For example, during the learning period of a new person on an assembly line, the individual may operate slowly and hamper the work of others. This may cause the productivity of several people to drop below normal and constitutes a cost of lost productivity attributable to training.

Example of Training Cost Measurement. The Electrosonics Corporation is a manufacturer of sophisticated radar and other equipment. Its principal customer is the Department of Defense. The firm requires highly trained technicians. Even though an individual may be experienced in the industry, he or she may still require a lengthy period of on-the-job training. The learning curve for one type of technician is shown in Figure 3-2.*

As Figure 3-2 shows, the individual is not expected to achieve standard productivity until the ninetieth day employed. This means that the difference between standard productivity and the actual productivity

*A learning curve shows the pattern of performance over time as a person learns a task.

Figure 3-2

INVESTMENT IN TRAINING DURING LEARNING PERIOD

The Electrosonics Corporation

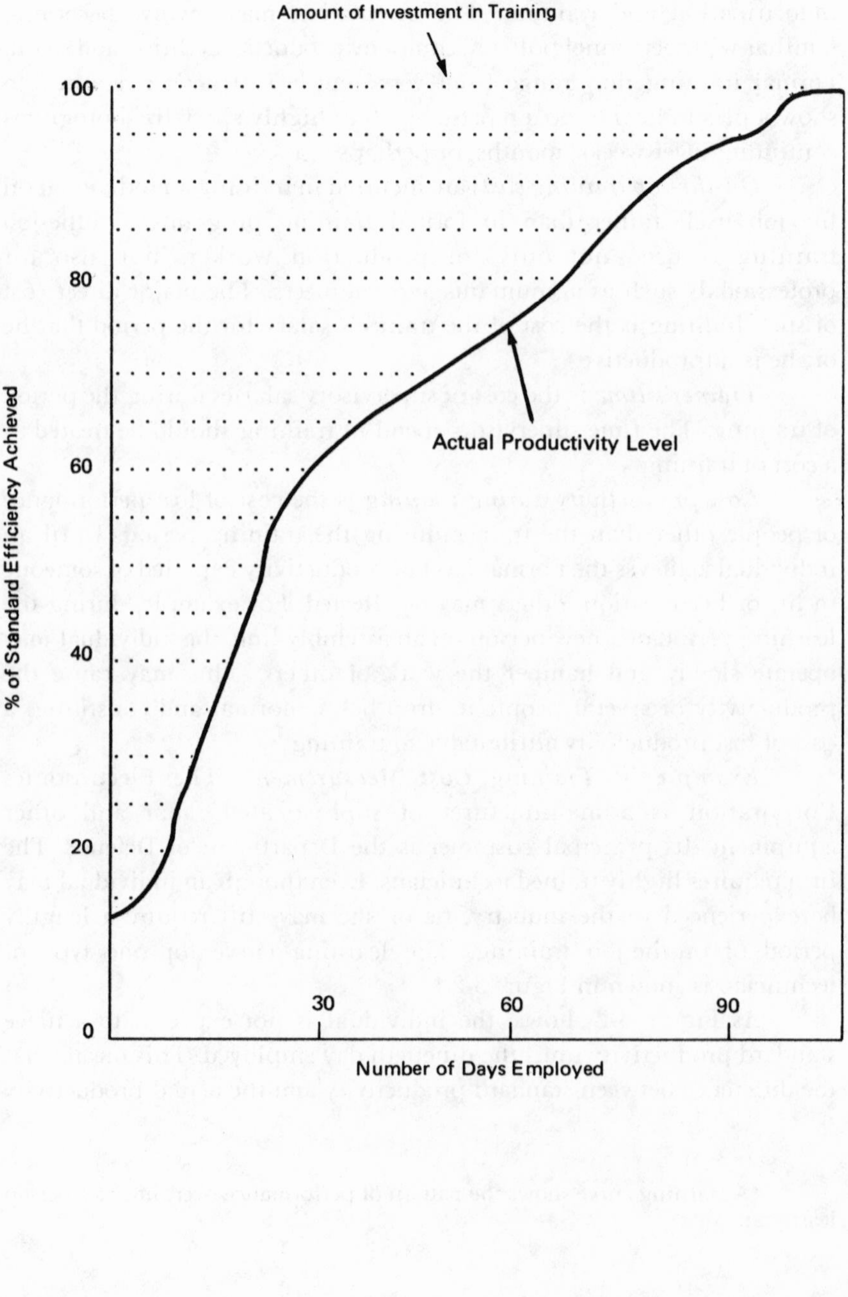

achieved by an individual is a cost of learning. This learning cost is essentially an investment made by an organization to develop its technicians. It is an investment in human assets.

Measurement of Replacement Cost of Human Resources

The concept of the replacement cost of human resources has been defined here as the sacrifice that would have to be incurred today to replace human resources presently employed. It was also noted that there is a dual notion of replacement cost: positional and personal. In this section we deal with the measurement of both types of replacement costs.

Positional Replacement Cost. The concept of positional replacement cost refers to the sacrifice that would have to be incurred today to replace a person occupying a specified position with a substitute capable of rendering equivalent services *in the given position.* As shown in Figure 3-3, there are three basic elements of positional replacement cost: acquisition costs, learning costs, and separation costs. The first two of these costs have been discussed previously; the third is examined here.

Separation costs are the costs incurred as a result of a position holder leaving an organization. They may include both direct and indirect components.

During a period of searching for a replacement, an organization may incur an indirect cost of separating a position holder because the responsibilities of the vacant position are not being performed. If performance in one position has an impact upon performance in other positions, holders of the latter may perform less effectively when the former is vacant. In an insurance company, for example, the performance of a claims investigator influences the performance of other investigators as well as adjusters, examiners, and the claims manager. The loss of an investigator results in a greater than normal cost during the period in which there is a search for a replacement. This difference can be conceived of as the *cost of a vacant position.* Similarly, during the period of searching for a new salesperson an opportunity cost may be incurred because of a loss of sales that would otherwise have accrued to the organization. This too is a cost of a vacant position.

Another element of separation costs is the cost of lost productivity prior to the separation of an individual from an organization, assuming that there is a tendency for performance to decrease at such a time.

Personal Replacement Cost. In contrast to positional replacement costs, the concept of personal replacement cost refers to the sacrifice that

Figure 3-3

MODEL FOR MEASUREMENT OF HUMAN RESOURCE REPLACEMENT COSTS

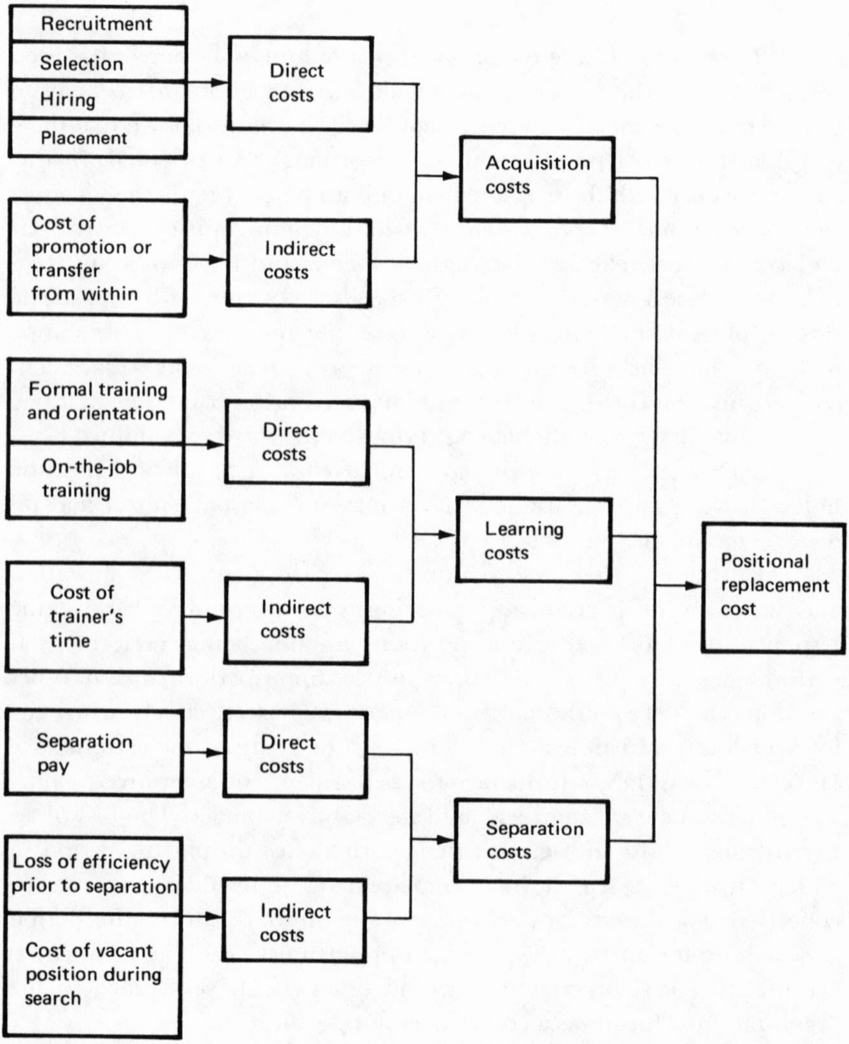

SOURCE: Eric G. Flamholtz, "Human Resource Accounting: Measuring Positional Replacement Costs," *Human Resource Management*, Spring 1973, p. 11. Reprinted by permission of the Graduate School of Business Administration, University of Michigan.

would have to be incurred today to replace a person with a substitute capable of providing a set of services equivalent to that of the individual being replaced. This construct refers to the cost of replacing a person with a functionally equivalent substitute rather than the cost of replacing him or her with the best available substitute.

In principle, the concept of personal replacement can be extended to individuals, groups, and even the total human organization. For example, we can attempt to replace the general manager of an automotive dealership or we can attempt to replace an entire organizational unit such as an aerospace engineering team.

The notion of personal replacement cost is quite similar to the concept of economic value. This similarity is intentional. Because of their close relation, and for other reasons to be discussed, we shall deal with the measurement of personal replacement cost in Chapter Seven.

Summary

This chapter has presented the basic concepts and measurement techniques required to account for human resource costs. Human resource costs are sacrifices incurred to acquire or replace people. They have expense and asset components, just as any other cost does. The original cost of human resources is the sacrifice that was actually incurred to acquire and develop people. It typically includes costs of recruitment, selection, hiring, placement, orientation, and on-the-job training. Replacement costs refer to the sacrifice that would have to be incurred today to replace human resources presently employed. They typically include acquisition, learning, and separation costs. Both original and replacement costs consist of direct and indirect costs as well as outlay and opportunity costs. Direct costs are costs traceable to a specified activity, while indirect costs are incurred for general use and are allocated to the activity. Outlay costs are actual cash expenditures, while opportunity costs refer to revenue forgone in acquiring or replacing people.

Case 3-1: Excellent Electronics Company (A)

Excellent Electronics Company was formed in 1975 to develop and manufacture new types of electronic home entertainment products. One of its main products was audio equipment.

The firm's president, Sanford Harris, anticipated a growing market for the company's products due to the increased affluence of U.S. consumers. From its inception in 1975 through 1980, the company experienced rapid growth. Sales in 1975 were $600,000, and in 1980 they exceeded $24 million. During this period the firm's work force increased in size to approximately 1,000 persons, including 100 managers. Many of its workers were highly skilled, and Harris felt that an effectively functioning team had been put together. As he stated:

> Our first few years were quite successful. Not only has our profitability increased, but we have developed a first-rate management and work force. And after all, in addition to our reputation people are our most valuable asset.

In 1981, the company began to experience decreasing sales. For the year as a whole, sales were forecast at $22 million. In addition, the company also experienced increasing costs. In March, Harris expressed concern that profits would be significantly affected:

> If present trends continue for the rest of the year, we're really going to be hurting. We may, in fact, have to perform some surgery on the organization. We've got a lot of fixed costs in salaried personnel, and we may have to lay off some of the work force and have the rest make up the slack. I hope we don't have to go that far.

By May, business conditions had not improved, and Harris asked the company's controller to estimate the payroll savings from a layoff of 10 percent of the work force for periods of three, six, nine, and twelve weeks. The controller's estimate is shown in Table 3-1. It was estimated that seasonal sales would increase in twelve to fourteen weeks and most of the employees would be rehired.

Before making a decision, Harris called a meeting of top management on May 12, 1981. The financial vice-president, Carter Roberts, agreed with the controller's estimates and felt that a layoff of nine weeks would substantially help the firm's profit for the year. He stated: "We need a layoff of nine weeks to save $270,000. That would make the bottom line look reasonable for the year." However, the

Table 3-1

ESTIMATE OF PAYROLL SAVINGS FROM LAYOFF OF 10% OF WORK FORCE

Layoff Period (weeks)	*Payroll Savings*
3	$ 90,000
6	180,000
9	270,000
12	360,000

personnel manager, Jay Barker, objected to the layoff decision. He argued that:

> A layoff will hurt us in the long run more than it will help us today. We've built a good organization, but a layoff will hurt morale. In addition, we will need these people by the end of August. But by that time some will have found jobs elsewhere and we won't be able to get them back. If we have to recruit, hire, and train replacements for many people who do not return, we will have to incur substantial costs.

The president listened intently to the personnel manager's arguments, and then he turned to the controller: "What do you think about this, Hal?" The controller replied: "Well, it makes sense to me, but none of Jay's arguments are backed up by specifics. I *know* we can save $270,000 for a nine-week layoff—less, of course, the costs Jay has mentioned. But we don't know how much those costs would be. I suppose we will just have to factor that as an intangible into our final decision."

Questions

1. Based on the information currently available to management, do you recommend a layoff for three, six, nine, or twelve weeks? Explain.
2. What information would you need to quantify the "intangible costs" of the layoffs cited by the personnel manager?

Case 3-2: Excellent Electronics Company (B)

During its meeting on May 12 the company discussed a proposed layoff decision that was intended to reduce payroll costs and increase profitability. The company's personnel manager, Jay Barker, had argued against the proposal on the grounds that it might not be economically advantageous if all costs were considered. The president, Sanford Harris, decided to postpone a decision until Barker "put some numbers on his arguments." Barker was scheduled to report back to the Executive Committee on May 19.

During the May 19 meeting Barker presented his report:

> I have tried to estimate what it will cost us to start up operations again at the end of three, six, nine, and twelve weeks. I have prepared estimates for "optimistic," "pessimistic," and "most likely" conditions as shown in Tables 3-2 through 3-4.

Barker noted that he had made the following assumptions:

1. We will not make a layoff for a period greater than twelve weeks because of the expected increase in seasonal demand in about twelve to fourteen weeks.
2. The cost of rehiring an employee is equal to one week's salary. This is the cost to get the employee back up to normal productivity, but this is only a "guesstimate."
3. The cost of replacing one of our workers who did not return following the layoff is equal to half a year's salary. This is the cost of recruiting, selecting, and training replacements. This figure was derived from some rough calculations based on past experience, but it is conservative.
4. The cost of decreased morale among employees not laid off was not considered. This is another conservative assumption.
5. Optimistic, most likely, and pessimistic estimates of the percentage of workers who would return after the layoff were also made. For purposes of aggregating the data, I assumed that there was a 0.10,

Note: For a description of Excellent Electronics Company and events prior to the May 12, 1981, meeting, see Case 3-1.

Table 3-2

ESTIMATED COST OF RETRAINING AND REPLACING WORK FORCE AFTER LAYOFF

Cost Elements	3-Week Layoff Optimistic	3-Week Layoff Most Likely	3-Week Layoff Pessimistic	6-Week Layoff Optimistic	6-Week Layoff Most Likely	6-Week Layoff Pessimistic
1. Estimated % employees rehired	95	80	65	90	75	60
2. Total retraining cost of rehires*	$ 28,500	$ 24,000	$ 20,500	$ 27,000	$ 22,500	$ 18,000
3. Total replacement cost of force lost†	37,500	150,000	267,500	75,000	187,500	300,000
4. Total cost of layoff	$ 66,000	$174,000	$288,000	$102,000	$210,000	$318,000

Cost Elements	9-Week Layoff Optimistic	9-Week Layoff Most Likely	9-Week Layoff Pessimistic	12-Week Layoff Optimistic	12-Week Layoff Most Likely	12-Week Layoff Pessimistic
1. Estimated % employees rehired	85	70	55	80	65	50
2. Total retraining cost of rehires*	$ 25,500	$ 21,000	$ 16,500	$ 24,000	$ 20,500	$ 15,000
3. Total replacement cost of force lost†	112,500	225,000	337,500	150,000	267,500	350,000
4. Total cost of layoff	$138,000	$246,000	$354,000	$174,000	$288,000	$365,000

*Assuming cost of retraining an employee is equal to one week's salary.
†Assuming cost of replacing an employee is equal to one-half of a year's salary.

Table 3-3

CALCULATION OF EXPECTED COST OF REHIRING AND REPLACING WORK FORCE

Layoff Period (weeks)	Optimistic Total Cost*	Optimistic Probability	Most Likely Total Cost*	Most Likely Probability	Pessimistic Total Cost*	Pessimistic Probability	Expected Cost
3	$ 66	.10	$174	.80	$288	.10	$174,600
6	102	.10	210	.80	318	.10	210,000
9	138	.10	246	.80	354	.10	246,000
12	174	.10	288	.80	365	.10	284,300

*Thousands.

Table 3-4

COMPARISON OF COSTS AND BENEFITS OF LAYOFF DECISION

Period of Layoff (weeks)	*Estimated Payroll Savings*	*Estimated Cost of Rehiring and Replacement*	*Net Benefit (Cost)*
3	$ 90,000	$174,600	$(84,600)
6	180,000	210,000	(30,000)
9	270,000	246,000	24,000
12	360,000	284,300	75,700

0.80, and 0.10 chance of the optimistic, most likely, and pessimistic conditions occurring, respectively.

"I think the data are interesting," Barker concluded. "What do you think?"

Questions

1. Assume that you are the company's controller and that the president has asked you to comment on the report the personnel manager presented. What would you say to him?
2. Would you recommend a layoff? If you recommend a layoff, should it last for three, six, nine, or twelve weeks? Explain.

Case 3-3: The University of Michigan (B)

During the spring of 1971, the University of Michigan was facing budgetary problems. There was an apparent gap between its budgeted needs and the recommended state budget for the university.

The university's salary position relative to comparable institutions had been slipping over the past five years. Moreover, pressure to increase faculty work loads was anticipated.

In *The University of Michigan Today,* the following article appeared:

HUMAN RESOURCES WORTH?—$1.7 BILLION

Suppose that U-M had to start over, that President Fleming had to rebuild the human organization of U-M back to where it is today, an effectively functioning human organization including faculty and nonacademic staff, students, and an international reputation. How much would it cost in terms of payroll?

Rensis Likert, recently retired director of the Institute of Social Research, posed this question to the executive officers and deans. Their responses agreed with responses to similar questions posed to leaders of technologically complex industrial firms.

The median response was that the cost would be equivalent to ten times the annual payroll. For the university, last year's payroll was $172 million; therefore, the estimated cost for replacement of the institution's human resources could be $1.7 billion.

"If highly valuable scientists and scholars leave the university because of the pressure and constraints they feel from restricted budgets," Likert said, "the decrease in the value of the human organization may be so great as to make the year both costly and highly inefficient so far as the university's total operation is concerned. Such effects can be costly and be felt over extended periods of time."[1]

Questions

1. Assuming that you are a state legislator who is analyzing the budget requested by the university together with the budget proposed by the governor, what is your opinion of the comments made by Rensis Likert?
2. Assuming that you think Likert's comments are valid, how should you take them into account in making decisions on the university's budget?

Case 3-4: Barter Automotive Products Limited (A)

Barter Automotive Products Limited of Winnipeg is one of the oldest established manufacturers and distributors of automotive parts and supplies in Canada. The company was incorporated in 1927 and like so many other prairie-based manufacturers achieved only moderate success until the end of World War II. After World War II, Barter expanded its automotive supply business in order to have national coverage in Canada. As Barter grew more prosperous, over the years, it also diversified into other industries.

In 1959 the company's management anticipated a snowmobile craze and as a result decided to pioneer this potential growth industry in Western Canada. A wholly owned subsidiary company, Alberta Snowmobiles Ltd., was incorporated in January 1, 1960. The company had been formed to manufacture and distribute snowmobiles and accessory equipment. As of December 31, 1969, Alberta had achieved only average results by Barter's standards (see Tables 3-5 and 3-6).

The senior management of the subsidiary as of December 31, 1969, consisted of:

President:	Jack Davis, aged 42
Vice-President:	
Marketing:	Ross Walker, aged 38
Production:	Fred Johnson, aged 35
Finance:	Bruce Marshall, aged 37

All of the executives were native Albertans and had been with the company since its formation in 1960. In addition to these senior executives the company employed ten middle-level managers, fifteen first-line supervisors, and approximately sixty plant, sales, and office staff.

Although the senior executives had been with the company since its inception, the development into a cohesive organization had been a slow process due to the vagaries and extreme competition in the embryo snowmobile industry. In fact, the middle-level managers

Note: This is a slightly modified version of a case prepared by W. Daryl Lindsay. It is printed with the permission of the author.

Table 3-5

ALBERTA SNOWMOBILES LTD.

Income Statement Year Ended December 31, 1969

Sales	$600,000
Cost of goods sold*	280,000
Gross margin	320,000
Selling and administrative expenses	170,000
Net income before income taxes	150,000
Income taxes	75,000
Net income	$ 75,000

*Includes depreciation charge of $40,000 in 1969.

Table 3-6

ALBERTA SNOWMOBILES LTD.

Balance Sheet December 31, 1969

Current assets:		
Cash		$ 50,000
Accounts receivable		100,000
Inventories		50,000
Total current assets		200,000
Plant, net		800,000
		$1,000,000
Accounts payable		$ 85,000
Due to parent company		215,000
Shareholders' equity:		
Common stock	$500,000	
Retained earnings	200,000	700,000
		$1,000,000

and first-line supervisors, on the average, had been with Alberta just two years.

The Economic Development Council of the state of Montana had been attempting to entice Barter's senior management into moving the snowmobile operations to that state for the past few years. To make the move more attractive the council had offered to advance Barter a development loan equal to Barter's initial capital investment in the state.

During 1969 Barter engaged Ace Market Consultants to conduct a survey of the potential snowmobile market in the upper northwest states. The consultants projected the income and financial position of the company for the subsequent four years, assuming that it moved to Montana. The parent company also had Alberta supply its pro forma statements for the next four years, assuming that the company would remain in Alberta.

Because the projected return on investment and the size and timing of the net operating cash inflows were far superior for Montana, the subsidiary was relocated in the United States.

Operating Results. Subsequent to the December 31, 1971, year end of the two-year-old Montana Snowmobiles, Inc. (Montana), the senior management of Barter received the comparative financial statements of the subsidiary (Tables 3-7 and 3-8).

Although the sales had turned out to be in line with the forecasts of Ace Market Consultants, the total operating results were discouraging to the parent company. Since Barter's senior management wished to discover the reasons for these disappointing results they engaged the Corwin Consulting Group to analyze the operations of Montana Snowmobiles, Inc. Corwin assigned Mike Martin, one of its most experienced consultants, to the project.

During the course of an initial discussion, Jack Davis, president of Montana, indicated to Martin that Davis was the only member of senior management who had moved from Alberta to Montana. Most of the other senior staff members had young families. Davis pointed out that the men believed the economic future of the province of Alberta to be brighter than that of the state of Montana. Davis also indicated to Martin that he had encountered similar growth pains in starting Alberta Snowmobiles Ltd. He implied that he thought Alberta's operations actually were far superior than the records had indicated.

Martin decided to investigate Alberta Snowmobiles Ltd.'s operations prior to reviewing the results of Montana Snowmobiles, Inc. Martin's investigation of Alberta Snowmobiles Ltd. revealed interesting information regarding the personnel development and start-up costs of the subsidiary.

Investments in Human Assets by Alberta. The parent company, Barter Automotive Products Limited, had charged the subsidiary $56,000 in 1960 as the cost of recruiting, selecting, and hiring the senior executive members of Alberta. This amount was charged off against operations by Alberta in 1960. Davis and Martin further calculated that the subsidiary

Table 3-7

MONTANA SNOWMOBILES, INC.

Income Statement Year Ended December 31

	1970	1971
Sales	$1,250,000	$1,500,000
Cost of goods sold*	630,000	730,000
Gross margin	620,000	770,000
Selling and administrative expenses	490,000	610,000
Net income before income taxes	130,000	160,000
Income taxes	65,000	80,000
Net income	$ 65,000	$ 80,000

*Includes annual depreciation charge of $50,000.

Table 3-8

MONTANA SNOWMOBILES, INC.

Balance Sheet December 31

	1970	1971
Current assets:		
Cash	$ 20,000	$ 50,000
Accounts receivable	220,000	230,000
Inventory	110,000	120,000
Total current assets	350,000	400,000
Plant, net	950,000	900,000
	$1,300,000	$1,300,000
Accounts payable	235,000	255,000
Development loan	500,000	400,000
Common stock	500,000	500,000
Retained earnings	65,000	145,000
	$1,300,000	$1,300,000

had incurred an average annual cost of $7,000 per senior manager for each of the years 1961 to 1969 over and above normal salary costs. They determined that these costs were incurred for formal orientation and training, on-the-job training, familiarization, and individual development. Davis also stated that the organization was just becoming cohesive in 1970 and that he had included $10,000 in the projections for each of the years 1970, 1971, 1972, and 1973 to enable the company to become more completely fused. He commented to Martin that in his opinion the company would only be as strong as the human resources within the organization.

Davis further demonstrated to Martin's satisfaction that the subsidiary had expended $42,000 in acquiring and developing the middle-level managers and first-line supervisors employed as of December 31, 1969. Davis also had included $4,000 in each of the projections from 1970 to 1973 to cover additional personnel development costs, which he thought would benefit future operations.

Martin realized that this buildup of human assets had not been accounted for, since all the expenditures had been written off in the year they were incurred.

Martin recognized that expenditures for the development of human resources are as vital to each company's long-term operations as any other capital expenditures on physical plants. He analyzed the data that Davis and he had collected regarding expenditures on human resources which had a deemed long-term expected benefit to the company but had been expensed as incurred.

Martin summarized the data as shown in Table 3-9. He also determined that the company had charged an additional $49,000 to salary expense in 1969, which should have been capitalized and amortized over fourteen years. The amortization of human resources for the year ended December 31, 1969, should have been $22,600 (amortization expense per year). Based on this information, he adjusted the data presented in Table 3-9 as shown in Table 3-10. He proposed that the company should have made the following adjustment to its records as of December 31, 1969:

Human Resource Assets, net	$239,500	
Amortization Expense	22,600	
Salary Expense		$49,000
Retained Earnings		213,100

Martin recast the 1969 financial statements of the subsidiary based on these data, and he also changed the projections for the years 1970 to 1973. He took into consideration that an additional $14,000 was to be capitalized each year, and amortized on a straight-line basis over fourteen years, instead of being charged directly to expense annually (Tables 3-11 and 3-12). The original operating results for Alberta Snowmobiles Ltd. are shown in Table 3-13.

Table 3-9

SUMMARY OF SUBSIDIARY'S INVESTMENTS IN HUMAN ASSETS

Year	*Description*	*Expenditure ($)*	*Expected Useful Life (Years)*
1960	Start-up costs charged by parent company	56,000	35*
1961–1968	Training, familiarization and development costs of senior management ($28,000 x 8 yrs)	224,000	14†
1968	Training, familiarization and development costs of middle-level managers and first-line supervisors	21,000	14†
		$301,000	
Total straight-line amortization accumulated to December 31, 1968: $87,900.			

*Assumed to have an expected useful life of 35 years because average age of executives at date of incorporation was 29. (Lesser period could have been assumed due to the probability of turnover, death, or retirement before age 65 of any members of the group.)

†Assumed to have a shorter expected useful life due to necessity of continuously upgrading the qualifications of management.

Table 3-10

SUBSIDIARY'S NET INVESTMENT IN HUMAN ASSETS

	Human Resources Assets	*Accumulated Amortization*
1960 to 1968	$301,000	$ 87,900
Additions during 1969	49,000	22,600
Balance, December 31, 1969	$350,000	$110,500

Investments in Human Assets by Montana. Utilizing the knowledge and experience he had gained from his analysis of Alberta, Martin investigated the records of Montana for the past two years. He was able to accumulate data on the human assets, as shown in Table 3-14.

Martin knew that Barter's senior management had received financial statements which did not include any explicit recognition of the human resource assets that were being built up. He realized that the operating results also were understated by the amount spent on developing human resources which were expected to enable the subsidiary to achieve long-term economic benefits. The statements he prepared are shown in Tables 3-15 and 3-16.

Table 3-11

ALBERTA SNOWMOBILES LTD.

Income Statement Year Ended December 31

	Actual	*Pro Forma*			
	1969	*1970*	*1971*	*1972*	*1973*
Sales	$600,000	$700,000	$800,000	$900,000	$1,000,000
Cost of goods sold*	271,000	316,000	346,000	376,000	406,000
Gross margin	329,000	384,000	454,000	524,000	594,000
Selling and administrative expenses	130,000	170,000	200,000	220,000	250,000
Net income before amortization and income taxes	199,000	214,000	254,000	304,000	344,000
Amortization—human resources	22,600	23,600	24,600	25,600	26,000
Net income before income taxes	176,400	190,400	229,400	278,400	317,400
Income taxes†	75,000	100,000	120,000	145,000	165,000
Net income	$101,400	$ 90,400	$109,400	$133,400	$ 152,400

*Includes annual depreciation charge of $40,000.

†Amortization of Human Resources not deemed an allowable deduction for income tax purposes. Assumed effective income tax rate of 50%.

Table 3-12

ALBERTA SNOWMOBILES LTD.

Balance Sheet December 31

	Actual	Pro Forma			
	1969	*1970*	*1971*	*1972*	*1973*
Current assets:					
Cash	$ 50,000	$ 70,000	$ 65,000	$ 90,000	$ 110,000
Accounts receivable	100,000	100,000	135,000	140,000	150,000
Inventory	50,000	70,000	80,000	90,000	100,000
Total current assets	200,000	240,000	280,000	320,000	360,000
Plant, net	800,000	760,000	720,000	680,000	640,000
Human resources, net	239,500	229,900	219,300	207,700	195,100
	$1,239,500	$1,229,900	$1,219,300	$1,207,700	$1,195,100
Accounts payable	$ 85,000	$ 85,000	$ 65,000	$ 100,000	$ 100,000
Due to parent	215,000	115,000	35,000	—	—
Common stock	500,000	500,000	500,000	500,000	500,000
Retained earnings	439,500	529,900	619,300	607,700	595,000
	$1,239,500	$1,229,900	$1,219,300	$1,207,700	$1,195,100

Table 3-13

ALBERTA SNOWMOBILES LTD.

Pro Forma Income Statement Year Ended December 31

	1970	*1971*	*1972*	*1973*
Sales	$700,000	$800,000	$900,000	$1,000,000
Cost of goods sold*	320,000	350,000	380,000	410,000
Gross margin	380,000	450,000	520,000	590,000
Selling and administrative expenses	180,000	210,000	230,000	260,000
Net income before income taxes	200,000	240,000	290,000	330,000
Income taxes†	100,000	120,000	145,000	165,000
Net income	$100,000	$120,000	$145,000	$ 165,000

*Includes annual depreciation of $40,000.
†Assumed effective income tax rate of 50%.

Table 3-14

INVESTMENTS IN HUMAN ASSETS BY MONTANA

	1970		*1971*	
	Expenditure ($)	*Expected Useful Life (Years)*	*Expenditure ($)*	*Expected Useful Life (Years)*
Recruiting, selecting and hiring:				
Senior managers	$ 70,000	25*	$ 7,500	25*
Middle-level managers	15,000	25	15,000	25
First-line supervisors	7,500	25	7,500	25
Formal orientation, training and familiarization	14,000	14†	21,000	14†
	$106,500		$51,000	
Amortization expense	$ 4,700		$ 7,400	

*Assumed to have an expected useful life of 25 years because average age of executives at date of incorporation was 40. (Lesser period could have been assumed due to the probability of turnover, death, or retirement before age 65 of any members of the group.)

†Assumed to have a shorter expected useful life due to necessity of continuously upgrading the qualifications of management.

Table 3-15

MONTANA SNOWMOBILES, INC.

Income Statement Year Ended December 31

	1970	*1971*
Sales	$1,250,000	$1,500,000
Cost of goods sold*	594,000	713,000
Gross margin	656,000	787,000
Selling and administrative expenses	419,500	576,000
Net income before amortization and income taxes	236,500	211,000
Amortization—human resources	4,700	7,400
Net income before income taxes	231,800	203,600
Income taxes†	65,000	80,000
Net income	$ 166,800	$ 123,600

*Includes annual depreciation charge of $50,000.

†Amortization of Human Resources not deemed an allowable deduction for income tax purposes. Assumed effective income tax rate of 50%.

Table 3-16

MONTANA SNOWMOBILES, INC.

Balance Sheet December 31

	1970	*1971*
Current assets:		
Cash	$ 20,000	$ 50,000
Accounts receivable	220,000	230,000
Inventory	110,000	120,000
Total current assets	350,000	400,000
Plant, net	950,000	900,000
Human resources, net	101,800	145,400
	$1,401,800	$1,445,000
Accounts payable	$ 235,000	$ 255,000
Development loan	500,000	400,000
Common stock	500,000	500,000
Retained earnings	166,800	290,400
	$1,401,800	$1,445,400

Question

Assume that you are Mike Martin of the Corwin Consulting Group. Prepare a report to Barter Automotive Products interpreting and evaluating the performance of Alberta and Montana.

FOUR

First-Generation Accounting Systems for Human Resource Costs

During the late 1960s, business firms began to apply the concepts of human resource accounting to their own operations. A few organizations developed systems of accounting for their *investments* in human resources, while others began to account for the *replacement cost* of their human resources. This chapter surveys selected cases of these initial attempts to develop systems of accounting for human resource costs and examines the intended use of these systems in managing human resources. These pioneering studies are significant not only for historical reasons but also to illustrate the applications of human resource cost accounting that were initially envisioned. The next chapter discusses more recent attempts to use human resource accounting.

Accounting for Human Resource Investments: A Professional Athletic Organization

Human resources are of paramount importance to professional athletic teams, so it is not surprising that the first reported attempt to account for people as assets was made by a professional athletic enterprise, the Milwaukee Braves baseball organization. (At least, it is the first attempt known to this author.)

In 1962, "Milwaukee Braves, Inc." was incorporated to acquire and operate the Milwaukee Braves Baseball Club. In 1963, the corporation began to treat its investments in future team development as an asset to be capitalized and amortized over its expected useful life rather than as an expense in the period incurred. Thus the company chose to account for its investments in people as assets for purposes of financial reporting.[1]

The Milwaukee Braves system seems to have been intended primarily for financial reporting purposes. More recently, there have been attempts to develop systems for managerial purposes in industrial as well as in service organizations.

In the subsequent discussion, we shall examine systems of accounting for human resource costs in three different types of enterprises: manufacturing, public accounting, and insurance. These systems should be viewed as case studies in establishing systems of accounting for human resource costs rather than as ideal systems; different systems may well be required by firms in different industries, or firms of varying sizes, and so on.

Accounting for Human Resource Investments: A Manufacturing Company

In late 1966, William Pyle together with the management of R. G. Barry Corporation initiated a pioneering effort to develop a system of accounting for the firm's investment in its human assets on a current cost basis.* Under Pyle's direction, the firm formulated a set of concepts and procedures for measuring recruiting, acquisition, training, development, and other costs incurred as investments in human assets. This section describes the R. G. Barry system in order to exemplify the concepts and methods of accounting for investments in people.[2]

Company Background. R. G. Barry Corporation, a public company listed on the American Stock Exchange, produces and manufactures a variety of soft goods. Its products include slippers and other footwear, robes, and pillows. The company markets its products through manufacturer's representatives in department, specialty, chain,

*Members of Barry's management who participated in the research included Gordon Zacks, president; Edward Stan, treasurer; Richard Burrell, controller; and Robert L. Woodruff, Jr., vice-president in charge of human resources.

discount, and food store channels of distribution. In 1971 R. G. Barry had approximately 1,700 employees. Sales for the year were $34 million and the company's assets (conventionally defined) totaled about $18 million.[3]

Motivation for Human Resource Accounting. In an article describing the company's human resource accounting system, Robert L. Woodruff, Jr., rhetorically asked:

> Why in the world is a little company with good—but unspectacular—growth, good—but unromantic—products, good—but unsophisticated—technology, good—but undramatic—profitability interested in the development of a system of accounting for the human resources of the business? This is a fair question and deserves an answer.[4]

The answer to this question, as we shall see, is largely attributable to three interrelated factors: the economics of the business in which Barry operates, the company's managerial philosophy, and certain perceived limitations of conventional accounting.

R. G. Barry's technology is basically similar to that of the apparel industry. In 1970, 85 percent of the company's production was sewn footwear. The basic technology consists of sewing machines. This means that neither technology per se nor financial requirements constitute a significant barrier to competitive entry into the company's markets. Indeed, apparel companies have the lowest capital per employee and the lowest sales per employee of any of *Fortune* 500 corporations.

The major component of unit manufacturing costs in apparel companies is labor rather than materials or depreciation costs. This results because it is a people-intensive rather than an equipment-intensive industry. Thus the company's management was well aware that the firm's human resources could potentially constitute the competitive difference in its industry. As R. G. Barry's president, Gordon Zacks, stated: "From the very beginning, then, we recognized that if we were to be unique, the only uniqueness we could bank upon was the people power in our company."[5]

Recognizing the crucial role played by human resources in its industry, R. G. Barry adopted a managerial philosophy based on the premise that people are valuable organizational resources. In Woodruff's words: "Like many companies, Barry, over the years, had placed great philosophical emphasis on the value of people to the corporation."[6] Similarly, Zacks stated: "I think that the characteristic philosophy of our firm, and a philosophy that has characterized our company even from the beginning, is one which emphasizes the value of people in the organization."[7] It should be noted, however, that the company's managerial philosophy does not treat people as the only important resource; rather, people are viewed as an integral part of a mix of resources. As Gordon Zacks observed:

> We believe that it is the job of the manager to plan, organize, and control the utilization of three types of assets—*human assets, customer loyalty assets,* and *physical assets*—and to employ these in such a way that he generates a profit by creating new assets. Furthermore, he should manage his profit in such a way as to remain solvent.[8]

This philosophy led Barry to identify five key "result areas" for which managers are held responsible: profit, solvency, physical resources, human resources, and customer loyalty. Thus the firm's managerial philosophy was consistent with the underlying premise of human resource accounting—that people are valuable organizational resources.

The third factor contributing to Barry's interest in developing a system of accounting for its human resources was the recognition that management did not receive sufficient information to manage its human resources effectively. The company's accounting information system did not provide the data required to facilitate certain decisions involving human resource planning and utilization. Similarly, it did not provide managers feedback to permit the evaluation of the company's effectiveness in utilizing its human resources. Barry also recognized that the behavior of managers is influenced by the kind of feedback they receive about their performance and that people tend to direct attention toward the aspects of their performance on which they are evaluated. This means that if managers do not receive performance reports on their effectiveness in managing people, they are likely to concentrate upon the measured aspects of performance while neglecting the unmeasured aspects. Barry's top management was concerned, for example, that a manager could sacrifice long-term profitability for short-term increases in reported net income by either driving people too hard or eliminating training expenditures; yet there was no way to monitor the economic impact of such mismanagement.

For all these reasons, Barry's top management felt the need to develop a system of measurements of the cost and value of its human resources. Its ultimate aim was to develop an information system that provided data to facilitate planning and control of the management of human resources.

The System's Objectives and Scope. The company's specific objectives in developing a human resource accounting system, as cited by Woodruff, were:

1. To provide Barry managers with specific feedback information on their performance in managing the organizational assets and customer loyalty assets entrusted to their care
2. To provide Barry managers with additional information pertaining to human resources which would assist in decision making
3. To provide the organization with a more accurate accounting of its return on total assets employed, rather than just physical assets, and to enable management to analyze how changes in the status of the assets employed affect the achievement of corporate objectives.[9]

The system's purpose, in other words, was to provide the information needed by managers to facilitate decisions involving human resources, to provide feedback on their performance in managing human resources, and to reflect investments in human resources in financial statements prepared for internal purposes.

The company planned ultimately to account for all of its personnel. The initial effort, however, was limited to an accounting of approximately "100 exempt salaried employees."* The system's scope was limited for three reasons. First, this was done to make the problem more tractable. Second, it was anticipated that the experience gained in accounting for the exempt personnel would probably be helpful in extending the system to other people. Finally, these 100 people were

*"Exempt salaried employees" refers to those salaried employees (as opposed to hourly personnel) who are not covered by the U.S. Wage and Hours Law.

thought to constitute one of the most valuable segments of the company's human resources.

In 1969, the system was extended to include factory and clerical employees in two of the company's plants. In 1970, the R. G. Barry Corporation reported a net investment of $1,765,000 in human resources.[10] This total was the sum of investments made in 425 factory and clerical personnel.

For reasons of feasibility, the system's scope was limited to accounting for the original cost of human resources. It was felt that there were significantly fewer measurement problems involved in accounting for human resource costs than in measuring human resource value, because the approach used to measure costs could be borrowed from conventional accounting. As Brummet, Flamholtz, and Pyle stated: "It is significant to note that many of the concepts and much of the terminology being used in developing human resource accounting are being adopted from conventional accounting. They are merely being applied to a problem that has been relatively ignored."[11] The problem of valuation was deferred to the future.

The Measurement System Developed. The system developed to account for the investments made in the firm's managerial (exempt) resources is shown schematically in Figure 4-1. The total costs of the firm are first classified into two components: human resource costs and other costs. The human resource costs are then separated into their expense and asset components. For a cost to be treated as an asset, it must be expected to provide benefits to the company beyond the current accounting period. If its benefits are expected to be fully consumed during the current period, it is treated as an expense. The human assets are then classified into functional categories such as recruiting, acquisition, informal training, and development. These functional costs are traced to specified individuals and recorded in individualized accounts for manager *A*, *B*, . . . , *N*. Rules and procedures have been developed to depreciate these investments over their expected future service life.

There are seven functional accounts for exempt personnel in the R. G. Barry system. These accounts differ from the general taxonomy of functional accounts presented previously in Figure 3-1. The primary difference is that Barry's system differentiates the broad categories of acquisition and learning costs into several finer components. The seven functional accounts are:[12]

Figure 4-1

MODEL OF HUMAN RESOURCE ACCOUNTING SYSTEM FOR INVESTMENTS IN INDIVIDUALS AT R. G. BARRY CORPORATION

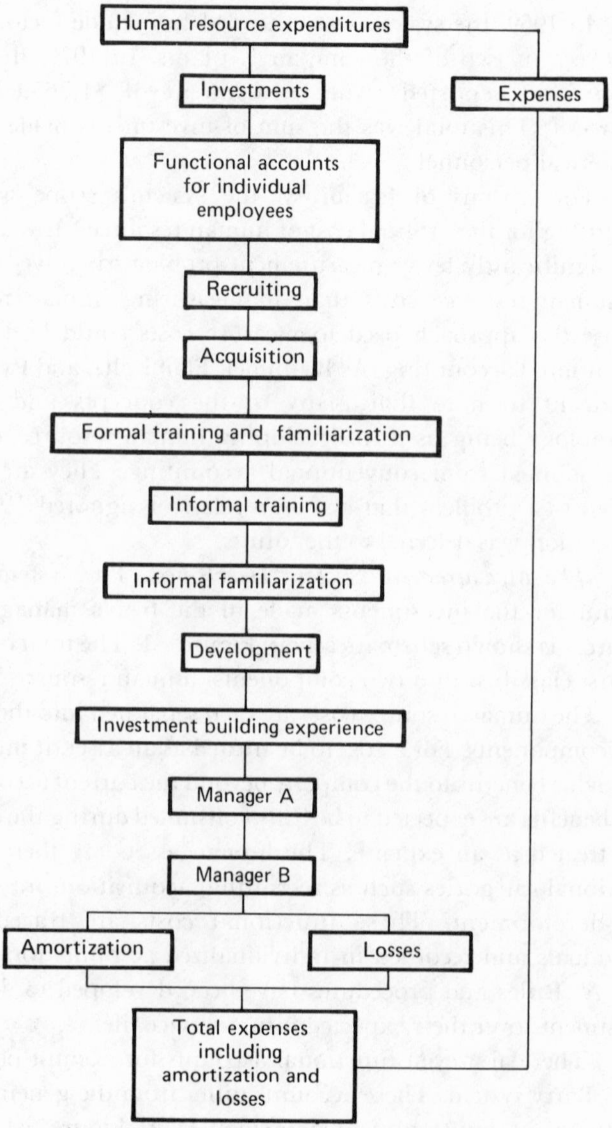

SOURCE: Adapted from William C. Pyle, "Implementation of Human Resource Accounting in Industry," in R. Lee Brummet, Eric G. Flamholtz, and William C. Pyle (editors), *Human Resource Accounting: Development and Implementation in Industry* (Ann Arbor: Foundation for Research on Human Behavior, 1969), p. 43. Reprinted by permission of Foundation for Research on Human Behavior.

1. *Recruiting outlay costs* are costs associated with locating and selecting new (management) personnel. This category includes search fees, advertising, interviewer or interviewee travel expense, allocations of personnel and acquiring department time for internal screening and interviewing, and testing and evaluation expense. Outlay costs for unsuccessful candidates are allocated to the cost of obtaining the candidate hired.*
2. *Acquisition costs* are costs incurred in bringing a new person on board. This category includes placement fees, moving costs, physical examination, allocation of personnel, and acquiring department time in placing a person on the payroll and situating him or her with the necessary equipment to perform the job.
3. *Formal training and familiarization costs* are costs normally incurred immediately after hire or possible transfer from one location to another. They refer to formal orientation program, vestibule training, and so forth.
4. *Informal training costs* are associated with the process of teaching a new person to adapt *existing* skills to the new job. The costs related to this process are normally salary allocations only and vary with each position depending upon the level of the job in the organization, number of subordinates, interaction patterns outside the department, and so on.
5. *Informal familiarization costs* are those associated with the complex process of integrating a new manager into the organization to the point where he or she can be a fully effective member of the organization. Such costs include learning the company's philosophy, history, policies, objectives, communication patterns, past practices, precedents, and understanding of the people with whom the new position holder regularly interacts. The costs, which can be sizable depending on the level and scope of the position, also consist of salary allocations.
6. *Investment building experience costs* are those investments in on-the-job learning that occur *after* the initial familiarization period and are expected to have value to the company beyond the current accounting period. Investment building experience is the development of a capability that would not reasonably be expected as a normal part of the person's job.

*For example, if ten candidates for a sales position are interviewed, the total recruiting outlay costs incurred are allocated to the one selected and hired.

7. *Development costs* are associated with investments in increasing a manager's capabilities in areas beyond the specific technical skills required by the position. In this category are management seminars and university programs or courses.

The functional accounts for exempt personnel differ from those used for factory and clerical personnel because both the nature and scale of investments are significantly different. Three functional accounts are used for the latter group: acquisition, orientation, and training costs.

Data Collection. It was not feasible to determine the past costs incurred as investments in the company's human resources. Instead, the system was developed to account for *future* investments in people, and estimates were made of actual past expenditures. As Robert Woodruff explained:

> Although it was possible to develop the means to accrue and account for future organizational assets *[sic]* outlay costs, records were not available to reconstruct investments in long service management members. Consequently, standards were developed for the above seven functional areas in order to establish beginning balances for the individual accounts. As accumulated experience provides accurate actual costs in the functional area, modification of the original standards may become necessary.[13]

The company modified its existing personnel forms to collect the required data. For example, development costs were collected by means of a "Training and Development Requisition."[14]

Depreciation Methods. As previously noted, investments in human resources are depreciated over their expected useful life. Certain items such as recruiting and acquisition costs are depreciated over the expected organizational tenure of the individual because they are expected to provide benefits as long as the person remains in the company. Other items such as training and development are depreciated over the period of expected utility, which is typically less than the person's expected tenure.

Moreover, individual employee asset accounts are reviewed periodically to determine whether obsolescence or health deterioration warrants recognition of a loss of human assets. Clearly, obsolescence is difficult to assess. When turnover occurs, the undepreciated balance of a person's account is written off as a charge to current earnings.

Selected Data. This system was able to provide management with several types of data that were not available previously. First, personnel management was able to obtain information on the typical investments made in people. In 1969, for example, about $3,000 was typically invested in first-line supervisors while more than $30,000 was invested in a top-level manager. Selected investments for that year are shown in Table 4-1. Management was able to use this information in planning and controlling certain personnel activities as well as in strategic planning.

Table 4-1

MEAN INVESTMENTS IN INDIVIDUALS

R. G. Barry Corporation
1969

Types of Personnel	*Mean Investment*
First-line supervisor	$ 3,000
Engineer	10,000
Middle manager	15,000
Top manager	35,000

SOURCE OF DATA: Robert L. Woodruff, Jr., "Human Resource Accounting." *Canadian Chartered Accountant,* September 1970, p. 5.

The system also provided personnel management with information on the investments being made in different human resource management functions such as recruiting and on-the-job training. Thus it monitored the company's investment in certain essential personnel functions and could be used for planning and control. Selected data on the company's investment in personnel functions are shown in Table 4-2.

The system not only provided personnel management with information; it also provided information to operating people. For example, the company's "Human Resource Accounting Quarterly Reports" were created to inform operating people about the monetary losses attributable to turnover. Management believed that by representing

Table 4-2

INVESTMENTS IN HUMAN RESOURCE MANAGEMENT FUNCTIONS

R. G. Barry Corporation
1969

Functions	*Investment*
1. Acquisition cost†	$110,000
2. On-the-job training	120,000
3. Familiarization	155,000
4. Formal development	50,000

†Cost of new hires, transfers, and promotions.
SOURCE OF DATA: Robert L. Woodruff, Jr., "Human Resource Accounting," *Canadian Chartered Accountant*, September 1970, p. 5.

turnover in monetary terms rather than merely by rates, the economic losses incurred by the company when people exit could be "clearly dramatized to the operating people."

For internal management purposes, the company also developed a set of financial statements that reflect the impact of human resource accounting. This means that expenditures made as investments in people who are expected to have a useful life of more than one year should be capitalized and depreciated rather than expensed during the current accounting period. By this method, Woodruff stated, "the effect of various investments in, and write-offs of, human resources on the income stream is more truly representative of the performance of the company than that which conventional accounting data presently indicate."[15]

Financial statements reflecting the difference between human resource accounting and conventional accounting treatments of income and assets for 1970 and 1971 are shown in Tables 4-3 and 4-4. These financial statements are taken from the company's 1970 and 1971 annual reports.

The 1970 balance sheet shows a net investment in human resources of more than $900,000, while the 1971 report shows net investments of approximately $1,600,000. This means that total assets as conventionally defined were understated because they were prepared according to generally accepted accounting principles.

The income statement for 1970 shows a net decrease in human assets of about $44,000. This is the difference between new investments

Table 4-3

"THE TOTAL CONCEPT"

R. G. Barry Corporation and Subsidiaries
1970 (Pro Forma)
(Conventional and Human Resource Accounting)

BALANCE SHEET	*1970 Conventional and Human Resource*	*1970 Conventional Only*
Assets		
Total current assets	$10,944,693	$10,944,693
Net property, plant and equipment	1,682,357	1,682,357
Excess of purchase price of subsidiaries over net assets acquired	1,188,704	1,188,704
Net investments in human resources	942,194	–
Other assets	166,417	166,417
	$14,924,365	$13,982,171
Liabilities and Stockholders' Equity		
Total current liabilities	$ 3,651,573	$ 3,651,573
Long term debt, excluding current installments	2,179,000	2,179,000
Deferred compensation	77,491	77,491
Deferred federal income taxes based upon full tax deduction for human resource costs	471,097	–
Stockholders' equity:		
Capital stock	1,087,211	1,087,211
Additional capital in excess of par value	3,951,843	3,951,843
Retained earnings:		
Financial	3,035,053	3,035,053
Human resources	471,097	–
Total stockholders' equity	8,545,204	8,074,107
	$14,924,365	$13,982,171
STATEMENT OF INCOME		
Net sales	$28,164,181	$28,164,181
Cost of sales	18,252,181	18,252,181
Gross profit	9,912,000	9,912,000
Selling, general and administrative expenses	7,546,118	7,546,118
Operating income	2,365,882	2,365,882
Other deductions, net	250,412	250,412
Income before federal income taxes	2,115,470	2,115,470
Net increase (decrease) in human resource investment	(43,900)	–
Adjusted income before federal income taxes	2,071,570	2,115,470
Federal income taxes	1,008,050	1,030,000
Net income	$ 1,063,520	$ 1,085,470

NOTE: The information presented on this page is provided only to illustrate the informational value of human resource accounting for more effective internal management of the business. The figures included regarding investments and amortization of human resources are unaudited and you are cautioned for purposes of evaluating the performance of this company to refer to the conventional certified accounting data further on in this report.

SOURCE: *R. G. Barry Corporation 1970 Annual Report,* p. 13.

Table 4-4

"THE TOTAL CONCEPT"

R. G. Barry Corporation and Subsidiaries
1971 (Pro Forma)
(Conventional and Human Resource Accounting)

BALANCE SHEET	*1971 Conventional and Human Resource*	*1971 Conventional Only*
Assets		
Total current assets	$12,810,346	$12,810,346
Net property, plant and equipment	3,343,379	3,343,379
Excess of purchase price over net assets acquired	1,291,079	1,291,079
Net investments in human resources	1,561,264	—
Other assets	209,419	209,419
	$19,215,487	$17,654,223
Liabilities and Stockholders' Equity		
Total current liabilities	$ 3,060,576	$ 3,060,576
Long term debt, excluding current installments	5,095,000	5,095,000
Deferred compensation	95,252	95,252
Deferred federal income taxes based upon full tax deduction for human resource costs	780,632	—
Stockholders' equity:		
Capital stock	1,209,301	1,209,301
Additional capital in excess of par value	5,645,224	5,645,224
Retained earnings:		
Financial	2,548,870	2,548,870
Human resources	780,632	—
Total stockholders' equity	10,184,027	9,403,395
	$19,215,487	$17,654,223
STATEMENT OF INCOME		
Net sales	$34,123,202	$34,123,202
Cost of sales	21,918,942	21,918,942
Gross profit	12,204,260	12,204,260
Selling, general and administrative expenses	9,417,933	9,417,933
Operating income	2,786,327	2,786,327
Other deductions, net	383,174	383,174
Income before federal income taxes	2,403,153	2,403,153
Net increase in human resource investment	137,700	—
Adjusted income before federal income taxes	2,540,853	2,403,153
Federal income taxes	1,197,850	1,129,000
Net income	$ 1,343,003	$ 1,274,153

NOTE: The information presented on this page is provided only to illustrate the informational value of human resource accounting for more effective internal management of the business. The figures included regarding investments and amortization of human resources are unaudited and you are cautioned for purposes of evaluating the performance of this company to refer to the conventional certified accounting data further on in this report.

SOURCE: *R. G. Barry Corporation 1971 Annual Report,* p. 17.

in human resources and depreciation plus write-offs for turnover and other losses. Thus in 1970 net income before income taxes was *lower* under human resource accounting than under conventional accounting by approximately $44,000. The income statement for 1971 shows a net increase in human resource investments of approximately $138,000. In this year net income under human resource accounting is *greater* than income as calculated under conventional accounting, because the latter treats investments in human capital as expenses of the current period.

These differences in accounting treatments of investments in people have important managerial implications because they affect the calculation of the company's rate of return on investment (ROI). (This point is discussed fully in Chapter One.) These different accounting conventions affect both the numerator and the denominator of ROI. The impact of this difference for the year 1971 is shown in Table 4-5.

Table 4-5

DIFFERENCE IN RETURN ON INVESTMENT

R. G. Barry Corporation
1971 (Pro Forma)
(Conventional and Human Resource Accounting)

Accounting Methods	*Net Income*	*Total Assets*	*ROI*
Conventional	$1,274,000	$17,654,000	7.2%
Human resource	1,343,000	19,215,000	6.9%
Difference	69,000	1,561,000	

SOURCE: *R. G. Barry Corporation 1971 Annual Report,* p. 17.

The system developed at R. G. Barry also provided a human resource capital budget and a report upon performance as measured against plans. This information was intended to assist managers in the management of human resources. This report and its uses are described in Case 4-1.

The System's Uses and Benefits. R. G. Barry's system of accounting for human resource costs had important applications and benefits. The system was useful in human resource planning because it provided management with historical costs of recruiting, hiring, training, and so on. These historical costs of personnel functions were used as estimates for budgeting personnel costs. For example, a company may be planning to expand its operations and open a new plant requiring the addition of personnel, including ten first-line supervisors, two middle managers, and one top manager. By using historical data, the company can budget its personnel activities more reliably, as shown in Table 4-6.

Table 4-6

CAPITAL BUDGET FOR HUMAN RESOURCES

Classifications	*Number*	*Cost per Individual*	*Total Budgeted Costs*
First-line supervisor	10	$ 3,000	$30,000
Middle managers	2	15,000	32,000
Top manager	1	35,000	35,000
			$97,000

SOURCE: *R. G. Barry Corporation 1969 Annual Report,* p. 15.

The system can also be employed in strategic planning for the company as a whole. The company's president, Gordon Zacks, has described the application of human resource accounting in formulating strategy:

> We use human resource accounting information in strategic decision making. The information is employed in evaluating alternative investment opportunities. We have rejected the conventional return-on-assets approach because it does not recognize human investments. In evaluating a project, we take the physical assets into account as everyone else does, but we also add to that the investment to be made in the human resources required to support the opportunity. And when we develop relationships to profit, it is the relationship of all those resources, tangible and human, to a particular profit opportunity.[16]

Thus R. G. Barry was attempting to use the notion of expected return on investment on *all* its resources (human as well as conventionally defined assets) as a criterion for strategic decision making. Its human resource accounting system helped management implement this concept by providing data about human resource costs that are essential inputs to this criterion. In contrast, management could not have operationalized this criterion if it had only had data from a conventional accounting system.

The system was also helpful in control. It has two different but related control functions: (1) to motivate managers to conserve (or, more properly, not to liquidate unnecessarily) the company's human assets and (2) to provide a means of evaluating management's conservation of its human resources. Specifically, the company feared that under conventional accounting managers might be motivated to pressure subordinates in order to increase current profitability at the expense of losing their long-term motivation and loyalty. As a result of being driven, people might become increasingly dissatisfied and leave the organization. Thus a manager might show reported increases in earnings while he or she was actually liquidating the company's human assets and, accordingly, diminishing long-term profitability. This situation is analogous to depreciating a machine and failing to charge the expired costs to earnings. The result is that net income is overstated. Without human resource accounting, then, managers may have a built-in motivation to liquidate human resources in order to look good.

This is a classic example of unintended harmful effects of a measurement system, and it can be avoided by using a human resource accounting system. With Barry's accounting system, the unamortized cost of human resources is written off as a loss when turnover occurs. This practice reduces reported net income. In principle, it eliminates the potential incentive to deplete human assets in order to increase profitability.

R. G. Barry's personnel management was able to monitor the extent to which human resources had been conserved by means of a quarterly report that accounted for "increases" and "decreases" in human resource investments as shown in Table 4-15 (Case 4-1) at the end of this chapter. The report shows decreases in human resource investments attributable to turnover. Because the monetary loss of human assets attributable to turnover was reported, management could obtain a better understanding of the economic effects of turnover than if only rates were reported.

Potentially, the system has another major control function—to provide a means of evaluating the personnel department's efficiency. Specifically, the cost standards for the addition and replacement of people can be compared with actual costs. Variances, if any, should be explained.

Discussion of the System. R. G. Barry's system of accounting for investments in people as organizational resources should be viewed as a case study. It is the product of one company's attempt to apply the concepts of human resource accounting. As such, it was most certainly a pioneering effort. The system described does, however, have certain limitations.

One potential limitation of the system is the reliability of the cost data used as inputs. Because of the lack of historical records, it was necessary for management to estimate the parameters of the costs that had been incurred as investments in people. These estimates should therefore be viewed as approximations because their reliability was not assessed.

A second possible limitation involves the validity of the taxonomy of seven functional accounts. In principle, there is no scientific way to determine whether five, six, seven, or some other number of accounts is appropriate. In practice, however, the greater the number of classifications of costs, the greater the difficulty of measuring costs. It is less difficult to measure the two concepts of formal and informal (on-the-job) training cost, for example, than to measure costs of formal training and familiarization, informal training and familiarization, investment building experience, and so on. The greater the specificity of accounts, the greater the opportunity for introducing error. There is, then, a potential trade-off between the degree of detail sought by the system and the potential for error.

A third aspect of the system that requires further study is its utility for management planning and control. At present, there have been no documented studies of the effects of the system upon management decision making. The uses and benefits previously described are all anticipated or hypothesized; there have been no published tests to determine whether human resource accounting actually makes a significant difference in management decisions.

There was some evidence, however tenuous, that the system had an impact on R. G. Barry. According to management, there seemed to be a greater awareness throughout the organization of the importance of human resources. Nevertheless, this awareness may have been stimulated merely because the company made a formal attempt to monitor its investments in people and because those measures of human resource costs directed attention to the issue.

Accounting for Human Resource Investments: A CPA Firm

Pioneering attempts to apply the idea of accounting for investments in people occurred not only in manufacturing organizations such as R. G. Barry Corporation but in service organizations as well. The Montreal office of Touche Ross & Co. (a Big Eight CPA firm), for example, developed a system of accounting for investments in its personnel. It is to this system that we now turn our attention.

The Firm's Motivation. The rationale for the firm's interest in developing a system of accounting for investments in people has been described by Michael Alexander:

> A public accounting firm is, by its very nature, human resource intensive and represents an ideal proving ground for the application of human resource accounting concepts. The primary assets of such a firm are its clients and the human capabilities of its people. The financial or physical assets represent a relatively minor part of the firm's total value and consist largely of cash, receivables, financial capital, and office equipment. As a result, conventional accounting systems which deal with these elements alone are of limited use for managing the all-important human resources.[17]

Thus the firm believed that because people are its most important assets, it was necessary to account for investments in people.

Information Desired. To manage human resources effectively in a public accounting firm, certain information is necessary or at least desirable. Information about costs of recruitment, selection, and training is required because public accounting firms incur substantial expenditures to recruit, hire, and train people. These costs constitute an investment, and one that may not be recovered for several years. Information about the cost of turnover and the replacement cost of people is also necessary for two reasons. First, turnover rates are typically quite high in public accounting. For example, assume that a firm had hired 100 staff accountants in 1973. By 1978 it could have expected that no more than 30 percent would still be with the firm.* Second, the investment in people lost as a result of turnover can be substantial. Similarly, the cost of replacing people as a result of turnover can be significant. For these reasons, it is important to CPA firms to monitor the rate and cost of turnover.

Because a CPA firm is human capital intensive, its long-term survival depends to a great extent upon the development of its human resources. Younger members of the professional staff must be effectively trained in order to provide replacements of senior members of the firm as well as to provide for growth in the firm. This means that managers must be motivated to devote time, energy, and resources to training and development. However, there is typically an opportunity cost to training—time devoted to training in the current period may require a sacrifice of income that otherwise could have been earned. This suggests that CPA firms require some measure of the return expected to be derived on its investments in people in order to facilitate the rational allocation of time to be devoted to development. At a minimum, a firm might simply account for the time allocated to various activities. As Alexander stated:

> The traditional yardstick of performance in a public accounting firm has normally been chargeable hours—the time an employee devotes to client service. Unfortunately, however, the use of this fact as a single measurement may discourage investment in human resources, since the latter is often seen as a feat which is only accomplished at the expense of chargeable hours.[18]

There are, of course, other needs for information about human resources in a CPA firm. For example, information is needed about the effectiveness of hiring and training policies and programs and about the profitability of manpower allocation decisions. For all these reasons, the firm began to develop a system of accounting for investments in people.

The System's Design and Output. The system was designed to measure the investment in people as individuals. Both outlay costs (out-of-pocket expenditures) and opportunity costs (billings forgone) were

*Turnover in public accounting is quite high, but the example cited is based on the actual experience of one firm (not Touche Ross) and may, of course, not be typical of CPA firms generally.

estimated in measuring the investment in each individual since the firm had no published data about these investments.

Data collection problems were minimized to some extent because the firm was already generating all of the information required as inputs to the human resource accounting system. In Alexander's words:

> The cost of time or opportunity costs were developed from time records regularly filled out by each employee. These records show how each hour of the day was spent and whether or not it was chargeable to a client. The out-of-pocket or outlay costs were easily obtained with only minor reclassification of existing cost accounts.[19]

According to Alexander, the output of the system consisted of a set of reports to management. These reports monitored various aspects of the firm's investment in its people. Four of the reports generated by the firm's system were the cost of time analysis report, the summary of human resource investments, the statement of human resource flows, and the contribution report.

The *cost of time analysis report,* shown in Table 4-7, presents the planned and actual allocation of time for the period ended December 31, 1970. The major reason for such a report is that the services of people in a CPA firm are closely correlated with time. *Chargeable hours,* or time billed to clients, represent a direct contribution to a firm's income. Time is the common denominator for investment in human asset development. Thus it is important to monitor its use.

As shown in Table 4-7, the firm identified three dimensions of the output or product of professional staff time: chargeable, investment, and maintenance. Chargeable time has already been defined. *Investment* time represents the time that is devoted to building human assets. *Maintenance* time is the portion of time that is an "expense" and presumably has no future service potential.

This report indicates the planned as well as actual hours for the various activities and reports variances from two primary causes. The manpower variance reflects a different number of people actually on the staff than planned, while the hours variance indicates the difference between planned and actual hours for the specified activity.

The main functions of such a report are planning and control of human services. Most likely, the very fact that standards for each component of a person's time must be set will lead to more systematic

Table 4-7

COST OF TIME ANALYSIS REPORT

For Year Ending December 31, 1970

	Total Office			
	Plan	*Man. Var.*	*Hr. Var.*	*Actual*
Chargeable	$738,952	$(7,230)	$(24,724)	$706,998
Investment				
Recruiting	11,500	622	868	12,990
Orientation	11,000	69	1,931	13,000
Counseling and dev.	10,000	579	1,421	12,000
Formal training courses	35,000	100	7,000	42,100
Research	15,500	42	(284)	15,258
Total	$ 83,000	$ 1,412	$ 10,936	$ 95,348
Maintenance				
Practice development	8,694	(124)	(5,850)	2,720
Prof. affairs and PR	3,064	19	6,825	9,908
Administration	36,864	237	(310)	36,791
Holidays and vac.	102,000	(742)	(25,892)	75,366
Sickness and per.	28,932	(68)	8,877	37,741
Total	$179,554	$ (678)	$(16,350)	$162,526
Total	$1,001,506	$(6,496)	$(30,138)	$964,872

SOURCE: Michael O. Alexander, "Investments in People," *Canadian Chartered Accountant,* July 1971, p. 41. Reprinted by permission of the *Canadian Chartered Accountant.*

and rational planning. Similarly, the very fact that variances from plan are recorded and reported will tend to motivate people to pay attention to the allocation of time.

The *summary of human resource investments,* shown in Table 4-8, presents the sum of investments made in people during the year. It compares planned with actual investments and identifies both the outlay and the opportunity cost components of investments. The report does not present the variances; although they can be calculated from the data provided, good reporting procedures require reporting variances per se.

The source of outlay costs is the firm's conventional accounting system, modified slightly in order to accumulate human resource costs incurred. The opportunity costs are derived from the cost of time report.

The summary of human resource investments can be used to monitor the effectiveness of the firm's human resource investment (human capital budgeting) programs. The effectiveness of the firm's plans can be partially assessed in terms of whether stated goals have been

Table 4-8

HUMAN RESOURCE INVESTMENTS

For Year Ending December 31, 1970

	Plan			*Actual*		
	Outlay	*Opport.*	*Total*	*Outlay*	*Opport.*	*Total*
Recruiting	$ 500	$11,500	$12,000	$1,420	$12,990	$ 14,410
Orientation	2,500	11,000	13,500	2,200	13,000	15,200
Counseling and development	1,600	10,000	11,600	400	12,000	12,400
Formal training courses	5,000	35,000	40,000	3,500	42,100	45,600
Research	1,400	15,500	16,900	1,200	15,258	16,458
Total	$11,000	$83,000	$94,000	$8,720	$95,348	$104,068

SOURCE: Michael O. Alexander, "Investments in People," *Canadian Chartered Accountant*, July 1971, p. 41. Reprinted by permission of the *Canadian Chartered Accountant*.

achieved. For example, formal training was planned at an estimated cost of $40,000 for 1970, as shown in Table 4-8. Was this training objective actually achieved? Did the firm, in other words, do what it intended to do? In addition, the efficiency of training can be assessed. Was the actual cost incurred in training greater than, less than, or equal to planned cost of the specified activities? In other words, the variance from plan can be used as a measure of efficiency of human resource investments.

The *statement of human resource flows*, shown in Table 4-9, presents changes in human resources during the year. The report measures such changes both in units of manpower and in monetary terms. It compares planned changes with actual changes, but it does not report variances.

This report, according to Alexander, is intended to "emphasize the importance of human resource development, and it allows managers to assess their performance in this context."[20] This statement of purpose does not fully describe the report's uses. Basically, the report enables management to monitor the firm's inventory of people and the investments associated with that inventory. The opening balance represents the stock of human resources on hand at the beginning of the year. During the year, there are specified planned additions such as transfers into the office or new recruits. There are also anticipated reductions in human assets attributable to transfers-out and turnover. The investments portion of this report deals with the monetary stock of human capital. Changes in investments in people are caused by all of the

Table 4-9

STATEMENT OF HUMAN RESOURCE FLOWS

For Year Ending December 31, 1970

	Manpower		*Investments*	
	Plan	*Actual*	*Plan*	*Actual*
Opening balance	29	29	$112,532	$112,532
Add:				
Transfers in (other offices)	4	3	13,000	10,321
Investments:				
Recruiting	10	10	12,000	14,410
Investments in existing personnel during period	—	—	82,000	89,658
Total	14	13	$107,000	$114,389
Less:				
Transfers out (other offices)	6	5	30,000	26,449
Departures	9	8	34,000	33,498
Amortization	—	—	32,000	36,381
Total	15	13	$ 96,000	$ 96,328
Closing balance	28	29	$123,532	$130,594

SOURCE: Michael O. Alexander, "Investments in People," *Canadian Chartered Accountant,* July 1971, p. 41. Reprinted by permission of the *Canadian Chartered Accountant.*

changes in physical inventory just described; but they are also affected by changes in the existing stock of people through training and amortization. In essence, then, this report can more accurately be labeled a *human capital inventory*. It is an inventory both in physical quantities and in monetary units.

One aspect of this report worthy of special attention is *amortization*. In describing the system, Alexander stated that "human resource amortization is based upon the same principles as those used to systematically record the expiration or depreciation of a firm's other assets."[21] Amortization for any component of investment in human resources is based upon either the individual's expected tenure in the organization or the expected useful life of the investment per se. Operationally speaking, the investment is either depreciated during the period of a person's expected tenure or the expected life of the investment. For example, an investment in training that is expected to benefit an individual for three years will be depreciated during that period if the individual is expected to remain in the firm for *at least* three years. If the person were expected to remain only for two years, however, the investment would be depreciated over a two-year period.

The *contribution report,* shown in Table 4-10, is based on the notion that the firm's human resources comprise a profit center. Conceptually, the firm is conceived of as a set of service centers, and the contribution of each center is measured and compared against the plan. The report identifies a manpower and an hour variance.

Table 4-10

CONTRIBUTION REPORT

For Year Ending December 31, 1970

	Total Office			
	Plan	*Man. Var.*	*Hr. Var.*	*Actual*
Chargeable hours X standard billing rates	$738,743	$ (6,537)	$(25,220)	$706,986
Less:				
Salaries and fringe benefits	240,000	(13,107)		253,107
Amortization of human resource investment	32,000	(4,381)		36,381
Departures	34,000	502		33,498
Standard operating contribution before overhead	$432,743	$(23,523)	$(25,220)	$384,000

SOURCE: Michael O. Alexander, "Investments in People," *Canadian Chartered Accountant,* July 1971, p. 42. Reprinted by permission of the *Canadian Chartered Accountant.*

Benefits of the System. The system of accounting for investments in people at the Touche Ross office reportedly provided management with information that improved the ability to manage human resources. Specifically, the system provided information that was necessary for decision making in such areas as employee turnover, optimum staff mix, and hiring policies. According to Alexander, the system "provided the firm with a number of facts which have led to some reassessment of its traditional approach to staff mix and resource allocation."[22] The system indicated that profit contributions per employee were somewhat different than what had been assumed. This finding implies that the firm changed its personnel allocation decision rules. Thus the firm was in a better position to determine optimal staff mix because of the information it had about personnel contributions.

Discussion of the System. The information available about the system developed at the Touche Ross office is not sufficient to permit an assessment of its validity, reliability, or utility. Nevertheless, the very fact of the system's implementation indicates that managers in various industries were beginning to sense the need to account for human resources. Moreover, it was certainly a pioneering effort in human resource accounting and made a significant contribution to the field.

Accounting for Human Resource Replacement Costs: An Insurance Company

At present, there are still relatively few organizations with systems of accounting for the positional replacement cost of human resources. Where such systems do exist, the costs of replacing people tend to be understated because some components of replacement are typically overlooked. This section describes a pioneering effort to develop a system for measuring positional replacement costs in an insurance company. This organization will be called the "Midwestern Insurance Company."[23]

At the time the system was developed, Midwestern Insurance Company was a medium-sized mutual insurance firm engaged in business throughout the United States. It had more than 4,000 full-time employees, about 25 percent of whom were salespeople. Its assets exceeded $250 million.

The system of measuring positional replacement costs was developed in a branch of Midwestern located in a large city in the Midwest. At that time, the branch had 110 employees. A partial branch organization chart is presented in Figure 4-2. The branch had four sales teams, each consisting of approximately fifteen salespeople, and twenty-two inside and outside claims personnel (investigators, adjusters, examiners, and others).

The Company's Motivation. One of the major reasons for the company's interest in accounting for the replacement cost of its human resources was the high rates and cost of turnover among salespeople in the insurance industry in general and at Midwestern in particular. The firm typically experienced high turnover among salespeople and claims investigators during their first year of employment—approximately one third of all new salespeople left the firm during the first twelve months. Thus the firm was interested in measuring the cost of replacing sales and claims personnel to determine the magnitude of these costs and the

Figure 4-2

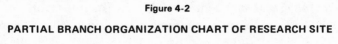

PARTIAL BRANCH ORGANIZATION CHART OF RESEARCH SITE

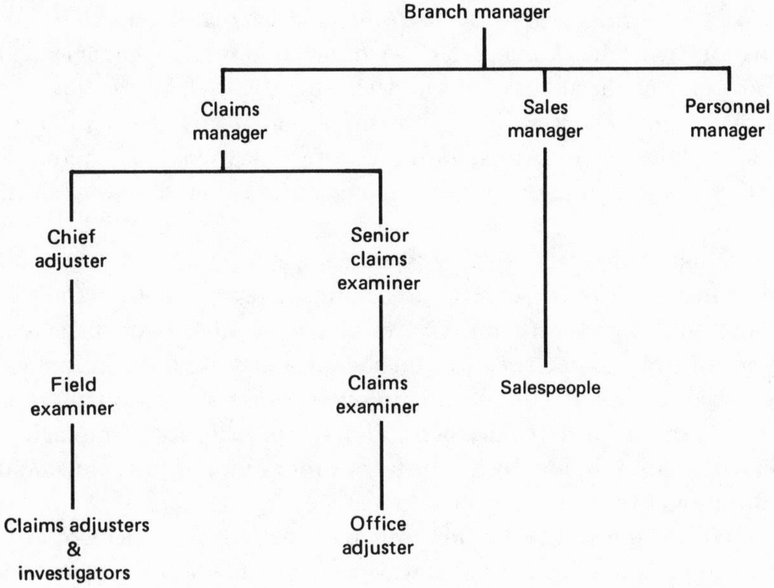

SOURCE: Eric G. Flamholtz, "The Theory and Measurement of an Individual's Value to an Organization," (Ph.D. dissertation, University of Michigan, 1969), p. 47.

potential for cost savings from reducing turnover. The firm was also interested in the possible use of measures of human resource replacement cost in various personnel policy decisions. For example, the firm found it difficult to motivate high-performing salespeople to accept promotions to sales manager because the job change would typically involve a reduction in the individual's earnings. A sales manager's salary in this firm was fixed, while a salesperson's commissions could well exceed the manager's salary. Thus one issue of concern was: How valuable are sales managers to the organization? A related issue was: If they are as valuable as we think they are, how can we modify compensation policy to reflect their value and, in turn, motivate high-potential salespeople to become managers?

The Measurement System. The measurement of positional replacement costs was based on the model discussed in Chapter Three (see Figure 3-3). The form used to collect the data specified in this model, shown in Appendix 4-1, was developed and evaluated on the basis of discussions with the claims, sales, personnel, and branch managers. The purpose of such discussions was to determine if all relevant components of replacement cost were being measured and if any items should be excluded. Thus the measurement procedure was assessed as having face validity to management; that is, management believed it was a valid system.

Some of the data required were collected from objective sources such as historical records, time sheets, and wage rates. However, it was also necessary to obtain subjective estimates of other data such as the amount of time people spend in on-the-job learning, the percentage of decreased productivity of other employees when a position is vacant during a search for a replacement, and the probability of replacing a specified position holder by a transfer, a promotion, or from outside the organization.

Where subjective estimates were required, the management group was asked to indicate the persons who were capable of making the most reliable estimates of the data required. Where feasible, the estimates were obtained from two or more persons to assess their reliability. The estimates obtained thus had face validity to management in a dual sense. First, they were made by people who were selected as the best available source of the data. Second, management was prepared to accept the data as the best available.

In this pilot study, it was assumed that these estimates were reasonable approximations of the data required. The major concern was to obtain reasonable estimates, and resource constraints prevented an attempt to obtain similar estimates from a different branch in order to assess the reliability of the data.

Data Collection. Positional replacement cost data were collected in two forms: anticipated costs and standard costs. *Anticipated positional replacement costs* refer to the costs actually expected to be incurred to acquire the best available substitute. The best available substitute may or may not be the most desirable substitute. A *standard positional replacement cost* refers to the cost to replace an individual assuming he or she is replaced by the natural or most desirable substitute. For example, in an insurance company the *natural substitute* for a claims examiner may be an office adjuster. However, it may not be possible to replace the claims examiner with an office adjuster. As a result, it may be necessary to use the *best available substitute,* such as a claims adjuster. This may result in a difference between standard positional replacement cost (based upon replacement by an office adjuster) and anticipated positional replacement costs (based upon replacement by a claims adjuster). The difference between these costs may be attributable to differences in the amount of training required by the two alternative substitutes to replace the examiner effectively.

Selected Data. The positional replacement costs obtained for the sales and claims groups, respectively, are presented in Tables 4-11 and 4-12.

These tables include estimates of both standard and anticipated positional replacement costs. Standard and anticipated costs are equivalent in almost all cases, with the exceptions of the field and claims examiners and the sales manager. The differences are attributable to expected difficulties involved in replacing these position holders with their natural or most desirable substitutes. As a result, various components of their respective replacement costs are anticipated to exceed standard costs. These cost differentials are attributable to manpower planning policies and practices. In order to understand the causes of differences between standard and anticipated positional replacement costs, it is helpful to examine the cost elements themselves.

As shown in Table 4-13, the anticipated cost of replacing a sales manager exceeds standard for two of the three cost components: learning and separation costs. The anticipated training cost exceeds standard by $75,800 and the anticipated separation cost exceeds standard by $19,300, a total of $95,100 more than standard. This difference is attributable to the difficulty forecast by management in obtaining a natural substitute for a sales manager (a sales management trainee) and the corresponding need to replace the manager with a salesperson. First, it will require some time to locate a suitable candidate and, in the meantime, the organization will incur opportunity costs attributable to the vacant managerial position. Second, while the sales manager's position is vacant during his or her training, the company can anticipate decreased productivity (in sales retention and new business development) from many of its salespeople, but especially among its more inexperienced personnel. In addition, the candidate is expected to require a significantly greater amount of time before he or she achieves the normal level of effectiveness as sales manager. This means that the anticipated costs of learning, direct as well as indirect, can be expected to exceed standard.

Table 4-11

POSITIONAL REPLACEMENT COSTS

Sales Personnel

Positions	Positional Replacement Costs: Anticipated Costs	Positional Replacement Costs: Standard Costs
Salespeople		
1. Below-average performance	$ 31,600	$31,600
2. Average performance	44,100	44,100
3. Above-average performance	56,800	56,800
Sales manager trainee	51,700	51,700
Sales manager	185,100	90,000

SOURCE: Eric G. Flamholtz, "Human Resource Accounting: Measuring Positional Replacement Costs," *Human Resource Management*, Spring 1973, p. 13. Reprinted by permission of the Graduate School of Business Administration, University of Michigan.

Table 4-12

POSITIONAL REPLACEMENT COSTS

Claims Personnel

Position	Positional Replacement Costs: Anticipated Costs	Positional Replacement Costs: Standard Costs
Claims investigator	$ 6,000	$ 6,000
Claims adjuster	6,000	6,000
Office adjuster	7,800	7,800
Field examiner	24,700	12,800
Claims examiner	9,700	8,700
Senior examiner	15,900	15,900
Chief adjuster	15,100	15,100
Claims manager	18,700	18,700

SOURCE: Eric G. Flamholtz, "Human Resource Accounting: Measuring Positional Replacement Costs," *Human Resource Management*, Spring 1973, p. 14. Reprinted by permission of the Graduate School of Business Administration, University of Michigan.

In Table 4-14, the anticipated cost of replacing a field examiner exceeds standard by $11,900. This differential is expected to arise because of the predicted difficulty of obtaining a natural substitute. Specifically, management estimates a low probability of replacing a field examiner by a transfer of an office adjuster (the natural substitute). If the field examiner is replaced by a claims adjuster, acquisition costs will be $1,600

Table 4-13

POSITIONAL REPLACEMENT COSTS: STANDARD AND ANTICIPATED

Sales Personnel

	Standard Positional Replacement Costs				*Anticipated Positional Replacement Costs*			
Positions	*Acquisition*	*Learning*	*Separation*	*Total*	*Acquisition*	*Learning*	*Separation*	*Total*
Salespeople								
Below average	$ 600	$13,900	$17,100	$31,600	$ 600	$ 13,900	$17,100	$ 31,600
Average	900	19,400	23,800	44,100	900	19,400	23,800	44,100
Above average	1,100	25,000	30,700	56,800	1,100	25,000	30,700	56,800
Sales management								
Trainee	1,000	22,700	27,900	51,700	1,000	22,700	27,900	51,700
Sales manager	51,700	38,300	–0–	90,000	51,700	114,100	19,300	185,100

SOURCE: Eric G. Flamholtz, "Human Resource Accounting: Measuring Positional Replacement Costs," *Human Resource Management,* Spring 1973, p. 15. Reprinted by permission of the Graduate School of Business Administration, University of Michigan.

Table 4-14

POSITIONAL REPLACEMENT COSTS: STANDARD AND ANTICIPATED

Claims Personnel

	Standard Positional Replacement Costs				*Anticipated Positional Replacement Costs*			
Positions	*Acquisition*	*Learning*	*Separation*	*Total*	*Acquisition*	*Learning*	*Separation*	*Total*
Claims investigator	$ 600	$4,000	$1,400	$ 6,000	$ 600	$ 4,000	$1,400	$ 6,000
Claims adjuster	600	4,000	1,400	6,000	600	4,000	1,400	6,000
Office adjuster	5,600	1,100	1,100	7,800	5,600	1,100	1,100	7,800
Field examiner	8,600	3,300	900	12,800	7,000	16,700	1,000	24,700
Claims examiner	7,100	1,000	600	8,700	6,600	2,500	600	9,700
Chief adjuster	11,300	3,000	900	15,200	11,300	3,000	900	15,200
Senior examiner	11,300	3,500	1,100	15,900	11,300	3,500	1,100	15,900
Claims manager	14,900	3,800	–0–	18,700	14,900	3,800	–0–	18,700

SOURCE: Eric G. Flamholtz, "Human Resource Accounting: Measuring Positional Replacement Costs," *Human Resource Management,* Spring 1973, p. 15. Reprinted by permission of the Graduate School of Business Administration, University of Michigan.

less than standard, because it is less costly to replace a claims adjuster than an office adjuster. However, $13,400 greater learning costs will be incurred if the replacement is a claims adjuster rather than an office adjuster, as a result of a significantly longer period of on-the-job learning. The difference in separation costs between the two positions (only $100) is not significant.

Table 4-14 also shows that the anticipated cost of replacing a claims examiner exceeds standard by $1,000. This cost differential is also attributable to predicted difficulty in replacing the position holder with the natural substitute.

As already noted, positional replacement costs are composed of opportunity as well as outlay costs. In this instance, opportunity costs are more significant for sales personnel than for claims personnel.

The primary opportunity costs are associated with the learning and separation components of positional replacement cost. For example, 55 percent of the learning costs of a salesperson are opportunity costs. Similarly, 100 percent of the separation costs of a salesperson are opportunity costs. These are costs of a vacant position during a search for a replacement.

The System's Potential Uses. A system of accounting for positional replacement costs potentially has both direct and indirect uses in the human resource management process. It can be helpful in planning and controlling the use of human resources and also in developing surrogate measures of a person's value to an organization. The former use is examined below; the latter is treated in Chapter Seven.

Measures of positional replacement costs can play a significant role in budgeting personnel requirements, in controlling personnel acquisition, learning, and separation costs, and in evaluating the effectiveness of personnel planning policies and practices.

The process of personnel planning not only involves forecasting the number of people required in various staff classifications, but also estimating the monetary costs of recruiting, selecting, hiring, and developing personnel resources in terms of a personnel budget. Anticipated and standard positional replacement costs can facilitate the preparation of such budgets.

Moreover, standard positional replacement costs, like all standard costs, can help control personnel costs. Thus the personnel function in organizations can be treated as a cost center; standard costs act as criteria for cost control.

The comparisons of standard and anticipated costs can also serve as a means of monitoring the effectiveness of personnel planning policies and practices. In the insurance company previously cited, anticipated positional replacement costs exceeded standard for the field and claims examiner and sales manager positions. The reason in all three cases was the predicted difficulty of obtaining natural substitutes. This is an indication that the organization is incurring an opportunity cost attributable to personnel planning practices.

Similarly, analyses of the components of such replacement costs may indicate areas for cost savings. In the Midwestern Insurance Company, for example, 100 percent of separation costs associated with salespeople were costs of a vacant position during a search for a replacement. These costs ranged from $17,100 for a below-average-performing salesperson to $30,700 for an above-average salesperson. The magnitude of these costs, together with the relatively high rate of turnover of insurance salespeople (about 20 percent annually for new hires), seems to indicate the desirability of investigating alternative methods of reducing such costs. The opportunity cost that can occur in one year from turnover of new hires can run into hundreds of thousands of dollars. Assume a firm hires 100 salespeople in a given year, has a first-year turnover rate of 20 percent, and all of the salespeople who turn over are below average. Considering only separation costs, the total expected cost attributable to turnover would be $342,000 (20 × $17,100). If we now consider total positional replacement cost, expected turnover cost would be $632,000. Of course, these costs would increase if average and above-average salespeople were included in the 20 percent first-year turnover rate, as some undoubtedly are.

Discussion of the System. Midwestern Insurance Company's system of accounting for human resource replacement costs should be viewed as a case study. It is the product of a pilot study to apply a model for measurement of positional replacement costs.

One of the system's limitations is the reliability of some of the data used to obtain measures of positional replacement cost. Just as in the R. G. Barry system, it was necessary to obtain subjective estimates for some data. These estimates must be viewed as approximations since their reliability was not assessed. Another limitation is that no attempt was made in this study to study the use of the data derived in management decisions; rather, recommendations were made to the company about how this information might be applied in the personnel management process.

Summary

This chapter has surveyed selected cases of pioneering attempts to develop systems of accounting for human resource costs. The R. G. Barry Corporation, a manufacturing enterprise, developed a system of accounting for its human assets for managerial purposes. The nature of the company's industry, its managerial philosophy, and management's need for information about its human assets all contributed to its effort to develop the system. Initially, the system included only exempt personnel, but it was later extended to hourly employees. For reasons of feasibility, the system was limited to accounting for costs and does not account for value. The company perceived several benefits from the system—not only in its personnel activities but also in strategic planning for the company as a whole. The company included unaudited pro forma financial statements prepared according to the conventions of human resource accounting in its annual reports to illustrate the system's informational value.

A public accounting firm (Touche Ross & Co.) also developed a system of accounting for investments in its personnel. The firm felt the need to account for its human resources because CPA firms are, by their nature, human resource intensive. Touche Ross & Co. believed that information about investments in people was required in order to facilitate their effective management. The firm's Montreal office provided managers with a set of reports designed to monitor aspects of investments in people and their utilization as organizational resources.

At Midwestern Insurance Company, an effort was made to develop a pilot system of accounting for human resource replacement costs. The firm was motivated to measure the replacement cost of its human resources because turnover rates among salespeople and certain claims personnel were felt to be quite high. Measurements of standard and anticipated replacement costs were developed. A system of accounting for positional replacement costs can be helpful in planning and controlling the use of human resources, especially in budgeting personnel requirements, controlling personnel costs, and evaluating the efficiency of personnel planning policies and practices.

Case 4-1: R. G. Barry (B)

In the July 1970 issue of Michigan Business Review, *an article by William C. Pyle of the University of Michigan discussed some aspects of his research with the R. G. Barry Corporation to develop human resource accounting. Part of that article dealt with the use of human resource accounting for internal managerial purposes. As an example of the R. G. Barry system's utility, Pyle cited its applicability to "capital budgeting for human resources." That discussion is reproduced here:*

It was noted earlier that conventional accounting practice impedes the acquisition and development of human capabilities by treating all such expenditures as business expenses to be charged against revenue in one year. For internal management purposes, the Barry Corporation has changed this practice. In the latter part of 1969, the firm prepared what is believed to be industry's first capital budget for human resources. Expenditures undertaken with the objective of building long-term capabilities are charged against revenue over the period of expected benefit.

Based upon the plans they have submitted, managers receive quarterly human resource reports indicating the "book value" of investments in their subordinates at the beginning and end of the quarter. Increases and decreases occurring during the period are also highlighted. The report form presented in [Table 4-15] indicates the type of information which R. G. Barry's executives are now using to guide the management of human resources. The firm's vice-president of personnel, Robert L. Woodruff, Jr., describes how this new information is being used:

> Capital budgeting for human resources, together with reporting actual performance against the plan, gives the manager an additional perspective on the total effectiveness of his unit. Investments made in additional personnel, replacement personnel, training and development as well as write-offs incurred through turnover and obsolescence of prior investments are reported against the manager's plan. The transfer of human assets from one department to another is also planned. For the corporation as a whole "transfers in" must equal "transfers out."
>
> This quarterly report informs the manager whether planned developmental investments are in fact being made

Note: Reprinted from William C. Pyle, "Monitoring Human Resources—'On Line,'" *Michigan Business Review,* July 1970, pp. 26-27. Reproduced by permission of the *Michigan Business Review* and the author.

Table 4-15

HUMAN RESOURCE CAPITAL BUDGET 1970

Quarter Ending: June 30, 1970 | **Beginning Balance $1,325,000** | **Location: Corporate Total**

New Investments | **Supervisor: President**

Year-To-Date

Actual # People	Dollars Plan	Dollars Actual	MANAGEMENT PERSONNEL	Dollars Plan	Dollars Actual	12 Month Plan
3	$ 25,000	$ 19,500	Additions	$ 40,000	$ 30,000	$110,000
7	42,000	51,000	Replacement	84,000	90,000	168,000
18	11,500	10,000	Development	20,000	17,800	60,000
3	21,000	14,000	Transfer in	42,000	35,000	84,000
121	120,000	130,000	Hourly personnel	250,000	264,500	510,000
	$219,500	$225,100*	Total	$436,000	$437,300	$932,000
			WRITE-OFFS MANAGEMENT PERSONNEL			
	$ 17,250	$ 19,100	Amortization	$ 34,500	$ 36,000	$138,000
3			Turnover losses			
3	10,000	11,000	Voluntary	20,000	24,000	80,000
1	7,500	4,800	Involuntary	15,000	11,400	60,000
—	17,000	800	Obsolescence	2,500	1,100	5,000
3	21,000	14,000	Transfer out	42,000	35,000	84,000
111	120,000	117,400	Hourly personnel	230,000	251,000	480,000
	$192,750	$167,100	Total	$344,000	$359,100	$847,000
			Ending Balance $1,383,000			

*Numbers in this column do not total $225,100. Error is in original report.

SOURCE: William C. Pyle, "Monitoring Human Resources—'On Line,'" *Michigan Business Review*, July 1970, p. 27. Reproduced by permission of the *Michigan Business Review* and the author.

> as planned, and whether write-offs of investments due to separations are exceeding his original expectations. For each profit center, the net of new investment less write-offs is applied as an adjustment to the conventional profit figure which reflects either a positive or a negative impact on the important bottom line number.

Human resource accounting techniques are employed not only to evaluate the performance of current operations, but are also used in analysis and selection of new business opportunities. The firm's president, Gordon Zacks, describes this application:

> We use human resource accounting information in strategic decision making. The information is employed in evaluating alternative investment opportunities. We have rejected the conventional return-on-assets approach because it does not recognize human investments. In evaluating a project, we take the physical assets into account as everyone else does, but we also add to that the investment to be made in the human resources required to support the opportunity. And when we develop relationships to profit, it is the relationship of all of those resources, tangible and human, to a particular profit opportunity.

In this regard, the firm's controller, Richard Burrell, adds: "Human resource accounting data provide still another tool to evaluate the allocation of resources among profit opportunities to maximize the return on all corporate resources." The report format seen in [Table 4-15] may also be used as a device to evaluate new business opportunities. The required capital expenditures for human resources (and write-offs of prior investments) may be projected and included along with similar information for the physical resources associated with each option under consideration. When a particular opportunity is selected, these data then serve as the plan against which actual experience is reported. In addition to special-purpose analyses such as these, human resource data are also being integrated with the firm's conventional financial statements for internal management purposes.

Questions

1. Does the report presented in Table 4-15 meet the company's objective of providing information for capital budgeting of human resources? Explain.
2. What changes, if any, would you recommend in the report's content and its format?

Case 4-2: R. G. Barry (C)

During the past year work continued on the development of Barry's human resource accounting system. The basic purpose of the system is to develop a method of measuring in dollar terms the changes that occur in the human resources of a business that conventional accounting does not currently consider.

Basic Concept. Management can be considered as the process of planning, organizing, leading, and controlling a complex mix of resources to accomplish the objectives of the organization. Those resources, we believe, are physical resources of the company as represented by buildings and equipment, financial resources, and human resources which consist of the people who comprise the organization and proprietary resources which consist of trademarks, patents, and company name and reputation.

In order to determine more precisely the effectiveness of management's performance it is necessary to have information about the status of investments in the acquisition, maintenance, and utilization of all resources of the company.

Without such information, it is difficult for a company to know whether profit is being generated by converting a resource into cash or conversely whether suboptimal performance really has been generated by investments in developing the human resources which we expensed under conventional accounting practice.

Definition. Human resource accounting is an attempt to identify, quantify, and report investments made in resources of an organization

Note: In the 1969 corporate annual report of the R. G. Barry Corporation, pro forma financial statements adjusted to reflect human resource accounting concepts were included, as shown in Table 4-16. Excerpts from the 1969 annual report, which describe the system, are presented here.

Table 4-16

"THE TOTAL CONCEPT"

R. G. Barry Corporation and Subsidiaries
1969 (Pro Forma)
(Financial and Human Resource Accounting)

BALANCE SHEET	*1969 Financial and Human Resource*	*1969 Financial Only*
Assets		
Total current assets	$10,003,628	$10,003,628
Net property, plant and equipment	1,770,717	1,770,717
Excess of purchase price of subsidiaries over net assets acquired	1,188,704	1,188,704
Net investments in human resources	986,094	—
Other assets	106,783	106,783
	$14,055,926	$13,069,832
Liabilities and Stockholders' Equity		
Total current liabilities	$ 5,715,708	$ 5,715,708
Long term debt, excluding current installments	1,935,500	1,935,500
Deferred compensation	62,380	62,380
Deferred federal income taxes as a result of appropriation for human resources	493,047	—
Stockholders' equity:		
Capital stock	879,116	879,116
Additional capital in excess of par value	1,736,253	1,736,253
Retained earnings:		
Financial	2,740,875	2,740,875
Appropriation for human resources	493,047	—
Total stockholders' equity	5,849,291	5,356,244
	$14,055,926	$13,069,832
STATEMENT OF INCOME		
Net sales	$25,310,588	$25,310,588
Cost of sales	16,275,876	16,275,876
Gross profit	9,034,712	9,034,712
Selling, general and administrative expenses	6,737,313	6,737,313
Operating income	2,297,399	2,297,399
Other deductions, net	953,177	953,177
Income before federal income taxes	1,344,222	1,344,222
Human resource expenses applicable to future periods	173,569	—
Adjusted income before federal income taxes	1,517,791	1,344,222
Federal income taxes	730,785	644,000
Net income	$ 787,006	$ 700,222

NOTE: The information presented on this page is provided only to illustrate the informational value of human resource accounting for more effective internal management of the business. The figures included regarding investments and amortization of human resources are unaudited and you are cautioned for purposes of evaluating the performance of this company to refer to the conventional certified accounting data further on in this report.

that are not presently accounted for under conventional accounting practice. Basically, it is an information system that tells management what changes over time are occurring to the human resources of the business. It must be considered as an element of a total system of management—not as a separate device or gimmick to focus attention on human resources.

Objectives. Broadly, the human resource accounting information system is being designed to provide better answers to these kinds of questions: What is the quality of profit performance? Are sufficient human capabilities being acquired to achieve the objectives of the enterprise? Are they being developed adequately? To what degree are they being properly maintained? Are these capabilities being properly utilized by the organization?

As expressed in our 1968 annual report, our specific objectives in development of human resource accounting are: (1) to provide Barry managers with specific feedback information on their performance in managing the organizational resources entrusted to their care so that they can make proper adjustments to their pattern of operations to correct adverse trends or further improve the condition of these resources; (2) to provide Barry managers with additional information pertaining to human resources to assist in their decision making; and (3) to provide the organization with a more accurate accounting of its return on total resources employed, rather than just the physical resources, and to enable management to analyze how changes in the status of the resources employed affect the achievement of corporate objectives.

Approach. The approach used has been to account for investments in securing and developing the organization's human resources. Outlay costs for recruiting, acquiring, training, familiarizing, and developing management personnel are accumulated and capitalized. In accordance with the approach conventional accounting employs for classification of an expenditure as an asset, only those outlays which have an expected value beyond the current accounting period deserve consideration as investments. Those outlays which are likely to be consumed within a twelve-month period are properly classified as expense items. The investments in human resources are amortized over the expected useful period of the investment. The basic outlays in connection with acquiring and integrating new management people are amortized over their expected tenure with the company. Investments made for training or development are amortized over a much shorter period of time. The system now covers all locations of the corporation.

Research and development of the system began in late 1966 as a joint effort between the Institute for Social Research, of the University of Michigan, and R. G. Barry.

Applications. There are many potential applications for human resource accounting. Considering outlays for human resource investments which have a useful life over a number of years would have an impact upon the current year's revenue. By recognizing investments in human resources and their useful lives, losses resulting from improper maintenance of those resources can be shown in dollar terms. Estimating the useful lives of investments also provides a basis for planning for the orderly replacement of human capabilities as they expire, supplementing conventional manpower planning. Finally, recognizing investments in human resources will allow management to calculate dollar return on investment on a more comprehensive resource base for a particular profit center.

Summary. From the standpoint of management, knowledge of the human resource investments, maintenance, and returns is necessary for proper decision making and planning long-range corporate growth. As industry becomes increasingly technical, and management becomes progressively more complex, we believe conventional accounting practice will come to recognize human resource accounting in financial reporting.

At this stage, the human resource accounting system at R. G. Barry is best regarded as a potentially important tool of the overall management system. It is not an end in itself and needs continuing refinement and development.

Question

In early 1970, an investor in R. G. Barry Corporation was reviewing the firm's 1969 annual report and came across the foregoing material. He decided to write a letter to the firm's chairman of the board commenting on this study and giving his reactions. Assuming you are the investor, prepare the letter to the firm's chairman of the board.

Case 4-3: R. G. Barry (D)

As part of its human resource accounting system, the R. G. Barry Corporation has developed various forms for collecting data on

Table 4-17

R. G. BARRY FORM FOR RECRUITMENT AND ACQUISITION COSTS

REQUEST FOR PERSONNEL

Position: QUALITY CONTR. MGR. Salary Grade: 37 Name GORDON DANIELS Number

Date: 2/28/68

Date to Start: 2/28/68 Age: 36

Column 1	2	3	4	5	6	7	8	9	10	11
Functional Classifications	General Costs		Candidates							Totals
"O" - Outlay Cost "S" -- Standard Cost	Internal	External	1	2	3	4				
A. RECRUITING:										
1. "S" Internal Screening	150									
2. "S" Personnel Dept. Time			75	75	75	75				300
3. "S" Acquiring Dept. Time			—	150	150	150				450
4. "O" Advertising										
N.Y. TIMES		440								
5. "O" Search Fees										
6. "O" Interview Travel Expense			—	123	148	92				363
Interviewee:										
Interviewer:										
7. "O" Testing/Evaluation					70					70
8. "O" Other										
9. Non-hire Allocation					1330					
10. TOTALS	150	440	75	348	1773	317				
B. ACQUISITION:										
1. "S" Personnel Dept. Time					40					
2. "S" Acquiring Dept. Time					50					
3. "O" Agency Fees					1350					
4. "O" Moving Costs					700					
5. "O" Temporary Living Expense					540					
6. "O" Temporary Travel Allowance					180					
7. "O" Physical Examination					70					
8. "O" Other										
9. TOTAL					2930					

	Standard	Outlay	Variance Favorable	Variance Unfavorable
Recruiting Cost	$2025	$1773	$252	
Acquisition Cost	$2380	$2930		$550

SOURCE: Robert L. Woodruff, Jr., "Development of a Human Resource Accounting System at the R. G. Barry Corporation," in *Human Resource Accounting: Development and Implementation in Industry,* edited by R. Lee Brummet, Eric G. Flamholtz, and William C. Pyle (Ann Arbor: Foundation for Research on Human Behavior, 1969), p. 76. Reprinted by permission of the Foundation for Research on Human Behavior.

investments in people. The company's form for collecting recruitment and acquisition costs is shown in Table 4-17.

Questions

1. Are there any items of cost shown in this form that you would not include in calculating the firm's investment in recruiting and acquisition of a quality control manager?
2. Explain the source and the meaning of the $1,330 "nonhire allocation" shown on line 9, column 6.
3. What changes, if any, would you suggest in this form?

Case 4-4: Midwestern Insurance Company

This chapter has discussed the Midwestern Insurance Company's system of accounting for positional replacement costs. Refer to Tables 4-11 through 4-14. Analyze the data presented in these tables.

Questions

1. What problems for personnel management do the data suggest?
2. What actions should management take to either avoid or overcome these problems? Explain.

Appendix 4-1: Measuring Positional Replacement Costs

Exhibit 4-1

REPLACEMENT COST SURVEY FORM

Position ______ Selection Ratio ______ Number Hired ______

Position Number ______ Promotion Channel Code ______

Replacement From (check one): Promotion ___ Company Pool ___ Outside ______

Position From Which Replacement Is Selected	Probability	Estimates Made By Name	Title

Cost Classifications	Estimated Time	Average Cost of Time	Total Cost
I. Acquisition Cost			
A. Recruitment and selection			
1. Hiring supervisor's time:			
Title: ______	______	______	______
2. Time of others involved:			
Title: ______	______	______	______
3. Allocated common costs	______	______	______
B. Hiring costs			
1. Agency fees			______
2. Moving expenses			______
3. Moving salary allowance	______	______	______
4. Other	______	______	______
C. Cost of vacant territory during search (1)	______	______	______
D. Cost of replacing from within (2)			______
E. Total acquisition cost			______ *
II. Training Cost			
A. Orientation training			
1. Trainer's time			
Title: ______	______	______	______
2. Trainee's time	______	______	______

3. Time of others directly involved:

Title: ________ ________ ________ ________

Title: ________ ________ ________ ________

Title: ________ ________ ________ ________

4. Indirect cost of training (3)

B. On-the-job training

1. Trainer's time

Title: ________ ________ ________ ________

2. Trainee's time (4) ________ ________ ________

3. Time of others directly involved:

Title: ________ ________ ________ ________

Title: ________ ________ ________ ________

Title: ________ ________ ________ ________

4. Indirect cost of training (5) ________

C. Advanced training

1. Home office charges ________

2. Trainee's costs ________

3. Other ________

D. Total training cost ________

III. Separation Cost

A. Loss of efficiency prior to separation:

1. Position holder ________ ________ ________

2. Others affected (4) ________ ________ ________

B. Total separation cost ________ *

IV. Total Replacement Cost ________ **

SOURCE: Eric G. Flamholtz, "The Theory of Measurement of an Individual's Value to an Organization," (Ph.D. dissertation, University of Michigan, 1969), pp. 136–139.

Exhibit 4-2. SCHEDULE 1.

Cost of Vacant Territory During Search for Replacement

Positions Affected	% Negative Efficiency	Average Cost of Time	Total Cost Per Month
		Total	

Exhibit 4-3. SCHEDULE 2.

Cost of Replacing Position Holder from Within Company

Replacement From	Total Replacement Cost	Less Separation Cost	Cost RPFW	Probability	Expected Cost
				Total	

Exhibit 4-4. SCHEDULE 3.

Indirect Cost of Training

Positions Affected	% Negative Impact on Efficiency	Average Cost of Time	Total Cost Per Month
		Total	

Exhibit 4-5. SCHEDULE 4.

Loss of Efficiency Prior to Separation

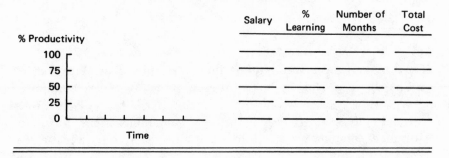

1. Position holder:

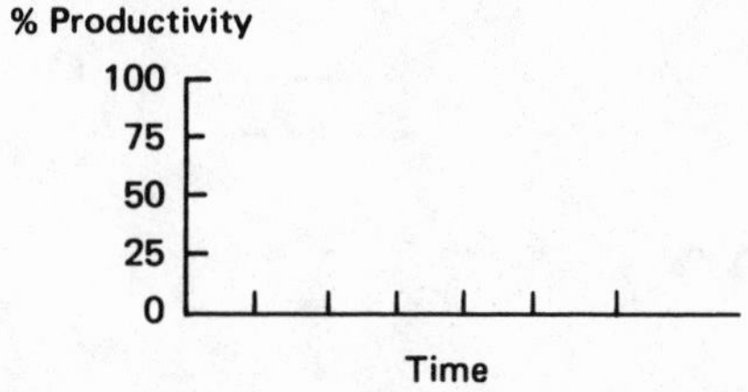

Salary	% Loss	Number of Months	Total Cost

2. Others affected (same as Schedule 1)

Exhibit 4-6. SCHEDULE 5.

Cost of Trainee's Learning On-the-Job

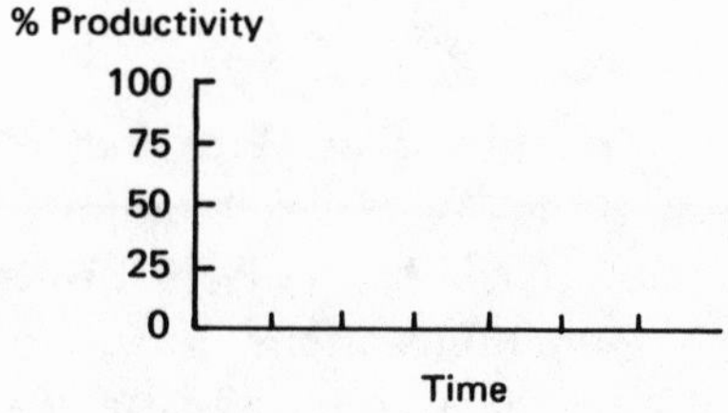

Salary	% Learning	Number of Months	Total Cost

FIVE

Second-Generation Accounting Systems for Human Resource Costs

The initial attempts to account for human resource costs were described in Chapter Four. During the past decade, efforts to apply the notion of human resource cost accounting have continued. A variety of profit-oriented enterprises in such industries as communications, aerospace, brokerage, computers, oil refining, and advertising, to cite just a few, began accounting for their investments in people and the replacement cost of people on an experimental basis to deal with specific managerial issues of interest to their companies. Moreover, nonprofit organizations such as hospitals, educational institutions, and governmental agencies began to develop human resource cost accounting systems.

As a sample of this second generation of developmental work, this chapter presents two case studies of the application of human resource accounting to the measurement of personnel replacement costs. These two studies are representative of the major second-generation applications of human resource cost accounting.

Accounting for Human Resource Costs: A Financial Institution

As noted in the previous chapter, there are few published accounts of systems for measuring personnel replacement costs in spite of a growing body of literature proposing their utility. This section describes the development and application of a method of personnel replacement cost measurement in a large international bank we shall call "Metro Bank."[1] This study is significant not only as an illustration of the application of human resource accounting technology, but also because it was one of the first attempts by a major American corporation to apply human resource accounting.

Company Background. Metro Bank is a large financial institution. At the time this study was conducted, the organization had over 18,000 employees and assets exceeding $15 billion. The company had seven major divisions throughout the state in which it operated. At the time of the study there were over 2,000 tellers and 500 management associates—management trainees, recruited after graduation from college—employed by the firm.

Company Motivation. There were a number of reasons why Metro Bank was interested in accounting for the replacement costs of its human resources. First, there was concern for the potential investment loss due to high turnover rates among both tellers and management associates. Second, various studies conducted by the bank had unsuccessfully attempted to quantify the costs involved, but the issue of how much it actually costs to replace a teller remained unresolved in the minds of senior management personnel. Some managers argued, for example, that the cost of replacing tellers was virtually nothing, and that "anybody" could be a teller. Others argued that it exceeded $10,000. Finally, the positions in question had high visibility, not only to those within the organization but to customers as well. Individuals occupying these positions, then, were viewed as important assets to the company.

The Study's Objective. In brief, the operational objective of the study was to measure the cost per hire of tellers and management associates. The broad managerial objective was to help resolve the debate over the true cost of tellers and management associates. This information, in turn, would be useful for future decisions involving the choice between tellers and automated teller machines.

Model for Replacement Cost Measurement. The basic approach to measurement of replacement costs was based on the model discussed in Chapter Three (see Figure 3-3). However, the operational objective of measuring cost per hire of selected personnel classifications necessitated some modifications in the model. Cost per hire is defined as the cost to recruit, select, hire, and develop a person to bring him or her to the performance level typically expected in the given position or classification.

Figure 5-1 presents the model for calculation of cost per hire. It is composed of two elements: acquisition costs and development costs. Each of these elements is explained in the following paragraphs.

Figure 5-1

MODEL FOR CALCULATION OF COST PER HIRE

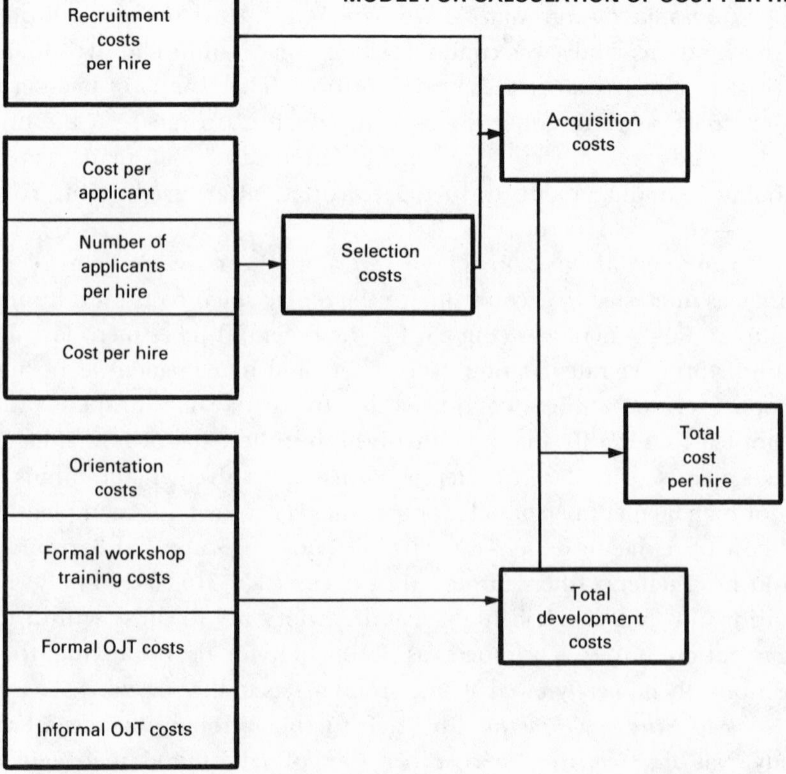

In the model developed, *acquisition costs* are restricted to recruitment costs per hire and selection costs. (Hiring placement costs are ignored.) At Metro Bank, *recruitment costs* include providing a formal requisition to alert those involved that an opening exists, listing the opening with the government's Employee Development Department (as required by law), and determining which search method to use (newspaper, radio/television, employment agency, and so on).

The other component of acquisition costs, *selection costs,* is determined by three factors: cost per applicant, number of applicants per hire, and cost per hire. *Cost per applicant* is a function of the various steps in the selection process, such as reception of application, initial interview, employment tests, in-depth interview, and reference checks. The *number of applicants per hire* acts as a multiple of the prior computation to determine the *cost per hire* (selection phase).

Development costs are costs that must be incurred to bring the new employee up to an acceptable level of performance. (These are referred to as learning costs in the generic model presented in Chapter Three.) In this study, total development costs are made up of four basic components: orientation costs, formal workshop training costs, formal on-the-job training (OJT) costs, and informal OJT costs. *Orientation costs* are associated with the introduction that normally takes place in an organization. This process usually includes discussion of the organization's history, policy and procedures, benefits, and so forth. *Formal workshop training costs* are those incurred for standard classroom situations where the employee is provided with instruction regarding the position he or she will occupy. The cost for this instruction is usually significant, since productivity is almost always zero during training. *Formal* and *informal OJT costs* are those incurred to train an individual on the job itself rather than in a classroom. The difference between the two is that formal training occurs when training is supplemented with specific written instructions and a schedule. Informal training involves no written material and possibly no fixed schedule. While both types of OJT may occur after formal workshop training, the informal type is more prevalent.

Data Collection. To apply the models, the next step involved collection of the input data. First a list of the steps involved in recruiting, selection, and training of tellers and management associates was developed through interviews with line personnel. The composite list of steps was then returned to the individuals involved for review and approval. This procedure assured that nothing had been overlooked and that there was agreement on the steps. The steps for recruiting, selection, and training of tellers and management associates are presented in Appendix 5-1.

Next, cost components associated with each step were determined in a fashion similar to that outlined above. Three basic cost categories were identified: materials, labor, and services. Materials refers to any supplies used in the process of recruiting, selection, or training; labor refers to personnel time directly expended in these processes; services refers to indirect labor or charges for telephone, computer, or related services.

Finally, forms were developed by this process to collect the data on cost per hire, as shown in Appendix 5-2. These forms were distributed to the personnel officers of all seven divisions of the firm to be circulated to those in each division who were in the best position to provide the data. Individual telephone calls were made to determine two factors not shown on the survey form. These were the allocation ratio (the amount of time spent by current employees with the new employees) and the percentage nonproductive (the percentage of time either the current employee or new employee was nonproductive in primary assignments).

Illustrative Human Resource Replacement Costs. A summary of cost per hire for tellers is shown in Table 5-1. It should be noted that the information in this table has been disguised in order to protect the confidentiality of the organization involved. This table provides cost per hire information for each division and for all divisions combined. These costs are divided into the two components (acquisition and development costs) to assist management in determining which component accounts for cost variations between individual divisions and divisions locally based and outlying. The information provided in this table forms the basis for Case 5-1.

Table 5-1

SUMMARY OF COST PER HIRE (TELLERS) BY DIVISION

Divisions	*Acquisition Cost*		*Development Cost*		*Total Cost*
	$	%	$	%	$
Locally based divisions					
Division A	200	3	5,600	97	5,800
Division B	800	29	2,000	71	2,800
Division C	400	11	3,400	89	3,800
Average	467	11	3,666	89	4,133
Outlying divisions					
Division D	2,000	71	800	29	2,800
Division E	1,000	20	4,000	80	5,000
Division F	1,200	40	1,800	60	3,000
Division G	600	33	1,200	67	1,800
Average	1,200	38	1,950	62	3,150
Average—all divisions	886	25	2,686	75	3,572

NOTE: To preserve confidentiality, cost amounts were significantly adjusted to reflect current price levels.

Benefits and Limitations. The system of accounting for personnel replacement costs developed at Metro Bank was a significant step in the development of human resource cost accounting. It was one of the first applications attempted by a large corporation listed on the New York Stock Exchange. It is a direct attempt to improve the quality of information available to management for decision-making purposes.

Such information, however, may need to be viewed in a somewhat different light than traditional costs. For example, training (development) costs in one division could vary by several hundred percent from those in another division. In the case of Metro Bank, the figures initially created concern at lower levels of management because they pointed out disparity in costs being incurred by different divisions. The natural assumption was that high costs were negative, while low costs were positive. This was not necessarily the case. In the training example cited, higher costs could indicate higher-quality training. A nonjudgmental perspective should therefore be encouraged in such circumstances.

Discussion of the System. Metro Bank's system of accounting for human resources should be viewed as a case study. It is an attempt to apply a model of replacement costs to a financial institution. It seems to indicate that such information can have an effect on decision making as exemplified by management's concern over disparity of costs among divisions. In this case, high costs were viewed as negative when in reality they could very well be positive. This experience suggests that with the creation of human resource costing systems, there may also be a need for re-education of management, teaching them to view the figures not necessarily in strict cost terms but in terms of what those costs represent—for example, higher costs for more training or higher-quality training.

It is clear that the model's application was successful in increasing management's awareness of turnover costs. Although further research is needed to determine the reliability and validity of results, the model developed here is applicable elsewhere, both inside and outside the financial environment.

Accounting for Human Resource Replacement Costs: The U.S. Navy

A system of accounting for replacement costs of human resources can be of value to both the private and public sectors. The previous section described a system for determining costs per hire in a financial institution. This section examines the development and application of a model for measuring the personnel replacement costs of industrial engineers (the civilian sector) in the U.S. Navy.[2]

Information Desired. In the U.S. Navy, as in other organizations, considerable investment is made in the recruitment, selection, and training of people. Costly recruiting and selection procedures may have to be undertaken in order to acquire needed human resources. Furthermore, the training reflected in the development of experienced personnel can typically represent an even greater organizational investment. This training can be provided either by the hiring organization itself or essentially "purchased" by obtaining more experienced personnel from the outside at a higher starting salary.

Employee turnover, then, can result in substantial organizational costs, the magnitude of which is frequently unknown to management. Human resource replacement cost data can provide the information necessary for wise decision making with regard to human resources. In particular, the present study examines the relevance of replacement cost data to decision making involving such issues as training personnel internally versus the hiring of experienced outside personnel.

For the purposes of this study, cost data on a specific position, GS-12 supervisory industrial engineer, were collected from two different navy installations. Two research sites were used as a basis for cross-checking the reliability of the data derived. The following sections describe each site and present site-specific descriptions of the position of GS-12 supervisory industrial engineer.

Model for Replacement Cost Measurement. Positional replacement cost, as stated previously, is operationally defined as the cost of recruiting, selecting, and developing an individual in order to bring him or her up to a performance level typically expected in a given position. The model developed to account for human resource positional replacement cost in this study is based upon that described in Chapter Three. In this case, however, the model needed to be sensitive to the fact that the targeted position is not entry level, and required the accumulation of replacement costs along a career path.

The model used in this study is shown in Figure 5-2. The total replacement cost can be regarded as comprising two components: acquisition costs and development costs. The manner in which each of these costs was used in the study is described in the following section.

Acquisition Costs. These costs must be calculated somewhat differently from the manner outlined in Chapter Three, since the targeted position of GS-12 supervisory industrial engineer is not an entry-level

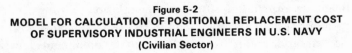

Figure 5-2
MODEL FOR CALCULATION OF POSITIONAL REPLACEMENT COST OF SUPERVISORY INDUSTRIAL ENGINEERS IN U.S. NAVY
(Civilian Sector)

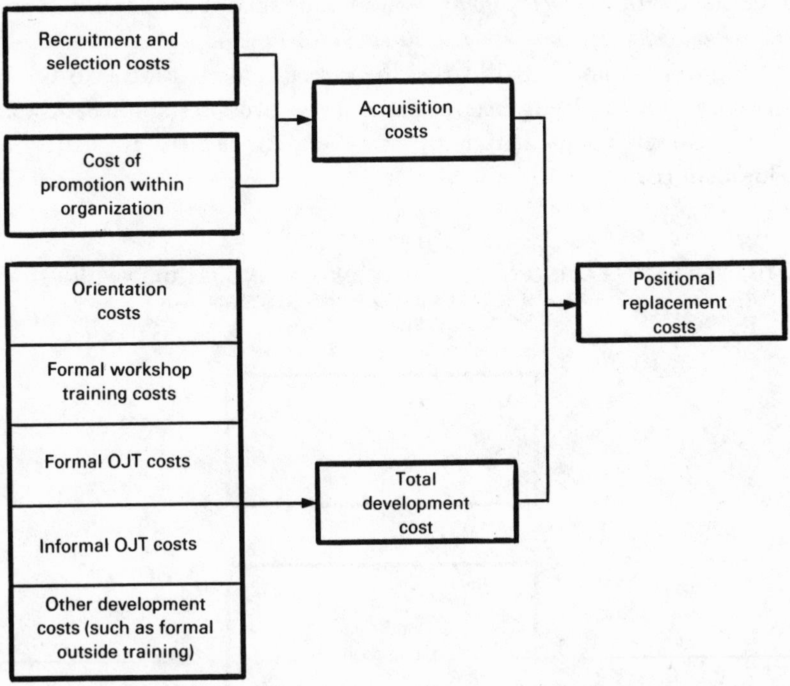

position. In this case, the acquisition cost component is the positional replacement cost of a GS-11 industrial engineer, the position which under normal circumstances will have to be refilled upon promotion to GS-12 status.

If and when such promotion does occur, or if the acquisition cost for an entry-level position needs to be determined, recruitment and selection costs must be calculated. In this case, *recruitment costs* range from the costs for requisitions to hire to the screening of applicants by a staffing specialist. *Selection costs* include labor costs associated with candidate review by a branch head and preliminary orientation of the new hire.

Development Costs. These costs comprise the expenditures necessary to bring an employee up to the expected level of performance. Development costs associated with the career ladders leading to GS-12 supervisory industrial engineer are made up of five components, although not all five are found at each stage of the career ladder. The five components are orientation costs, formal workshop training costs, formal OJT costs, informal OJT costs, and other costs associated with outside education and training. All but the last of these components have already been defined. *Other development costs* include such items as tuition and travel associated with classwork at outside colleges.

Figures 5-3 and 5-4 illustrate the career ladders leading to GS-12 supervisory industrial engineer at each of the two sites studied. As can be seen, career paths differ by site, which results in differing development costs.

Figure 5-3

CAREER PATH LEADING TO GS-12 SUPERVISORY INDUSTRIAL ENGINEER AT A U.S. NAVAL WEAPONS STATION (Site 1)

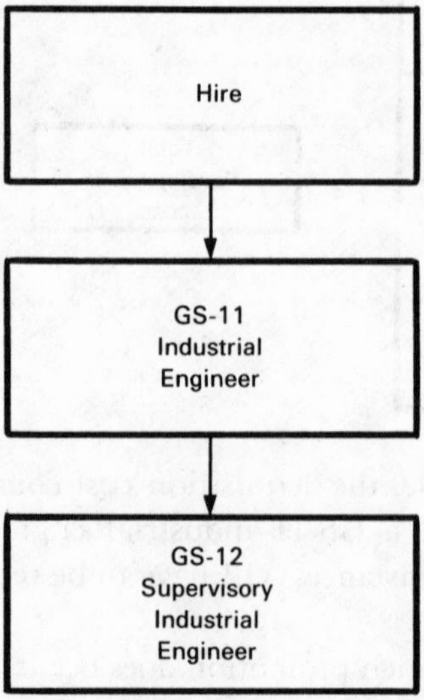

Data Collection. Positional replacement cost data were collected through interviews with appropriate personnel at both sites. This process entailed gathering information on recruiting, selection, and training costs for all positions necessary to bring the employee up to an acceptable level of performance since the targeted position is not entry level. The cost components for each position so identified are presented in Appendix 5-3.

Site 1 is a naval weapons station. The positions are located in the Industrial Engineering Division, which serves as consultant and adviser to all departments on the application of industrial engineering and

Figure 5-4

CAREER PATH LEADING TO GS-12 SUPERVISORY INDUSTRIAL ENGINEER AT A U.S. NAVAL AIR REWORK FACILITY (Site 2)

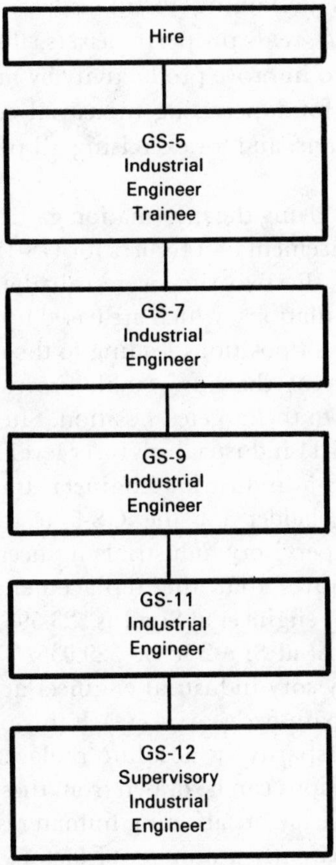

productivity principles and techniques. The division administers programs that provide evaluation, development, and implementation of methods, equipment, and facilities. Its objective is to provide services that will upgrade capabilities and enhance productivity while enabling employees to work in a setting that does not contribute to environmental pollution. The position itself carries responsibility for administrative direction, technical control, and decision authority for operation of one of the branches of the Industrial Engineering Division.

Site 2 is a naval air rework facility, a tenant activity of the naval air station. The positions are located in the Facilities Management

Branch of the Facilities Engineering Division. The Facilities Management Branch provides engineering services pertaining to the justification, design, construction, use, and maintenance of command facilities. The position itself carries responsibility for providing multidiscipline engineering services pertaining to all aspects of the use of covered building space and real property assets, for preparing detailed engineering studies to improve productivity by modifications to existing shop arrangements, for supervising industrial engineers and industrial engineering technicians, and for exercising all personnel administration responsibilities.

Selected Data. Using the information gathered through the process outlined above, replacement cost figures for GS-12 supervisory industrial engineers at each of the two sites were calculated. Tables 5-2 and 5-3 summarize these calculations, which are based upon the accumulation of the replacement costs of positions leading to the targeted position.

A comparison of these two tables reveals that there is not a standard career path to the targeted position. Site 1 typically hires at the more experienced GS-11 industrial engineer level, while Site 2 hires at the less experienced GS-5 industrial engineer trainee level and has a multiple-step career ladder for the GS-5 to reach GS-11 industrial engineer or GS-12 supervisory industrial engineer.

Table 5-2 shows that the replacement cost for the GS-12 supervisory industrial engineer at Site 1 is $23,596, while Table 5-3 shows the corresponding cost at Site 2 to be $29,035. The higher replacement cost for GS-12 supervisory industrial engineer at Site 2 is accounted for by the longer career path necessary to reach this position at this site.

Although a disparity in absolute replacement cost figures does exist, no firm conclusions can be drawn from these data without analysis of the nonquantitative factors affecting human resource decision making at the two sites. Apparently a number of factors account for differences in career paths leading to GS-12 supervisory industrial engineer at the two sites. The three factors that seem most prominent are labor market conditions, environmental factors, and internal development strategy.

Site 1's management reported that it has not been possible to recruit GS-5's or GS-7's because the government salary schedule is not competitive with corresponding entry-level jobs in the commercial sector. This site, however, has been able to recruit industrial engineers either at the GS-11 level or at the GS-12 level who are willing to accept a downgrade to GS-11. Site 2, on the other hand, has had at least some success in recruiting of GS-5's or GS-7's and consequently operates with this entry-level position.

Table 5-2

SUMMARY OF REPLACEMENT COST CALCULATIONS FOR GS-12 SUPERVISORY INDUSTRIAL ENGINEERS
Site 1

	Cost	*Cumulative Total Investment*
Acquisition costs	$ 653	$ 653
Development costs*		
GS-11 industrial engineer	3,317	3,970
GS-12 supervisory industrial engineer	19,626	$23,596
Total development costs	22,943	
Total replacement cost	$23,596	

*The cost of developing a GS-12 supervisory industrial engineer includes the cost of developing a GS-11 industrial engineer plus the differential cost to make the developmental transition to performance at the GS-12 level. The costs incurred at the GS-11 level to develop a GS-12 engineer are $3,317, and the costs at the GS-12 level are $19,626.

Table 5-3

SUMMARY OF REPLACEMENT COST CALCULATIONS FOR GS-12 SUPERVISORY INDUSTRIAL ENGINEERS
Site 2

	Cost	*Cumulative Total Investment*
Acquisition costs	$ 870	$ 870
Development costs*		
GS-5 industrial engineer trainee	5,303	6,173
GS-7 industrial engineer	5,885	12,058
GS-9 industrial engineer	492	12,550
GS-11 industrial engineer	4,633	17,183
GS-12 supervisory industrial engineer	11,852	$29,035
Total development cost	28,165	
Total replacement cost	$29,035	

*The cost to develop a GS-12 supervisory industrial engineer includes the cost of development incurred at lower levels.

The fact that Site 1 has successfully recruited GS-12's who were willing to take a downgrade to GS-11 suggests that underlying factors such as site location and overall work atmosphere may be aiding recruitment efforts here. Site 1, in fact, hires primarily local applicants while Site 2 hires recent college graduates from various locations (even out of state).

Site 2's strategy for human resource development for industrial engineers reflects an internal development strategy whereby an employee normally spends approximately one year at each of the following positions: GS-5, GS-7, GS-9, and GS-11. Site 1's strategy may in large part result from the previously mentioned labor market and environmental conditions. However, it may be that independent of these two factors Site 1 is deciding to hire more experienced personnel, thus reducing training costs. Such a strategy could have particular appeal if one assumed turnover to be inevitable, as "lost" training costs would be minimized.

The influence of these qualitative factors on replacement costs is evident when costs are subdivided into acquisition and development costs. These costs are shown in Tables 5-4 and 5-5. At least part of the difference in recruiting and selection costs between the two sites may be accounted for by environmental and labor market factors. Site 2, for example, hires primarily recent college graduates, which necessitates incurring additional travel costs for out-of-state candidates whereas Site 1 hires primarily local applicants.

The differences in training costs between the two sites result from similar factors. The training and development costs involved in an engineer's progression from GS-5 or GS-7 to GS-12 are costs incurred to the navy at Site 2 while at Site 1 more experienced engineers are hired who have been trained at another organization's expense.

The System's Potential Uses. The system of accounting for replacement costs of human resources that was developed in this study has a number of potential uses. These will be discussed at two levels of human resource management: the operational and the strategic.

At the operational level, replacement cost information can facilitate acquisition/development trade-off decisions. Is it more cost effective to recruit relatively inexperienced people and train them internally or to buy more experienced people?

Based upon cost information previously presented, Tables 5-6 and 5-7 provide the data necessary to make such a decision. For the GS-11 position, the buying of outside people (if this option is available)

Table 5-4

COMPARISON OF ACQUISITION COSTS AT SITE 1 AND SITE 2

	Site 1	*Site 2*
Labor costs		
Requisition	$ 1	$ 8
Personnel Dept.	137	52
Selection	310	148
Personnel Dept.-Processing	14	76
Orientation	6	60
	468	344
Benefits (30%)	141	103
	609	447
Other costs		
Computer services	5	0
Printed materials	39	0
Travel and per diem	0	423
Total Recruitment and Selection Costs	$654	$870

NOTE: Costs are rounded to whole numbers for presentation. Hence small differences due to rounding with Appendix 5-3 may exist.

Table 5-5

COMPARISON OF DEVELOPMENT COSTS AT SITE 1 AND SITE 2
For GS-11 Industrial Engineers and GS-12 Supervisory Industrial Engineers

	GS-11		*GS-12*	
	Site 1	*Site 2*	*Site 1*	*Site 2*
Labor				
Formal workshop training	$ 99	$ 1,495	$ 1,793	$ 2,118
Informal OJT	2,452	0	11,304	6,799
	2,551	1,495	13,097	8,917
Benefits	766	449	3,929	2,675
	3,317	1,944	17,026	11,592
Other costs				
Tuition	0	800	500	,260
Travel and per diem	0	1,890	2,100	0
	$ 3,317	$ 4,634	$19,626	$11,852

significantly reduces training costs.* The cost spread shrinks, however, for the GS-12 position, evidently because more extensive training is necessary for a supervisor who has not come up through the ranks.

Table 5-6

COMPARISON OF REPLACEMENT COSTS FOR GS-11 INDUSTRIAL ENGINEERS
Site 1 and Site 2

	Site 1	%	*Site 2*	%
Acquisition costs	$ 653	16	$ 870	5
Development costs	3,317	84	16,313	95
Total	$3,970	100	$17,183	100

Table 5-7

COMPARISON OF REPLACEMENT COSTS FOR GS-12 SUPERVISORY INDUSTRIAL ENGINEERS
Site 1 and Site 2

	Site 1	%	*Site 2*	%
Acquisition costs	$ 653	3	$ 870	3
Development costs	22,943	97	28,165	97
Total	$23,596	100	$29,035	100

Replacement cost information can also aid management in decisions surrounding pay increases and bonuses. In this study, knowing replacement cost information can aid in analyzing whether a reenlistment bonus is cost effective to the navy. Suppose, for example, that a GS-12 supervisory industrial engineer has an associated $29,000 replacement cost and that other considerations argue for the retention of this person. Assume that we make an offer of a three-year reenlistment bonus of $3,000 per year, or a total cost of $9,000 for the three-year period. If effective in increasing retention, this reenlistment bonus would produce a savings of the $29,000 replacement cost for the three-year period. Assume that the interest rate or cost of capital is 10 percent. Is there a net financial benefit to the navy of paying a reenlistment bonus

*Some restraint must be exercised in unequivocally asserting this conclusion since data are compared across sites.

Table 5-8

COSTS AND BENEFITS OF REENLISTMENT BONUS

(1) Year	(2) Interest Rate	(3) Bonus Payment	(4) Present Value Factor*	(5) = (3)X(4) Present Value of Bonus	(6) = Amount Earned by Postponing $29,000 Replacement Cost
1	10%	$3,000	0.909	$2,727	2,900
2	10%	$3,000	0.826	$2,478	$3,190
3	10%	$3,000	0.751	$2,253	$3,509
Total (3 years)				$7,458	$9,599†

*This amount represents the present (discounted) value of $1 to be paid at a specified future time at 10 percent interest.

†This is the amount that would be earned by investing $29,000 for three years at 10 percent.

of $3,000 per year ($9,000) in order to postpone a payment today of $29,000? As shown in Table 5-8, the answer is yes.

Assume that the $3,000 reenlistment bonus payments will be paid at the end of each year. This means that the series of three bonus payments amount to an annuity to be paid by the navy over a three-year period. The present value (time-adjusted value of money) of these payments is actually only $7,458, as shown in Table 5-8. Thus the net cost of the bonus to the navy is $7,548 and not $9,000. Moreover, the navy will earn 10 percent on the $29,000 replacement cost that it can postpone for three years. As shown in Table 5-8, this amounts to $9,599. The net return to the navy on the reenlistment bonus is $2,141 ($9,599 - $7,458). Although this method of analysis makes certain simplifying assumptions, it does indicate that an organization can derive a net financial benefit from an innovative effort to control turnover by using a human resource accounting perspective.

The strategic level of human resource decision making is at the cutting edge of future research in human resource management. Determining an optimal personnel mix is but one example of a decision for which replacement cost information can be of value. Replacement cost information can provide management with standard replacement costs relating to various personnel classifications. Such information is central for management to use in answering the question: Given the mission of our department, what types of people should we hire and in what mix?

In this study, for example, Site 1's management in the Industrial Engineering Division must decide on an optimal mix of industrial engineers and industrial engineer technicians (nondegreed). Such cost-effective analysis can only be done if the lingua franca of replacement cost data is included in the analysis.

Discussion of the System. This study represents one attempt to develop and apply a model for measuring human resource replacement costs. This system's usefulness in providing information for both operational and strategic human resource decision making suggests that continued research is warranted.

One area to be addressed in such research is that of computer-based human resource accounting information systems. To be used effectively, replacement cost data for targeted positions must be readily available and current. Computer systems must replace manual data collection procedures for this to occur.

A second area involves the analysis of the behavioral implications of using cost information. This analysis should study changes in the attitude and behavior of managers when presented with replacement cost information relating to their employees. This study involves "impact evaluation" of replacement cost information on management processes.

Finally, future research should look at the utilization of replacement cost information in human resource decision making. Replacement cost data "monetize" the information necessary for cost-effective human resource operational and strategic decisions. Further research needs to be conducted on how this information is used in formulating policies related to acquisition, development, allocation, conservation, evaluation, and reward of human resources. The uses of human resource replacement cost information in personnel planning and forecasting are a particularly important area for future research.

Summary

This chapter has presented accounts of two recent efforts to develop and apply systems of accounting for human resource costs. Both systems discussed in this chapter were attempts to improve the quality of information available to management for decisions regarding human resources.

Metro Bank, a large financial institution, developed a system of accounting for the replacement cost of selected personnel. A high level of turnover in the selected positions and the need to quantify the amount of lost investment led to the organization's desire to develop such a system. Among the benefits of this system are a new awareness on the part of management as to how high turnover translates into high costs. The study also suggests that care must be exercised in interpreting replacement cost information—high costs should not necessarily be viewed as negative. Management must learn to view the figures produced by such efforts in not only a quantitative but also a qualitative light.

A similar human resource accounting system was developed for the U.S. Navy. In this case, one position was studied and a comparison of replacement costs was made between two sites. A disparity in replacement cost figures was found to exist between the two sites. It was suggested that this disparity could be accounted for, at least in part, by labor market conditions, environmental factors, and managerial strategy. The information provided by application of the model can be of use at both the operational and the strategic levels of decision making—in "make versus buy" decisions, in decisions regarding pay increases or bonuses, in forecasting future personnel needs, and in determining the optimal personnel mix.

Case 5-1: Metro Bank

On March 3, 1981, Jerome Robinson was appointed director of personnel for the Central Western area of Metro Bank. Robinson was the youngest vice-president ever appointed to this position. His career thus far has been marked by insights into problems and potential problems that Metro Bank has experienced. He is known for both his intuitiveness and his progressive stance toward problem solving.

Metro Bank is a large international bank that employs more than 18,000 people and whose assets exceed $15 billion. There are seven major divisions—three urban and four suburban—in the Central Western area. Within the seven divisions there are a total of 2,000 tellers and 500 management trainees.

In keeping with his innovative reputation, Robinson is well aware of a set of problems that few have considered thus far. The switch in emphasis from goods to services that the U.S. labor force has shown in recent years has created new problems for management—problems that management does not possess the information to deal with effectively.

These problems concern such topics as "human assets" or "human capital" management. Costs of selecting employees, wage and salary administration, turnover, and even who should and should not be laid off at slack times—all are, for the most part, unanswered questions. In short, human resource replacement costs provide both an analytical approach and a common language to management. Robinson believes that to manage human resources effectively he needs information about the costs of acquiring, training, and replacing people.

Shortly after taking office, Robinson engaged a consulting firm to prepare a report on human resource replacement costs for the tellers in the Central Western area. This report was to be presented in terms of costs per hire in all seven divisions (both urban and suburban areas). A breakdown of the various components of total cost per hire was presented earlier in the chapter (Figure 5-1). Appendix 5-1 explains each one of the components.

The consulting firm gathered data from the controller's department, corporate personnel, and line personnel divisions. Data were captured in the form of a standard survey taken at each division. The survey sought to determine the cost components at each step from acquisition of an employee to bringing that employee to an acceptable level of performance. Each of these steps was then further divided into the three cost categories of labor, materials, and services. The consultants make individual calls to ascertain the allocation ratio (the amount of time spent by current employees with the new employees) and the percentage of nonproductive time (the percentage of time when either the current employee or new employee was not productive in his or her primary assignment).

The data given to Jerome Robinson are summarized in Appendix 5-2. Additional information concerning tellers at Metro Bank is provided in Appendix 5-2.

Robinson is now faced with the problem of determining what the data mean and how the information might be put to its best use. For example, the costs per hire differ greatly between the local divisions and outlying divisions—what does this tell him? There is also a question about the relationship of the percentages between the acquisition and development costs across divisions. Does the information mean anything or is it just an artifact? Are the tellers being overtrained—or undertrained? When should a teller be terminated for low productivity? These are just a few of the questions that face Robinson at this point.

Questions

1. If you were in Robinson's position, what would be your next step? How would you use the information? What kinds of changes would you make? Are there any other possibilities or implications in the data that Robinson has overlooked? What are some of the hidden benefits or pitfalls involved in relying on the data?
2. Suppose that you are the manager of a suburban division. How would you view the results? Should you worry about inferences that management might make concerning the efficiency (or inefficiency) of your operations? How could you use the data in Appendixes 5-1 and 5-2 to help you decide whether or not to terminate a teller? (*Hint:* Compare cost per hire to monthly salary by percentage of productivity—Appendix 5-3.)

Appendix 5-1: Steps in Recruitment, Selection, and Training

Exhibit 5-1

DEFINITION OF RECRUITMENT STEPS

Step	*Description*	*Explanation*
1-1	Requisition for a teller position	Decision to replace a teller and completion of the Requisition Form (08195-0), including obtaining authorized signatures.
1-2	Listing with EDD	Placing the appropriate order with the Employment Development Department.
1-3	Selection of search methods	Determining how we are going to find people for this opening: newspaper advertisement, list of internal candidates, list of prior applicants, job posting, etc.
1-4	Implement recruiting	Execution of step 1-3.
1-5	Other steps	Any other step related to this process not included above.

Exhibit 5-2

DEFINITION OF SELECTION—RECRUITMENT CENTER

Step	*Description*	*Explanation*
2-1	Reception of applicant	Determining the individual's status, the fact that he or she is applying for the job, and which job. Completion of application form by applicant.
2-2	Initial interview	Screening interview to determine whether the person is an applicant for the job in question.
2-3	Employment test	Administering the standard bank tests (clerical, numerical, etc.).
2-4	In-depth interview	Determining fully the applicant's qualifications for the job.
2-5	Reference checks	Verifying the information the applicant has provided (by phone, letter, or both).
2-6	Decision to refer, reject, or decline	Reviewing candidates interviewed to determine the one most qualified to be referred to the branch.
2-7	In-depth interview by branch	Determining fully the applicant's qualifications for the job.
2-8	Hire/decline	Notifying the most qualified applicants of acceptance, and notifying the others of the decline.
2-9	Other steps	Any additional steps in the selection process that are not listed above.

Exhibit 5-3

DEFINITION OF SELECTION—SELECTION CENTER

Step	*Description*	*Explanation*
2-1	Reception of applicant	Determining the individual's status, the fact that he or she is applying for the job, and which job. Completion of application form by applicant.
2-2	Initial interview	Screening interview to determine whether the person is an applicant for the job in question.
2-3	Employment test	Administering the standard bank tests (clerical, numerical, etc.).
2-4	In-depth interview	Determining fully the applicant's qualifications for the job.
2-5	Reference checks	Verifying the information the applicant has provided (by phone, letter, or both).
2-6	Selection decision	Reviewing candidates interviewed to determine the one most qualified.
2-7	Hire/decline	Notifying the most qualified applicants of acceptance, and notifying the others of the decline.
2-8	Other steps	Any additional steps in the selection process that are not listed above.

Exhibit 5-4

DEFINITION OF TRAINING STEPS

Step	*Description*	*Explanation*
3-1	Orientation	Initial introduction to the bank's policies and procedures.
3-2	Formal workshop training	Any classroom training or instruction that the staff member receives.
3-3	Formal OJT	Training utilizing the OJT package.
3-4	Informal OJT	The period of training required to bring the staff member up to acceptable levels of productivity.
3-5	Other steps	Any other type of training.

Exhibit 5-5

MANAGEMENT TRAINEE RECRUITMENT

Step	*Description*	*Explanation*
1	Division determines number of trainees quarterly	Internal staff planning to determine the number of trainees that will be needed.
2	Formal requisition sent to corporate personnel	Completion of the formal requisition for hire, including obtaining the authorized signatures.
3	Internal applicants reviewed by division	Review of potential applicants that the division has on file. These people are usually recommended by branch personnel.
4	External sources known to division are reviewed	Reviewing files that have been screened in the selection process. These are potential trainees from outside the division. They may be staff members from another division or from outside the bank.
5	Check transfers	Review of transfer requests listed with the Transfer Section.
6	Listing with EDD	Placing the appropriate order with the Employment Development Department.
7	College recruiting files (pending files including referrals—also ongoing)	Files maintained by employment, basically the result of on-campus interviews.
8	Selection of search methods	Determining how we are going to find people for this opening: agencies, job posting, newspaper advertising, etc.
9	Implement recruiting	Execution of steps 2 to 8.
10	Other steps	Any other step related to this process not included above.

Exhibit 5-6

MANAGEMENT TRAINEE SELECTION—INTERNAL

(Employees Already Working for the Bank)

Step	*Description*	*Explanation*
1	Referral by management	Decision and preparation of the recommendation (usually by an office manager) that a staff member be considered for the training program.
2	Interview by training officer	Interview to determine whether the person is qualified for further consideration for the training program.
3	Decision to be referred on—accept/decline	Decision whether the person is qualified for the training program.
4	Interviewed by division (optional)	Another interview of the potential trainee.
5	Group decision by division and training officers	Group meeting to determine which candidates will be selected to make up the next group of management trainees.
6	Accept/decline	Notifying the most qualified applicants of acceptance, and notifying the others of decline.
7	Other steps	Any additional steps not listed above.

Exhibit 5-7

MANAGEMENT TRAINEE SELECTION—EXTERNAL
(Hired from Outside the Bank)

Step	*Description*	*Explanation*
1	Reception of applicant	Determining the individual's status, the fact that he or she is applying for the job, and which job; includes completion of the application form.
2	In-depth interview	Determining fully the applicant's qualifications for the job.
3	Reference checks	Verifying the information the applicant has provided (by phone, letter, or both).
4	Decision to refer, reject, or decline	Deciding whether the person is qualified for the training program.
5	In-depth interview by division	Determining fully the applicant's qualifications for the job.
6	Hire/decline	Notifying the most qualified applicants of acceptance, and notifying the others of decline.

Exhibit 5-8

MANAGEMENT TRAINEE TRAINING

Step	*Description*	*Explanation*
1	Initial orientation	Initial introduction of the staff member is to the bank's policies and procedures.
2	Formal workshop training	Any classroom training or instruction that the staff member receives.
3	Formal OJT	Training that is formally scheduled and supervised while the staff member is physically working.
4	Training and counseling sessions—coaching	Time spent outside the classroom pointing out areas for improvement and bank practices.

Appendix 5-2: Forms Used in Data Collection

Exhibit 5-9

COST PER HIRE OF THE RECRUITING PROCESS
(For the Typical Teller Opening)

Date Completed: ____________
Organization Name: ____________
Number: ____________

STEPS		LABOR			MATERIALS (Forms, Letters, Manuals, etc.)		SERVICES (Travel, Phone, Premises, etc.)	
Step	*Description*	*Who in Division or Office (Branch) Staff Is Involved (Supervisor, V.P., etc.) in Activity?*	*Weekly Salary Rate of Division or Office (Branch) Staff Member Involved in Activity?*	*Average Time Spent by Staff Member of Division or Office (Branch) in Activity?*	*What*	*Cost*	*What*	*Cost*
1-1	Requisition for a teller position				Requisition form	6¢		
1-2	Listing with EDD							
1-3	Selection of search method							
1-4	Implement recruitment							

Date Completed: ____________
Organization
Name: ____________
Number: ____________

Exhibit 5-10

COST PER APPLICANT OF THE SELECTION PROCESS—RECRUITMENT CENTER

STEPS		*LABOR*			*MATERIALS* *(Forms, Letters, Manuals, etc.)*		*SERVICES* *(Travel, Phone, Premises, etc.)*	
Step	*Description*	*Who in Division or Office (Branch) Staff Is Involved (Supervisor, V.P., etc.) in Activity?*	*Weekly Salary Rate of Division or Office (Branch) Staff Member Involved in Activity?*	*Average Time Spent by Staff Member of Division or Office (Branch) in Activity?*	*What*	*Cost*	*What*	*Cost*
2-1	Reception of applicant				Application	6¢		
2-2	Initial interview							
2-3	Employment test				Clerical and numerical tests	5¢		
2-4	In-depth interview							
2-5	Reference checks							
2-6	Selection decision							
2-7	In-depth interview by branch							
2-8	Hire/decline							
2-9	Other steps							

NOTE: Assume that the applicant makes it through the entire selection process.

Exhibit 5-11

COST PER APPLICANT OF THE SELECTION PROCESS—SELECTION CENTER

Date Completed: ______
Organization
Name: ______
Number: ______

STEPS		*LABOR*			*MATERIALS* (Forms, Letters, Manuals, etc.)		*SERVICES* (Travel, Phone, Premises, etc.)	
Step	*Description*	*Who in Division or Office (Branch) Staff Is Involved Supervisor, V.P., etc.) in Activity?*	*Weekly Salary Rate of Division or Office (Branch) Staff Member Involved in Activity?*	*Average Time Spent by Staff Member of Division or Office (Branch) in Activity?*	*What*	*Cost*	*What*	*Cost*
2-1	Reception of one applicant				Application	6¢		
2-2	Initial interview							
2-3	Employment test				Clerical and numerical tests	5¢		
2-4	In-depth interview							
2-5	Reference checks							
2-6	Selection decision							
2-7	Hire/decline							
2-8	Other steps							

NOTE: Assume that the applicant makes it through the entire selection process.

Exhibit 5-12

COST PER HIRE OF TRAINING PROCESS
(For the Typical Teller)

Date Completed: ____________
Organization Name: ____________
Number: ____________

STEPS	*LABOR*			*MATERIALS* *(Forms, Letters, Manuals, etc.)*		*SERVICES* *(Travel, Phone, Premises, etc.)*	
Step Description	*Who in Division or Office (Branch) Staff Is Involved (Supervisor, V.P., etc.) in Activity?*	*Weekly Salary Rate of Division or Office (Branch) Staff Member Involved in Activity?*	*Average Time Spent by Staff Member of Division or Office (Branch) in Activity?*	*What*	*Cost*	*What*	*Cost*
3-1 Orientation				Orientation forms	$1.35		
3-2 Formal workshop training							
3-3 Formal OJT							
3-4 Informal OJT							
3-5 Other steps							

Exhibit 5-13

COST PER HIRE OF THE RECRUITING PROCESS

(For the Typical Management Trainee)

Date Completed: ____________

Organization

Name: ____________

Number: ____________

STEPS		*LABOR*			*MATERIALS* (Forms, Letters, Manuals, etc.)		*SERVICES* (Travel, Phone, Premises, etc.)	
Step	*Description*	*Who in Division or Office (Branch) Staff Is Involved (Supervisor, V.P., etc.) in Activity?*	*Weekly Salary Rate of Division or Office (Branch) Staff Member Involved in Activity?*	*Average Time Spent by Staff Member of Division or Office (Branch) in Activity?*	*What*	*Cost*	*What*	*Cost*
1-1	Division determines no. of trainees quarterly							
1-2	Formal requisition sent to corporate personnel							
1-3	Internal applicants reviewed by division							
1-4	External sources known to division are reviewed							
1-5	Check transfers							
1-6	Listing with EDD							
1-7	College recruiting files (pending files including referrals—also ongoing)							
1-8	Selection of search method							
1-9	Implement recruiting							

Date Completed: ____________
Organization
Name: ____________
Number: ____________

Exhibit 5-14

COST PER HIRE OF THE SELECTION—INTERNAL
(For the Typical Management Trainee)

STEPS		*LABOR*			*MATERIALS* (Forms, Letters, Manuals, etc.)		*SERVICES* (Travel, Phone, Premises, etc.)	
Step	*Description*	*Who in Division or Office (Branch) Staff Is Involved (Supervisor, V.P., etc.) in Activity?*	*Weekly Salary Rate of Division or Office (Branch) Staff Member Involved in Activity?*	*Average Time Spent by Staff Member of Division or Office (Branch) in Activity?*	*What*	*Cost*	*What*	*Cost*
2A-1	Referral by management							
2A-2	Interview by training officer							
2A-3	Decision to be referred on accept/decline							
2A-4	Interviewed by division (optional)							
2A-5	Group decision by division and training officers							
2A-6	Accept/decline							

Exhibit 5-15

COST PER HIRE OF THE SELECTION—EXTERNAL
(For the Typical Management Trainee)

Date Completed: ______________
Organization Name: ______________
Number: ______________

STEPS		*LABOR*			*MATERIALS* (Forms, Letters, Manuals, etc.)		*SERVICES* (Travel, Phone, Premises, etc.)	
Step	*Description*	*Who in Division or Office (Branch) Staff Is Involved (Supervisor, V.P., etc.) in Activity?*	*Weekly Salary Rate of Division or Office (Branch) Staff Member Involved in Activity?*	*Average Time Spent by Staff Member of Division or Office (Branch) in Activity?*	*What*	*Cost*	*What*	*Cost*
2B-1	Reception of applicant							
2B-2	In-depth interview							
2B-3	Reference checks							
2B-4	Decision to refer, reject, or decline							
2B-5	In-depth interview by division							
2B-6	Hire/decline							

Exhibit 5-16

COST PER HIRE OF THE TRAINING

(For the Typical Management Trainee)

Date Completed: ______________
Organization Name: ______________
Number: ______________

STEPS		*LABOR*			*MATERIALS* (Forms, Letters, Manuals, etc.)		*SERVICES* (Travel, Phone, Premises, etc.)	
Step	*Description*	*Who in Division or Office (Branch) Staff Is Involved (Supervisor, V.P., etc.) in Activity?*	*Weekly Salary Rate of Division or Office (Branch) Staff Member Involved in Activity?*	*Average Time Spent by Staff Member of Division or Office (Branch) in Activity?*	*What*	*Cost*	*What*	*Cost*
3-1	Initial orientation							
3-2	Formal workshop training							
3-3	Formal OJT							
3-4	Training and counseling sessions—coaching							

Exhibit 5-17

HUMAN RESOURCE COST OF RECRUITMENT AND SELECTION

Seal Beach

Components	*Who?*	*(1) Salary Rate ($)*	*(2) How Much Time? (Hours)*	*(3) (1) x (2)*	*(4) Allocation Ratio (Note 1)*	*(5) x (3) x (4) Cost ($) (Note 2)*
Labor Costs						
Requisition	GS-5 clerk	6.80	0.1	0.68	2	1
Personnel						
(Distribution of announcement)	GS-5 typist	6.80	2	13.60	2	27
(Screening, rating, etc.)	GS-11 staffing spec.	12.46	4	49.84	2	100
(Print shop)	WP-10	9.68	0.5	4.84	2	10
Selection						
(Candidate review)	GS-12 branch head	14.94	0.8	11.95	3	36
(Justification)	GS-12 branch head	14.94	0.25	3.74	3	11
(Interviews)	GS-12 branch head	14.94	3.5	52.29	3	157
	GS-13 dept. head	17.76	2	35.52	3	107
Personnel						
(Processing)	Clerk	5.52	2.5	13.80	1	14
Orientation	GS-12 branch head	12.46	0.5	6.23	1	6
Cost Subtotal—Labor						468
Total Labor Cost = Cost subtotal x (1 + benefits loading = 1.3)						609
Other costs						
Computer services						5
Printed materials						39
Total recruitment and selection costs						653

Exhibit 5-18

HUMAN RESOURCE COST OF TRAINING
GS-11 (INDUSTRIAL ENGINEER)
Seal Beach

Components	*Who?*	*(1) Salary Rate ($)*	*(2) How Much Time? (Hours)*	*(3) (1) x (2)*	*(4) Allo-cation Ratio*	*(5) (3) x (4)*	*(6) % Non-productive (Note 3)*	*(7) (5) x (6) Cost ($)*
Formal workshop training								
	GS-11 IE	12.46	7	87	1	87	100	87
	GS-11/12 trainer	13.45	14	188	0.07	12	100	12
Informal OJT	GS-11 IE	12.46	480	5,981	1	5,981	25	1,495
	GS-12 branch head	14.94	480	7,171	1	7,171	5	359
	GS-11 IE (peer)	12.46	480	5,981	1	5,981	10	598
Training cost subtotal								2,551
Total training cost = cost subtotal x (1 + benefits loading = 1.3)								3,317

Exhibit 5-19

HUMAN RESOURCE COST OF TRAINING
GS-12 (SUPERVISORY INDUSTRIAL ENGINEER)
Seal Beach

Components	*Who?*	*(1) Salary Rate ($)*	*(2) How Much Time? (Hours)*	*(3) (1) x (2)*	*(4) Allo-cation Ratio*	*(5) (3) x (4)*	*(6) % Non-productive (Note 3)*	*(7) (5) x (6) Cost ($)*
Formal workshop training								
	GS-12 supervisor IE	14.94	120	1,793	1	1,793	100	1,793
OJT								
	GS-12 supervisor IE	14.94	2,000	29,880	1	29,880	20	5,976
	GS-13 dept. head	17.76	2,000	35,520	1	35,520	15	5,328
Training cost—labor subtotal								13,097
Total training cost (labor) = labor subtotal x (1 + benefits loading = 1.3)								17,026
Other training costs								
Tuition								500
Travel								2,100
Total training costs								19,626

Exhibit 5-20

HUMAN RESOURCE COST OF RECRUITMENT AND SELECTION
North Island

Components	*Who?*	*(1) Salary Rate ($)*	*(2) How Much Time? (Hours)*	*(3) (1) x (2)*	*(4) Allo-cation Ratio*	*(5) (3) x (4) Cost ($)*
Labor costs						
Requisition	GS-5 clerk	6.80	0.2	1.36	1	1
(IE to IRD)	GS-14 div. director	20.99	0.1	2.10	1	2
	GS-15 dept. head	24.69	0.1	2.47	1	2
	GS-11 position mgr.	12.46	0.1	1.25	1	1
	0-5 exec. officer	19.32	0.1	1.93	1	2
Wage and classification	GS-11 staffing spec.	12.46	0.1	1.25	1	1
(IRD to Placement	GS-5 clerk	6.80	0.1	0.68	1	1
Office)	GS-11 staffing spec.	12.46	4	49.84	1	50
Selection						
(Phone calls)	GS-11	12.46	0.25	3.12	10	31
(Interviews)	GS-12 sec. head	14.94	2	29.88	3	90
	GS-12 branch head	14.94	0.25	3.74	3	11
	GS-14 div. director	20.99	0.25	5.25	3	16
Hiring						
(Physical exam)	GS-5 clerk	6.80	0.1	0.68	1	1
	GS-13 medical officer	17.76	0.75	13.32	1	13
(Security review)	GS-11 security officer	12.46	4	49.84	1	50
(Preprocessing)	GS-5 clerk	6.80	1.75	11.90	1	12
General orientation	GS-12 sec. head	14.94	4	59.76	1	60
Cost subtotal						344
Total labor cost = cost subtotal x (1 + benefits loading = 1.3)						447
Other costs						
Travel for interviewees (3 interviewees per selection)						198
Per diem for interviewees (3 interviewees per selection)						225
Total recruitment and selection costs						870

Exhibit 5-21

HUMAN RESOURCE COST OF TRAINING
GS-5 (INDUSTRIAL ENGINEER TRAINEE)
North Island

Components	*Who?*	(1) *Salary Rate ($)*	(2) *How Much Time? (Hours)*	(3) *(1) x (2)*	(4) *Allo-cation Ratio*	(5) *(3) x (4)*	(6) *% Non-productive*	(7) *(5) x (6) Cost ($)*
Orientation								
	GS-12 supervisor IE	14.94	4	60	1	60	100	60
	GS-5 trainee	6.80	4	27	1	27	100	27
Formal workshop training								
	GS-12 IE	14.94	44	657	0.066	43	100	43
	GS-5 trainee	6.80	22	150	1	150	100	150
Formal OJT								
	GS-11/12 IE	13.45	160	2,152	0.166	357	40	143
	GS-5 trainee	6.80	160	1,088	1	1,088	20	218
Informal OJT								
	GS-11/12 IE	13.45	800	10,760	0.166	1,786	25	447
	GS-5 trainee	6.80	800	5,440	1	5,440	55	2,992
Training cost subtotal								4,079
Total training cost = cost subtotal x (1 + benefits loading = 1.3)								5,303

Exhibit 5-22

HUMAN RESOURCE COST OF TRAINING
GS-7, 9, 11 (INDUSTRIAL ENGINEER)
North Island

Components	*Who?*	*(1) Salary Rate $*	*(2) How Much Time? (Hours)*	*(3) (1) x (2)*	*(4) Allocation Ratio*	*(5) (3) x (4)*	*(6) % Nonproductive*	*(7) (5) x (6) Cost ($)*
Formal workshop training								
	GS-7 IE	8.68	120	1,042	1	1,042	100	1,042
	GS-9 IE	9.99	24	240	1	240	100	240
	GS-11 IE	12.46	120	1,495	1	1,495	100	1,495
Training costs—labor subtotal								2,777
Total training costs labor = labor subtotal x (1 + benefits loading = 1.3)								3,610
Other training costs								
GS-7:	Tuition							1,600
	Travel							1,190
	Per diem							1,740
GS-9:	Tuition							180
	Travel							0
	Per diem							0
GS-11:	Tuition							800
	Travel							540
	Per diem							1,350
Total training costs								11,010

Exhibit 5-23

HUMAN RESOURCE COST OF TRAINING
GS-12 (SUPERVISORY INDUSTRIAL ENGINEER)
North Island

Components	*Who?*	(1) *Salary Rate ($)*	(2) *How Much Time? (Hours)*	(3) *(1) x (2)*	(4) *Allo-cation Ratio*	(5) *(3) x (4)*	(6) *$ Non-productive*	(7) *(5) x (6) Cost ($)*
Formal workshop training								
	GS-12 supervisor IE	14.94	136	2,032	1	2,032	100	2,032
	GS-11/12 trainer	13.45	160	2,152	0.04	86	100	86
OJT								
	GS-13 branch head	17.76	800	14,208	1	14,208	10	1,421
	GS-12 supervisor IE	14.94	800	11,952	1	11,952	45	5,378
Training cost—labor subtotal								8,917
Total labor cost = labor subtotal x (1 + benefits loading = 1.3)								11,592
Other training costs								
Tuition								260
Travel								0
Per diem								0
Total training costs								11,852

SIX

Determining Human Resource Value: Concepts and Theory

One of the major objectives of human resource accounting is to develop valid and reliable methods of measuring the value of an organization's human resources. Both monetary and nonmonetary measures are needed for use in decision making involving the acquisition, development, and allocation of human resources and in monitoring and evaluating the degree to which management has effectively and efficiently utilized human resources.

To develop methods of measuring human resource value, it is necessary to understand what human resource value is and to identify the factors influencing its magnitude and fluctuations. An understanding of the nature and determinants of human resource value will help us develop measurement capabilities by identifying the variables that determine the value of people and by explaining the interrelationships among these variables. This will aid in measuring human resource value in nonmonetary as well as in monetary terms.

The purpose of this chapter is, therefore, to develop a theoretical framework that explains the nature and determinants of the value of people to organizations. This framework is called *human resource value theory.* It draws upon economic, social, and psychological variables. We shall first examine the economic concept of value and then apply it to people to develop the notion of human resource value. Next we shall consider the factors that influence the value of individuals to organizations.[1] Finally, we shall examine the factors that determine the value of groups of people to organizations.[2] We must attempt to understand the value of people as individuals and as groups because in organizations (unlike geometry) the whole does not always equal the sum of its parts.*

The Economic Concept of Value

Despite its many applications, the concept of *value* has essentially two different meanings. It expresses the usefulness of a particular resource and the power of purchasing goods which possession of that resource facilitates. In other words, one type of value is *utility* and the other is *purchasing power*. The former is termed "value in use" or "use value," and the latter is termed "value in exchange" or "exchange value."

All economic theories of value are based explicitly on the premise that the attribute determining whether and to what extent an object possesses value is the perceived ability to render future economic utility, benefits, or services. Thus Ludwig Von Mises, a noted economist, wrote that "whoever wants to construct an elementary theory of value and price must first think of utility."[3] Similarly, Irving Fisher proposed that:

> No one will dispute that the buyer of any article of capital will value it for its expected services to him, and that "at the margin" of his purchases, the price he will pay is the equivalent to him of these expected services, or, in other words, is their "present worth," their "discounted value," or "capitalized value."[4]

If an object is not capable of rendering future economic services, it has no value. In these terms, an object's value is typically defined as the present worth of the services it is anticipated to render in the future.[5]

*For example, the value of a business enterprise as a going concern may be different from the value of its individual assets. This differential value is created by *synergism:* the cooperative action of discrete agencies such that the total effect is greater than the sum of the effects of the agencies acting independently.

The Concept of Human Resource Value

The concept of *human value* is derived from general economic value theory. Like all resources, people possess value because they are capable of rendering future services. In principle, then, we can define the value of people, like that of other resources, as the present worth of their expected future services. The concept of human resource value can be extended to individuals, groups, and the total human organization. Thus an individual's value to an organization can be defined as the present worth of the set of future services the person is expected to provide during the period he or she is anticipated to remain in the organization. Similarly, a group's value to an organization may be defined as the present value of its expected future services. Finally, the value of the human organization as a whole is the present worth of its expected future services to an enterprise.

The Determinants of an Individual's Value

In this section, we shall examine the determinants of an individual's value to an organization. Our objective is to formulate a model that identifies these determinants and explains their interrelationships. The model is shown schematically in Figure 6-10. Since it is complex, the reader may find it helpful to refer to it now to obtain an overview for the subsequent discussion.

Two Aspects of Individual Value. Unlike other resources, human beings are not owned by organizations, and hence they are relatively free to supply or withhold their services. From an organization's viewpoint, this means that the probability of realizing an individual's services is typically less than certainty. This also suggests that there is a dual aspect to an individual's value: (1) the amount the organization could potentially realize from his or her services if the person maintains organizational membership during the period of his or her productive service life and (2) the amount actually expected to be derived, taking into account the person's likelihood of turnover. The former is the individual's *expected conditional value* and the latter is the person's *expected realizable value.* The ultimate measure of a person's value is expected realizable value, because this concept is equivalent to the general notion of a resource's *economic value*—the present value of its expected future services.

Determinants of Expected Realizable Value. An individual's expected realizable value to an organization is thus multidimensional and composed of two interacting variables: the individual's conditional value and the probability that the individual will maintain membership in the organization. An individual's *conditional value* is the present worth of the *potential* services that could be rendered to the organization if the individual maintained organizational membership throughout his or her expected service life. The probability that the individual will maintain membership in the organization is the complement of the probability of turnover or exit. It determines the extent to which the organization will realize the individual's potential services or conditional value. The product of these two variables is thus the individual's expected realizable value—the present worth of services actually expected to be derived during the individual's anticipated tenure in the organization, as shown in Figure 6-1.

Figure 6-1

VARIABLES INTERACTING TO PRODUCE AN INDIVIDUAL'S EXPECTED REALIZABLE VALUE

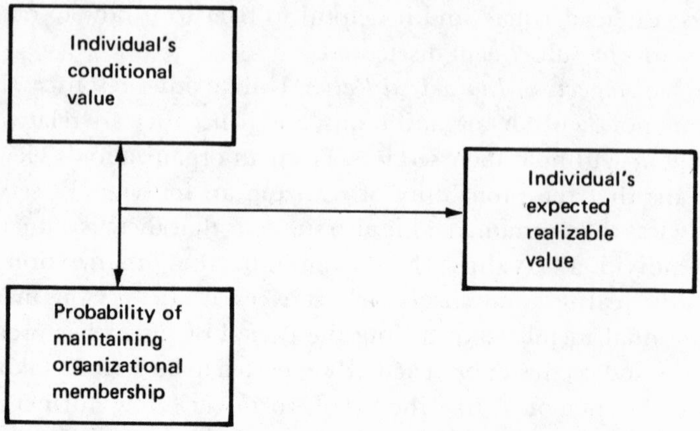

SOURCE: Eric Flamholtz, "Toward a Theory of Human Resource Value in Formal Organizations," *The Accounting Review,* October 1972, p. 669. Reprinted by permission of *The Accounting Review.*

Conditional Value. An individual's conditional value is a multidimensional variable composed of three factors: productivity, transferability, and promotability.* *Productivity* refers to the set of services an individual is expected to provide while occupying his or her present position. A synonym for productivity is performance. *Transferability* is the set of services an individual is expected to provide if and when he or she transfers to other positions at the same level in a different promotion channel. *Promotability* represents the set of services the individual is expected to provide if and when he or she occupies higher-level positions in the present or different promotion channels. Productivity, transferability, and promotability are, in other words, subsets of the "services" the person is expected to render, which are the elements of conditional value, as shown in Figure 6-2.

Figure 6-2

ELEMENTS OF CONDITIONAL VALUE AND THEIR INTERRELATIONSHIPS

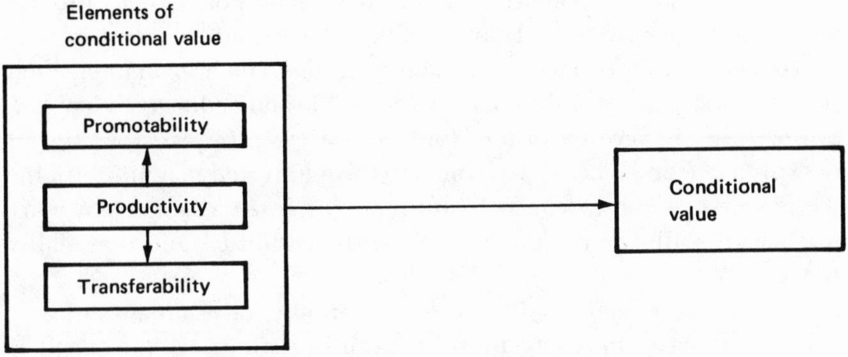

SOURCE: Eric Flamholtz, "Toward a Theory of Human Resource Value in Formal Organizations," *The Accounting Review,* October 1972, p. 669. Reprinted by permission of *The Accounting Review.*

The hypothesized relations among the elements of conditional value are also indicated in Figure 6-2. In this model, productivity is the central or causal variable. It is hypothesized to influence both promotability and transferability. Productivity influences promotability—or, more accurately, *perceived* promotability—because it affects an

*It should be noted that the model implicitly assumes that the services embodied in these variables are net of costs incurred to generate these services.

individual's eligibility for promotion. That is, because promotion practices in formal organizations are at least in part a function of past performance or prior services rendered, an individual's promotability is affected by evaluations of his or her past and expected future productivity. Similarly, transferability is influenced by productivity, which may affect the likelihood that the organization will consider the individual for a possible transfer. In some cases, transfer may also indicate promotion eligibility. For example, the rotation of "high-potential" MBAs through various jobs, functional areas, and geographical locations may indicate grooming for future promotion.

Determinants of Elements of Conditional Value. The elements of individual conditional value are the product of certain attributes of the individual and certain dimensions of the organization. The major *individual determinants* of conditional value are the individual's skills and activation level. The major *organizational determinants* of conditional value are the individual's role and the nature of organizational rewards. We turn now to each of these variables.

We begin with the *individual determinants.* The individual's "skills" represent his or her currently developed potential to provide services to an organization. Drawing upon Floyd Mann, we are primarily concerned with a trio of technical, administrative, and human interaction skills.[6] These general skills are relatively stable and enduring. They can, however, be changed by various forms of training. In principle, the set of skills a person possesses sets limits to the nature and magnitude of the services he or she can render to an organization. At a more elementary level, such skills are the product of cognitive abilities and personality traits.

The individual's *activation level* is another determinant of his or her conditional value. Activation level can be defined as "the extent of release of the stored energy of the organism through metabolic activity in the tissues."[7] In other words, it is the neuropsychological counterpart of the notion of "motivation." The level of activation is a major variable influencing human behavior. An individual's activation level is not constant and may vary as a result of changes in physiological and psychological determinants.

It is hypothesized that an individual's skills and activation level (motivation) interact to determine the person's potential for rendering services to an organization. Although an individual's skills set a theoretical limit upon the services that he or she can render, in practice the person's activation level is probably also a crucial determinant of the potential services to be realized by an organization. Individuals can compensate to a great extent for a lack of specific skills by increasing their activation level. An individual possessing a high degree of technical, administrative, and interpersonal skills, however, may provide less service to an organization than warranted by his or her potential because of a relatively low activation level. In either case, the relation between skills and activation level in producing productivity is quite complex. The relationship among these determinants and conditional value is shown in Figure 6-3.

Figure 6-3

RELATION OF INDIVIDUAL DETERMINANTS TO CONDITIONAL VALUE

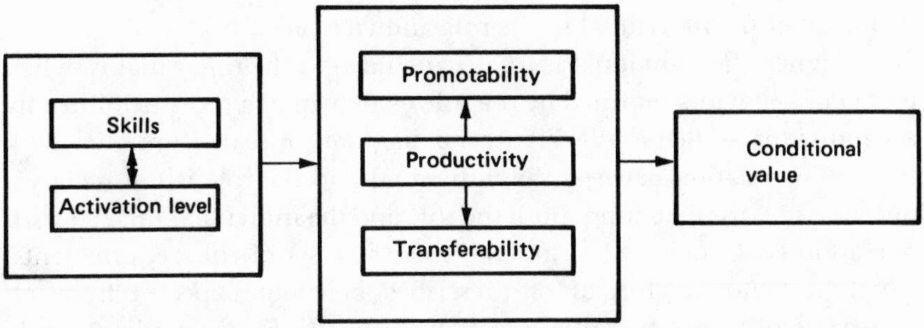

SOURCE: Eric Flamholtz, "Toward a Theory of Human Resource Value in Formal Organizations," *The Accounting Review,* October 1972, p. 671. Reprinted by permission of *The Accounting Review.*

We turn now to the *organizational determinants.* These individual determinants of conditional value also interact with certain organizational determinants. Although an individual may possess a set of skills and the motivation to apply them, the organizational role he or she occupies influences the extent to which he or she is offered the opportunity to render potential services. In this context a *role* refers to the set of behaviors expected from all persons occupying a specified position in an organization. For example, a person with a high degree of administrative skill may occupy the role of engineer, or the individual with great skill in solving mathematical problems may occupy the role of salesperson. In either case, the individual's conditional value to the organization is determined, in part, by the interaction between skill and organizational role. In other words, the individual is included in his or her role on only a partial or segmental basis. This occurrence is probably quite typical in organizations, for, as Katz and Kahn observe: "Unlike the inclusion of a given organ in the body in the biological system, not all of the individual is included in his organizational membership. The organization neither requires nor wants the whole person."[8]

To clarify the nature of the interaction between the individual and his or her organizational role as a determinant of a person's conditional value, their relationship is shown schematically in Figures 6-4, 6-5, and 6-6. In Figure 6-4, a set diagram shows two subsets, P and R (with P representing a person and R a role). From the diagram it can be seen that $P \cap R = E$, where E denotes the empty set. That is, there is no overlap or intersection between the person and the role. The skills available are simply not required by the role to which he or she is allocated.

In Figure 6-5, the situation can be expressed as $P \cap R \neq E$; the intersection of the person and the role is not empty. There is some inclusion of the individual in the role and vice versa.

When the individual is totally included in the role—that is, when the set of behaviors required by the role exactly match those exhibited by the individual—then $P = R$. Figure 6-6 diagrams this situation.

The relation between the individual and the role is not merely a question of fit or matching. Both the role and the individual interact with one another. Considered abstractly, there is a set of role requirements, which refer to the formal or prescribed behavior expected from *all* occupants of a specified role, position, or office. For example, the role of manager generally connotes certain universal expectations, and in a particular organization these expectations are made even more precise by systemic values, traditions, and norms. However, the perceptions of the role incumbent also affect the role. The set of attributes of the role perceived by the incumbent may or may not correspond closely to the role's formal requirements—newly promoted managers may bring with them a set of activities that were typically associated with their previous position.

The role and the individual also interact in other ways. Role prescriptions, as mechanisms specifying the tasks and jobs that people are to perform, are important influences upon an individual's activation level. William E. Scott has reviewed several neuropsychological studies on the determinants of activation and has suggested their implications for a better understanding of the relation between the structure of tasks and the degree of activation of an individual. Scott cites studies which give some evidence that there are several aspects of a task structure which

Figure 6-4

NO INTERSECTION BETWEEN PERSON AND ROLE

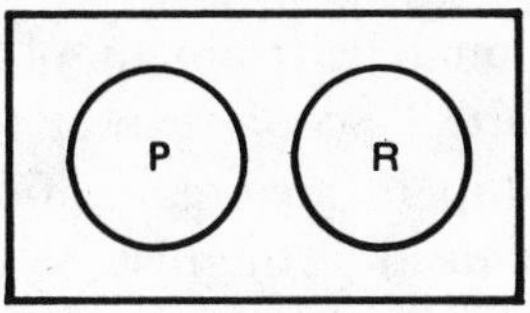

$P \cap R = E$

SOURCE: Eric Flamholtz, "Toward a Theory of Human Resource Value in Formal Organizations," *The Accounting Review,* October 1972, p. 671. Reprinted by permission of *The Accounting Review.*

Figure 6-5

SOME INCLUSION OF PERSON IN ROLE

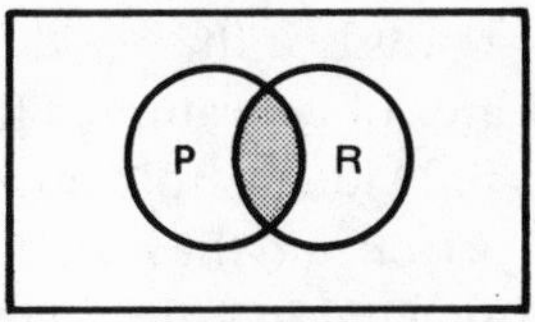

$P \cap R \neq E$

SOURCE: Eric Flamholtz, "Toward a Theory of Human Resource Value in Formal Organizations," *The Accounting Review,* October 1972, p. 671. Reprinted by permission of *The Accounting Review.*

Figure 6-6

TOTAL INCLUSION OF PERSON IN ROLE

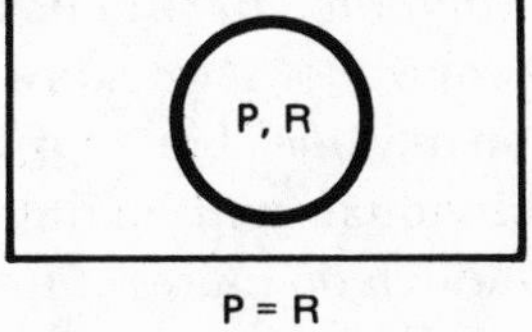

$P = R$

SOURCE: Eric Flamholtz, "Toward a Theory of Human Resource Value in Formal Organizations," *The Accounting Review,* October 1972, p. 672. Reprinted by permission of *The Accounting Review.*

may be determinants of activation level, including such variables as stimulus variation, intensity, complexity, uncertainty, and meaningfulness.[9]

Another organizational determinant of an individual's conditional value is the "rewards" people expect to derive from different aspects of their membership in an organization. As Daniel Katz has pointed out, "it is important to distinguish between rewards which are administered in relation to individual effort and performance and the system rewards which accrue to people by virtue of their membership in the system."[10] *Instrumental individual rewards*—rewards that are administered in relation to individual effort—are intended to motivate optimal role performance. *Instrumental system rewards*—rewards that accrue by virtue of membership in the system—are more effective for holding people within the organization, but they will not necessarily lead to higher productivity.

In terms of the proposed model, it is hypothesized that instrumental individual rewards influence the individual's conditional value by affecting the degree of activation. The rewards associated with behavior required by an individual's role influence the extent to which there is a fit between the person and the role. That is, the extent to which task performance is instrumental in satisfying an individual's needs will determine the likelihood that he or she will fulfill role requirements. This is the essence of the "path-goal hypothesis" presented by Georgopoulos, Mahoney, and Jones.[11] Thus it is hypothesized that the more likely it is that the behavior required by a given role will lead to rewards perceived to be instrumental in satisfying an individual's needs, the greater the inclusion of the person in the role and, therefore, the greater the individual's conditional value to an organization. The hypothesized relations among the variables that determine an individual's conditional value are shown schematically in Figure 6-7.

Probability of Maintaining Organizational Membership. Because people can leave an organization, we must consider not only the determinants of conditional value, but also the determinants of the probability that an individual will maintain membership in an organizational system. Research on causes of turnover has suggested that there is an inverse relationship between need satisfaction and the likelihood of exiting. Ross and Zander, for example, found that "the degree of satisfaction of certain personal needs supplied by an individual's place of employment has a significant direct relationship to his continuing to work for that company." They concluded that

Figure 6-7

RELATIONS AMONG VARIABLES DETERMINING AN INDIVIDUAL'S CONDITIONAL VALUE

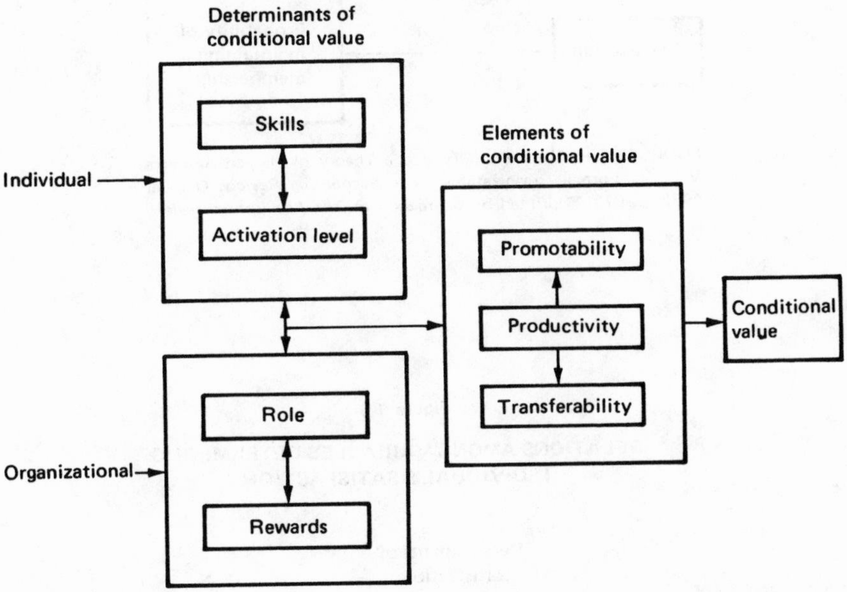

SOURCE: Eric Flamholtz, "Toward a Theory of Human Resource Value in Formal Organizations," *The Accounting Review*, October 1972, p. 673. Reprinted by permission of *The Accounting Review*.

"workers whose personal needs are satisfied on the job are more likely to remain in the organization."[12] Similarly, in reviewing the findings of research on the relation between job satisfaction and turnover, Fournet, Distefano, and Pryer concluded that the findings consistently show turnover negatively related to job satisfaction.[13] Thus there is evidence to support the general relation between these variables, as depicted in Figure 6-8.

To the extent that satisfaction with organization membership is related to the perceived opportunity to satisfy individual needs, it is hypothesized that satisfaction is the product of the interaction between the individual and organizational determinants of an individual's value. This means that satisfaction is presumed to be caused by the same *process* that produces an individual's value—the interaction between the

Figure 6-8

DETERMINANTS OF THE PROBABILITY OF MAINTAINING ORGANIZATIONAL MEMBERSHIP

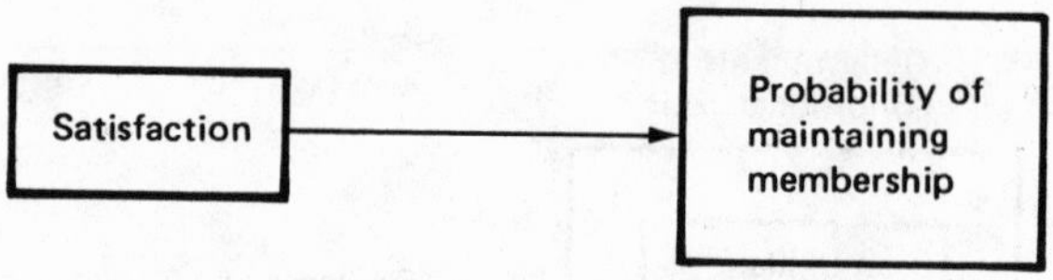

SOURCE: Eric Flamholtz, "Toward a Theory of Human Resource Value in Formal Organizations," *The Accounting Review*, October 1972, p. 673. Reprinted by permission of *The Accounting Review.*

Figure 6-9

RELATIONS AMONG VARIABLES DETERMINING INDIVIDUAL'S SATISFACTION

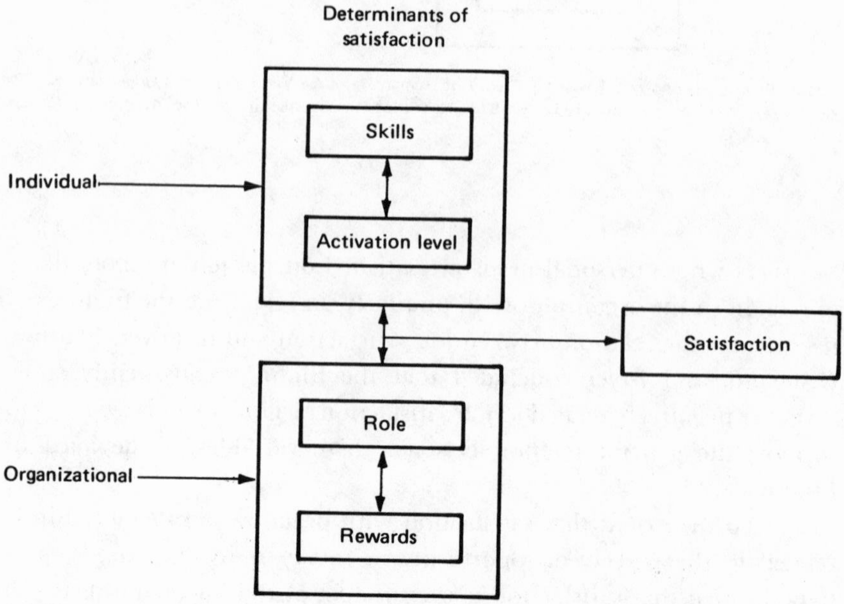

SOURCE: Eric Flamholtz, "Toward a Theory of Human Resource Value in Formal Organizations," *The Accounting Review*, October 1972, p. 674. Reprinted by permission of *The Accounting Review.*

individual's skills, activation level, and role, and the organizational reward structure. These hypothesized relations are shown schematically in Figure 6-9.

It should be noted that satisfaction is a global construct. Thus satisfaction is really a composite of several separate variables such as satisfaction with pay, satisfaction with working conditions, and satisfaction with supervision.

In addition to the relation between satisfaction and the probability of remaining in an organization, there is also a possible relation between satisfaction and one of the determinants of an individual's conditional value—for example, productivity. Research findings have generally tested the hypothesized relation between productivity and satisfaction from the viewpoint that the latter is a determinant of the former. Unfortunately, in reviewing and analyzing the results of such studies, Brayfield and Crockett argued that "we expect the relation between satisfaction and job performance to be one of concomitant variation rather than cause and effect." In addition, they conclude that "satisfaction with one's position in a network of relationships need not imply strong motivation to outstanding performance within that system."[14] Although many researchers expected to find a positive relationship between satisfaction and productivity, some have found a negative relationship. Obviously the relation between these variables is quite complex, and it is likely that there are other variables which moderate their effect upon each other. Accordingly, there is presently insufficient evidence to support a hypothesis on the nature of the relation between these variables.[15] It may be just as likely that satisfaction is caused by productivity as it is that productivity is determined by satisfaction.[16]

The Model as a Whole. The model of the nature and determinants of an individual's value developed above is shown schematically in Figure 6-10. Taken as a whole, it represents a framework for understanding the factors influencing an individual's value to an organization.

One of the most significant aspects of this preliminary theory of human resource value is that its constructs indicate the kinds of variables that must be considered in developing a measure of an individual's value. The model's specific measurement implications are presented next.

Figure 6-10

MODEL OF THE DETERMINANTS OF AN INDIVIDUAL'S VALUE TO A FORMAL ORGANIZATION

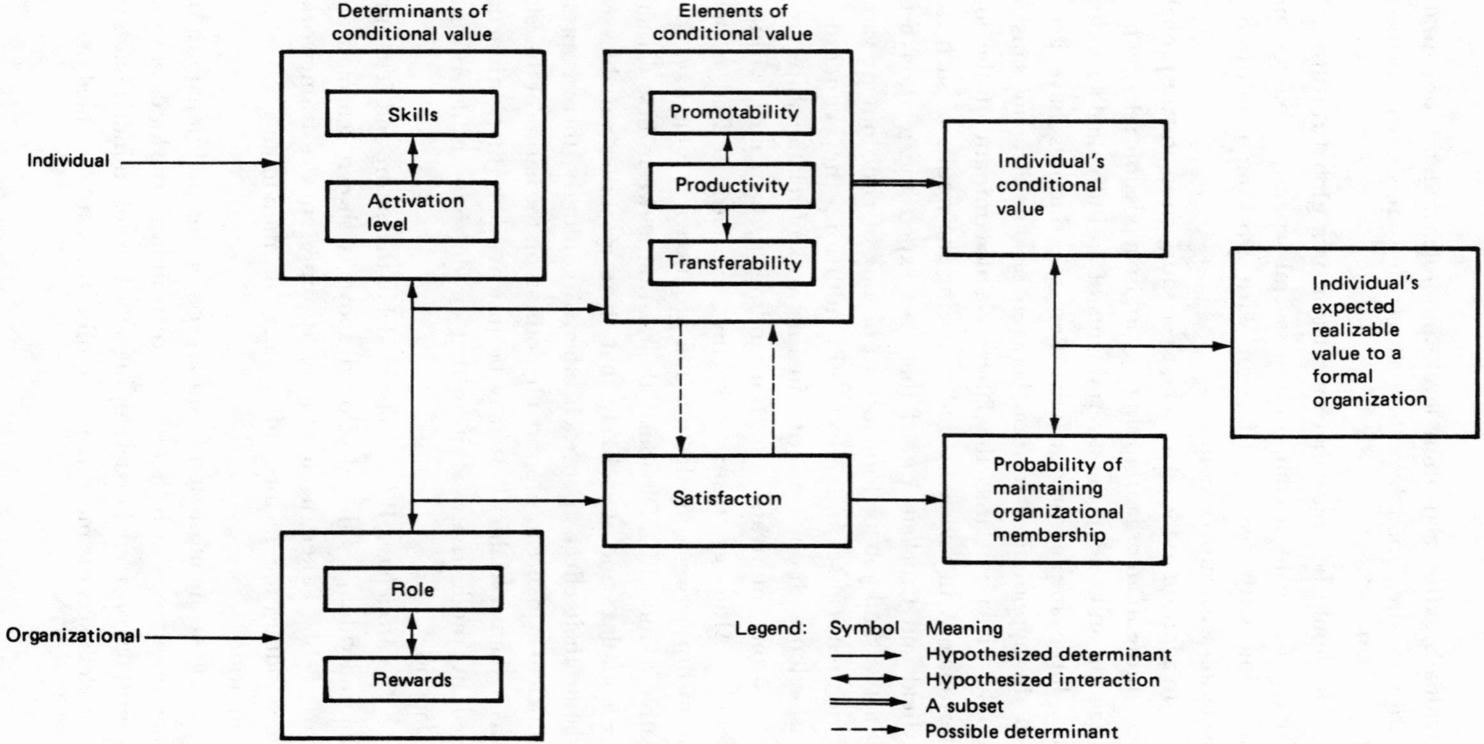

SOURCE: Eric Flamholtz, "Toward a Theory of Human Resource Value in Formal Organizations," *The Accounting Review*, October 1972, p. 668. Reprinted by permission of *The Accounting Review*.

The Model's Measurement Implications. The model shows that the ultimate measure of a person's worth to an organization is his or her expected realizable value. It also shows that conditional value is a penultimate measure. This is an important measurement implication because it is contrary to the conventional notion of a person's value, which does not distinguish between these two value dimensions. Specifically, there is a tendency to think of a person's value in terms of his or her potential (conditional) worth to a firm rather than in terms of anticipated (realizable) worth. For example, a personnel manager may prefer to hire the individual with the greatest potential value rather than the one with the greatest anticipated value considering the likelihood of turnover. If the personnel manager were trying to optimize the value of human resources, he or she would hire people with the greatest realizable value. In practice, both variables should be measured and reported to personnel management.

The model also shows us how to obtain a measure of the opportunity cost of turnover. If expected conditional value measures the maximum potential value of people to a firm, then the difference between it and expected realizable value represents the opportunity cost of turnover. Thus this differential also represents the amount an organization can spend in order to reduce turnover to zero. It is not, of course, always desirable to reduce turnover to zero.

Conceptually, the model permits us to understand the value of increasing, and the opportunity cost of decreasing, employee satisfaction. It shows that changes in satisfaction affect the probability of people maintaining membership in an organization; this in turn influences the extent to which an organization will actually derive a person's potential services. Thus the model shows that satisfaction is an important determinant of a person's value and suggests the need for this variable to be measured and reported to management.

Another of the model's measurement implications is that an individual's worth is not merely a function of personal attributes; it is the product of a set of interacting economic, social, and psychological variables. Thus a person's value is a function not only of his or her skills and activation level, but also of the person's organizational role.

The model also provides a broader concept of the elements of conditional value than that commonly held. It suggests that productivity and promotability are not the only elements of conditional value; transferability is also an element. Productivity and promotability are typically measured in organizations, but not transferability. The model makes this variable more visible and suggests the need for it to be taken into account in measuring individual value.

The model's most important contribution for the monetary measurement of human resource value is its implication that a person's value is a product of both the attributes of the individual per se and the characteristics of the organization. This implication provides the underlying premise for our conceptualization of the individual valuation problem, as discussed in Chapter Seven.

In regard to nonmonetary measurement of human resource value, the model identifies several variables for measurement. It also shows the relationship of these variables to the ultimate and penultimate measures of a person's worth.

Mathematical Statement of Model. In algebraic terms, the model can be restated:

$$\text{ERV} = \text{ECV} \times P(R) \qquad (1)$$
$$P(R) = 1 - P(T) \qquad (2)$$
$$\text{OCT} = \text{ECV} - \text{ERV} \qquad (3)$$

where ERV = expected realizable value
ECV = expected conditional value
$P(R)$ = probability of maintaining organizational membership
$P(T)$ = probability of turnover
OCT = opportunity cost of turnover

Using these variables, the human resource professional can analyze the costs and benefits of turnover control, or the differential effects of different management styles on the expected opportunity costs of turnover. Assume, for example, that the conditional value of the human resources for a division of a large industrial enterprise is $10 million at the beginning of the year 19X6 and that the probability of turnover is 10 percent. Then the opportunity cost of turnover will be $1 million:

$$\text{ERV} = \$10{,}000{,}000 \times (0.90) = \$9{,}000{,}000$$
$$\text{OCT} = \$10{,}000{,}000 - \$9{,}000{,}000 = \$1{,}000{,}000$$

If, however, a turnover control program were introduced at the beginning of 19X6 and reduced the rate of turnover from 10 percent to 5 percent, the savings to the organization would be $500,000. The reader should verify this savings by using the formulas provided above.

In brief, the model provides a quantitative framework that may be used to analyze a wide variety of human resource actions in terms of their impact on the value of human resources. It can be used to quantify the effect of human resource management strategies and actions upon ECV, ERV, or OCT—the key variables affected by managerial decisions.

Testing the Model's Validity. Many of the model's variables have been studied in different contexts for some time. However, the author knows of no previous attempt to link them to individual value. Thus we must raise the following issues: Are the variables actually determinants of a person's value to an organization? In other words, are the hypothesized determinants of an individual's value really valid? Are there any variables not contained in the model that are determinants of a person's value? Finally, are the hypothesized relations among the variables valid?

Discussion of the Model. The model is intended as a first step toward a theory of human resource value in formal organizations. Its scope is restricted to the nature and determinants of an individual's value to an organization.

The model treats an individual's value as an independent or marginal phenomenon. The validity of this treatment depends upon several variables, including the nature of the organization and the degree of interdependence of organizational roles. Accordingly, this model does not fully take into account the dynamic aspects of organizational life. An individual's promotability, for example, may be determined not only by his or her own skills, activation level, and expected service potential, but also by the promotability of others. Thus it should not be inferred that the model purports to explain the value of groups of people in formal organizations.

Similarly, it should not be inferred that the model fully explains the nature of individual value. Future research may find that other variables should be included or that present variables are unnecessary. The validity of the hypothesized relations among the variables also needs to be assessed.

The Determinants of Group Value

We have examined the determinants of individual value to an organization as an independent phenomenon both because the individual is an important unit of study per se and because this treatment helps to reduce the complexity of explaining the nature of human value.

It is, however, well recognized that for many reasons the individual is not always the appropriate unit of organizational analysis. In fact, many management theorists tend to argue that the *group* rather than the individual should be the primary focus of study.

In this section, we examine the determinants of a group's value to an organization. Our objective, as in the case of individuals, is to present a model that shows the key variables affecting the value of a group of people to an organization.

Rensis Likert and David G. Bowers have presented a model (shown in Figure 6-11) that identifies variables which have been found to influence the effectiveness of a human organization. The model is intended to represent "the productive capability of the human organization of any enterprise or unit within it (that is, a work group)."[17] The model, Likert and Bowers suggest, can be used as a basis for measuring changes in the value of the productive capability of a human organization. It is based upon work by Likert, Bowers, Seashore, and others at the University of Michigan's Institute for Social Research to identify and measure the determinants of effective organization structures and management styles.[18]

The Model's Variables. The model is organized in terms of three broad classes of variables: causal, intervening, and end result:

1. The *causal* variables are independent variables that determine the course of developments within an organization and the results achieved by the organization. These causal variables include only those that are controllable by the organization and its management. General business conditions, for example, although an independent variable, are *not* viewed as causal since they are not controllable by the management of a particular enterprise. Causal variables include the structure of the organization and management's policies, decisions, business and leadership strategies, skills, and behavior.
2. The *intervening* variables reflect the internal state, health, and performance capabilities of the organization; that is, the loyalties, attitudes, motivations, performance goals, and perceptions of all members and their collective capability for effective action, interaction, communication, and decision making.

Figure 6-11

RELATIONSHIP AMONG HUMAN ORGANIZATIONAL DIMENSIONS

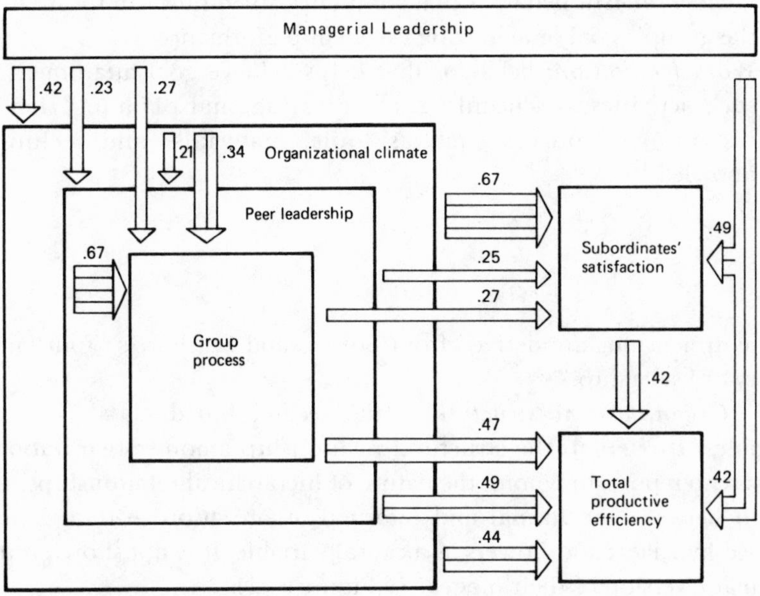

NOTE: Width of arrow shows magnitude of relationship.
Copyright by Rensis Likert Associates, Inc., 1972. Used by permission. No further reproduction authorized.

3. The *end-result* variables are the dependent variables that reflect the results achieved by that organization, such as its productivity, costs, scrap loss, growth, share of the market, and earnings.[19]

Causal Variables. The model hypothesizes that there are two different types of causal variables: managerial behavior and organization structure.

Managerial behavior (denoted as "managerial leadership" in Figure 6-11) refers to the dimensions of supervisory behavior influencing group effectiveness. Specifically, Likert and Bowers cite four dimensions or components of managerial behavior that are hypothesized to influence group effectiveness:

1. *Support:* behavior that enhances someone else's feeling of personal worth and importance

2. *Team building:* behavior that encourages members of the group to develop close, mutually satisfying relationships
3. *Goal emphasis:* behavior that stimulates an enthusiasm for meeting the group's goal or achieving excellent performance
4. *Work facilitation:* behavior that helps achieve goal attainment by such activities as scheduling, coordinating, and planning, and by providing resources such as tools, materials, and technical knowledge

These dimensions are derived from Bowers and Seashore's "four-factor theory of leadership."[20]

Organizational structure is the second broad class of causal variables. It refers to the structural relationship among organizational roles: who reports to whom, the nature of hierarchical relationships, and the fit between the formal and informal organization. Although it is defined by Likert and Bowers as a causal variable, it is not shown in the schematic version of their model (see Figure 6-11).

Intervening Variables. Taken together, the two classes of causal variables (managerial behavior and organizational structure) influence the intervening variables. There are four types of intervening variables: group processes, peer leadership, organizational climate, and subordinates' satisfaction.

Work group processes relate to the interpersonal processes that characterize a work group per se.[21] They refer to group processes of planning, coordinating efforts, decision making and problem solving, information sharing, and similar factors, as shown in Table 6-1.

Peer leadership refers to the support, interaction facilitation, work facilitation, and goal emphasis provided by the subordinate peer group. In other words, this concept refers to the leadership behavior exhibited by the peer group. Peer leadership includes the same four factors that comprise managerial leadership but it refers to behavior directed by subordinates toward subordinates rather than by managers toward subordinates.

Organizational climate refers to the social and psychological climate that people perceive about an organization. It refers to several critical social-psychological dimensions of the organization, including

Table 6-1

ITEMS USED TO MEASURE HUMAN ORGANIZATIONAL DIMENSIONS

Managerial Leadership—Extent manager displays the following:

- *Support*
  - friendly
  - pays attention to what you are saying
  - listens to your problems
- *Goal Emphasis*
  - encourages best effort
  - maintains high standards
- *Help with Work*
  - shows ways to do a better job
  - helps you plan, organize, and schedule
  - offers new ideas, solution to problems
- *Team Building*
  - encourages subordinates to work as a team
  - encourages exchange of opinions and ideas

Group Process—extent of:

- planning together, coordinating efforts
- making good decisions, solving problems
- knowing jobs and how to do them well
- sharing information
- wanting to meet objectives
- having confidence and trust in other members
- ability to meet unusual work demands

Peer Leadership—Extent peers display the following:

- *Support*
  - friendly
  - pays attention to what you are saying
  - listens to your problems
- *Goal Emphasis*
  - encourages best effort
  - maintains high standards
- *Help with Work*
  - shows ways to do a better job
  - helps you plan, organize, and schedule
  - group shares with each other new ideas, solutions to problems
- *Team Building*
  - encouragement from each other to work as a team
  - emphasis on team goal
  - exchange of opinions and ideas

Satisfaction with

- your fellow workers
- your superior
- your job
- this organization compared with others
- your pay
- progress you've made in the organization up to now
- your chances for getting ahead in the future

Organizational Climate

- *Communication Flow*
  - you know what's going on
  - those above are receptive
  - you are given information to do jobs well
- *Decision-Making Practices*
  - you are involved in setting goals
  - decisions are made at levels of accurate information
  - persons affected by decisions are asked for their ideas
  - know-how of people of all levels is used
- *Concern for Persons*
  The organization:
  - is interested in the individual's welfare
  - tries to improve working conditions
  - organizes work activities sensibly
- *Influence on Your Department* from
  - lower level supervisors
  - employees who have no subordinates
- *Technological Adequacy*
  - improved methods are quickly adopted
  - equipment and resources are well managed
- *Motivation*
  - differences and disagreements are accepted and worked through
  - people in organization work hard
    - for money, promotions, job satisfaction, and to meet high expectations from others
    - encouraged by policies, working conditions and people

SOURCE: Rensis Likert and David G. Bowers, "Improving the Accuracy of P/L Reports by Estimating the Change in Dollar Value of the Human Organization," *Michigan Business Review,* March 1973, pp. 15–24.

the processes of communication, decision making, control, motivation, and others, as shown in Table 6-1.

Subordinates' satisfaction refers to the satisfaction of subordinates with various dimensions of their membership in the organization: satisfaction with pay and advancement opportunities, satisfaction with their jobs, satisfaction with the company, satisfaction with supervisor, and satisfaction with peer group.[22]

Although quite complex, the hypothesized relationships among these variables and the causal variables can be described briefly: Managerial leadership determines organizational climate. Together, these two classes of variables determine peer leadership. Together, these three variables determine group processes. Managerial leadership also determines subordinates' satisfaction. The latter variable is also influenced by organizational climate, peer leadership, and work group processes. The direction of the relationships among these variables is shown by arrows in Figure 6-11, and their magnitude is indicated by the coefficient of determination on each arrow.*

End-Result Variables. The end-result variable (total productive efficiency) is composed of costs, sales, earnings, and the like. The model hypothesizes that the causal and intervening variables determine the result of "total productive efficiency."

Discussion of the Model. This model is an important step toward understanding a group's value to an organization. It should neither be inferred that the model is fully validated nor that it represents all the major dimensions of a group's value to an organization. The model consists of several hypotheses about which variables influence the value of a human organization, as well as certain hypotheses about the variables' interrelationships.** Chapter Eight presents evidence of the validity of these hypotheses.

Although this model of the determinants of a group's value to an organization is tentative, it is a major contribution to human resource value theory and, in turn, to human resource valuation. The model

*The coefficient of determination (r^2) is the square of the coefficient of correlation (r).

**In a personal communication, Likert questioned my use of the term "hypothesized" in referring to the model's relationships. He noted that the model's relationships are based on substantial bodies of data and believes that the term "findings" would be more accurate.

specifies the key variables influencing the value of a group of people to an organization. It also presents hypotheses about the interrelationships among these variables. Although research on the relation of these variables to organizational effectiveness has been conducted for quite some time, Likert was the first to recognize that they could be used to explain the determinants of the value of people to organizations.[23]

At present, the model's most important contribution is to the nonmonetary measurement of human resource value. It identifies several variables that can be measured by attitude surveys, as described in Chapter Eight.

Potentially the model may make a significant contribution to the monetary measurement of human resource value, because Likert has suggested that measurements of the model's variables may ultimately be used to forecast changes in the financial situation of organizations attributable to changes in the value of human resources. We shall examine this application of the model in Chapter Seven.

In the author's judgment, one potential limitation of the model is that it is derived from a specific theory of management.* The model is an outgrowth of the research by Likert and his colleagues (notably Bowers, Katz, Kahn, Morse, Tannenbaum, and Seashore) at the University of Michigan's Institute for Social Research on the determinants of managerial and organizational effectiveness. The metatheory underlying the model is closely related to Likert's notion of the "system 4" style of management, a form of participative management.[24]

The potential limitations of the model are suggested by the following questions: Does the model's validity depend on the validity of Likert's theory of management? Is the model consistent with other theories of management (for example, "system 1," an autocratic theory of management)? These questions cannot be answered at present, but they are issues to which future research must be directed.

*In a personal communication, Likert disagreed with these statements about the relation of the model to his metatheory of management. He stated that the model is not based on his "system 4" but is derived from findings of a large number of studies. Readers are referred to the original studies to form their own judgment. See James C. Taylor and David G. Bowers, *Survey of Organizations* (Ann Arbor: University of Michigan, 1972).

Summary

In this chapter we examined the determinants of human value in an organization. *Value,* in this context, is defined as the present value of future services. Similarly, *human resource value* is the present worth of the future services that people are expected to provide. Two models of the determinants of human resource value were presented: one, by the author, explains the determinants of individual value; the other, by Likert, explains the determinants of group value.

In my model, the ultimate measure of a person's value is expected realizable value. This is composed of two variables: conditional value (potential value) and the probability that the person will remain with the firm during his or her expected service life. The conditional value of a person depends on his or her promotability, transferability, and productivity. These in turn depend on both the skills and the activation level of the individual. The organizational determinants of a person's conditional value include the degree to which the role assignment corresponds with the employee's skills and personal goals and the reward system used by the company. The probability of a person staying in an organization is directly related to the degree of job satisfaction that the employee feels.

The Likert and Bowers model was used to represent the variables that affect a group's value to an organization. Causal variables (those controllable by the organization) and intervening variables (reflecting organizational capabilities) determine the end-result variables of the company. The causal variables include managerial behavior and organizational structure. The intervening variables include group processes, peer leadership, organizational climate, and subordinates' satisfaction. The end results are the total productive efficiency of an enterprise.

Each of these models identifies variables that determine the value of people to organizations. These variables must be taken into account in measuring the value of people as organizational resources, as we shall see in the following chapters dealing with human resource valuation methods.

SEVEN

Monetary Measurement Methods

This chapter deals with the measurement of the value of people as organizational resources in monetary terms. The primary goal is to provide a method for measuring the two major dimensions of a person's value to an organization (expected conditional value and realizable value) that were presented in Chapter Six. Our initial focus will be on the problem of measuring an individual's value to an organization. In principle, the value of a group or the total human organization can be determined by merely aggregating the values of the individuals comprising the larger unit. However, we shall also consider some specific problems of group valuations. Moreover, we shall summarize some of the other approaches to the measurement of human resource value that have been proposed in the literature of human resource accounting.

Conceptualization

As noted in Chapter Six, people are of value to organizations because they are capable of rendering future services. The services that people render to an organization are determined by their productivity, promotability, transferability, and probability of retention, as defined in Chapter Six. In brief, the services that people render to a company depend on the set of present and potential roles they may occupy in an organizational hierarchy as well as the likelihood that they will actually occupy those roles.

Assume, for example, that a person is currently a staff accountant for a CPA firm during 19X6. Based on the firm's experience, we have determined that this person has a specified probability of doing one of four possible things during the coming year: remaining in his or her present position, being promoted to the next higher position, being transferred to a different office, and leaving the firm (either voluntarily or by request).

The value of the person to the firm depends on the value of each of the four possible things the person might do during the coming year. Each possibility represents what we shall call a *service state*. Service states are different conditions an individual might occupy in a firm and perform different levels of service. If the person who is currently a staff accountant remains a staff accountant during the next year, that is one level of service. If the person is promoted to the next job classification (semisenior), that is a second level or state of services. If the person leaves the firm, we also view that as a service state (the state of exit). If the person remains a staff accountant, the firm might, for example, derive a value of $40,000 for the coming year, while if the person became a semisenior the firm might derive a value of $55,000. If the person left the firm at the beginning of the next year, however, the firm would derive a value of zero, while if he or she left sometime during the year, the firm would derive some value from the services that the person performed while still a member of the firm.

As seen in the foregoing illustration, the value of an individual to a firm depends on the value of the service states the person will occupy in an organizational hierarchy (present position, next higher position, exit, and so on) as well as the probabilities that the person will occupy each possible service state. This means that the value of human resources to a firm is based on a stochastic (probabilistic) process.

A *stochastic process* refers to any natural system that operates in accordance with probabilistic laws. For example, the weather is a stochastic process. On a given day, there is a certain probability that it will be clear, that there will be rain, that there will be snow, and so forth. Similarly, the movement of people through an organizational hierarchy is a stochastic process. In time, people move through the organizational hierarchy from one service state to another. These movements from state to state are termed *state transitions* or, more simply, *transitions*.

In certain stochastic processes, *rewards* are derived as the system's elements make transitions from one state to another.[1] The rewards are, in other words, the benefits derived by the system. This type of stochastic process is termed a *stochastic process with rewards*.

In the organizational hierarchy, people move from one role to another in a probabilistic manner. As people occupy specified organizational roles, they render services (rewards) to an organization. Thus the movement of people from one role to another in an organization is a stochastic process with rewards.

The Stochastic Rewards Valuation Model

Based on the preceding concepts, one method that has been proposed for measuring a person's value to an organization is termed the *stochastic rewards model* for human resource valuation. This section describes the formal model and explains how it can be used to measure an individual's expected conditional and realizable values to an organization.[2]

Elements of the Model. We can measure an individual's expected conditional and realizable value to an organization by means of a stochastic rewards valuation model. To do this, we must:

1. Define the mutually exclusive set of states an individual may occupy in the system (organization).
2. Determine the value of each state to the organization.
3. Estimate a person's expected tenure in an organization.
4. Find the probability that a person will occupy each possible state at specified future times.
5. Discount the expected future cash flows to determine their present value.

The first step is to define the states of the system. The states should be defined to include the various organizational roles and the state of exit, as shown in Figure 7-1. Because we are dealing with a stochastic process with rewards, we shall call each of these states *service states.* This implies that we expect to derive a specified quantity of services when an individual occupies a particular service state for a given time period.* The second step is to determine the value the organization derives when an individual occupies each service state for a specified time period. We call these values *service state values.* The third step is to estimate a person's future tenure in the organization—this is the valuation period.

*This is true even for exit, because the quantity of services expected when an individual occupies this service state is zero.

The fourth step is to estimate the probability that a person will occupy each possible state at specified future times. For example: What is the probability that a person who is presently a first-line supervisor in marketing will still be a first-line supervisor in marketing at the end of one year? What is the probability that he will be a first-line supervisor in manufacturing? What is the probability he will be a middle manager? What is the probability that he will have left the firm? Finally, we must determine the present value of the expected future benefits by discounting future values to be derived.

Figure 7-1

SERVICE STATE MATRIX

Organization Levels	*Organization Groups*: Marketing	Manufacturing	Finance
Top management			
Middle management			
First-line supervisors			
Operating personnel			
		Exit	

Stated symbolically, the model requires that we define the set of i possible service states, where $i = 1, 2, \ldots, m$, and m is the state of exit. Second, we must determine the value to the organization of each of the i service states, where R_i *denotes the set of* i possible service state values: $R_1, R_2 + \ldots + R_m$. Since, by definition, R_m denotes the state of exit, the service state value of R_m will be zero—a person who occupies the state of exit is of no value to an organization. Third, we must estimate a person's expected service life (tenure) in the organization, where t denotes expected tenure. Next we must find the probability that a person will occupy each of the i possible positions at a specified future time. This is the probability that the organization will derive the rewards associated with different service states. It is denoted $P(R_i)$, which includes $P(R_1) + P(R_2) + \cdots + P(R_m)$. Finally, we must discount the expected future cash flows derived from service state values to their present worth (discounted value).

Measurement of Expected Conditional Value. Drawing upon this model, we can now symbolically define a person's expected conditional value as

$$E(CV) = \sum_{t=1}^{n} \left[\frac{\sum_{i=1}^{m-1} R_i \cdot P(R_i)}{(1 + r)^t} \right] \tag{1}$$

where E(CV) is the expected conditional value; R_i is the value R to be derived by the organization in each possible service state *i; $P(R_i)$* is the probability that the organization will derive R_i (the probability that a person will occupy state *i*); *t* is time; *m* is the state of exit; and $(1 + r)^t$ is the discount factor for money. In words, this expression simply means that an individual's expected conditional value is the discounted mathematical expectation of the monetary worth of the future rewards (services) the person is expected to render to an organization in the future roles (positions) expected to be occupied, when we ignore (hold constant) the probability of turnover.

Expression (1) tells us how to measure conditional value. It literally says: For each time period ($t = 1$ to n), calculate the discounted mathematical expectation (expected value) of the rewards a person will generate for an organization $[\Sigma R_i \cdot P(R_i)/(1 + r)^t]$, assuming that the person will *not* leave the organization. Recall that by definition the variable expected conditional value is the present worth of the potential services that are expected to be rendered to the organization if the individual maintains organizational membership throughout his or her expected service life.

Measurement of Expected Realizable Value. Drawing on the model, we can symbolically define a person's expected realizable value as

$$E(RV) = \sum_{t=1}^{n} \left[\frac{\sum_{i=1}^{m} R_i \cdot P(R_i)}{(1 + r)^t} \right] \tag{2}$$

where all symbols have the same meaning as in Expression (1). The difference between these two expressions is that the service states include the state of exit ($i = m$) in the latter expression but not in the former. Recall that by definition the variable expected realizable value is the present worth of the services an organization actually expects to derive from an individual during the person's anticipated tenure in the organization. Conceptually, it is the product of conditional value and the probability that the person will maintain organizational membership.

Relation Between the Variables. A person's expected conditional and realizable values can be equal if, and only if, the person is certain to remain in the organization throughout his or her expected service life. If the probability of turnover exceeds zero, expected conditional value must exceed realizable value, as shown in Table 7-1. This table illustrates the calculation of these measures for an individual in an insurance company, assuming an expected service life of one year. As the table shows, the probability of exit is 0.10. To calculate expected conditional value, the probabilities of occupying each position must be transformed, so that their sum is 1.00. The transformation simply involves dividing each individual probability by the sum of the probabilities of occupying the three positions (0.10 + 0.50 + 0.30 = 0.90). For example, the conditional probability of occupying the position of office adjuster is 0.11 (0.10/0.90). Thus the difference between the person's expected conditional and realizable value in the example is $1,110 ($11,270 - $10,160). This is, of course, attributable to a probability of turnover of 0.10.

Table 7-1

ILLUSTRATION OF CALCULATION OF EXPECTED CONDITIONAL AND REALIZABLE VALUE

I. Expected Conditional Value

(1) Service States	(2) Expected Service State Values	(3) Conditional Probabilities of Occupying Each State	(4) Product (2) X (3)
Office adjuster	$ 7,800	.11	$ 860
Claims examiner	9,700	.56	5,430
Senior examiner	15,100	.33	4,980
Expected Conditional Value			$11,270

*II. Expected Realizable Value**

(1) Service States	(2) Expected Service State Values	(3) Realizable Probabilities of Occupying Each State	(4) Product (2) X (3)
Office adjuster	$ 7,800	.10	$ 780
Claims examiner	9,700	.50	4,850
Senior examiner	15,100	.30	4,530
Exit	0	.10	0
Expected Realizable Value			$10,160

*Probability of exit = .10.

Application of the Stochastic Rewards Valuation Model

To apply this model in an actual organization it is necessary to define a set of service states, derive a measure of the value of each state, and estimate an individual's expected service life and the probabilities that the individual will occupy each service state at each point during his or her expected service life. The basic problem involved in applying this model in real organizations is the difficulty of obtaining valid and reliable data inputs of the value of a service state, a person's expected tenure, and the probabilities of occupying states at specified times. The problems of measuring each of these elements of the model are discussed below.

Measurement of Service State Values. Ideally, the appropriate measure of the value derived when an individual occupies a specific service state for a time period is the discounted future earnings contributed to the firm (or what accountants call *economic value*). In principle, this can be measured by either the price-quantity method or the income method. The *price-quantity method* involves determining the product of the price per unit of human services and the quantity of expected services. For example, in a CPA firm, we can obtain measurements of the product of a person's "net chargeable hours" to clients and his or her applicable billing rate. This is a measure of the gross contribution to profit that the individual makes. (We must, of course, deduct payments to the individual for salary to derive a measure of his or her net contribution.) The *income method* involves forecasting the expected earnings of a firm and allocating them between human and other resources and further allocating them among specified people.

In human capital intensive organizations (service organizations such as aerospace, CPA, and advertising firms), the problems of measuring service state values are relatively small. However, there are many organizations in which it is very difficult, if not impossible, to obtain a measure of a service state's value by either the price-quantity or the income methods. In these companies, we may use a surrogate or proxy measure of a service state's value such as compensation. The use of surrogates is described in the next section. As an alternative approach, we may use transfer pricing as a means of developing the service state values. A *transfer price* is an internally designated price for the exchange of goods or services within an organization.

Measurement of Expected Service Life. The model uses a valuation period equal to a person's expected service life. Service life is influenced by many factors, including the individual's natural life expectancy, his or her health and emotional state, the organization's retirement policies, and the person's interorganizational mobility. Since these factors cannot be known with certainty, we must measure the individual's service life probabilistically. We refer, therefore, to *expected service life,* meaning the mathematical expectation of service life.

There are two ways to measure a person's expected service life: by using historical experience to develop actuarial predictions and by subjective forecasts of future probabilities. Both methods were described in Chapter Six.

Measurement of Mobility Probabilities. A critical input required to apply the stochastic rewards valuation model is the human resource mobility probabilities or transition probabilities. These probabilities can be measured or derived by two methods: actuarial prediction and subjective prediction.

The actuarial method, based on the use of Markov transition matrices, is described here. The subjective method is described in Chapter Nine, where we deal with a case study of the application of the model in a CPA firm.

There are three steps involved in the calculations of the mobility probabilities:

Step 1: The firm must compile a data base of personnel hires, transfers, promotions, and exits for all employees.

Step 2: The data must be aggregated to determine the transitions from one side to another.

Step 3: The mobility or transition probabilities can then be derived from the frequency count of the state-to-state transitions.

Each of these steps will now be explained in greater detail.

The organization must first compile a historical data base dealing with the movement of people in the firm. This data base must indicate the person's positions in the firm during each year since he or she was hired. As shown in Table 7-2, for example, Mr. A. Abel was hired during 1982 as an assistant accountant. In 1983 he was still an assistant. In 1984 he became a "semisenior," and he left the firm in 1985.

From this historical data base (Table 7-2), the number and types of state-to-state transitions made during each year must be counted. (Counting may be done manually or, preferably, with a computerized data base program.) Table 7-3 shows a state transition matrix. The matrix

Table 7-2

HISTORICAL DATA BASE FOR HUMAN RESOURCES

Person	*1982 Job Level*	*1983 Job Level*	*1984 Job Level*	*1985 Job Level*
Abel	Assistant	Assistant	Semi senior	Exit
Barry	Senior	Senior	Exit	Exit
Cando	Semi senior	Senior	Senior	Senior
Donenow		Assistant	Assistant	Exit

Table 7-3

FREQUENCY COUNT OF TRANSITIONS

	Year T + 1				
Year T	*Senior*	*Semisenior*	*Assistant*	*Exit*	*Total*
Senior	30	0	0	20	50
Semisenior	20	20	0	20	60
Assistant	0	20	10	10	40
Exit	0	0	0	40	40

shows that there are four possible service states: assistant, semisenior, senior, and exit. The matrix has the same set of rows and columns. It should be interpreted as follows: How many people who were in a given state in year T will be in any of the four service states in the next year ($T + 1$)? For example, there were fifty seniors in year T; of those fifty, thirty will still be seniors and twenty will exit by year ($T + 1$). Similarly, there were forty assistants in year T; of these, ten will still be assistants, twenty will be semiseniors, none will be seniors, and ten will exit by year ($T + 1$). Thus the transition matrix shows the frequency of state-to-state transitions during a time period (for example, one year).

The mobility probabilities can be directly derived from the frequency count of the transitions. Suppose the frequency count is as in Table 7-3. (Note that this count represents totals from several years of historical data.) These frequencies are transformed into probabilities, as shown in Table 7-4. For example, the probability that a staff assistant will make the transition to a semisenior in the following year would be 20/40 or 50 percent. Similarly, there is a 25 percent (10/40) chance that the person will remain a staff assistant and a 25 percent chance of exit

Table 7-4

TRANSITION MATRIX

	Year T + 1			
Year T	Senior	Semisenior	Assistant	Exit
Senior	60%	0	0	40%
Semisenior	33%	33%	0	33%
Assistant	0	50%	25%	25%
Exit	0	0	0	100%

(or turnover rate) from the firm. The transition matrix in this example would be as shown in Table 7-4.

Summary of the Model's Application. As described above, the application of the stochastic rewards valuation model is a five-step process:

Step 1: Define the service states that people will occupy, including the state of exit.

Step 2: Calculate the transition matrix required to determine the probabilities of movement from state to state in the organizational hierarchy.

Step 3: Measure the value of each service state to the firm.

Step 4: Determine the discount rate or cost of capital.

Step 5: Calculate the values of human resources by using the data derived in steps 1 to 4.

Illustration of the Model. This section illustrates the application of the stochastic rewards valuation model described above. The illustration continues our example of the value of a staff member in a CPA firm. A CPA firm is being used as the context for illustration because it is an example of a human capital intensive firm, because an example in this type of firm can be generalized to other human capital intensive firms including all professional organizations (law firms, engineering firms, and the like), and because such firms typically have most of the data available to apply the model in a relatively straightforward manner. The model can also be applied in other types of firms, but additional procedures must be developed to facilitate the application.

We shall use the audit department of a CPA firm for this illustration. The firm has seven service states, as shown in Table 7-5. These states include the state of exit as well as six other job classifications an individual may occupy.

Each of these states has a gross and net service state value. The *gross service state value* is the amount of the expected chargeable hours of services to be rendered by the staff member to clients multiplied by that person's billing rate. It is a measure of the gross revenue contribution of the individual to the firm and thus involves treating the individual as a revenue center. The *net service state value* is the difference between gross service state value and the cost of the individual to the firm. In principle, this difference is attributable to the process of having a person provide services to clients. Net service state value is, therefore, a measure of an individual as a profit center. The gross and net service state values for our illustrative CPA firm are shown in Table 7-6.

To determine a person's value to a firm, it is necessary to calculate probabilities that the individual will occupy each possible service state at specified future times. This information is derived from the transition matrices described above. The information concerning the expected mobility of Robert Walker, one of the firm's staff, is shown in Table 7-7. To calculate a person's value to a firm, we also need information about the cost of money or discount rate. Assume that the firm's current cost of capital is 10 percent.

Given this information, it is feasible to calculate an individual's expected conditional and realizable value using the formulas shown previously in Expressions (1) and (2). The results of these calculations show that expected conditional value is $72,682 and expected realizable value is $48,611. The expected opportunity cost of turnover is $24,071, the difference between Expressions (1) and (2).

Other Models for Individual Valuation

Because of the difficulties encountered in measuring a service state's value, it may not always be feasible to apply the stochastic rewards valuation model described above. This suggests the need for other methods of measuring a person's expected conditional and realizable values.[3]

Table 7-5

SERVICE STATES

State Number	State Name
7	Exit
6	Partner
5	Manager—heavy*
4	Manager—light*
3	Senior
2	Staff—heavy*
1	Staff—light*

*The labels "heavy" and "light" refer to degrees of experience.

Table 7-6

SERVICE STATE VALUES

State Number	State Name	State Values Gross	State Values Net
7	Exit	–0–	–0–
6	Partner	60,000	15,000
5	Manager—heavy	45,000	14,000
4	Manager—medium	35,000	13,000
3	Senior	25,000	12,000
2	Staff—heavy	20,000	11,000
1	Staff—light	15,000	10,000

NOTE: These data are hypothetical.

Table 7-7

MOBILITY PROBABILITIES FOR ROBERT WALKER

Individual #1	States						
Year	1	2	3	4	5	6	7
1	.5	.3	0	0	0	0	.2
2	.1	.7	0	0	0	0	.2
3	0	.7	.1	0	0	0	.2
4	0	.4	.4	0	0	0	.2
5	0	.1	.6	0	0	0	.3
6	0	0	.4	.3	0	0	.3
7	0	0	.1	.5	0	0	.4
8	0	0	0	.5	0	0	.5
9	0	0	0	.3	.2	0	.5
10	0	0	0	0	.2	0	.8
11	0	0	0	0	0	0	1.0

There are several possible alternative bases for monetary measures of an individual's value to a formal organization: original cost, replacement cost, current cost, compensation, and opportunity cost. In the subsequent discussion, we will assess the feasibility of using each of these measures to develop a model for individual valuation.

Original Cost. The primary advantages of using original cost as a surrogate measure of an individual's value are that it would be consistent with the conventional accounting use of cost as an implicit surrogate of value, and it seems feasible to measure the costs actually incurred in acquiring people.[4] The primary limitation is that except at the date of acquisition, the cost incurred to acquire a resource may bear no significant relation to its value today.

Replacement Cost and Current Cost. The need for a surrogate measure of individual value is derived from the need for a surrogate input in human resource investment decisions and in the evaluation of human resource utilization. For these uses, replacement and current costs have greater relevance than historical costs because they are, by definition, more closely related to the market's current assessment of an asset's economic value. Indeed, R. J. Chambers once went beyond the argument that current costs are a surrogate measure of value and suggested that current cost *is* the market's estimate of economic value: "The price currently ruling for producer's goods is the market's assessment of the present value of expected income flows from their use at the present level of prices, for all potential users of such goods."[5] He argued that, barring imperfections in the market, current cost and value will be equal.

In principle both current cost and replacement cost reflect an individual's value to a formal organization. Drawing upon Chambers, *current cost* or *market value* is, by definition, the market's assessment of an individual's value as a resource. *Replacement* or *reproduction cost* is similar to current cost, except that it represents the sacrifice to be incurred by a single firm, rather than the market as a whole, in replacing its resources.

In choosing between replacement cost and current cost as possible surrogates, there is one factor of critical importance: the feasibility of obtaining observations of the surrogate in the real world. In other words, is it possible to obtain empirical measures of the surrogate? Since ours is not an economy typically engaged in the purchase and sale of people, measures of an individual's market value are generally not directly established.* Similarly, measures of an individual's replacement cost are not typically available. It is feasible, however, to develop measures of an individual's replacement cost. Thus it seems likely that replacement cost may ultimately be used as one possible surrogate measure of an individual's value. However, it will not be feasible to obtain measurements of current cost.

A primary limitation of replacement cost, like historical cost, is that it may not bear a significant relation to a resource's value. It is necessary, therefore, to empirically assess its validity as a value surrogate. In a 1969 study, I attempted to test the notion that replacement cost can be used as a surrogate measure of a person's value. I developed a replacement cost model for individual valuation. In addition, Hekimian and Jones have stated that although replacement cost is almost an ideal method of asset valuation, it suffers from two limitations:

1. Management may have some particular asset which it is unwilling to replace at current cost, but which it wants to keep using because the asset has a value greater than its scrap value. There must be some method of valuing such an asset.
2. There may be no similar replacement for a certain existing asset.[6]

Compensation. Compensation measures such as salary or commissions are another possible surrogate. *Compensation* is the price paid for the use of units of human services. On the surface, these measures purport to represent an organization's assessment of the value of an individual's services, and, therefore, they are potentially useful to develop a surrogate valuation model. However, compensation measures are sometimes inadequate value surrogates because they, too, may not necessarily bear a significant relationship either to an individual's value or to his or her current productivity, an element of conditional value. Since performance measures (which are used to measure productivity) are often utilized as a basis for compensation, an individual's salary may not reflect the dimensions of his or her value that are not included in the performance measures. In addition, salary may not reflect an individual's promotability. A variety of other factors such as organizational compensation policy, wage and salary structures, and the presence or absence of unions also affect the extent to which compensation measures

*There are exceptions, such as market value measures for professional athletes in football, baseball, and basketball.

such as salary accurately reflect individual value. Since in a specified instance compensation measures may or may not be satisfactory surrogates of individual value, we must, as with other measures, empirically assess their validity.

In spite of these possible limitations, there have been a few proposals to use a person's capitalized future salary as a surrogate measure of his or her value to a firm. This approach involves forecasting a person's future salary and discounting these expected earnings to their present worth.

Roger Hermanson proposed using the present value of the stream of future wage payments to people, adjusted by a performance efficiency factor, as a proxy measure of their value to a firm.[7] He calls this the "adjusted present value method." More descriptively, it might be termed the "adjusted discounted future wage method." This method is presented in Technical Appendix 7-1.

Baruch Lev and Aba Schwartz also proposed the use of compensation as a surrogate measure of a person's value.* Recognizing that the general economic valuation model presupposes a perfect knowledge of future income streams associated with a resource, they choose to measure a person's value to a firm in terms of his or her expected earnings. Thus the value of a person is the present value of his or her remaining future earnings from employment.[8] The Lev and Schwartz model is summarized in Technical Appendix 7-2.

Opportunity Cost. Another possible surrogate measure of a person's value is opportunity cost. *Opportunity cost* is the value of an asset in an alternative use. It is measured by the amount of net cash inflows that must be sacrificed in order to direct a resource from one use to another. Thus it is the value of an opportunity forgone. In the case of an individual, the opportunity cost is the value forgone by allocating the person to one job rather than to another.

The Hekimian and Jones method of applying the concept of opportunity cost to value people proposes to establish the values of people by establishing an internal labor market in a firm through the process of competitive bidding. Under their method, all managers of investment centers would be encouraged to bid for any scarce employee they want. According to Hekimian and Jones, "the manager who is

*Lev and Schwartz do not distinguish between the conditional and realizable dimensions of a person's value and implicitly use the term *value* to refer to *conditional value* as defined in Chapter Six.

successful in acquiring the service of a bid-for employee includes his bid price in his investment base. The benefit to the winning bidder is the increased profit he can earn with the service of that scarce employee." They suggest that only certain scarce employees should be valued in this manner, but that "employees of the type that can be hired readily from the outside should not be regarded as a scarce resource and should not, therefore, either be subject to a bid or form part of the asset base of the investment center."[9]

One of the key questions involved in the application of the opportunity cost concept to human resource valuation is: What procedure should be used by the manager to determine the amount to bid for a specified person? In principle, the manager should base his or her bid upon the present value of the differential earnings expected to be contributed by the addition of a human resource; unfortunately, the manager has no simple means of doing this. Indeed, this is precisely the reason for developing surrogate measures of a person's value! Consequently, there is a good deal of circularity in proposing to use the opportunity cost concept as a surrogate measure of an individual's value.

Validation of Surrogate Valuation Models. It is not sufficient to assert that there is an identity or even close correspondence between the true unknown economic value of individuals and surrogates such as replacement cost, compensation, or other proxy measures, and, having made this assumption, simply to utilize the purported surrogate in place of measures of value. Instead, these assertions should be reviewed as testable hypotheses. In these terms, the research question posed is: What is the relation between S_i and an individual's value to a specified organization? (S_i refers to the set of i possible surrogate measures of individual value.)

In one study [cited in the annotated bibliography (Flamholtz, 1969)] I attempted to assess the convergent and discriminant validity of compensation, replacement cost, and performance measures as surrogates of an individual's value to an organization.* The principal finding of the study was that certain measures of replacement cost, as well as compensation and performance measures, each possess convergent and

***Convergent validation* refers to the method of confirming a new measure of a given construct by assessing its agreement with independent measures of the same construct. *Discriminant validation* involves assessing the independence of a measure with respect to other measures from which it is intended and expected to differ.

discriminant validity as surrogates of individual value. The results were consistent for two independent samples (claims personnel and salespeople). Thus we have some assurance that the results of the study may well be generalizable and are not attributable to an unidentified spurious factor in a single sample.

Valuation of Groups

In principle, the value of a group is merely the sum of the value of the individuals comprising that group. Thus theoretically we can merely aggregate the value of individuals as measured by the stochastic rewards valuation model to calculate a group's value. However, the value of a group may not be equal to the sum of the values of the individuals comprising it. One major reason for the differential may be synergism. Thus we must develop methods for the valuation of groups per se; it is not valid merely to apply methods for individual valuation to group valuation.

Definition of Group. The term *group* can be defined in many ways, but it basically has two different connotative meanings. First, it represents, according to conventional usage, any collection of n people, where n exceeds 1. In other words, two or more people constitute a group. The term also has a sociological meaning. In this sense, it refers to a collection of people who *perceive* themselves to be a group; that is, they share a group identity. Thus the group represents a system—a so-called *human organization.*

These two notions of what constitutes a group have important implications for human resource accounting. For example, consider two groups of industrial workers in a tire manufacturing plant. One "group" merely consists of five individuals who have been assigned a joint task for a day. The other "group" consists of five people who have previously worked together and function as an effective team. In this situation it is quite likely that the latter group will be more productive than the former. The latter group is, in other words, more valuable than the former, because it is a true human organization. In this chapter, we shall use the term *group* in its sociological sense to refer to a true human organization. Human organizations range from face-to-face work groups, such as laboratory technicians or maintenance workers, to more complex groups such as management. Also included in this definition is the total group that constitutes a business enterprise. It is in this sense that a firm is a human organization.

Types of Groups. In business organizations there are several types of groups. One way of thinking about these groups is in terms of their organizational classification. For example, there are work groups, departments, plants, and divisions. Another way of thinking about groups is whether they comprise an expense center or a profit center.

In an *expense center,* inputs are measured in monetary terms, but no attempt is made to measure outputs in monetary terms. Expense centers typically render services to other subunits of an organization. For example, the personnel department is an expense center. Its expenditures for recruitment and training are measured in monetary terms, but its outputs are not measured.

In a *profit center,* both inputs and outputs are measured in monetary terms. For example, a division that is responsible for both manufacturing and sales constitutes a profit center.

This distinction is important for the valuation of groups because, in principle, it ought to be feasible to apply the normative stochastic rewards model to profit centers; by definition, *profit* is the principal measure required by economic valuation. In contrast, it will be necessary to employ surrogates for expense centers because, by definition, there is no measurement of their output or services in monetary terms.

Methods for Valuation of Profit-Center Groups. There has been relatively little research on the problem of measuring a group's value to an organization. Consequently, there is no well-developed normative model for group valuation. However, a few possible approaches to the problem have been suggested, including three that might be used to value groups constituting profit centers: the economic value approach, the unpurchased goodwill method, and the human organizational dimensions method. These methods are described below.

The Economic Value Approach. In principle, a resource's value is equal to the present worth of the future services it can be expected to provide. Theoretically, then, the value of a group of people should be determined by the present worth of their future services.

Drawing upon this notion, Brummet, Flamholtz, and Pyle have proposed that groups of human resources should be valued by estimating their contribution to the total economic value of the firm. This involves forecasting the firm's future earnings, discounting the earnings to determine the firm's present value, and allocating a portion to the human resources based upon their relative contribution. They suggest that one measure of the relative contribution of human resources to the value of the firm is the ratio of investment in human resources to total resources.

This approach is reputed to be used in the insurance industry to value sales forces at the time of mergers or sales of firms.[10]

To increase our understanding of this approach, we shall examine a simple illustration: Assume that the Automotive Parts Manufacturing Corporation has $15 million in assets, including $5 million in human assets. The firm's forecasted future earnings, discounted to their present worth, total $24 million. Table 7-8 shows the calculation of the economic value of human resources based on these data. Since human resources constitute one third of the firm's total assets, one third of the firm's value is allocated to them. Thus the value of the firm's human assets is $8 million (one third of $24 million).

Table 7-8

AUTOMOTIVE PARTS MANUFACTURING CORP.
ILLUSTRATION OF THE ECONOMIC VALUATION METHOD

1. Ratio of human to total assets:

$$\frac{\$5{,}000{,}000 \text{ (Human Assets)}}{\$15{,}000{,}000 \text{ (Total Assets)}} = 1/3$$

2. Present value of firm's expected future earnings: $24,000,000
3. Portion of firm's value allocated to human resources:

   (1) · (2) = $8,000,000

The Unpurchased Goodwill Method. Another proposed method of economic valuation is what Hermanson calls "the unpurchased goodwill method."* This approach is based on the argument that "the best available evidence of the present existence of unowned resources is the fact that a given firm earned a higher than normal rate of income for the most recent year.[11] In other words, Hermanson is proposing that supranormal earnings are an indication of resources not shown on the balance sheet, such as human assets. However, he has limited his search for supranormal earnings to the prior year because his method of valuing human resources is explicitly intended for use in published corporate

*This method was first purposed in Hermanson's pioneering doctoral dissertation. See Roger H. Hermanson, "A Method for Reporting All Assets and the Resulting Accounting and Economic Implications" (Ph.D. dissertation, Michigan State University, 1963). See also Roger H. Hermanson, *Accounting for Human Assets.*

financial statements rather than internal organizational uses. Given this intended use, any method must meet the test of "objectivity." Thus, Hermanson ruled out any attempt to apply economic valuation to its ultimate since this would be subject to the uncertainty involved in any forecast of future events. If applied to this degree, the method would involve forecasting future earnings and allocating any excess above normal expected earnings to human resources.

To take a simple illustration, assume that three firms comprise a given industry. Table 7-9 presents the data required to calculate the unpurchased goodwill of each firm: the amount of owned assets, net income after taxes, and the ratio of net income to total owned assets (excluding human assets). Table 7-9 shows that the average return earned on the industry's investment is 10 percent. The rates for the three firms comprising the industry vary from 5 percent (Firm B) to 20 percent (Firm A). Firm C is earning the average rate for the whole industry (10 percent).

Under Hermanson's proposed method, the differential earnings are allocated to human resources. His rationale is that "since the owned assets lying idle would earn nothing, the differences in rates of earnings can be ultimately traced to the efforts of the operational assets.* Also,

Table 7-9

UNPURCHASED GOODWILL

The Oly-Gopoly Industry

	Firm			*Total*
	A	*B*	*C*	*Industry*
Total owned assets	100,000	200,000	300,000	600,000
Net income	20,000	10,000	30,000	60,000
Ratio of net income to total owned assets	20%	5%	10%	10%

*According to Hermanson: "Assets are scarce resources (defined as services but grouped by and referred to as agents), operating within the entity, capable of being transferred by forces within the economy, and expressible in terms of money, which have been acquired as the result of some current or past transaction, and which have the apparent ability to render future economic benefits." He distinguishes between *owned assets* (which include all scarce resources, legally or constructively owned by the entity, that have a separate determinable market value and therefore could conceivably be directly used or converted for the payment of its debts) and *operational assets* (which consist of all scarce resources operating in the entity that are not owned). See Hermanson, *Accounting for Human Assets,* Occasional Paper No. 14 (East Lansing: Bureau of Business and Economic Research, Michigan State University, 1964), pp. 4–5.

since it can be argued that operational assets are primarily made up of various human resources, these two terms will be used interchangeably hereafter."[12] In other words, Hermanson concluded that human assets are the source of differential earnings rates and therefore measured their value in terms of such earnings differentials as those shown in Table 7-10.

As seen in Table 7-10, the differential earnings rates have been used to capitalize human assets. Since Firm A has a positive $100,000 variance from normal earnings, its imputed human assets are $100,000 (capitalized earnings). Since Firm C's earnings are equal to the industry average, no imputed human assets have been capitalized. Since Firm B's earnings are less than the industry average, we infer that its human resources are relatively inefficient and ineffective. The effect of this inefficiency is that the firm has $100,000 of assets that are earning no return on investment. Thus on paper Firm B has $200,000 of assets; however, in reality, its effective assets are $100,000 ($200,000 total owned assets less $100,000 of negative human assets).

This method has certain limitations. First, it only recognizes human assets when a firm's earnings exceed an industry's average earnings. Yet even the firm with so-called normal earnings must have some human resources, but these are ignored under this method. Thus since the method limits recognition of human resources to the amount of earnings in excess of normal, there is no recognition of the human resource *base* required to carry out "normal" operations. Consequently, human assets are understated by this method. Second, the method as described by Hermanson only uses the actual earnings of the prior period as a basis for calculating human assets. This is done to ensure that human resources no longer of significance to the firm are not included.*

The Human Organizational Dimensions Method. This method is based on the premise that the value of people, like that of all other resources, should be measured in terms of the present worth of their expected contribution to a firm's future earnings. The method attempts to overcome the difficulties involved in forecasting the firm's future earnings as well as to take into account the contribution made by human resources to such earnings.

This valuation approach is derived from the Likert–Bowers model of a group's value to an organization (examined in Chapter Six). The

*Because Hermanson's method is intended for external reporting to investors and others, he has emphasized verifiability and has chosen to employ only prior year's earnings. However, the method may be modified to use forecasts of future earnings, which are more relevant for managerial purposes.

Table 7-10

CALCULATION OF HUMAN ASSET VALUE BY THE UNPURCHASED GOODWILL METHOD IN THE OLY-GOPOLY INDUSTRY

	Firm		
	A	*B*	C
1. Total owned assets	$100,000	$200,000	$300,000
2. Normal net income at 10%	10,000	20,000	30,000
3. Actual net income	20,000	10,000	30,000
4. Variance	10,000	(10,000)	–0–
5. Human assets (capitalized at 10%)	100,000	(100,000)	–0–

approach is based on the hypothesized relationship among the so-called causal, intervening, and end-result variables. In other words, it is argued that causal variables such as managerial leadership and organization structure are determinants of organizational processes such as motivation, communication, decision making, coordination, and control. Taken together, the causal and intervening variables describe the internal state of the organization as a human system. They determine the productive capability of the system. Thus the causal variables influence the intervening variables, which, in turn, determine the organization's end results.

Drawing upon this conceptualization, Likert and Bowers have described a five-step method for computing a monetary estimate of the expected *change* in the value of a human organization.

1. The dimensions of the human organization are measured at specified time periods in nonmonetary terms. These "measurements" are the scaled responses of people to questionnaire items (such as the survey of organizations described in Chapter Eight). The measurements are typically made on a Likert scale, also described in Chapter Eight.
2. The scores (the scaled responses to questionnaire items) are then standardized by statistical methods to take into account the degree of variability of the set of responses.
3. The difference between two standardized scores from one period to the next is then calculated. This difference or change is called a *delta*. The delta represents the change in an index of specified dimensions of the human organization.
4. Given knowledge of the relation between a specific index (or a composite of all indices) and specified end results, the next step is

to estimate the expected future change in end-result variables from observed present changes in dimensions of the human organization. Specifically, for a given variable the delta is multiplied by the coefficient of correlation between that variable and an end-result variable. This provides an estimate in standard scores of the anticipated change in the end-result variable attributable to a change in the human organizational dimension hypothesized to cause that change.

5. The final step is to translate the standard scores into the measuring units of the end-result variables.[13]

In principle, this approach can be used to predict changes in any end-result variable, monetary or nonmonetary. For those measured in monetary terms (sales, costs), the estimated changes will be in monetary terms. "A single 'best' estimate can be computed," as Likert and Bowers state, "by using a multiple coefficient of correlation based on all of the coefficients of correlations between the causal variables and an index combining the scores for all of the performance variables."[14]

To increase our understanding of this approach, we shall examine a simple example. Table 7-11 shows hypothetical responses to a typical questionnaire item from the survey of organizations at two points in time. It also shows the method of calculating a score for the questionnaire item.

Once the scores for each time period have been calculated, the delta or change is simply the difference between the two scores. For example, the difference between scores for the first and second time period for the question shown in Table 7-11 is +0.15 (4.05 - 3.90).

The final step in calculating an estimated change in the value of human resources by this method is to multiply the delta by the coefficient of correlation between the dimension of the human organization and the end-result variable. If, for example, there is a correlation of 0.6 between these two variables, then estimated change in the end-result variable attributable to the change in the dimension of the human organization is 0.09 (0.15 multiplied by 0.6). Assuming that the end-result variable were "net profit," then net profit would be expected to increase in proportion to the 0.09 change in the human organizational dimension. If we assume, for example, that each 0.10 change in this human organizational dimension results in a $10,000 change in net profit, then the 0.09 change would be expected to increase net profits by $9,000.

Table 7-11

CALCULATION OF CHANGE IN A GROUP'S VALUE BY HUMAN ORGANIZATIONAL DIMENSIONS METHOD

Illustrative Questionnaire Item:
"How receptive are those above you to your ideas and suggestions?"

Response Categories	Response Scale	% Response at Time Period No. First	Second
To a very great extent	5	20	25
To a great extent	4	50	55
To some extent	3	30	20
To a slight extent	2	0	0
To a very slight extent	1	0	0
		1.00	1.00
Weighted mean score:*		3.90	4.05

*Calculated $X_i \cdot P(X_i)$, where X_i = Response scale for the i categories and $P(X_i)$ = % response in each category. Thus the mean score at the first time period is calculated: $(5 \cdot 20) + (4 \cdot 50) + (3 \cdot 30) + (2 \cdot 0) + (1 \cdot 0) = 3.90$.
SOURCE: James C. Taylor and David G. Bowers, *The Survey of Organizations: A Machine-Scored Standardized Questionnaire Instrument* (Ann Arbor: Institute for Social Research, 1972). Copyright © 1967, 1968, 1969, 1970, 1972 by the University of Michigan. Reprinted by permission.

This method is an interesting and potentially valuable approach to the monetary measurement of a group's value. However, there are certain difficulties involved in applying the method. First, it only permits measurement of the *change* in the value of a human organization; it does not facilitate valuation of the human organization as a whole. This is simply because the method is based on changes. Of course, this is simply a limitation of the method's applicability and not a defect in the method per se.

There are also some technical difficulties in the proposed method. Likert and Bowers use the coefficient of correlation to determine the degree of change in the end-result variable attributable to change in an intervening variable. This overestimates the relationship between the variables; instead, they should use the coefficient of determination or the square of the coefficient of correlation. In addition, the validity of their method depends on the validity of performance measures available, as

Likert and Bowers themselves recognize. Yet there are many problems involved in obtaining valid and reliable performance measurements. Third, the method can only be used to generate monetary measurement when financial performance data are available. (It might be used with surrogates such as compensation, but its validity when used with surrogates must be assessed empirically.) Finally, even if financial performance measurements are available, it is necessary to establish a relationship between changes in human organizational dimensions and changes in financial measures. For example, how do we know that a change of 0.10 in the human organizational dimensions will produce a change of $10,000 in net profits?

In spite of these difficulties, this method is worthy of future research. At present, however, its validity and feasibility have not yet been established.

Methods for Valuation of Expense-Center Groups. In profit centers, the principal inputs for the valuation of groups are typically available. However, where groups constitute expense centers, surrogate measures are required for their valuation. Application of the major surrogates to group valuation is discussed below.

In principle, the idea of capitalizing a person's salary and using it as a surrogate measure of human value can be applied to the valuation of groups as well as individuals. By this method, the value of the group would be estimated as the sum of the value of the individuals comprising the group.

This is not an ideal method of group valuation because of the possible effects of synergy. (The group's value may differ from the sum of the values of the individuals comprising it.) Still, the method may provide a valid first approximation or "ball-park estimate" of a group's value to a firm. At present, there has been no attempt to assess the validity of this method for the valuation of groups.

Another method of valuing groups involves using replacement cost as a surrogate. By definition, the *replacement cost* of a group is the sacrifice that would have to be incurred today to recruit, select, hire, train, and develop a substitute group capable of providing a set of services equivalent to that of a group presently employed.

*In a personal communication, Rensis Likert expressed his belief that the method is feasible where reliable and valid measurements of the coefficients of determination are available, and he indicated that the method has been applied in such instances.

The replacement of a group is a good example of the effects of synergism. Assume that the research department of a large chemical manufacturer has been organized and operating productively for some time. If one member of the research team were to leave, the firm would have to incur certain costs of recruitment, selection, and training to replace the person. In addition, the replacement would undergo a period of socialization and familiarization with other team members and the peculiarities of the research being conducted. This process would result in some opportunity costs of lost productivity of the team during the period of breaking in the new person. Now consider the effects if two members of the team were to leave and had to be replaced. Predictably, this might cause relatively greater disruption than the loss of a single person, but the remaining team members would probably still fit the replacements into the existing system. However, if the entire team resigned and had to be replaced, the company would no longer have an existing human organization. In this case, the firm would have to replace not only individuals per se but an existing sociotechnical system.

The economic importance of ongoing sociotechnical systems is well recognized in industry. For example, Alfred P. Sloan justified a substantial amount paid for "goodwill" when General Motors purchased Adam Opel A.G. by stating that: "For us to build or equip for manufacturing a new factory in Germany would require at least two or three years before operations could be put on an efficient and profitable basis. The amount paid Opel in excess of net assets would be returned within the time required to start from the ground up."[15] In such situations, it seems reasonable that a substantial portion of the value of a going concern is attributable to the existence of a well-developed human organization.

Expanding upon this premise, Likert attempted to obtain subjective estimates of the cost of replacing the human organizations of various firms. For example, he asked "some of the key managers" of an equipment manufacturer the following question:

> Assume that tomorrow morning every position in the firm is vacant, that all of the present jobs are there, all of the present plants, offices, equipment, patents, and all financial resources but no people. How long would it take and how much would it cost to hire personnel to fill all of the present jobs, to train them to their present level of competence, and to build them into the well-knit organization which now exists?[16]

According to Likert, the response was: "It would take us several years and it would cost us at least twice our annual payroll to build the human organization that we have today." Likert notes that their payroll is $350 million. Thus the managers believed it would cost an estimated $700 million to replace their human organization.[17]

Although one can question the validity of these managers' subjective estimates, the basic point is that replacement cost can be used as one possible surrogate measure of a group's value. At present, however, the replacement cost valuation methods that have been developed are for individuals rather than groups.

Another possible surrogate measure of a group's value is original cost. Conceptually this method would involve estimation of the original costs to recruit, select, hire, train, and develop a firm's existing human organization. The major difference between using original costs to value individuals and groups is the necessity of estimating the cost of developing an effectively functioning group. This is the cost of developing effective communication, decision making, coordination, and other organizational processes commonly referred to as "teamwork." However, at present, there are no methods of measuring the costs of developing organizational processes.

This section has examined some possible methods for the valuation of groups. Each method might be required if synergism exists and if the value of the group exceeds the value of the individuals comprising it. However, the stochastic rewards valuation model generally provides the optimal measure of a group's value to an organization. As a minimum, it will provide a conservative measure of a group's value in most situations. For all practical purposes, therefore, this method should be favored over the other methods described.

Valuation of the Total Human Organization

The problem of valuing the total human organization is virtually identical with the problem of valuing groups. If the organization is profit-oriented, the problem is essentially one of applying the concepts and methods that are appropriate for valuing profit centers. If it is a nonprofit organization, the problem is to apply the methods appropriate for an expense center.

Summary

This chapter has treated the problem of measuring the value of an organization's human resources in monetary terms. It has focused on the development of measures of value for individuals, groups, and the total human organization.

The problem of measuring an individual's value can be conceptualized as a stochastic process with rewards. The anticipated difficulties involved in applying this normative model suggest the need for surrogate measures. There are several possible surrogates, including original cost, replacement cost, compensation, and opportunity cost.

This chapter also treated the problem of valuing groups of human resources. We have examined various methods for valuation of groups constituting profit centers and expense centers. The methods for valuing profit centers include the economic value method, the unpurchased goodwill method, and the human organizational dimensions method. Methods for valuation of expense centers include capitalization of compensation, replacement cost valuation, and original cost valuation. The problem of valuing the total human organization was also considered.

As noted above, I have concluded that the optimal method for valuation of individuals, groups, and the total human organization is the stochastic rewards valuation model.

Case 7-1: National CPAs

National CPAs is a major international firm of certified public accountants. Harold K. Jones, the firm's national personnel partner, became interested in the idea of accounting for the firm's human resources after reading a few articles on the subject. He decided to experiment with the application of a stochastic rewards valuation model to his firm's personnel.

Jones first identified seven service states that personnel could occupy in the firm, as shown in Table 7-12. He then calculated the gross and net values of each service state. *Gross service state value* was assumed to be equal to the product of the average billing rate multiplied by average chargeable hours of personnel in the given service state. For example, the billing rate of an audit partner was $60 per hour and the partner was expected to generate approximately 1,000 "chargeable hours" (hours chargeable to clients). *Net service state value* was the difference between gross value and the person's compensation. For example, a partner with a gross value of $60,000 and a compensation of $45,000 had a net service state value of $15,000 (his expected annual contribution). The service state values at National CPAs are shown in Table 7-13.

Table 7-12

SERVICE STATES

State Number	State Name
7	Exit
6	Partner
5	Manager—heavy*
4	Manager—light*
3	Senior
2	Staff—heavy*
1	Staff—light*

*The labels "heavy" and "light" refer to degrees of experience.

Table 7-13

SERVICE STATE VALUES

State Number	State Name	State Values: Gross	State Values: Net
7	Exit	–0–	–0–
6	Partner	60,000	15,000
5	Manager—heavy	45,000	14,000
4	Manager—medium	35,000	13,000
3	Senior	25,000	12,000
2	Staff—heavy	20,000	11,000
1	Staff—light	15,000	10,000

NOTE: These data are hypothetical.

To experiment with the application of the stochastic rewards valuation model, Jones selected five subjects. He then estimated the probabilities that these staff members would occupy each possible service state during the period each was anticipated to remain in the organization. These probabilistic estimates are shown in Table 7-14. For example, individual 1 is expected to have a probability of 0.5 of occupying state 1, a probability of 0.3 of occupying state 2, and a probability of 0.2 of occupying state 7 during the coming year.

Having compiled these data, Jones was ready to calculate estimates of the value of these five members of his professional staff. He assumed that the cost of money was 7 percent per annum.

Table 7-14

MOBILITY PROBABILITIES

Individual #1				*States*			
Year	*1*	*2*	*3*	*4*	*5*	*6*	*7*
1	.5	.3	0	0	0	0	.2
2	.1	.7	0	0	0	0	.2
3	0	.7	.1	0	0	0	.2
4	0	.4	.4	0	0	0	.2
5	0	.1	.6	0	0	0	.3
6	0	0	.4	.3	0	0	.3
7	0	0	.1	.5	0	0	.4
8	0	0	0	.5	0	0	.5
9	0	0	0	.3	.2	0	.5
10	0	0	0	0	.2	0	.8
11	0	0	0	0	0	0	1.0

Individual #2				*States*			
Year	*1*	*2*	*3*	*4*	*5*	*6*	*7*
1	0	0	0	0	0	1.0	0
2	0	0	0	0	0	1.0	0
3	0	0	0	0	0	1.0	0
4	0	0	0	0	0	0	1.0

Individual #3				*States*			
Year	*1*	*2*	*3*	*4*	*5*	*6*	*7*
1	0	0	.8	0	0	0	.2
2	0	0	.9	0	0	0	.1
3	0	0	0	.5	0	0	.5
4	0	0	0	.5	0	0	.5
(pattern in year 4 continued years 5–15)							

Individual #4				*States*			
Year	*1*	*2*	*3*	*4*	*5*	*6*	*7*
1	0	.9	0	0	0	0	.1
2	0	.9	0	0	0	0	.1
3	0	.5	0	.4	0	0	.1
4	0	.2	0	.7	0	0	.1
5	0	0	0	.8	0	0	.2
6	0	0	0	.7	0	0	.3
7	0	0	0	.6	0	0	.4
8	0	0	0	.5	0	0	.5
9	0	0	0	0	.7	0	.3
10	0	0	0	0	.9	0	.1
11	0	0	0	0	0	1.0	0
12	0	0	0	0	0	1.0	0
13	0	0	0	0	0	1.0	0
(pattern continued to year 40)							

Individual #5				*States*			
Year	*1*	*2*	*3*	*4*	*5*	*6*	*7*
1	.6	0	0	0	0	0	.4
2	.5	0	0	0	0	0	.5
3	.2	0	0	0	0	0	.8
4	0	0	0	0	0	0	1.0

Questions

1. Compute the expected conditional value of the five staff members using Expression (1) shown on page 199.
2. Compute the expected realizable value of the five staff members using Expression (2) shown on page 199.
3. What are the major factors that explain the differences in the expected conditional and realizable value of these staff members at National CPAs?

Case 7-2: Barter Automotive Products Limited (B)

Barter Automotive Products Limited has national coverage in the automotive supply industry. By the end of 1968 the Toronto branch had grown to be very profitable. The population of the city of Toronto and surrounding area was expanding rapidly and was going to require more extensive service. Barter had to choose between enlarging the present branch or subdividing Toronto into two separate branches. A decision was made to divide the city and area into two distinct distribution centers.

The existing branch was retained in its present location in the east end of Toronto to service the growing Oshawa-Whitby area as well as eastern metropolitan Toronto. The other branch was located in the west end of Toronto to service western metropolitan Toronto and the burgeoning Oakville-Hamilton markets. Barter designated the two branches as Toronto-East and Toronto-West. Toronto-West is managed by the former assistant sales manager for the original Toronto branch.

The operating results and financial positions of the two branches for the years ended December 31, 1969 and 1970, are presented in Tables 7-15 and 7-16.

Barter was extremely disappointed with the results turned in by the Toronto-West branch. They were seriously considering reconsolidating the two branches. During the discussion of this possible consolidation they commented on the large new sales volume that they had been able to generate due to the opening up of a second branch. They realized that if the consolidation were to occur, some of this volume probably would be lost to competitors. Because they wished to avoid this possibility, they decided to have an analysis performed on the Toronto operations. Since management was pleased with the previous effort of the Corwin Consulting Group, they decided to engage Corwin to conduct the study of the Toronto branches.

Note: This is a slightly modified version of a case prepared by W. Daryl Lindsay. It is printed with the permission of the author.

Table 7-15

INCOME STATEMENTS FOR TORONTO BRANCHES

	Toronto-East December 31		Toronto-West December 31	
	1969	1970	1969	1970
Sales	$1,600,000	$2,000,000	$1,200,000	$1,800,000
Cost of sales	910,000	1,070,000	750,000	1,000,000
Gross margin	690,000	930,000	450,000	800,000
Selling and administrative expenses	290,000	430,000	390,000	710,000
Net income before income taxes	400,000	500,000	60,000	90,000
Income taxes	200,000	250,000	30,000	45,000
Net income	$ 200,000	$ 250,000	$ 30,000	$ 45,000

Table 7-16

BALANCE SHEETS FOR TORONTO BRANCHES

Current assets:				
Cash	$ 10,000	$ 10,000	$ 10,000	$ 10,000
Accounts receivable	160,000	255,000	120,000	180,000
Inventory	80,000	150,000	60,000	90,000
Total current assets	250,000	415,000	190,000	280,000
Warehouse, net	450,000	390,000	400,000	390,000
	$650,000	$805,000	$590,000	$670,000
Accounts payable	$150,000	$205,000	$ 90,000	$170,000
Due to head office	500,000	600,000	500,000	500,000
	$650,000	$805,000	$590,000	$670,000
Return on investment	30.8%	31.1%	5.1%	6.7%

The Problem. Corwin identified the situation in Toronto as being similar to the problems faced by both Alberta Snowmobiles, Ltd., and Montana Snowmobiles, Inc.* However, this situation was unique in that the Toronto-West branch had been started in 1969 with only the branch manager having had any experience with Barter's operations. The Toronto-East branch comprised, primarily, salespeople from the original Toronto branch. The Toronto-West branch was still in the process of developing a cohesive sales force and would be incurring large expenditures for this purpose for a number of years. The Toronto-East branch, on the other hand, had already developed a solid sales force. Unfortunately, they had not maintained sufficient records to indicate the

*See Case 3-4 for a discussion of Albert Snowmobiles, Ltd., and Montana Snowmobiles, Inc.

actual amounts they had expended on developing their human resources to the present stage.

Valuation of Human Assets. Mike Martin of the Corwin Consulting Group recognized the uniqueness of the Toronto problem. He decided to employ an outlay cost approach to determine the current cost of the sales force of the Toronto-West branch. However, to determine the current worth of the Toronto-East sales force he decided to utilize some form of present-value approach.

To value the human assets of the Toronto-East branch, Martin considered a present-value concept utilizing the following three decision factors:

1. Future wage payments for the next five years
2. Discount rate based on the rate of return on owned assets in the economy for the most recent year
3. The company's efficiency ratio—the firm's rate of return in relation to the average rate of return for the industry

He believed that there would be a meaningful correlation between salespeople's salaries and value to the company, since the salespeople's remuneration was dependent on performance (sales less costs, including credit losses, incurred in making sales). Martin therefore believed that this method would be a reasonable approach for determining the economic value of the sales force of the Toronto-East branch.

Together with the Toronto-East branch manager and the vice-president–finance of Barter, he was able to determine amounts representing expected total remuneration to salespeople, as shown in Table 7-17.

The most recent report of the Dominion Bureau of Statistics indicated that the average rate of return on owned assets in the economy was 8 percent in both 1969 and 1970. The reported rate of return for the industry was 24 percent in 1969 and 20 percent in 1970. Using the branches' original statements, Martin therefore computed efficiency ratios of 31/24 in 1969 and 31/20 in 1970. He prepared the data to compute the economic value of Toronto-East's human resources, as shown in Table 7-18.

Since the Toronto-West branch was still attempting to develop and strengthen its sales force into a cohesive unit, Martin thought that an outlay cost concept would be a realistic approach to valuing the human resource assets.

Table 7-17

EXPECTED SALESPEOPLE'S COMPENSATION

Toronto-East Branch

Year	*Estimated Compensation*
1970	$ 70,000
1971	80,000
1972	90,000
1973	100,000
1974	110,000
1975	120,000

Table 7-18

TORONTO-EAST
CALCULATION OF ECONOMIC VALUE OF HUMAN RESOURCES

8% Discount Factor	*Expected Remuneration*		*Present Value of Remuneration*	
	1969	*1970*	*1969*	*1970*
.926	$ 70,000	$ 80,000	$ 64,820	$ 74,080
.857	80,000	90,000	68,560	77,130
.794	90,000	100,000	71,460	79,400
.735	100,000	110,000	73,500	80,850
.681	110,000	120,000	74,910	81,720
			$353,250	$393,180

Economic Value = Present Value X Efficiency Ratio

1969: $\$353,250 \times \frac{31}{24} = \$456,300$ (rounded to $450,000).

1970: $\$393,180 \times \frac{31}{20} = \$609,400$ (rounded to $600,000).

A detailed analysis of the Toronto-West records for the past two years yielded the information with regard to human resources shown in Table 7-19. Martin proposed correcting entries to capitalize the human resources.

Because the Toronto-West branch was still in the development stage, Martin was of the opinion that the synergistic component of human asset value would be equivalent to the amount of amortization. He therefore did not recommend amortizing human assets at this time.

Corwin's Report to Management. The consultant's report to management included the financial statements shown in Tables 7-20 and 7-21. The branches' returns on investment based on these revised

Table 7-19

INVESTMENTS IN HUMAN ASSETS BY TORONTO-WEST

Year	*Description*	*Expenditure*
1969	Start-up costs incurred	$60,000
	Training, familiarization, and development costs	20,000
		$80,000
1970	Start-up costs incurred	$30,000
	Training, familiarization, and development costs	60,000
		$90,000

Table 7-20

INCOME STATEMENT

	Toronto-East December 31		*Toronto-West December 31*	
	1969	*1970*	*1969*	*1970*
Sales	$1,600,000	$2,000,000	$1,200,000	$1,800,000
Cost of sales	910,000	1,070,000	750,000	1,000,000
Gross margin	690,000	930,000	450,000	800,000
Selling and administrative expenses	290,000	430,000	310,000	620,000
Net income before income taxes	400,000	500,000	140,000	180,000
Income taxes (1)	200,000	250,000	30,000	45,000
Net income	$ 200,000	$ 250,000	$ 110,000	$ 135,000

(1) Toronto-West's taxable income estimated to be:

	1969	*1970*
Net income before income taxes	$140,000	$180,000
Less capitalization of human resources	80,000	90,000
Taxable income	$ 60,000	$ 90,000

(Assumed effective income tax rate of 50%.)

statements are shown in Table 7-22. The report recommended maintaining both branches. It stated that operating results were good considering the enlarged asset bases.

Questions

1. Do you think the approaches used by the consultant to value the Toronto-East branch and the Toronto-West branch were sound? Explain.

Table 7-21

BALANCE SHEET

	Toronto-East December 31		Toronto-West December 31	
	1969	*1970*	*1969*	*1970*
Current assets:				
Cash	$ 10,000	$ 10,000	$ 10,000	$ 10,000
Accounts receivable	160,000	255,000	120,000	180,000
Inventory	80,000	150,000	60,000	90,000
Total current assets	250,000	415,000	190,000	280,000
Warehouse, net	400,000	390,000	400,000	390,000
Human resources	450,000	600,000	80,000	170,000
	$1,100,000	$1,405,000	$670,000	$840,000
Accounts payable	150,000	205,000	90,000	170,000
Due to head office:				
Current	500,000	600,000	500,000	500,000
Capital	450,000	600,000	80,000	170,000
	$1,100,000	$1,405,000	$670,000	$840,000

Table 7-22

REVISED CALCULATION OF RETURN ON INVESTMENT

	Toronto-East		Toronto-West	
	1969	*1970*	*1969*	*1970*
Net income	$ 200,000	$ 250,000	$110,000	$135,000
Total assets	$1,100,000	$1,405,000	$670,000	$840,000
Rate of return	18.2%	17.8%	16.4%	16.1%

2. What, if anything, should Barter's management do on the basis of the data provided by the consultant?

Case 7-3: Retail Development Corporation Limited (A)

Retail Development Corporation Limited (RDC) is a public company engaged solely in retail store and shopping center development. The basic objective of the company is to assist major retail chain stores in locating and developing their new store sites. Once a site has been found and legal ownership of the property established, RDC in conjunction with the store's management designs the building and plans the layout including fixtures, merchandise displays, customer and merchandise logistics, maintenance and service facilities, and security. RDC also arranges to supervise the actual construction of the project. Due to the nature of its operations, RDC is primarily composed of highly skilled individuals. The company is divided into a head office and two operating divisions: Eastern and Western. Each division has a division manager and is staffed by a number of engineers, architects, interior designers, realtors, lawyers, financiers, and accountants.

The directors of RDC recognized that they employ highly skilled and very mobile people. Since the company's primary investment is in its personnel, the management has made concerted efforts, at all times, to develop and motivate the employees. In 1967 head office management engaged the Corwin Consulting Group to aid them in ascertaining the current value of this essential asset group.

The consultants recognized that the level of earnings achieved by an organization is generally the function of the way it manages and utilizes both its physical and human assets. However, in the case of RDC the physical assets are negligible and are considered to have an insignificant effect on earnings. The consultants therefore reasoned that if they were able to isolate and account for all changes in earnings caused solely by variations in general business conditions, they should be able to determine the relationship between the system of managing human assets and the level of earning generated by each division. They further assumed that once they discerned a meaningful correlation between those behavioral variables influenced by management and the trend in earnings, they would be able to forecast future earnings. Corwin proposed to determine the current value of each division's human assets by discounting the predicted earnings at an appropriate discount rate.

Since Rensis Likert has advanced a behavioral variables method of estimating the current value of a firm's human enterprise, Corwin decided to review his approach. Likert proposes to measure the present value of human resources by ascertaining the relationship among causal, intervening, and end-result variables.* These three variables were defined in Chapter Six.

Malcolm Forsyte, a social scientist associated with the Corwin Consulting Group, modified a questionnaire originally developed by Likert to obtain information regarding certain causal and intervening variables in each division of RDC. The characteristics he chose to assess include: motivational forces, communication processes, interaction-influence systems, decision-making processes, goal-setting procedures, control processes, and performance characteristics (productivity, quality of work, and so on).

Note: This is a slightly modified version of a case prepared by W. Daryl Lindsay. It is printed with the permission of the author.

*This approach is described in Chapter Eight.

The intent of each question was to inform Forsyte whether or not the management system utilized in each division could be deemed to be authoritarian, abdicratic, or supportive. He hypothesized that the level of earnings could be correlated over a period of time with the management system employed by the division, higher level of earnings being associated with a supportive management system. That is, as a management system approaches the supportive method over a period of time a higher level of earnings should be achieved and maintained.

To facilitate analysis, the questionnaire was scaled along a continuum from 1 to 15. That is, an individual question is assigned a value between 1 and 15 depending upon how a respondent answers the question. After all the questions are answered by each manager and subordinate interviewed, an arithmetic mean is computed. If the mean happens to be 5 or below, the management system is designated as being authoritarian. If the mean is greater than 5 but less than or equal to 10, the management system is considered to be abdicratic. If the mean turns out to be greater than 10, the management system is deemed to be supportive.

During the period March 15, 1967, to December 31, 1969, Forsyte performed measurements of the selected causal and intervening variables for the two operating divisions by having each manager and his subordinates complete the questionnaire quarterly. The consultants considered three years to be an adequate period of time for relatively stable relationships to develop or for a series of relationships to complete their entire cycle. After this time lapse they believed they had sufficient information to relate the causal and intervening variables' measurements to the earnings of the divisions. Corwin applied a linear regression analysis to determine a relationship among the causal, intervening, and earnings end-result variables. The consultants further refined the statistical analysis procedures to the point where they were reasonably assured they could estimate the future earnings of each division based upon its present scores on the causal and intervening variables. Their supposition was that these expected earnings would reveal the earning power of each division's human resources at the time of measuring the causal and intervening variables. At the same time they recognized that the estimated level of earnings might not be attained until subsequent periods. The analysis of the questionnaire and the accounting records yielded the data shown in Tables 7-23 and 7-24.

Corwin applied the method of least squares to the data. Although a multiple regression approach will permit a more sophisticated analysis,

Table 7-23

WESTERN DIVISION MANAGEMENT SYSTEM AND EARNINGS

Date of Measurement		*Results*	
Management System	*Quarterly Earnings*	*Management System (X)*	*Quarterly Earnings (Y) (000's)*
9-30-66	3-31-67	12.4	62
12-31-66	6-30-67	12.4	63
3-31-67	9-30-67	12.5	65
6-30-67	12-31-67	12.6	66
9-30-67	3-31-68	12.8	68
12-31-67	6-30-68	13.1	70
3-31-68	9-30-68	13.4	72
6-30-68	12-31-68	13.6	75
9-30-68	3-31-69	13.6	74
12-31-68	6-30-69	13.9	74
3-31-69	9-30-69	14.2	75
6-30-69	12-31-69	14.2	75

Table 7-24

EASTERN DIVISION MANAGEMENT SYSTEM AND EARNINGS

Date of Measurement		*Results*	
Management System	*Quarterly Earnings*	*Management System (X)*	*Quarterly Earnings (Y) (000's)*
9-30-66	3-31-67	12.5	120
12-31-66	6-30-67	12.7	120
3-31-67	9-30-67	13.2	121
6-30-67	12-31-67	13.8	123
9-30-67	3-31-68	14.0	123
12-31-67	6-30-68	14.1	123
3-31-68	9-30-68	14.2	123
6-30-68	12-31-68	14.2	124
9-30-68	3-31-69	14.2	124
12-31-68	6-30-69	14.3	125
3-31-69	9-30-69	14.3	125
6-30-69	12-31-69	14.3	126

a simple regression analysis was employed since a composite measurement score had been developed. The analysis was performed on a basis of a six-month lag between a change in the management system score and any change in earnings. In real life, the time lag may extend to a number of years. The following linear equations ($y^* = a + bx$) were derived for each division:

$$\text{Western: Quarterly earnings} = -21.415 + 6.906(X) \quad (1)$$
$$\text{Eastern: Quarterly earnings} = +85.13 + 2.747(X) \quad (2)$$

The management system for each division was predicted to be at the 14.3 level on the measurement scale. By utilizing the linear equations derived above, the consultants forecasted the annual earnings of each division to be at an estimated level of $300,000 for Western and $500,000 for Eastern. Because the industry sought a return on investment of at least 10 percent, this rate was used to calculate the asset value. The resulting calculations disclosed the estimated values of the human assets to be $3,000,000 at Western and $5,000,000 at Eastern.

Table 7-25 shows the return on investment for each division for 1970, as prepared by the head office.

Table 7-25

DIVISIONAL RETURN ON INVESTMENT

	Eastern Division	*Western Division*
Current estimated value of human resources	$5,000,000	$3,000,000
Net income	$ 750,000	$ 240,000
Return on investment:		
Actual	15%	8%
Target	10%	10%

Questions

1. Do you think that the approach used by the consultant to value the branches' human assets was sound? Explain.
2. How might this approach be improved?

Case 7-4: Retail Development Corporation Limited (B)

In December 1970, the Retail Development Corporation (RDC) held an annual meeting to review past operations and plan for the future. During the course of the annual meeting among various head office officials and division personnel, including the two division managers, the Western manager estimated that he could improve his net income by $280,000 in 1971. To do this, however, he said he would need to obtain a ten-person team of engineers, architects, and interior designers presently employed by the Eastern division. The Eastern division manager replied that his profits would diminish by $200,000 if he were to lose these people. His reasoning was based on the additional hiring and training costs his division would have to incur to replace the team it would lose.

The head office officials liked the idea of increasing income by $80,000. However, they were perplexed as to how to arrange the transfer of personnel and still give equitable treatment to each division manager. They decided to engage Mike Martin of the Corwin Consulting Group to formulate a reasonable solution to the problem.

Mike Martin recognized that it was a case of attempting to determine how one should go about allocating scarce resources to achieve optimum economic benefit for the total company. He decided to recommend an opportunity cost approach based on a competitive bidding method. Martin's plan was to develop a range of alternative bid prices rather than a single price for the group of people who might be approached about transferring to the West.

Martin's report to the management of RDC contained the data shown in Table 7-26. The report explained these data in the following general manner:

Table 7-26

CALCULATED VALUE OF HUMAN ASSETS TO EACH DIVISION

	Eastern Division	*Western Division*
Current estimated value of human resources	$5,000,000	$3,000,000
Net income	750,000	240,000
Return on investment:		
Actual	15%	8%
Target	10%	10%
Expected net income with addition of ten men	–	520,000
Expected net income after loss of ten men	550,000	–
Maximum bid to meet target return on marginal investment	2,000,000	2,800,000
Maximum bid to meet target return on total investment	2,500,000	2,200,000

Note: This is a slightly modified version of a case prepared by W. Daryl Lindsay. It is printed with the permission of the author.

1. The Western division manager could bid up to $2,200,000 for the ten people to meet his target rate of return. That is, 10 percent of $5,200,000 = $520,000. Of course, since he is currently earning 8 percent, any bid up to $3,500,000 will result in an improvement in his present rate of return (8 percent of $6,500,000 = $520,000). However, since the investment in the ten people only earns an incremental increase in net income of $280,000 he should not bid more than $2,800,000 to maintain his 10 percent target (10 percent of $2,800,000 = $280,000).
2. Since the Eastern division manager estimated that his division's income would decrease by $200,000 if it lost the ten people, he could bid $2,500,000 for their services and still meet his target rate of return of 10 percent. That is, 10 percent of $7,500,000 = $750,000. However, another interpretation of the same bid is that is represents an undertaking of a $2,500,000 increase in the investment base in order to receive an incremental rate of 8 percent or to save $200,000 in income. That is, 8 percent of $2,500,000 = $200,000. On an incremental basis this is below his target rate of return. Accordingly, the division manager may consider that $2,000,000 is a better bid in order to maintain his target return on investment. That is, 10 percent of $2,000,000 = $200,000.

Martin stated that eventually the two division managers will have to bid for the services of the ten people. If the Eastern division manager is the higher bidder, and thus retains the ten people in his organization, he will have to include their increased asset value (the winning bid price) in his division's investment base. On the other hand, if the manager of the Western division is the higher bidder, he will acquire the right to make an offer to the ten people. If they accept the offer, the Western division manager will then increase his division's investment base by the amount of the bid. At the same time, the asset base of the Eastern division will be decreased by the asset amount it had been carrying for the ten people. However, it will have to incur additional investment expenditures in human resources to hire and train new people to replace the ten transferred to the Western division.

Questions

1. Is the approach used by the consultant to value human assets sound? Explain.

2. Should the head office allocate the ten-person team to the Eastern or to the Western division? Explain.
3. Would your decision be different if a transfer of personnel from one division to another were *not* involved? Explain.
4. If the team is transferred, would you compensate the Eastern division? If so, how?

Technical Appendix 7-1: Hermanson's Adjusted Discounted Future Wages Method

In his pioneering monograph, *Accounting for Human Assets,* Roger H. Hermanson proposes using compensation (the present value of the future stream of wage payments to people) as a surrogate measure of a person's value to an organization. Hermanson adjusts this discounted future wage stream by an "efficiency factor" and terms his method "the adjusted present value method"; more descriptively, it might be termed "the adjusted discounted future wages method." This approach to the measurement of human resource value is described below.

Description of the Method. In brief, Hermanson proposes to adjust discounted expected future wage payments to people by what he calls an *efficiency factor.* This factor is designed to measure the relative effectiveness of the human resources of a given firm.

Conceptually, the efficiency factor is a ratio based upon the return on investment derived by the specified firm relative to all other firms in the economy for a specified period. Hermanson supports the use of this ratio by arguing that the differential earnings of a firm are attributable to human resources. Specifically, he states that "since the owned assets lying idle would earn nothing, the differences in rates of earnings can ultimately be traced to the efforts of operational assets. Also, . . . it can be argued that operational assets are primarily made up of various human resources."[18] Thus he suggests that one way to measure the value of human resources is on the basis of their expected compensation adjusted for their efficiency relative to the efficiency of other human resources operating in the economy.

To calculate the efficiency ratio, Hermanson proposes to use a weighted average of the firm's net income during the past five years. The efficiency ratio is calculated by the following expression:

Note: Adapted from Roger H. Hermanson, *Accounting for Human Assets,* Occasional Paper No. 14 (East Lansing: Bureau of Business and Economic Research, Graduate School of Business Administration, Michigan State University, 1964), by permission of the author and publisher.

$$\text{Efficiency ratio} = \frac{5\frac{RF0}{RE0} + 4\frac{RF1}{RE1} + 3\frac{RF2}{RE2} + 2\frac{RF3}{RE3} + \frac{RF4}{RE4}}{15} \qquad (1)$$

where RFO = rate of accounting income on owned assets for firm for current year

REO = average rate of accounting income on owned assets for all firms in economy for current year

RF4 = rate of accounting income on owned assets for firm for fourth year previous

RE4 = average rate of accounting income on owned assets for all firms in economy for fourth year previous

It should be noted that the efficiency ratio weights prior years' earnings. The current year is given a weight of 5, the preceding year receives a weight of 4, and so on. As Hermanson states: "The purpose for doing this is to use more than just one year's performance in the computation of the value of human resources, but at the same time to give more emphasis to recent performance than to past performance."[19]

This efficiency ratio is then used to adjust the present value of expected future wage payments over a five-year period in order to derive a surrogate measure of human resource value. In principle, this method can be applied to value individuals, groups, and the total human organization.

Illustration of the Method. There are three steps to calculate adjusted discounted future wages. The first step is to calculate unadjusted discounted future wage payments for a five-year period, as shown in Table 7-27. This table shows that the present value of future wage

Table 7-27

COMPUTATION OF THE PRESENT VALUE OF A FUTURE STREAM OF PAYMENTS TO HUMAN RESOURCES

Year	*Dollar Amount*	*Present Value of $1 Paid at the End of the Year at 6%*	*Present Value of the Future Payment Discounted at 6% (col. 2 X col. 3)*
1	$100,000	.943	$ 94,300
2	120,000	.890	106,800
3	135,000	.840	113,400
4	140,000	.792	110,880
5	150,000	.747	112,050
	$645,000		$537,430

SOURCE: Roger H. Hermanson, *Accounting for Human Assets,* p. 16.

payments is $537,430. The second step is to calculate the efficiency factor. Assume for purposes of this illustration that the efficiency ratio is 1.4. This means that the human resources of the firm returned a ratio of 1.4 earnings relative to the economy as a whole. The third step is to adjust the discounted wages by the efficiency factor: $537,430 × 1.4 = $752,402. Thus the present value of human resources under this approach would be $752,402.

Discussion of the Method. It should be noted that Hermanson merely presented this method for illustrative purposes to show how compensation might be used as a human value surrogate. The method has certain limitations. First, the valuation period selected is arbitrary. There is no necessary justification for five years; another period might well have been chosen. Second, the efficiency factor concept will be difficult, if not impossible, to apply in the real world. The data are simply not available. Third, the weighting scheme used in computing the efficiency factor is arbitrary. There is no theoretical or empirical justification for these weights. As a result, I believe that the highest level of measurement achieved by this factor is an ordinal level; this means that it will merely permit a ranking of the value of human resources of various firms. It should be noted here that Hermanson was *not* attempting to develop a method for managerial purposes; his concern was external reporting to investors.

In brief, the idea of using compensation as a surrogate for human resource value is sound. However, the method proposed by Hermanson has certain limitations.

Technical Appendix 7-2: Lev and Schwartz's Compensation Model

Lev and Schwartz have argued that the difficulties involved in determining the value of human capital under uncertainty make it necessary to use a person's future compensation as a proxy of his or her value. Based on this premise, they have formulated a model for the measurement of a person's value to a firm using the person's anticipated future earnings from employment as a surrogate measure of his or her economic value. Their model is described below.

Note: This research summary is adapted from Eric Flamholtz, "On the Use of the Economic Concept of Human Capital in Financial Statements: A Comment," *Accounting Review,* January 1972, pp. 148–152, by permission of *Accounting Review.*

The Measurement of Human Capital. According to Lev and Schwartz, "the value of human capital embodied in a person of age τ is the present value of his remaining future earnings from employment."[20] Their valuation model for a discrete income stream is

$$V_\tau = \sum_{t=\tau}^{T} \frac{I(t)}{(1+r)^{t-\tau}} \tag{1}$$

where V_τ = human capital value of a person τ years old
$I(t)$ = person's annual earnings up to retirement
r = discount rate specific to person
T = retirement age

They also state that "strictly speaking, expression (1) is an *ex post* computation of human capital value, since only after retirement is the series $I(t)$ known."[21]

Lev and Schwartz convert their *ex post* valuation expression to an *ex ante* model by replacing the observed (historical) values of $I(t)$ in Expression (1) with estimates denoted $I^*(t)$ of future annual earnings. They also suggest a means of obtaining the estimated future earnings data. According to them, the estimated human capital value of a person τ years old is thus[22]

$$V_\tau^* = \sum_{t=\tau}^{T} \frac{I^*(t)}{(1+r)^{t-\tau}} \tag{2}$$

They also indicate that Expression (2) ignores the possibility of death occurring prior to retirement age and suggest that this factor can be incorporated into the model.[23]

$$E(V_\tau{}^*) = \sum_{t=\tau}^{T} P_\tau(t+1) \sum_{i=\tau}^{t} \frac{I_i{}^*}{(1+r)^{t-\tau}} \tag{3}$$

where $E(V\tau^*)$ is the expected value of a person's human capital and $P\tau(t)$ is the probability of a person dying at age t.

Critique of the Model. A major limitation of the valuation model proposed by Lev and Schwartz is that it ignores the possibility and probability that the individual will exit from the organization for reasons other than death or retirement. Thus the application of the model may significantly overstate an individual's expected service life and, in turn, overstate or inflate the value of human capital. In other words, their so-called measure of the expected value of the person's human capital is actually a measure of the expected conditional value of a person's human capital—it is based on the implicit condition that the person will remain in an organization until death or retirement.

People leave organizations prior to death or retirement for a variety of reasons—both voluntarily and involuntarily. They leave to enter the armed forces, to return to school, to join another organization for a better job, because they are terminated, and so on. They may leave because they are dissatisfied with the organization's pay, promotion opportunities, or general policies. Although the rate of turnover varies from one industry to another and even varies among firms in the same industry, it is not reasonable to ignore this phenomenon.

Given the likelihood of turnover for reasons other than death or retirement, it is necessary to consider not only a person's expected conditional value but also the individual's expected realizable value—the present worth of services actually expected to be derived during the individual's anticipated tenure in the organization. The relations among these variables were shown previously in Figure 6-1.

Another major limitation of their valuation model is that it ignores the probability that people will make role changes during their careers. Lev and Schwartz implicitly assume that an industrial engineer will remain an engineer throughout his expected service life in an organization. This assumption is somewhat unrealistic. People may change the career channel they occupy in an organization one or more times depending upon age, education, skill, situational requirements, and so forth. For example, many young engineers obtain MBA degrees with the intention of ultimately moving into managerial positions—not only in engineering but also in other areas. For such people, engineering may merely be the entry position in an organization. Thus it is necessary for a valuation model to take the likelihood of such role changes into account.

Since the model proposed by Lev and Schwartz does not take this factor into account, it may significantly distort the value of a person's human capital. Consider, for example, a situation in which an individual is likely to transfer between promotion channels—for example, from the position of claims adjuster in an insurance company to the position of salesperson. If the value of a salesperson to the organization differed from that of a claims adjuster, the measure of human capital proposed by Lev and Schwartz would not reflect the difference. In fact, this example is a real one taken from the writer's experience in measuring the value of human resources in a branch of an insurance company.

Lev and Schwartz suggest that this model may be used to value individuals, groups, or the total human assets of an enterprise. However, it may not necessarily be valid simply to aggregate measures of the value of individuals to value groups because of synergism.

EIGHT

Nonmonetary Measurement Methods

This chapter deals with the problem of measuring the value of human resources in nonmonetary terms. It first examines the importance of nonmonetary measurement of human resource value. Next it presents certain concepts and techniques that may be used to measure human resource value in nonmonetary terms. Finally, the chapter discusses how these methods may be applied in measuring human resource value. Specifically, it examines how they can be used to measure the variables contained in the two models of human resource value presented in Chapter Six: the model of the determinants of group value and the model of determinants of individual value.

Importance of Nonmonetary Valuation

Although accounting has historically used money as its basic unit of measurement, an American Accounting Association committee has suggested that there is no reason why money should be the only unit of measurement used in accounting. The committee stated that "there is also no reason why the only measure applied should be 'value' in terms of dollars. It is entirely conceivable that accounting should deal with various measures and do so in a systematic form, say, a vector or number of measures."[1] The committee concluded that the future scope of accounting was likely to include nonmonetary as well as monetary measures.

In human resource accounting, nonmonetary measures of human resource value have significant uses. First, they may be used for decisions that do not require monetary measurements. Layoff decisions, for example, do not require monetary measures of human resource value. Second, nonmonetary measures may also be used as surrogates for monetary measures. For example, a ranking of people according to their conditional value may be used as a surrogate for the monetary measurement of conditional value. Third, nonmonetary measures may be used to predict monetary measures. (See the human organizational dimensions valuation method discussed in Chapter Seven.) Thus it is important to develop valid and reliable nonmonetary methods of measuring human resource value.

Nonmonetary Methods of Valuing Human Resources

There are several concepts and techniques that might be used as nonmonetary measures of human resource value. They include measurements commonly used in personnel research and personnel management. Skills inventories, performance evaluation methods, potential assessments, and attitude measurements are all familiar tools of personnel management, and each can be used as part of a system of accounting for human resources. The concept of *subjective expected utility* may also be used for the nonmonetary measurement of human resource value. These concepts and techniques are described below.

Skills Inventory. One of the most basic techniques for evaluating a firm's human resources is the *capability* or *skills inventory,* an enumeration of the capabilities of organizational members. It may identify education, knowledge, and experience in addition to skills.

The capability inventory represents a nominal level of measurement. It is a classification of people according to their skills and represents a type of balance sheet of the potential services that can be rendered by people at a specified time. A simple skills inventory is shown in Table 8-1.

Performance Evaluation Methods. There are several techniques to facilitate *performance evaluation,* including ratings, rankings, and checklists. The first two are relevant to human resource accounting.

Ratings are methods of assessing a person's performance in relation to a set of scales. For example, a supervisor may rate a person on the extent to which he or she possesses intelligence, technical knowledge, motivation, interpersonal skills, and judgment. The rating

Table 8-1

1971 ABT ASSOCIATES, INC., STAFF CAPABILITIES

	Education			*Years Experience*				
Education and Experience Area	*BS/BA*	*MS/MA*	*Ph. D.*	*0–2*	*3–5*	*6–10*	*11–15*	*16–25*
Social Sciences								
Economics	21	5	3		9	1	1	
Education	7	8	2	11	17	8	2	3
Law			6 (J.D.)		3	1		
Political science	26	8	3	2	1	4	2	
Psychology	4	3	3	2	1	1	1	
Sociology	13	8	2	6	15	5	1	2
Urban studies	2	1			3	1		
Subtotal	73	33	19	21	49	21	7	5
Management Sciences								
Business administration		22		2	5	4	4	
Marketing	1			2	5	2	1	1
Planning				1	5	3	1	
Public relations				2	3	4		
Subtotal	1	22	–	7	18	13	6	1
Physical Sciences								
Computer science	4	3	1	2	5	1	1	1
Engineering	7	4	1		6	5	1	1
Mathematics	3							
Physics	9	2	2		2	1		
Subtotal	23	9	4	2	13	7	2	2
Humanities								
Classics	1							
English	5	1		1	1			
French	2							
Spanish	1							
Fine arts	1				1	2		
History	16	3			2			
Journalism	1	3						
Philosophy	4							
Liberal arts	5	1	0					
Subtotal	35	9	0	1	4	2	–	–
Totals	132	73	23	31	84	43	15	8

NOTE: 24 staff members have training in at least two different disciplines, giving individuals interdisciplinary capabilities.

SOURCE: *Abt Associates, Inc. 1971 Annual Report,* p. 9.

physically consists of a numerical score on these or other characteristics.

Rankings are an ordinal form of rating. By this method, an evaluator ranks people on one or more dimensions. For example, a supervisor might be asked to rank subordinates on their "leadership potential."

Several procedures can be used to obtain rankings. The simplest is merely to rank people on the dimension being studied by selecting the highest, then the next highest, and so on. The *alternation ranking* method is a procedure designed to simplify the judgmental process involved in ranking and, in turn, increase its reliability. Under this method, we first select the person with the highest value, then the person with the lowest value. From the remaining people, we next select the person with the highest value and then the one with the lowest value, and so on. The *paired comparisons* method is a third procedure for deriving a ranking of people from a series of comparisons between pairs of individuals. It requires a comparison of each person with every other person. By a simple scoring technique, a rank ordering may be constructed from the paired comparisons. This method becomes cumbersome when the number of people to be compared exceeds ten. Research on the reliability of the alternation ranking and paired comparison methods shows they are equally reliable. Both are more reliable than the simple ranking method.

Assessment of Potential. Potential assessments are designed to determine a person's capacity for development and promotion. Their aim is to measure the services that people are potentially capable of rendering to an organization.

A major approach to the assessment of potential is a *trait approach.* Under this method, we attempt to identify the traits required for success in a given position and assess the extent to which people possess these traits. The assessment may be made either by judgmental or psychometric methods.

Attitude Measurement. Techniques for the measurement of *attitudes* are designed primarily to obtain information about the tendencies of people to express feelings about some object. By means of attitude surveys, organizations may assess the attitudes of people toward their job, pay, working conditions, or the organization as a whole. Thus the sources of employee satisfaction and dissatisfaction may be identified. For example, a questionnaire may include such statements as "I am often bored with my job." The respondent is asked to indicate the degree to which he or she agrees or disagrees with the statement. The responses may be scaled: (1) strongly agree, (2) agree, (3) undecided, (4) disagree, and (5) strongly disagree. These responses are typically scored by assigning a 5 to the highest or most favorable response, a 4 to the next most favorable response, and so on.

Subjective Expected Utility. The concept of *subjective expected utility* combines two more fundamental notions: utility and subjective probability.[2] *Utility* is the economic concept of subjective value. It is a resource's perceived value to its user. *Subjective probability* is the subjective estimation of an event's likelihood. It is a person's degree of belief in the likelihood of an event.

Psychophysical methods have been developed to measure utility and subjective probability directly.[3] These methods involve procedures for scaling subjective magnitudes. They include paired comparisons, rating methods, and *magnitude estimation*—a scaling procedure that purports to achieve a ratio level of measurement. Magnitude estimation involves assigning numerals to indicate the magnitude of a property or characteristic. Zero means that there is none of the property, while high numerals indicate a great deal of the property. If one object has twice as much of a property as another, its assigned numeral would be twice as high.

Application of Nonmonetary Methods. Each of the concepts and techniques described above can be used to measure human resource value in nonmonetary terms. The next section illustrates how these methods can be applied. First they are applied to measure the variables contained in the models previously described.

Measurement of Individual Value Determinants

Figure 6-10 presented a schematic representation of a model of the variables that determine an individual's value to an organization. In this section, we shall see how each of these variables can be measured in nonmonetary units.

Expected Realizable Value. This is the ultimate component of a person's value to an organization. It can be measured by applying certain personnel evaluation methods. One method is ranking. By this method, an evaluator would rank people according to their expected realizable value to a firm. The evaluator may be a supervisor, a peer, a subordinate, an independent expert, or possibly the person being evaluated. The ranking procedure results in an ordinal measure of people according to their *subjective expected realizable utility*. This is a measure of the gross value of people to a firm. A true measure of their economic value would reflect their net contribution, their gross value less their compensation, and other costs associated with their utilization.

Expected Conditional Value. This is the penultimate component of a person's value to an organization. It can also be obtained by ranking methods. Evaluators can be instructed to rank people according to their conditional value (utility) to an organization. For example, we might ask an evaluator: "Consider the services that each member of your staff can potentially provide to the firm during the next fifteen years. Assuming that they will not leave the firm, rank these people according to their value to the firm during this period. Rank the person with the highest value first and the person with the lowest value at the bottom."

Probability of Maintaining Membership. We can derive the probability that a person will remain in a firm for a specified time from two sources: actuarial probabilities and subjective probabilities. *Actuarial probabilties* can be obtained from the firm's past history; *subjective probabilities* can be derived from managerial judgment.

The firm's experience will indicate the rate of turnover. If we project past experience into the future, we can forecast the probability that people will remain in the firm. One method of doing this is to construct a stochastic model of the organization's mobility process. This stochastic model is based on the notion that people move among the organization's service states in accordance with probabilistic laws. Service states include all organizational positions and the state of exit, which people enter when they leave the organization. The model can be used to determine the probability that a person will make a transition from one state to another. It can be used to predict the probability that a given person will remain in a specified state or will move to other possible states in the future. Historical data are used to derive the transition probabilities, as described previously in Chapter Seven.

The calculation of the transition probabilities under the markovian assumption about mobility is illustrated in Table 8-2.* The data shown are for a hypothetical CPA firm. In this example, we see the probabilities that a staff accountant in 1984 will be a staff accountant, senior, manager, partner, or will have left the firm in 1985, 1986, and so on until 1991. At the end of one year, there is a probability of 0.57 that

*The markovian assumption is that the probability of occupying a specified state is a function of the state currently occupied and is not dependent on the states previously occupied.

Table 8-2

CALCULATION OF MARKOVIAN TRANSITION PROBABILITIES
FOR A STAFF ACCOUNTANT IN A CPA FIRM

	Probability of Occupying Each State at Future Times						
States	*1985*	*1986*	*1987*	*1988*	*1989*	*1990*	*1991*
Staff	.57	.25	.06	.01	0	0	0
Senior	.15	.27	.30	.23	.13	.05	.02
Manager	0	0	.01	.05	.09	.11	.11
Partner	0	0	0	0	0	0	0
Transferred	.03	.05	.06	.07	.07	.08	.08
Exit	.25	.43	.57	.65	.70	.76	.79

he or she will still be a staff accountant and a probability of 0.28 that he or she will have left the firm.

Another technique for obtaining these probabilities is by deriving *subjective probabilities,* which are an expression of the degree of belief that an event will occur. They are a numerical representation of a subjective or judgmental estimate of an event's likelihood.

Subjective probabilities can be measured in various ways. The simplest method is to ask a person to estimate the probability of an event—for example, "What do you think is the probability that you will be promoted next year?" *Magnitude estimation* is another technique used to measure subjective probabilities.[4]

Elements of Conditional Value. There are three hypothesized elements of a person's conditional value: productivity, transferability, and promotability. A great deal of personnel research is concerned with the measurement of these variables under the labels of performance and potential.

Performance refers to the contribution a person has already made in his or her current organizational role. It may be measured by either objective or subjective indicators. Some performance evaluation systems in organizations use objective measures of productivity such as units produced, efficiency, quality, scrap, and ability to meet schedules. Other systems are based on performance appraisals, where supervisors or others assess a person's performance by means of ratings or ranking methods.

Potential refers to the contribution a person is expected to make to an organization in the future. It is a person's potential capability—the potential to occupy positions of greater responsibility and transferability. It can be measured by subjective assessments and psychometric tests.

Subjective assessments of potential are quite common in organizations. Supervisors are asked to rate various personality characteristics such as intelligence, initiative, judgment, and leadership ability. They may also be asked to assess a person's overall promotability and the positions he or she may soon be ready to occupy. In addition, they may be asked which positions would be helpful in enhancing a person's promotability.

Psychometric tests are also commonly used to measure aspects of a person's potential. Tests of intelligence, personality, and aptitude may be used in promotion decisions. The tests may be scored in order to indicate a person's promotability in relation to others.

Satisfaction. This variable can be measured by means of attitude surveys. We can construct a global measure of satisfaction from a questionnaire aimed at determining the satisfaction of employees with their job, pay, supervisor, working conditions, peers, chances for promotion, and so on.

Instrumental Individual Determinants. These determinants consist of two variables: skills and activation level (motivation). A person's skills may be measured at a nominal level by means of a *capability inventory*. This is an inventory of the skills, experience, and education of organizational members.

Motivation may be measured by means of *attitude surveys.* For example, questionnaires may be designed to ask: To what extent do you agree with the following statements:

1. I am usually enthusiastic about my job.
2. I am usually bored by my work.

These questions may be combined to form an index of motivation. Of course, all questions must be tested to assess the validity and reliability with which they indicate the concept being measured. The concept is measured by scaling responses.

Instrumental Organizational Determinants. The primary hypothesized instrumental organizational determinants are a person's role and organizational rewards. Methods of job analysis can be used to measure the content of a job. We know that such job-related factors as stimulus variation, stimulus intensity, and meaningfulness are determinants of a person's activation level. Methods need to be developed to standardize measurement of these factors.

Rewards can be measured by attitude surveys. People can be asked to indicate their perceptions of the magnitude, desirability, and equitability of the organization's reward system.

Measurement of Group (Organizational) Value Determinants

The Likert–Bowers model of the determinants of a group's value to an organization (shown previously in Figure 6-11) tells us what variables to measure as indicators of the value of the human organization. To measure these variables, researchers at the University of Michigan's Institute for Social Research have designed and assessed the validity of an instrument called the *survey of organizations.*[5] The survey of organizations is a questionnaire based on the model's theoretical framework.* It is designed to measure what Bowers and Taylor call "organizational climate." (Likert has termed this the "state of the human organization.")

Organizational climate, as defined by William Evan, "is a multidimensional perception of the essential attributes or character of an organizational system."[6] Organizational climate is thus a concept that refers to organizational members' perceptions of the social-psychological context of the organization in which they exist. It refers to the social-psychological reality of the organization and is hypothesized to influence organizational behavior.

Indicators of Organizational Climate. The variables selected for measurement in the survey of organizations include leadership processes, the character of motivational forces, communication processes, interaction-influence processes, decision-making processes, goal-setting processes, and control processes. To measure these variables as they are perceived by members of an organization, a set of questions was formulated and organized into a questionnaire. The questionnaire contains a core of items designed to tap the causal and intervening

*In fact, the survey of organizations was based on an earlier version of the model (see Rensis Likert and David G. Bowers, "Organizational Theory and Human Resource Accounting," *American Psychologist,* 1969, 24, no. 6, (pp. 585–592), while the present model is based, in part, on the empirical research findings derived from the validation of the survey instrument. See James C. Taylor and David G. Bowers, *Survey of Organizations* (Ann Arbor: University of Michigan, 1972).

Table 8-3

ORGANIZATIONAL CLIMATE ITEMS

7. "To what extent is this organization generally quick to use improved work methods?" (Five-point extent scale)
8. "To what extent does this organization have a real interest in the welfare and happiness of those who work here?" (Five-point extent scale)
9. "How much does this organization try to improve working conditions?" (Five-point extent scale)
10. "To what extent does this organization have clear-cut, reasonable goals and objectives?" (Five-point extent scale)
11. "To what extent are work activities sensibly organized in this organization?" (Five-point extent scale)
12. "How adequate for your needs is the amount of information you get about what is going on in other departments and shifts?" (Five-point extent scale)
13. "How receptive are those above you to your ideas and suggestions?" (Five-point extent scale)
14. "To what extent are you told what you need to know to do your job in the best possible way?" (Five-point extent scale)
16. "How are differences and disagreements between units or departments handled in this organization?" (Descriptive response categories)
24. "Why do people work hard in this organization?" (Descriptive response categories)
27. "To what extent are there things about working here (people, policies, or conditions) that encourage you to work hard?" (Five-point extent scale)

"In general, how much say or influence does each of the following groups of people have on what goes on *in your department*?"

30. "Lowest-level supervisors (foremen, office supervisors, etc.)"
31. "Top managers (president, vice presidents, heads of large divisions, etc.)"
32. "Employees (people who have no subordinates)"
33. "Middle managers (department heads, area managers, etc.)" (Questions 30–33 have five-point extent scales)
34. "How are objectives set in this organization?" (Descriptive response categories)
35. "In this organization to what extent are decisions made at those levels where the most adequate and accurate information is available?" (Five-point extent scale)
36. "When decisions are being made, to what extent are the persons affected asked for their ideas?" (Five-point extent scale)
37. "People at all levels of an organization usually have know-how that could be of use to decision-makers. To what extent is information widely shared in this organization so that those who make decisions have access to all available know-how?" (Five-point extent scale)
38. "To what extent do different units or departments plan together and coordinate their efforts?" (Five-point extent scale)
39. "Which of the following best describes the *manner* in which problems between units or departments are generally resolved?" (Descriptive response categories)
104. "To what extent are the equipment and resources you have to do your work with adequate, efficient, and well-maintained?" (Five-point extent scale)

SOURCE: James C. Taylor and David G. Bowers, *Survey of Organizations: A Machine-Scored Standardized Questionnaire Instrument* (Ann Arbor: Institute for Social Research, 1972). © 1967, 1968, 1969, 1970, 1972 by the University of Michigan. Reprinted by permission of the Institute for Social Research and the authors.

variables contained in Likert's model. Table 8-3 shows a set of twenty-two questions that measure these variables.

The questions are designed to evoke perceptual responses. As Taylor and Bowers state, "they stimulate (or intend to stimulate) the responding participant to orient himself with specific facts and express his opinions as to how he perceives those facts, not whether he 'likes' them or not."[7]

The questionnaire limits the respondent to a set of five response categories, known as the Likert Scale. For example, the respondent is asked to indicate the degree to which he or she agrees or disagrees with a series of statements: "to a very great extent," "to a great extent," "to some extent," "to a slight extent," or "to a very slight extent."

The individual questionnaire items can be combined into indices for each of the variables being measured. Taylor and Bowers have constructed composite indices for various dimensions of organizational climate. Using the method of smallest space analysis, a technique for determining the relationship among several variables, Taylor and Bowers found five distinct and consistent clusters of variables: technological readiness, human resource primacy, communication flow, motivational conditions, and decision-making practices.[8]

The *technological readiness* index is the extent to which equipment, facilities, methods, and procedures are kept adequate, efficient, and up to date. It is a measure of technological capability. *Human resource primacy* refers to the degree of concern for human resources. At the high end of the scale, there is a central concern for human resources. At the low end, the index reflects a climate in which human resources are of secondary importance. *Communication flow* represents the direction of information flows in the organization. It measures the extent of upward, downward, and lateral communication. *Motivational conditions* refers to the major reasons leading employees to work hard and the barriers to motivation caused by interpersonal or interunit conflict. The final index, *decision-making practices,* refers to the character of decision-making processes.

Taylor and Bowers have studied the internal consistency reliability and discriminant validity of the five composite indices of organizational climate. They found that all of the indices except technological readiness have acceptable internal consistency reliability and discriminant validity. They suggest, therefore, that four of the indices may now be used in practice, while the index of technological readiness should not be used until further evidence is obtained.[9]

Reconceptualization of the Model. The survey of organizations was designed to measure the variables that comprise organizational climate. However, the studies by Taylor and Bowers of its validity and reliability led to a reconceptualization of the theory of organizational functioning underlying the measurement instrument. Since the Likert-Bowers model of the determinants of a group's value to an organization is an outgrowth of this same theory of organizational effectiveness, the Taylor-Bowers findings also stimulated a reconceptualization of their model. Thus the revised model (shown previously in Figure 6-11) reflects Taylor and Bowers' findings.[10]

Taylor and Bowers' findings on the validity of the model and the instrument used to measure the model's variables may not be conclusive, as the authors themselves suggest. However, both the model and the survey of organizations are important contributions toward the nonmonetary measurement of human resource value.

Conclusion

Although there is a need for nonmonetary measurement of human resource value, the current state of human resource accounting has not fully developed this measure. Since the need is great, we can expect to see further efforts to develop the nonmonetary measurement of human resource value.

Summary

This chapter has dealt with the measurement in nonmonetary units of the value of human resources. We have examined how each of the models of human resource value presented in Chapter Six can be measured.

Expected realizable and conditional value can be measured by ranking methods. The probability of maintaining membership can be measured by actuarial and subjective probabilities. The elements of conditional value (productivity, transferability, and promotability) can be measured by personnel research and appraisal methods as well as by certain objective measures. Productivity corresponds to measures of performance, and it can be measured by objective indices and by management appraisal. Promotability and transferability can be measured in terms of the measures of potential such as psychometric tests and subjective assessments. Satisfaction can be measured by attitude surveys. Skills can be measured by a capability inventory and motivation can be measured by an attitude questionnaire. A person's role can be measured by job analysis, while rewards can be measured through attitude surveys.

All of the variables contained in the Likert-Bowers model of the determinants of a group's value can be measured by the survey of organizations, an attitude questionnaire. Taylor and Bowers have conducted tests of the predictive validity and the internal consistency reliability of this instrument. Their findings led to a reconceptualization of an earlier version of the Likert-Bowers model and provide a foundation for the development of nonmonetary measurements of a group's value to an organization.

Case 8-1: Glass Products Corporation (A)

Glass Products Corporation, which manufactures glass jars and bottles, operates several plants throughout the United States. In 1971, the company was faced with increased competition, declining sales, increasing costs, and decreasing profitability.

To help remedy the situation, home office management issued instructions to all plant managers to cut manufacturing costs by 10 percent. The instructions were issued in March 1971, and by December the goal had been achieved. For the remainder of the year costs were kept down and profits improved. Plant managers received their regular bonuses for the year.

Questions

1. Do you agree with home office management's decision to instruct all plant managers to reduce manufacturing costs by 10 percent? Why?
2. Can you predict any possible harmful effects of this action? Explain.

Case 8-2: Glass Products Corporation (B)

During the spring of 1972, home office management of Glass Products Corporation again became concerned as costs crept up and manufacturing efficiency ratios deteriorated. When questioned about the

Note: For a description of the company, see Case 8-1.

deteriorating performance, several plant managers cited increased absenteeism, turnover, and poor morale. One plant manager said:

> The morale among the hourly employees and even the foreman is lousy. They have been under continuous pressure for the past year, and now it's beginning to show up. You just can't keep pushing people as hard as we have for as long as we have. I'm afraid some very good men will leave. The economy has turned up and these guys are mobile. If many do leave, it will cost us a helluva lot to replace them, and we won't be operating at normal efficiency for quite some time.

Questions

1. Should home office management have predicted this situation? Explain.
2. Assume that you are on the controller's staff in the home office. Prepare a memo outlining how this problem might have been avoided or at least minimized.

NINE

First-Generation Accounting Systems for Human Resource Value

This chapter presents a case study of an organization (Lester Witte & Company) that was one of the first to apply the concepts and methods discussed in Chapter Seven to develop a system of accounting for the value of its human resources. The study was intended as a research effort, and it is reported here because of its historical interest and because it illustrates the thinking involved in this pioneering application of human resource accounting.

Organizational Background

Lester Witte & Company is a firm of certified public accountants founded in 1924 in Chicago as a local practice. Its clients consist primarily of relatively small and medium-sized companies in a variety of businesses. At the time this resource study was conducted (1971–1972), the firm had offices in several major metropolitan areas in the United States and had also formed an international group. In 1972, its professional staff totaled approximately 275. The largest office was the firm's headquarters, Chicago, with forty professionals.

Each of the firm's area offices was organized according to function, as shown in Figure 9-1. The "auditing and accounting," "tax planning

Figure 9-1

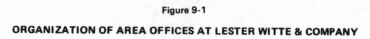

ORGANIZATION OF AREA OFFICES AT LESTER WITTE & COMPANY

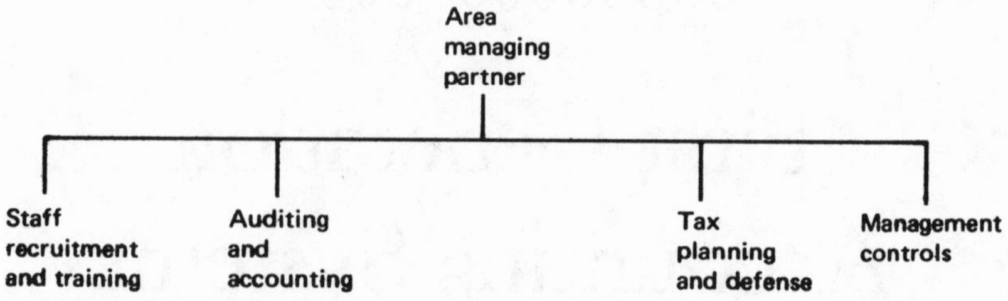

and defense," and "management controls" functions are client service centers. Each is directed by partners who are specialists in the particular service, and each constitutes a profit center. The "staff recruitment and training" function is an internal management service center. It performs the traditional personnel functions of staffing and training as well as the function of organizational development.

Motivation for Human Resource Accounting

What factors led to Lester Witte's interest in developing a system of accounting for the value of its human resources? The firm's interest was largely a product of the same factors that led R. G. Barry to develop its human resource accounting system: the nature of the firm, its managerial philosophy, and certain management information needs that could not be satisfied by the conventional accounting information system.

Nature of the Firm. In a CPA firm, human assets play a greater role than financial or physical assets because the services provided by CPA firms are the product of human rather than physical or financial capabilities. CPAs are trained professionals. The development of a certified public accountant requires several years of formal education and on-the-job training. During this developmental period, the individual is developing his or her own human capital: a set of skills and knowledge. Thus in CPA firms the major resource is truly people, or human capital.

In addition to the human capital that employees bring with them to a firm, all CPA firms make substantial investments in recruiting, selecting, training, and developing people with the expectation of building human capabilities or assets. A firm's investment in human capital is typically a product of both cash outlays and opportunity costs of revenue forgone during a CPA's developmental period.

For a variety of reasons, turnover is relatively high among professional staff in CPA firms. When turnover occurs, valuable human assets can be lost, and firms may have to incur outlay and opportunity costs to replace personnel.*

Given the economic importance of people to CPA firms, any tool that helps management acquire, develop, conserve, or utilize human assets more effectively and efficiently is of great benefit. Witte perceived human resource accounting to be a tool that could potentially help facilitate the management of its human resources in many of the ways discussed previously.

The Firm's Managerial Philosophy. Another major reason for Witte's interest in human resource accounting, especially human resource valuation, was that it seemed to be a logical extension of the firm's managerial philosophy. Their philosophy is closely related to what the late Abraham Maslow called "Eupsychian Management." Both Eupsychian Management and Witte's managerial philosophy are based on the notion of self-actualization. The term *self-actualization* was coined by psychologist Kurt Goldstein. As used by Maslow, it refers to the desire for self-fulfillment, or the tendency for a person to want to become what he or she is capable of becoming. More generally, it is the desire to actualize the potentiality of a person.

Drawing upon the notion of self-actualization, Maslow coined the word *Eupsychia* and defined it as the culture that would be generated by 1,000 self-actualizing people on some sheltered island where they would not be interfered with. It refers, in other words, to an ideal culture that might be created under the most favorable circumstances. Such an ideal culture, Maslow thought, would facilitate the self-actualization of people. Similarly, Maslow saw Eupsychian Management as a managerial philosophy that would create an environment in which people could achieve self-actualization through their work.

Maslow believed that the work lives of people were the central ingredient in achieving self-actualization. In his words:

*It should not be inferred that turnover is to be totally avoided; indeed, CPA firms encourage a certain degree of turnover for several reasons. For example, they often wish to place professional staff with clients. Since former staff are familiar with the CPA firm's procedures, the difficulty of audits is reduced.

> We can learn from self-actualizing people what the ideal attitude toward work might be under the most favorable circumstances. These highly evolved individuals assimilate their work into the identity, into the self, i.e., work actually becomes part of the self, part of the individual's definition of himself.[1]

Thus Maslow saw work, and hence management, as a vehicle to achieve the ends of individuals and organizations simultaneously.

Taking a more formal view of Eupsychian Management, its basic premise is that people can achieve self-actualization via their work. Based on this premise, the central hypothesis underlying Eupsychian Management is that the greater the degree of a person's self-actualization, the greater the person's economic value to an organization. This means that the more an individual has achieved what he or she is potentially capable of becoming, the more valuable the person is to the organization—which implies a mutually dependent relationship between the person and the organization. The more an organization helps people self-actualize, the more it derives benefits from human services. Similarly, the more an individual strives to achieve self-fulfillment through his or her work, the more valuable the person becomes to an organization. In game-theoretical terms, it is a win-win situation.

The Eupsychian hypothesis has been expressed differently in a previous section of this book. In Chapter Six, it was observed that a person might be totally included, partially included, or totally excluded from his or her organizational role. Our hypothesis was that the greater the degree to which the person is included in the role, the greater the individual's satisfaction and the greater his or her value to the organization. This simply means that a person's value is hypothesized to be determined, in part, by the fit between the person and his or her work role. This is essentially what Maslow meant when he stated (in discussing self-actualizing people) that "these highly evolved individuals assimilate their work into the identity."[2]

The role of the Eupsychian manager is to create an organizational environment in which people can achieve the optimal degree of self-actualization and, in turn, their optimal value to the enterprise. More specifically, the task of the Eupsychian manager is to optimize the value of all of an organization's resources: human, financial, and material. In turn, the manager must optimize the value of the firm's human resources. Optimizing human resource value means, in Maslow's terms, creating a

Eupsychian managerial culture—an organizational culture in which people are free to self-actualize. The underlying premise is, of course, that self-actualization will result in the optimal degree of goal congruence between individuals and the social organization as a whole.

Lester Witte's management perceived that human resource accounting might be a helpful tool to implement the firm's managerial philosophy. They saw that it could potentially provide a method of measuring management's progress in appreciating the value of people to the firm. They reasoned that managers could help the organization in two ways: first, by making a contribution to current profitability and, second, by building human assets which, in turn, would contribute to future profitability. Thus they desired a method of monitoring the value of the firm's human resources and its changes over time.

Interestingly, Maslow himself perceived the need for human resource accounting and saw it as an adjunct to Eupsychian Management. In his book *Eupsychian Management,* Maslow discussed the need for human resource accounting:

> The problem for the accountants is to work out some way of putting on the balance sheet the human assets of the organization: that is, the amount of synergy, the degree of education of all the workers in the organization, the amount of time and money and effort that has been invested in getting good informal groups to work together well like a good basketball team, the development of loyalties, the cutting down of hostilities and jealousies, the reduction of tendencies to restrict production, the lowering of the tendency to stay away when mildly sick, etc. This is quite apart from the values of these human assets to the town or city, state, or country, or to the human species.[3]

Thus Maslow clearly saw the linkage between his notion of Eupsychian Management and human resource accounting. He saw it as a need to redefine the concept of profit to reflect such intangibles as human assets.

Limitations of Conventional Information Systems. The third factor contributing to Witte's interest in developing a system of human resource accounting was based on certain limitations of conventional accounting information systems. Witte believed that it could provide information to improve the effectiveness and efficiency with which the firm managed its professional staff.

The firm anticipated two major applications of an operational system of human resource valuation: (1) a means of monitoring the effectiveness of the firm's development and conservation of human assets and (2) a tool to be used in various personnel decisions. Since the firm's managerial philosophy is based on the notion that the value of people must be developed and conserved, it seemed reasonable to ask: Is the firm appreciating, maintaining, or depleting the value of its human assets? The system that was developed was intended to help management answer this question. It was also anticipated that the ability to measure the value of human resources would facilitate a variety of personnel decisions, such as selection, development, placement, and compensation. For example, the firm wanted to base partner profit sharing, at least in part, on the extent to which human assets had been appreciated during a year. In this way, there would be a built-in motivation for the development of human resources on which the long-term profitability of the firm depends. If the value of human resource development is not measured, an office may face a conflict between current and future profitability. If the performance measurement system bases evaluations solely on current profitability, then time devoted to human resource development results in an opportunity cost of current earnings forgone. This may motivate management to emphasize current profitability to the detriment of the future. Thus the measure of human resource value permits the dimension of human asset building to be factored into the firm's performance appraisal system.

The firm was also interested in developing a human resource valuation system because of certain expected peripheral, yet important, benefits. For example, the fact that the value of people was being measured was expected to communicate the firm's belief that people are valuable resources. This is the familiar attention-directing function of measurement systems. Also, the knowledge and skill developed in valuing the firm's human resources were expected to help in assessing the value of professional staffs of merger candidates.

Research Objectives and Scope

Research Objectives. The ultimate objective of this research was to develop a system of accounting for the value of the firm's human resources that satisfied the criteria of validity, reliability, and practicality (feasibility). To accomplish this end, the system needed to be tested by the scientific method to demonstrate its empirical validity. The data used as input and derived as output also needed to be reliable—or at least the degree of their reliability needed to be known. Finally, it had to be feasible (practical) to implement the system at a cost that was less than its anticipated benefits.

Another major research objective was to assess the attitudinal impact of human resource accounting. More specifically, the aim was to determine whether the introduction of human resource accounting concepts and measurements had any effect on the way members of the firm thought about the management of human resources. Does human resource accounting influence attitudes toward managerial policies of recruitment, selection, compensation, development, and allocation?

Scope of Research. The project was conducted using three offices as research sites in order to facilitate a controlled field study. At the time the study was initiated, two of these offices, X and Y, were reasonably comparable in size—both in terms of the number of professional staff and in gross annual billings. In both offices, the system of accounting for human resources was applied and measures of the value of people to the firm were obtained. This information provided a basis of comparison for the data derived at each site.

To test the attitudinal impact of human resource accounting, a longitudinal study was begun. To facilitate this aspect of the research, the third office, Z, served as a control. Although an attitude questionnaire was administered in Z as well as in X and Y, there was no introduction of a human resource accounting system at Z; that is, no attempt was made to measure the value of people at Z.

It was hypothesized that attitudes would change in Offices X and Y as a result of the introduction of human resource accounting. However, attitudes would not change very much in Z, except to the extent that the effects of human resource accounting filter to the rest of the organization. Thus Office Z was intended to furnish a benchmark against which we could judge whether attitudes in X and Y had changed significantly as the result of the introduction of human resource accounting. In other words, it was intended to permit us to test for the so-called Hawthorne effect—change that occurs simply because people react to being part of an experiment. It should also be noted that there were differences in the managerial philosophy of each office. Offices Y and Z were perceived by members of the firm as being much closer in philosophy than either X and Y or X and Z. Thus it seemed that the best comparison for the purposes of assessing attitudinal change would be between Y and Z.

The attitude questionnaire, together with its instructions, is included in Appendix 9-1. This questionnaire was administered at all three offices prior to any attempt to apply human resource accounting. For purposes of the pilot study, only professional staff were included.

The Valuation Model

The method used to value the firm's personnel was based on the stochastic rewards valuation model described previously in Chapter Seven. In brief, the basic premise of this valuation model is that people generate or derive services for an organization as they occupy specified roles and perform the tasks associated with these roles.

Given this model, there are three major dimensions of a person's value to an organization: positional value, expected conditional value, and expected realizable value. *Positional value* refers to the value of a person in the current state he or she occupies. *Expected conditional value* refers to the expected value of a person in the current and future states he or she may occupy, given that he or she will not exit from the firm. *Expected realizable value* refers to the expected value of a person in the current and future states he or she may occupy, taking into account the likelihood of turnover.

As described in Chapter Seven, to measure these three dimensions the following information is required: the period during which a person is expected to render services, the service states he or she is expected to occupy, the value derived by the organization when each state is occupied for a specified time period, and the probability that each state will be occupied during a specified time period. The application of the valuation model at Lester Witte is described below.

Service States. The first step to apply the model is to identify the service states a person may occupy. There are three different kinds of service states: organizational roles, transferability, and exit. *Organizational roles* are simply the states people occupy when they render a given type of services to the firm. An organizational role is not equivalent to a position such as partner; there may be different kinds of partners. *Transferability* refers to the condition in which a person is transferred to a different office. *Exit* refers to the condition in which a person has left the firm. The service states defined in Lester Witte's system are described in Appendix 9-2.

Valuation Period. The valuation period used in the model is the person's expected service life in the firm. This means that the firm is attempting to value a person's expected services for the period he or she is expected to render services to the organization.

Service State Value Measure. The basic notion of a stochastic rewards valuation model is that if an individual occupies a service state for a specified period, the organization derives rewards or earnings. In principle, these rewards may be measured in dollars or other units of service.

A major problem in applying this model at Lester Witte & Company was to determine measures of the value of the service states. The principal difficulty was that the services of all personnel are not typically measurable directly in monetary terms. While some people provide services that are directly measurable in monetary terms, others do not, because there are different types of services provided by people in a business.

There are essentially three different classes of services provided by people in a firm such as Lester Witte & Company: direct revenue production, indirect revenue facilitation, and mixed services. *Direct revenue producers* are people whose primary service involves the production of revenue; sales personnel are direct revenue producers. At Lester Witte, assistant accountants are direct revenue producers. *Indirect revenue facilitators* are persons whose primary service facilitates the production of revenue, but whose primary responsibilities are not for revenue production. Accountants, personnel managers, and purchasing agents are revenue facilitators. In practice, it is not always possible to classify people as either revenue producers or revenue facilitators; certain people provide both types of services. These *mixed service personnel* are people whose services include elements of both revenue production and revenue facilitation. At Lester Witte, many partners are mixed service personnel. Although they do generate revenue, much of their activities are devoted to revenue facilitation activities such as obtaining clients and managing the firm's internal operations.

The existence of these three classes of services poses a problem for human resource valuation: to determine a method of measuring the value of each class. Since our primary objective is monetary valuation, the specific problem is to determine the monetary value of the expected future services of a particular class of services.

At the time this study was conducted, the valuation logic was as follows: For direct revenue producers, services are, by definition, already represented in monetary terms; therefore, their value should be measured in terms of the principal measure of economic value. This is the product of *net chargeable hours* (hours devoted to direct revenue production) multiplied by the applicable *billing rate* to clients.

In principle, it would be appropriate to value all classes of services by this approach: the value of an hour of services multiplied by the total number of hours of services rendered. Unfortunately, there is no predetermined value for the hourly services of indirect revenue facilitators. One possible approach to developing a monetary measure of the value of services provided by revenue facilitators is to develop transfer prices for those services. A *transfer price* is a rate charged for *units of services* rendered in intracompany transactions. It thus establishes the value of services rendered internally in an organization.[4]

There are two different bases for establishing transfer prices: market-based prices and cost-based prices. As Robert N. Anthony has stated: "The ideal transfer price is based on a well-established, normal market price for the identical product or service being transferred, a market price that reflects the same conditions (quantity, delivery, time, etc.) as the product or service to which the transfer price applies."[5] In the absence of market-based prices, transfer prices may be based on costs (standard or actual cost, full cost or variable cost).

In developing its system of human resource accounting, Lester Witte employed transfer prices for indirect service personnel. The transfer pricing subsystem was based on a combination of market and internally negotiated transfer prices.

The need for transfer pricing is not unique to human resource accounting. As stated by Anthony, Dearden, and Vancil:

> When products or services are sold outside the company, the measurement of revenue is relatively easy. For products or services furnished to another unit within the company, however, the problem is difficult, for the company must construct its own substitute for the market mechanism that establishes external value.[6]

Mobility Probabilities. Application of the valuation model also requires measurements of the probabilities that a given person will occupy each possible service state at specified future times. These mobility probabilities can be derived from two sources: historical probabilities, which can be derived by actuarial prediction based on the firm's past experience, and subjective probabilities, which represent degrees of belief about the likelihood of occurrence of future events and can be obtained by using management's judgment.

Both historical and subjective probabilities have certain theoretical advantages and limitations. In fact, there is presently a controversy over which is to be preferred. The primary advantage of historical probabilities is that they are objective, or capable of independent verification, and free from personal bias. Their primary limitation is that they are based on past experience that may not be relevant to present and future conditions. The primary advantage of subjective probabilities is that they represent judgments made in light of expected future conditions. For example, a manager may take into account some significant change in forming his or her judgment about the probability of an event. Their primary limitation is that they are not objective.

As a practical matter, a decision was made at Witte to use subjective probabilities rather than historical probabilities during the initial stages of the human resource accounting system. The use of historical probabilities was rejected because future mobility was not expected to be very similar to past patterns.

The form used to collect the subjective probabilities, together with its related instructions, is shown in Appendix 9-3. The method used to obtain the probabilities is *magnitude estimation.*

The mobility probabilities are clearly a significant element for the measurement of a person's value. It is important, therefore, to determine the degree to which we can rely on them. One method of assessing this element at Witte was to ask the people making the mobility estimates to indicate the degree to which they felt confidence in the validity of the probabilities assigned, as shown in Part II of the mobility assessment form (Appendix 9-3). This provided information on the assessor's confidence in the measurements and, in turn, provided a basis for the decision maker's judgment of their reliability. In time it would be possible to determine who was typically optimistic or pessimistic in making such assessments, and decision makers would then be able to use this information in judging the reliability of the data.

Whenever subjective probabilities are used, it is important to have more than one source of information, and this is being done at Witte.

Alternative Valuation Methods

The firm recognized that it might be difficult to apply this model to value all of its personnel. Accordingly, it planned to develop alternative methods of measuring human resource value.

These alternative methods comprise a set of surrogate measures of human resource value. Two possible surrogate measures are historical and replacement cost. For example, assume that a specialist in an area of taxation is presently irreplaceable and that it would require four or five years to develop a replacement. In this case, the cost of obtaining a replacement would seem to be a relevant surrogate measure of the person's value.

Outcome of the Pilot Study

What happened to the human resource valuation project at Lester Witte? Research to develop and apply this study at Lester Witte and Company proceeded for more than three years. Just about the time when the system was fully developed and ready to be applied, the firm began to experience a variety of organizational problems that had nothing to do with human resource accounting. These problems diverted management's attention away from further development and application of human resource accounting, and the study gave way to matters of greater urgency. Unfortunately, the system was never fully implemented with day-to-day operations, except on the pilot experimental basis, and ultimately the firm discontinued this research effort.

Summary

This chapter has described a case study of an attempt to develop a valid, reliable, and practical system of accounting for the value of a firm's human resources. The organization is Lester Witte and Company, a firm of certified public accountants.

Three major, interrelated factors led the firm to develop this system: the nature of CPA firms, the firm's managerial philosophy, and certain limitations of conventional accounting information systems. In CPA firms, people truly are one of the most valuable assets. The firm's managerial philosophy is based on this premise and stresses the importance of increasing the value of people. The firm's management perceived that human resource accounting might be a helpful tool to measure management's progress in appreciating the value of people to the firm.

The research at Lester Witte had a dual objective: to develop an operational system of accounting for human resource values and to assess the attitudinal impact of the system on members of the organization. The basic research question here was: Does human resource accounting influence attitudes toward managerial policies of recruiting, selection, compensation, development, and allocation?

The valuation model was based on the stochastic rewards valuation model described in Chapter Seven. The basic premise of the model is that people generate services for the organization as they fulfill the role requirements associated with specified service states. Some of the service states are intended to make a direct contribution to revenue production, while others are intended to make an indirect contribution by facilitating revenue production. The problems of applying the model to both types of services were discussed.

The research project described here was an ambitious effort by the firm. Although it is not currently in use by Lester Witte & Company, it remains of historical interest as the first reported attempt to develop a system of accounting for human resource value.

Appendix 9-1: Research Survey of Professional Staff Opinions on Matters of Personnel Management

PURPOSE OF THE QUESTIONNAIRE

This questionnaire is part of a research study being conducted at Lester Witte & Company. The purpose of this part of the study is to find out how people feel about various aspects of the management and utilization of professional staff at Lester Witte & Company.

This is not a study of individual persons. The questionnaire is designed so that we can identify the respondent's professional classification and office location. The results will be tabulated on a group basis: by office, and within each office by professional levels. Where there are less than three people in any classification by office, the data will not be reported to the firm.

The individual questionnaires will be held in strict confidence by the researcher, and will not be seen by any member of the firm. The tabulated group results will, of course, be reported to the firm. The questionnaires should be returned directly to the researcher in the envelope provided. You will note that the questionnaire has been assigned a code number by the researcher so that a follow-up letter can be sent to those individuals who fail to respond initially.

This is not a test. There are no "correct" answers or "trick" questions. You are simply requested to answer the questions candidly.

We wish to thank you for your participation in this study. We hope that it will be beneficial to Lester Witte & Company.

Instructions:

In the next section, you will find a series of statements about various aspects of the management and utilization of people at Lester Witte & Company. You are asked to indicate the degree to which you personally agree or disagree with the attitude expressed by each statement. Please indicate your agreement or disagreement by circling the item in the scale that best represents your attitude.

For example: Professional staff should make an effort to complete assignments on time.

Strongly Agree	(Agree)	Undecided	Disagree	Strongly Disagree

As previously indicated, there are no "correct" or "incorrect" answers. This is not a test. It is an attempt to determine your opinions.

QUESTIONNAIRE

PLEASE READ EACH QUESTION CAREFULLY BEFORE RESPONDING

Note: To help in the statistical analysis of the data, the following information is needed:

______ Classification	______ Office Location	Do not write in this box ______ code
(Partner, Manager, Staff Accountant less than one year, Staff Accountant more than one year)		

1. Supervisors should view their staff as human resources.

   Strongly Agree | Agree | Undecided | Disagree | Strongly Disagree

2. People should be compensated in relation to their value to the firm.

   Strongly Agree | Agree | Undecided | Disagree | Strongly Disagree

3. When an individual is transferred from one office to another, the recipient should not compensate the other office for a loss of human resources.

   Strongly Agree | Agree | Undecided | Disagree | Strongly Disagree

4. An individual should feel responsible for developing his (or her) own skills.

   Strongly Agree | Agree | Undecided | Disagree | Strongly Disagree

5. A supervisor should not feel responsible for developing the skills of professional staff.

   Strongly Agree | Agree | Undecided | Disagree | Strongly Disagree

6. The firm should attempt to measure the dollar value of its human resources.

   Strongly Agree | Agree | Undecided | Disagree | Strongly Disagree

7. Professional staff should not typically be assigned to the engagement best suited to the individual's development.

   Strongly Agree | Agree | Undecided | Disagree | Strongly Disagree

8. The most qualified professional staff member available should typically be assigned to an engagement.

   Strongly Agree | Agree | Undecided | Disagree | Strongly Disagree

9. The firm should evaluate its effectiveness in developing people.

   Strongly Agree | Agree | Undecided | Disagree | Strongly Disagree

10. The firm should not think of its personnel as a valuable resource.

Strongly Agree | Agree | Undecided | Disagree | Strongly Disagree

11. Supervisors should view a staff member primarily as a means to get a task done.

Strongly Agree | Agree | Undecided | Disagree | Strongly Disagree

12. The firm should not be willing to make substantial expenditures to recruit and select staff.

Strongly Agree | Agree | Undecided | Disagree | Strongly Disagree

13. Supervisors should not be concerned about staff members' satisfaction with the firm as long as they get their job done.

Strongly Agree | Agree | Undecided | Disagree | Strongly Disagree

14. The firm should not be willing to sacrifice current profitability in order to insure future staff development.

Strongly Agree | Agree | Undecided | Disagree | Strongly Disagree

15. The firm should attempt to hire people with the greatest long-run value rather than those with the greatest immediate value.

Strongly Agree | Agree | Undecided | Disagree | Strongly Disagree

16. Supervisors should attempt to provide staff the opportunity to fully utilize their abilities.

Strongly Agree | Agree | Undecided | Disagree | Strongly Disagree

17. Professional staff turnover should not be minimized.

Strongly Agree | Agree | Undecided | Disagree | Strongly Disagree

18. A professional staff member's compensation should not be an important indication of the person's value to the firm.

Strongly Agree | Agree | Undecided | Disagree | Strongly Disagree

Appendix 9-2: Service States Descriptions

State No.	*Name*	*Description*
1.	Staff accountant (A)	0-1 year experience; works as assistant on audit, tax or Management Controls engagements; may be responsible on one-person engagements; no supervisory responsibilities; may have light client contact.
2.	Staff accountant (B)	Generally 1-2 years experience; works on either one-person managements or may have one assistant; has significant client responsibility in technical areas; client business and financial consulting generally in unsophisticated areas.
3.	Staff accountant (C)	Generally 3-4 years experience; in charge of all engagements he or she handles; has number of assistants necessary to complete assignments; significiant client contact at both technical and advisory levels; generally limited partner contact on engagements except at highest levels of sophistication; definite partner potential; responsible for development of all subordinates.
4.	Manager	Handles all levels of client contact normally held by partner; partner surrogate; management of numerous client engagements including technical review, client advisory contact; substantial administrative responsibility in area of specialty; counseling responsibility for all subordinates he or she deals with; will be a strong technical specialist and/or be responsible for significant inputs of new clients and/or total client management responsibility for a significant group of clients; definite short-term partner potential.
5.	Partner (A)	Ultimate responsibility for clients including technical review, consulting, marketing, specific office administrative responsibilities including some new client acquisition and human resource development.
6.	Partner (B)	Responsibility for major (in fee volume and client size) clients of firm; either partner in charge of office, recognized authority within firm in area of expertise (technical or administrative) including human resource development and/or responsible for substantial productive marketing efforts for the firm.
7.	Transfered	This service state is occupied when a person is transferred to another office.
8.	Exit	This service state is occupied when a person leaves the firm.

Appendix 9-3: Instructions for Form 1 Assessment of Mobility

Background Information

1. The time period to be covered by this forecast of mobility is the period the person under assessment is expected to remain in the firm.
2. As used in this context, "service states" are the staff classifications which an individual can occupy and the state of exit (left the firm). The services states are described in Appendix 9-2.

Part I Instructions for Estimating Probabilities

1. You are requested to assess the expected mobility of the specified individual during the period he (she) is expected to remain in the firm.
2. First, you are requested to look forward from today to one year in the future and indicate the probability that at the specified point in time the individual will (a) occupy each possible staff classification, (b) transfer to another office, or (c) have left the organization. In other words, you are asked to estimate: how likely is the individual to be in his present classification? How likely is he to be in other classifications? And how likely is he to have left the organization?
3. Next, look ahead two years in the future, then three years, and so on.
4. In making these estimates, please use the following procedure:
   a. You are asked to assign a number that indicates the probability that the individual will occupy each of the possible service states enumerated in Part I.
   b. You may use any numbers you wish.
   c. But we want you to use smaller numbers to indicate that the individual is less likely to be in a specified service state and larger numbers to indicate that he or she is more likely to be in a service state.
   d. Also, if it is impossible that he or she will occupy a particular service state, assign a zero. This means that the probability of his or her occupying a service state at the specified point in time is zero.
   e. Further, if the probability that an individual will be in a particular service state is twice as great as the probability that he or she will occupy another service state, assign a number twice as large. In other words, assign a number to indicate the individual's chances for occupying a service state in proportion to his or her chances for occupying all other possible service states.
   f. It may be helpful to assign a number to indicate the probability that the person will occupy a given state and then assign other numbers in relation to the first number as a bench mark.
5. Example: John Johnson is presently a Staff Accountant (A). Looking forward one year, he is very likely to be a Staff Accountant (B). We assign the number 10 to indicate this probability (any numbers are possible). It is impossible that he will still be a Staff Accountant (A), so we assign a zero. He is very likely to remain in the firm, but there is some chance of turnover: about 1/10 the likelihood that he will be a Staff Accountant (B). We assign a 1 to indicate the likelihood of turnover. It is not possible that he will occupy any other service state so we assign zeros to indicate the probabilities that he will occupy each of the other possible states.
6. If a person is likely to be transferred to another office, you are requested to indicate the probability that he (she) will occupy each possible staff classification *after* the transfer.

Instructions for Part II

The purpose of Part II of Form I is to ask you to indicate the degree to which you are confident that the probabilities you assigned in Part I are valid. Check the statement that most closely represents the extent to which you feel confident that the probabilities are valid.

FORM I

ASSESSMENT OF FUTURE MOBILITY
Lester Witte & Company

Name of individual assessed	Year under assessment	Office
Staff classification	Assessment by	Date

Part I. Looking forward__________ year(s) to July 1, 19______, what is the probability that the individual named above will:

Item No.	Service State	Probability Assigned
	A. Occupy the staff classification of:	
1.	Staff accountant (A)	________
2.	Staff accountant (B)	________
3.	Staff accountant (C)	________
4.	Manager	________
5.	Partner (A)	________
6.	Partner (B)	________
7.	B. Transfer to another office (*)	________
8.	C. Exit	________
	(*) To which office might the person be transferred?	________
	If transferred, what is the probability that the person will occupy the following staff classifications after the transfer:	
	1. Staff accountant (A)	________
	2. Staff accountant (B)	________
	3. Staff accountant (C)	________
	4. Manager	________
	5. Partner (A)	________
	6. Partner (B)	________

Part II. Confidence in Probabilities

A. For the service state the person is most likely to occupy, to what extent do you feel confident that the probability you assigned is valid? (check one):

1. To a very great extent ________
2. To a great extent ________
3. To some extent ________
4. To a slight extent ________
5. To a very slight extent ________

B. For the service state the person is next most likely to occupy, to what extent do you feel confident that the probability you assigned is valid? (check one):

1. To a very great extent ________
2. To a great extent ________
3. To some extent ________
4. To a slight extent ________
5. To a very slight extent ________

TEN

Second-Generation Accounting Systems for Human Resource Value

During the decade since Lester Witte & Company initiated their pioneering attempt to develop a system of human resource valuation, there has been growing recognition of the value of human assets and the need to account for them. This chapter presents a recent case study of an organization that has applied a system of accounting for the value of human resources. The study involves valuation of human assets for corporate income tax purposes.

Executives as Intangible Assets

This section describes the development and application of a model to value a pool of human assets. Specifically, the study described here was undertaken to determine the fair market value and related depreciation of a select group of personnel for tax purposes.

The Problem. A major financial services corporation purchased the assets and liabilities of a securities brokerage firm for a price in excess of net book value. A portion of the purchase price premium was attributable to the (unmeasured) value of an intangible asset acquired by the purchaser—the human capital or human assets represented by the acquired pool of registered representatives (account executives) employed by the brokerage firm.

If such an intangible asset can be depreciated for tax purposes, a corporation can realize a cash flow savings that represents a significant economic benefit. However, this type of asset can only be depreciated when certain conditions are met. According to Revenue Ruling 64-456, 1974-2 C.B. 65, it must be established that the asset "(1) has an ascertainable value separate and distinct from goodwill; and (2) has a limited useful life, the duration of which can be ascertained with reasonable accuracy."

This study was designed to determine both the value and the useful life of the acquired pool of account executives in order to meet these conditions. Once this information was acquired, an appropriate amortization schedule would be developed to depreciate the assets over their useful life.

The Study. The study was originally designed to determine the value of all registered representatives employed by the brokerage firm as of the date of acquisition. Industry studies and discussions with management indicated, however, that institutional representatives controlled such a small portion of their accounts that the impact on the firm would be immaterial in the event of their termination. Since the human resource valuation model used in this study is based on the value contributed by a specific pool of account executives, the decision was made to limit its application to those individuals whose presence or absence would directly affect the fair market value of the firm (through account maintenance or loss to another firm)—that is, retail registered representatives.

The Valuation Model. The model used to determine the fair market value and related depreciation of the brokerage firm's registered retail representatives was the stochastic rewards valuation model described in Chapter Seven. This study did not, therefore, involve the development of a new model but used one that had been previously designed to facilitate the valuation of a firm's assets.

Applying the Model. The specific model used was

$$D_T = \sum_{n=1}^{N} D_n \qquad (1)$$

In words: The total depreciable value of the human asset is the discounted sum of future earnings. The annual depreciable value is then estimated to be

$$D_n = S \frac{\sum_{j=1}^{m} \pi_{jn} V_{jn}}{(1+d)^n} \tag{2}$$

where π_{jn} = probability of an account executive being in state j during year n

V_{jn} = undiscounted value of profit attributable to sales effort of an account executive in state j during year n

d = discount rate

s = number of account executives with firm at time of acquisition

N = practical upper limit on number of years account executive might remain in the organization

m = the number of states

The values of the π_{jn} are found by employing the one-step transition probabilities and the Chapman–Kolmogorov equations, which may be found in Hillier and Lieberman:[1]

$$\pi_{jn} = \sum_{i=1}^{m} \pi_{io} P_{ij}^{(n)} \qquad \text{for } j = 1, 2, \ldots, m \tag{3}$$

where π_{io} = probability of an account executive being in state i at beginning of first year

$P_{ij}^{(n)}$ = n-step transition probability (conditional probability that an account executive starting in state i in first year will be in state j after n years)

The specific steps involved in applying the model to the brokerage firm's situation described here are outlined below.

The first step in applying this model was to classify the possible production levels, or service states, that a retail registered representative could occupy. Four service states were identified: low producers (low), medium producers (medium), high producers (high), and terminated individuals (exit). Low producers were those individuals whose gross production contributed to the lower third of the total retail gross production for any given year. Similarly, medium producers contributed to the middle third and high producers contributed to the top third of total retail gross production.

In delineating service states, floating cutoff points (of one third high, one third medium, and one third low producers) were used rather than fixed cutoff points (say, high = $250,000 and over; low = under $250,000) to accommodate possible economic conditions that could cause total gross production to increase or decrease drastically in any given year and, in turn, impair the comparability of the data. The exit state includes individuals who were terminated during the year, and the value assigned to that service state is assumed to be zero regardless of the date of termination during that year. Table 10-1 shows the service state classifications, gross production cutoff points, and the number of retail registered representatives in each service state for the years studied.

Valuation Period. As can be seen from Table 10-1, the valuation period for each individual is the six years prior to the acquisition date. This period is used to meet the acquiring firm's aim of placing a value on the human assets obtained.

Service State Value Measures. We turn now to the manner by which an expected *net* profit contribution, or service state value, was

Table 10-1

SERVICE STATE CLASSIFICATIONS

Year	*Low* $	*Low* No.	*Medium* $	*Medium* No.	*High* $	*High* No.	*Exit (No.)*
19X1	$35,400 and below	154	$35,400–95,000	55	$95,000 and above	31	16
19X2	$23,000 and below	146	$23,000–130,900	74	$130,900 and above	31	65
19X3	$27,800 and below	181	$27,800–149,100	70	$149,100 and above	30	90
19X4	$45,200 and below	176	$45,200–153,600	71	$153,600 and above	30	133
19X5	$31,300 and below	193	$31,300–135,400	74	$135,400 and above	33	158
19X6	$28,500 and below	193	$28,500–123,700	73	$123,700 and above	35	206

NOTE: The numbers in this table have been disguised and are for illustrative purposes only.

determined for high, medium, and low service states. Low, medium, and high production categories were determined by dividing the total gross production figure for each year into thirds. Management reports on gross production per individual were used to facilitate this process. These reports also provided the information necessary to classify each registered representative into the low, medium, high, or exit category based upon his or her earnings for the year.

Having classified individuals according to service states, an aggregate gross production figure attributable to low, medium, and high producers could be calculated for each year by adding the individual earnings in each category. Since this model utilizes the net profit contribution of individuals to the firm, however, the *net* production and profit figures for each service state needed to be calculated.

To facilitate this calculation, the number of registered representatives in each possible service state had to be derived. Unfortunately, records from the brokerage firm did not include complete information about all the firm's registered representatives for the period 19X1 to 19X6; therefore, a sample of registered representatives was taken that included no less than 82.2 percent of the total actual retail income of all registered representatives in any given year. It was assumed that the registered representatives who were not included in the sample were distributed in the production categories in relatively the same proportion as the sample.

Having assigned individuals to their respective categories, a net production figure was calculated for each service state by allocating all related income and expenses to the low, medium, high, and exit categories. Several different allocation methods were used (all of which were determined through consultation with the brokerage firm's management): number of registered representatives in each service state, number of transactions made in each service state, and average production incomes in each service state.

Net production figures were used to calculate future annual net profit of low, medium, and high producers. This was done by determining a yearly average over the four year period (19X0–19X3). This calculation is shown in Table 10-2.

These future expected net profit figures must be adjusted by a control factor in order to calculate the net service state values. This factor is represented by the percentage of account control for low, medium, and high producers—that is, the percentage of gross production that a representative in a specific production category can take with him should he leave one brokerage firm to join another.

Table 10-2

CALCULATION OF NET PROFIT CONTRIBUTIONS

Year	*High*	*Medium*	*Low*
19X3	$ 80,000	$ 50,000	$ 10,000
19X4	85,000	50,000	15,000
19X5	70,000	40,000	2,000
19X6	90,000	60,000	25,000
Total	325,000	200,000	52,000
Yearly average 19X0–19X3	$ 81,250	$ 50,000	$ 13,000

NOTE: All numbers have been disguised to preserve confidentiality and are for illustrative purposes only

Information pertaining to the magnitude of these percentages was obtained from both the brokerage's management and the 1980 Securities Industry Association's special report entitled "Registered Representative Turnover and Retention." Both sources indicated that termination of high producers results in a larger customer loss for the brokerage firm than termination of low producers.

High producers generally possess professional qualities that foster client loyalty, and when a termination results in a relocation of the registered representative at another brokerage firm, as is frequently the case, a portion of the clientele follows the individual. Low-producing registered representatives control a smaller number of accounts. This factor, combined with a likelihood that termination of low producers often leads to exit from the brokerage industry itself, results in a smaller client loss for the firm.

Despite the presence of individual account control, a portion of the customer base usually remains with the original firm when a registered representative terminates employment. Therefore the marginal value of a registered representative equals only that portion of production income which leaves the firm when the individual terminates. Table 10-3 presents this portion of control information for low, medium, and high producers in the brokerage firm. These figures can then be used to adjust

Table 10-3

RETAIL REGISTERED REPRESENTATIVE CONTROL FACTOR

Service State	*Portion of Control*
High	0.90
Medium	0.60
Low	0.40

NOTE: These numbers are for illustrative purposes only.

Table 10-4

NET SERVICE STATE VALUES

Service State	*Value*
High	$73,125
Medium	30,000
Low	5,200

NOTE: These numbers are for illustrative purposes only.

the future expected net profit contributions (from Table 10-3) to derive the net service state values (shown in Table 10-4).

Mobility Probabilities. In order to apply the stochastic rewards valuation model, it is necessary to calculate the probability that low, medium, and high-producing retail registered representatives will occupy each possible service state (including the state of exit) at specified future points in time. In this instance, estimation of the required future mobility probabilities was based on the historical experience of the brokerage firm (for the period January 19X1 through October 19X6).

The pattern of mobility of registered representatives was determined by using a sample of individuals classified into low, medium, high, and exit service states according to their gross production income records, which were obtained from the firm. The relative frequency (probability) of occupancy of each service state was calculated on the basis of this sample for the period January 19X1 through October 19X6. These historical patterns were then used to estimate future mobility patterns. From this information, a transition matrix showing movement between service states including exit was constructed to establish attrition rates for registered representatives. This transition matrix is shown in Table 10-5.

Discount Rate. The discount rate used to determine the net present value of the future net profit contribution of the assets acquired was calculated on the basis of the capital assets pricing model (see Appendix 10-1), which uses the *historical return on the market* less the *historical risk-free rate* to determine a price of risk. This price of risk is then multiplied by a figure representing the *quantity of risk* to determine the risk premium of the purchased asset. A future expected risk-free rate of return is added to arrive at a required rate of return for the asset.

In this study, the *historical return on the stock market* was obtained by using Standard & Poor's Index of 500 stocks and calculating the amount of change from year to year for thirty-five years. The total return was calculated by adding the percentage of change to a given

Table 10-5

TRANSITION MATRIX
Probabilities of Transition Between Service States from Year T to Year T + 1

		Year T + 1		
Year T	*High*	*Medium*	*Low*	*Exit*
High	0.75	0.10	0.10	0.05
Medium	0.10	0.70	0.15	0.05
Low	0.00	0.10	0.65	0.25
Exit	0.00	0.00	0.00	1.00

NOTE: This matrix shows the probability that a registered representative who is in each service state in year *T* will be in each service state in year *T* + 1. For example, a registered representative who is in the high state in year *T* has a 0.75 probability of being in the high state, a 0.10 probability of being in the medium state, 0.10 probability of being in the low state, and a 0.05 probability of being in the exit state in year *T* + 1 (the subsequent year). All numbers have been disguised to preserve confidentiality.

dividend yield. The arithmetic average return for the thirty-five years 1947–1981 was taken to represent the historical return on the stock market.

The same method was used to obtain the *historical risk-free rate of return*. The average yield of U.S. government bonds during the thirty-five years 1947–1981 was used in this calculation.

The *quantity of risk* (beta) shows the extent to which the returns on a given investment move with the stock market. The measurement pertaining to the brokerage firm was obtained by taking an average of beta for the seven publicly traded brokerage firms as published in *Value Line*.

For the purposes of this study, it was assumed that the *future expected risk-free rate of return,* the final component of the capital assets pricing model, is the same as the yield to maturity on long-term treasury bonds. On January 1, 19X7, the *Wall Street Journal* published the yield to maturity on treasury bonds held for twenty-nine years. For conservative purposes, the average of the two longest-term bonds (maturing in May and November of the year 2011) was taken to represent the future expected risk-free rate of return.

Using these figures in the manner described above, a required rate of return for the asset described in this study was found to be 18.5. Discount rates were determined by adjusting this figure for expected inflation (7.7 percent).

Value of the Acquired Retail Registered Representatives. Based on the use of the stochastic rewards valuation model described above, the fair market value of the brokerage firm's registered representatives was determined as of the date of acquisition. Although the actual fair market value has been disguised, a representative illustration is shown in Table 10-6.

Appropriate Method of Amortization. Having established a fair market value for the acquired pool of registered representatives, their useful life needed to be determined in order to recommend an appropriate amortization schedule. This was, essentially, the last phase of the study. The useful life of the assets acquired was determined to be fourteen years. Ninety-five percent of the value of human assets acquired will be realized by the end of the thirteenth year after the date of acquisition. Less than 5 percent of the original asset value will remain after the fourteenth year, and that remainder should be realized in the fourteenth year.

Accelerated amortization, to reflect reasonable anticipated registered representative attrition, is appropriate through the ninth year.

Exhibit 10-6

VALUE OF ACCOUNT EXECUTIVES

Year	*Expected Number of High RR's**	*High-Income Streams†*	*Expected Number of Medium RR's**	*Medium-Income Streams***	*Expected Number of Low RR's**	*Low-Income Streams‡*	*Net RR Income Streams*	*Dis-Count Factor°*	*Discounted Estimated Income Streams Per Year*
1	7	$508,219	17	$519,000	34	175,760	$1,202,979	0.909091	$1,093,617
2	7	507,670	16	485,550	25	131,352	1,124,572	0.826446	929,399
3	7	499,105	15	436,492	20	101,613	1,037,211	0.751315	779,272
4	7	460,724	13	384,644	16	80,947	946,315	0.683013	646,345
5	6	454,300	11	335,673	13	66,034	856,007	0.620921	531,513
6	6	422,545	10	291,706	11	54,880	769,131	0.564474	434,154
7	5	388,012	8	253,191	9	46,261	687,464	0.513158	352,776
8	5	352,724	7	219,841	8	39,412	611,978	0.466507	285,492
9	4	316,130	6	191,097	7	33,842	543,069	0.424098	230,314
10	4	285,177	6	166,344	6	29,228	460,749	0.385543	185,350
11	3	254,429	5	145,003	5	25,351	424,783	0.350494	148,864
12	3	226,166	4	126,566	4	22,058	374,789	0.318631	119,419
13	3	200,475	4	110,600	4	19,236	330,312	0.289664	95,679
14	2	177,315	3	96,743	3	16,805	290,863	0.263331	76,593
15	2	156,567	3	84,689	3	14,699	255,956	0.239392	61,274
16	2	138,068	2	74,186	2	12,870	225,125	0.217629	48,994
17	2	121,634	2	65,020	2	11,276	197,930	0.197845	39,159
18	1	107,074	2	57,009	2	9,885	173,968	0.179859	31,290
19	1	94,202	2	50,002	2	8,669	152,873	0.163508	24,996
20	1	82,839	1	43,867	1	7,605	134,311	0.148644	19,965
21	1	72,822	1	38,493	1	6,673	117,988	0.135131	15,944
22	1	63,999	1	33,782	1	5,856	103,638	0.122846	12,731
23	1	56,234	1	29,652	1	5,140	91,025	0.111678	10,166
24	1	49,403	1	26,028	1	4,512	79,943	0.101526	8,116
25	1	43,397	1	22,850	1	3,961	70,207	0.092296	6,480
26	1	38,117	1	20,060	1	3,477	61,654	0.083905	5,173
27	0	33,477	1	17,612	1	3,053	54,142	0.076278	4,130

28	0	29,401	1	15,463	1	2,680	47,544	0.069343	3,297
29	0	25,820	0	13,577	0	2,353	41,750	0.063039	2,632
30	0	22,674	0	11,921	0	2,066	36,661	0.057309	2,101
31	0	19,911	0	10,467	0	1,814	32,192	0.052099	1,677
32	0	17,485	0	9,190	0	1,593	28,268	0.047362	1,339
33	0	15,354	0	8,069	0	1,399	24,822	0.043057	1,069
34	0	13,482	0	7,085	0	1,228	21,796	0.039142	853
35	0	11,839	0	6,221	0	1,078	19,139	0.035584	681
36	0	10,396	0	5,463	0	947	16,805	0.032349	544
37	0	9,128	0	4,797	0	831	14,756	0.029408	434
38	0	8,015	0	4,212	0	730	12,957	0.026735	346
39	0	7,038	0	3,698	0	641	11,378	0.024304	277
40	0	6,180	0	3,247	0	563	9,990	0.022095	221
41	0	5,427	0	2,851	0	494	8,772	0.020086	176
42	0	4,765	0	2,504	0	434	7,703	0.018260	141
43	0	4,184	0	2,199	0	381	6,764	0.016600	112
44	0	3,674	0	1,930	0	335	5,939	0.015091	90
45	0	3,226	0	1,695	0	294	5,215	0.013719	72
46	0	2,833	0	1,488	0	258	4,579	0.012472	57
47	0	2,487	0	1,307	0	227	4,021	0.011338	46
48	0	2,184	0	1,148	0	199	3,531	0.010307	36
49	0	1,918	0	1,008	0	175	3,100	0.009370	29
50	0	1,684	0	885	0	153	2,722	0.008519	23
51	0	1,479	0	777	0	135	2,390	0.007744	19
Fair market value (sum of the discounted income streams)									$6,213,498

NOTE: The numbers are for illustrative purposes only.

*Expected numbers of representatives are rounded to the nearest whole numbers for presentation purposes only. Calculations use unrounded expected values.

†The service state value for a high-producing registered representative is $73,125.

**The service state value for a medium-producing registered representative is $30,000.

‡The service state value for a low-producing registered representative is $5,200.

°The discount rate is 10 percent. Income streams are discounted from the end of the year back to the date of acquisition.

Table 10-7

AMORTIZATION SCHEDULE

Year	*Annual Amortization*	*Cumulative Amortization*
1	$1,093,617	$1,093,617
2	929,399	2,023,016
3	779,272	2,802,288
4	646,345	3,448,633
5	531,513	3,980,146
6	434,155	4,414,300
7	352,778	4,767,078
8	285,492	5,052,570
9	230,314	5,282,885
10	186,123	5,469,008
11	186,123	5,655,131
12	186,123	5,841,254
13	186,123	6,027,377
14	186,121	6,213,498*

NOTE: These numbers are for illustrative purposes only.

*Amortization was reduced during the final year by $2 to equal total fair market value of acquired pool of account executives per Table 10-6.

Thereafter, the straight-line amortization equivalent will reflect the reasonably anticipated registered representative attrition. Table 10-7 shows the calculated amortization schedule.

Discussion of the System. In this study, the stochastic rewards valuation model was used to establish the fair market value of acquired human assets. An amortization schedule was also determined, based on the expected life of the assets. Given these results, it seems that the pool of registered representatives acquired by the financial institution qualifies for a depreciation allowance since it meets the criteria set by the Internal Revenue Service.

The Study's Implications

The attribution of value to a pool of human assets obtained through an acquisition has obvious tax implications. Specifically, if the acquiring firm can depreciate the human assets acquired, it will generate significant cash savings.

The amortization allowance obtained by determining a value for the asset can be an important consideration in *ex ante* acquisition analysis and valuation, for if human capital can be depreciated, the effective cost of an acquisition is decreased.

The use of the stochastic rewards valuation model in forecasting the future number of account executives in service states would seem to be a major factor in meeting the Internal Revenue Service's criteria for depreciation allowance—that is, limited useful asset life that can be determined with reasonable accuracy and asset value separate and distinct from goodwill.

Given the growing appreciation of the importance of human assets in organizations, valuation of these assets seems not only reasonable but necessary. In a human capital intensive economy, much of the value of the firm is composed of human rather than physical or financial assets.

Summary

This chapter has described a recent application of the stochastic rewards valuation model. In this case, the model was used to determine the value of human assets purchased by one company from another. It was used to establish the fair market value of these assets, which along with an appropriate amortization schedule would qualify these intangible assets for a tax depreciation allowance. This allowance could result in a significant economic benefit for the purchasing firm through a cash flow savings.

Case 10-1: Worldwide Consultants

Worldwide Consultants is an international management consulting firm specializing in the financial aspects of strategic planning. Phil Valeur, the partner in charge of human resources, recognized the human capital intensiveness of his firm. He is interested in obtaining some measures of the human resource value of the professional staff and managerial personnel.

Note: This case was prepared by George Geis. Used by permission of the author.

Listed here are the five service states of interest to Valeur:

State Number	*State Name*
1	Consultant
2	Senior consultant
3	Manager
4	Partner
5	Exit

Valeur calculated the gross and net service state values associated with each service state. He assumed that the gross service state value for a given state was equal to the product of the average billing rate and the average chargeable hours for that state. Hence the $120,000 gross state value of a senior consultant reflected an average billing rate of $100/hour and an expected 1,200 chargeable hours per year. Net service state value is equal to the difference between gross service state value and expenses attributable to the state, including the compensation associated with the service state as well as an allocation of other company expenses.

Finally, Valeur derived what he termed a "separate value" for each of the states. To calculate this value he estimated the average percentage of business controlled by the employees of a given service state. For example, he estimated that the managers controlled (that is, could theoretically take with them if they left Worldwide) about 40 percent of their business. A summary of the data related to service state value follows:

State Number	*State Name*	*Gross Value*	*Net Value*	*Control*	*Separate Value*
1	Consultant	$ 70,000	$ 5,000	10%	$ 500
2	Senior consultant	120,000	20,000	20%	4,000
3	Manager	125,000	15,000	40%	6,000
4	Partner	180,000	25,000	60%	15,000
5	Exit	0	0	N/A	N/A

Using historical data from the past five years, Valeur developed the following matrix, which gives the probabilities of moving from one service state to another in any given year:

	To State				
	1	2	3	4	5
From State					
1	0.4	0.2	0.1	0	0.3
2	0.1	0.3	0.2	0	0.4
3	0	0.1	0.4	0.1	0.4
4	0	0	0	0.7	0.3
5	0	0	0	0	1.0

As of January 1, 1983, Worldwide has 100 consultants, 75 senior consultants, 50 managers, and 25 partners. Valeur used a 10 percent cost of capital as a discount rate.

Questions

1. What value would you place on the pool of consultants as of January 1, 1983? On the pool of senior consultants? On the pools of managers and partners? What interpretation would you give to these values?
2. What possible applications does Valeur's concept of separate value have?
3. What costs, other than compensation, should be included in calculating net service state value from gross service state value?
4. Do you think that the gross service state value of managers and partners should be calculated in the same way as for consultants and senior consultants? Explain.

Appendix 10-1: The Discount Rate Determined by the Capital Pricing Model

The capital assets pricing model states that the required rate of return on any asset is equal to the risk-free rate of return plus a risk premium. The risk premium is the price of risk multiplied by the quantity of risk. Hence

$$\text{Required return} = R_{FE} + (K_M - R_{FH}) \times \beta$$

where R_{FE} = future expected risk-free rate of return; that is, U.S. government bonds yield to maturity: 10.5% (source: *Wall Street Journal,* November 1, 1982)

K_M = historical return on stock market: 11.0% (35-year average return)

R_{FH} = historical risk-free rate of return; that is, U.S. government bonds average historical yield: 6.0%

β = quantity of risk; that is, average beta of publicly traded brokerage firms: 1.6

The discount rates were calculated by using the capital assets pricing model, which states that:

Historical return on the market in general	11.0%
Less the historical risk-free rate	–6.0
Equals the risk premium of the market in general (price of risk)	5.0%
Times the riskiness of the purchased asset (beta coefficient; quantity of risk)	× 1.6
Equals the risk premium of the purchased asset	8.0
Plus the future expected risk-free rate of return (includes future expected inflation rate)	+ 10.5
Equals the required return on the asset	18.5%

Note: All numbers in this appendix have been disguised and are for illustrative purposes only.

This rate was reduced by the amount of the future expected inflation rate because our expected future income streams did not include an inflation factor. Hence

1 + (required return on equity)	1.185
Divided by 1 + (expected future inflation)	1.077
Equals 1 + (discount rate)	1.100
Discount rate	10.0%

ELEVEN

Designing and Implementing Human Resource Accounting Systems

This chapter deals with the problem of designing and implementing systems of accounting for human resources. It provides guidelines for use in developing human resource accounting systems in organizations. The chapter first focuses on the problem of defining the content of a proposed system and then examines the phases in the design and implementation process. It is intended to be used by human resource professionals working together with accounting-information specialists to design their organization's human resource accounting system.

Human Resource Accounting Systems I–V

Different organizations require different degrees of human resource accounting capability. One firm may require only the most rudimentary system, while only the most advanced capability may be satisfactory for another company. Similarly, the human resource accounting capability appropriate for a firm at one stage may be quite inadequate at a later stage.

To illustrate the different types of human resource accounting capability, Table 11-1 presents five human resource accounting systems. This table shows various functions of human resource management

Table 11-1

HUMAN RESOURCE ACCOUNTING SYSTEMS I–V

Human Resource Management Functions	*System I* — *Prerequisite Personnel System*	*System II* — *Basic HRA System*	*System III* — *Intermediate HRA System*	*System IV* — *Advanced HRA System*	*System V* — *Total HRA System*
I. Human Resource Planning	Personnel skills inventory Replacement tables	Estimated costs of recruiting, training, etc.	Replacement costs	Standard and actual personnel costs Stochastic personnel mobility models Personnel simulations	Stochastic rewards valuation model Human resource value simulations
II. Human Resource Decision making: A. Budgetary	Personnel Costs included in "General and Administrative" expense	Personnel costs budgeted separately	Budgetary system for recruitment, training, etc. Budget replacement costs	Budget standard and actual costs Original and replacement costs	Human capital budgeting Budget ROI on human capital investment
B. Policy	Traditional selection, training, and placement methods	Value-oriented selection decisions	Recruitment vs. training trade-off analyses	Personnel assignment optimization models	Value-based compensation
III. Human Resources Conservation: A. After-the-fact	Turnover rates	Turnover cost	Replacement cost	Opportunity cost	Human resource value depletion
B. Before-the-fact	N.A.	Attitudinal data	Expected turnover cost (replacement)	Expected opportunity costs Human resource accountability	Expected conditional and realizable value depletion
IV. Human Resource Evaluation	Performance and potential ratings	Perceived value rankings	Psychometric predictions of potential value Interval scaling of value	Measurements of economic value of groups	Measurement of economic value of individuals
V. Human Resource Management Efficiency Control	N.A.	Comparison of actual costs with historical costs	Comparison of budgeted and actual costs Variance analysis	Comparison of actual costs against standard Variance analysis	Interunit comparison of costs

(human resource planning, decision making, conservation, and so on) and the human resource accounting capabilities provided by each system level.

An organization with a *System I* human resource accounting capability possesses most of the personnel systems that are prerequisite for the implementation of human resource accounting. System I consists of nominal but very elementary human resource accounting capability; that is, it consists of personnel systems which are aimed at the same functions of more sophisticated human resource accounting systems but which lack the advanced capabilities.

In *System II,* the human resource planning function incorporates estimates of costs of recruitment and training. Personnel costs are budgeted separately and not merely lumped in "general and administrative" expenses. Personnel policy decisions are based on a cost-value calculus. For example, personnel selection decisions are based on such criteria as a person's expected value to the firm. Decision makers are more aware of the trade-offs between one person with a high expected conditional value and another with a high expected realizable value. In a System II organization, management not only has data on turnover rates; it also has data on the *cost* of turnover. Thus turnover is expressed in a meaningful common denominator. Attitudinal data, such as measures of satisfaction and perceived motivation, are available, and they are used as leading indicators to forecast probable changes in turnover. Under System II, human resource evaluation is based on criteria of perceived value that are obtained by alternation-ranking (totem pole) methods. The efficiency of the human resource management process is assessed, and reports compare actual costs with historical costs of similar activities.

Under *System III,* there is intermediate human resource accounting capability. Human resource planning incorporates replacement costs as well as original costs. Budgetary and policy decision making for human resources is subject to more systematic analysis. There is a formal system for budgeting recruitment, training, and so forth. Personnel needs are planned as a formal part of overall corporate planning, and not just on an ad hoc basis. Policy decisions involving trade-offs between human resource variables are subjected to analyses. For example, the choice between recruitment of experienced workers versus hiring and training entry-level personnel is subjected to trade-off analysis. In System III, the replacement cost of turnover is measured and reported. Managers may be requested to explain controllable turnover. The human resource evaluation process is based on psychometric predictions of a person's potential, and value is assessed in nonmonetary terms using interval scaling methods. The efficiency of the overall human resource management process is based on a comparison of budgeted and actual personnel costs, and explanations of variances are required.

An organization with a *System IV* capability has an advanced human resource accounting system. In such organizations, human resource planning is based on standard personnel costs. Stochastic models are used to forecast personnel mobility and predict future human resource needs. The computer is used to run human resource planning simulations, and parameters in the models are varied so that sensitivity analyses can be performed. In the decision-making process, budgets are based on standard costs. Optimization models are used for personnel policy decisions; for example, personnel assignment may be based on optimization methods. Human resource conservation is assessed not only in terms of historical and replacement cost, but also in terms of the opportunity cost of human resources. The organization has an ongoing system of human resource accountability, and one criterion used to evaluate managers is human resource conservation. The firm also has an ongoing turnover control program, and it uses measures of expected opportunity cost of turnover as a basis for turnover control decisions. Under System IV, the organization accounts for the value of groups of people but not for individuals. The efficiency of the human resource management process is evaluated by comparing actual costs against standard, and there is a formal system for reporting and explaining variances.

System V represents total human resource accounting capability. Human resource planning is based on a stochastic rewards valuation model, and simulations of the effects of overall corporate plans on human resource value are performed. In the decision-making process, there is formal human capital budgeting. Return on investment is the criterion used to assess capital expenditures in human resources just as it is used for other resources. Personnel policy decisions are based fully on a cost-value calculus; for example, compensation is based on a person's expected value to the firm. Human resource conservation is controlled both before and after the fact. Anticipated human resource depletion is measured in terms of expected conditional and realizable replacement cost. Turnover control programs are initiated when expected depletion is too high. The System V organization has a human resource accountability subsystem, and managers are charged with the opportunity cost of controllable human value depletion. They are expected to conserve human as well as physical and financial assets entrusted to them. The human resource evaluation process includes the measurement of the economic value of individuals per se as well as that of aggregates such as departments, plants, or divisions. Finally, the efficiency of the human resource management function is assessed not only by comparison of actual against standard costs, but also by comparison among comparable organizational units. In sum, System V represents maximal human resource accounting capability.

These five systems of human resource accounting can be thought of as different levels of capability. At a particular time, System II may be more appropriate for a given firm than System III or IV. The systems can also be viewed as stages in the development of a firm's human resource accounting capability. A firm may presently be in the first stage of human resource accounting capability and desire ultimately to reach the fifth stage. It may be reasonable, however, to move gradually from stage to stage and incrementally increase the firm's capability. Alternately, the conditions may be appropriate for designing a System IV or V capability.

Choosing a System

The next question facing an organization that is interested in designing a human resource accounting system is: What factors should we consider to determine the degree of human resource accounting capability required? Four major factors must be considered: type of organization, size and structure of organization, existing human resource accounting capability, and availability of data for developing human resource accounting. Each of these variables is examined below.

Type of Organization. The key variables that influence the types of organizations in which human resource accounting is applicable are the degree of human capital intensiveness, the number of highly educated or skilled personnel, and the number of people occupying similar positions.

The more an organization is people-intensive, the greater the need for human resource accounting. Thus service organizations, which are very people-intensive, are likely to need to account for human resources. Typical examples are aerospace, advertising, banking, consulting, CPA, electronics, insurance, and retailing firms. In addition, a human resource accounting system may be required not only in human capital intensive firms but also in any organization with a substantial investment in human assets, such as airlines, communications, or automotive manufacturing.

Another key variable is the existence of a group of valuable human resources within an organization. Examples are airline pilots, loan officers, research engineers, or a management team. Each of these groups consists of highly trained personnel, and each typically represents a major organizational investment.

The third variable is the number of people who occupy similar positions. In a large bank, for example, there may be more than 3,000 loan officers, each performing virtually identical functions. In an aerospace company, there may be many thousand engineers occupying relatively homogeneous positions. In a retail store, there may be fifty sales personnel with comparable responsibilities. This factor is important because large numbers provide a basis for statistical prediction and the comparability of positions provides a basis for comparability of performance and potential. The type of organization, as we shall see, also influences the data available for human resource accounting.

Size and Structure of Organization. The size of an organization has both direct and indirect influences on the type of human resource accounting capability required. The smaller the organization, the more likely it is that management can exercise personal control over human resource management. In very small organizations (fewer than 500 employees) there may be no need for human resource accounting because management has personal knowledge of operations.

The larger the organization, the more likely it is to be decentralized; and the greater the degree of decentralization, the greater the need for human resource accounting. In decentralized organizations, corporate management lacks personal knowledge of local operations. It relies, instead, upon formal systems of financial reporting to provide knowledge and control over operations. In such cases, unless the financial control system monitors human resources, it is very likely that important aspects of human resource development and conservation will be neglected. The reason for this is well known to managers: "Things that get measured get counted." Thus a human resource accounting system must be designed as a subsystem to the overall management information system.

Existing Human Resource Accounting Capability. A company's existing personnel systems and human resource capability will also influence the choice of a human resource accounting system. A company with inadequate personnel systems is unlikely to be able to digest more than System I capability. An organization with a computer-based human resource information system is in a fine position to develop System V capability.*

Potential for Developing Human Resource Accounting. Another major factor influencing the choice of a human resource accounting system is the potential for actually developing given levels of capability. In some cases, all the necessary data are either presently available or easily accessible. In other cases, some data may simply be unobtainable.

In some organizations, notably service organizations, data on human resource costs, historical data on personnel mobility, social-psychological measurements, and value data (billing rates, chargeable time, and so on) are very likely to be available. This occurs because human services are the primary product of the organization, and these data are available as a routine aspect of business operations.

In other organizations (including service organizations), some or all of these data are simply not available. In these cases, the potential for developing human resource accounting is to intermediate (System III) or advanced (System IV) capability but probably not higher.

Designing and Implementing a System

The typology of the five general classes of human resource accounting systems is intended principally for illustrative purposes; it is unlikely that a specific organization's human resource accounting needs will exactly match System I, II, and so on. Instead, a system will very likely have to be tailored to a firm's needs. This section describes the phases involved in designing and implementing a human resource accounting system. It provides a step-by-step approach to the development of such a system.

The phases in the design and implementation of a system are shown schematically in Figure 11-1. These phases are common to the development of any human resource accounting system, whether it is System I or System V. As shown in Figure 11-1, the five phases in the development of a system are to (1) identify human resource accounting objectives, (2) develop human resource accounting measurements, (3)

*There are, of course, exceptions to these general statements. An organization may wish to move directly from minimal to advanced human resource accounting capability.

Figure 11-1

GENERALIZED MODEL OF PROCESS DESIGN AND IMPLEMENTATION OF A HUMAN RESOURCE ACCOUNTING SYSTEM

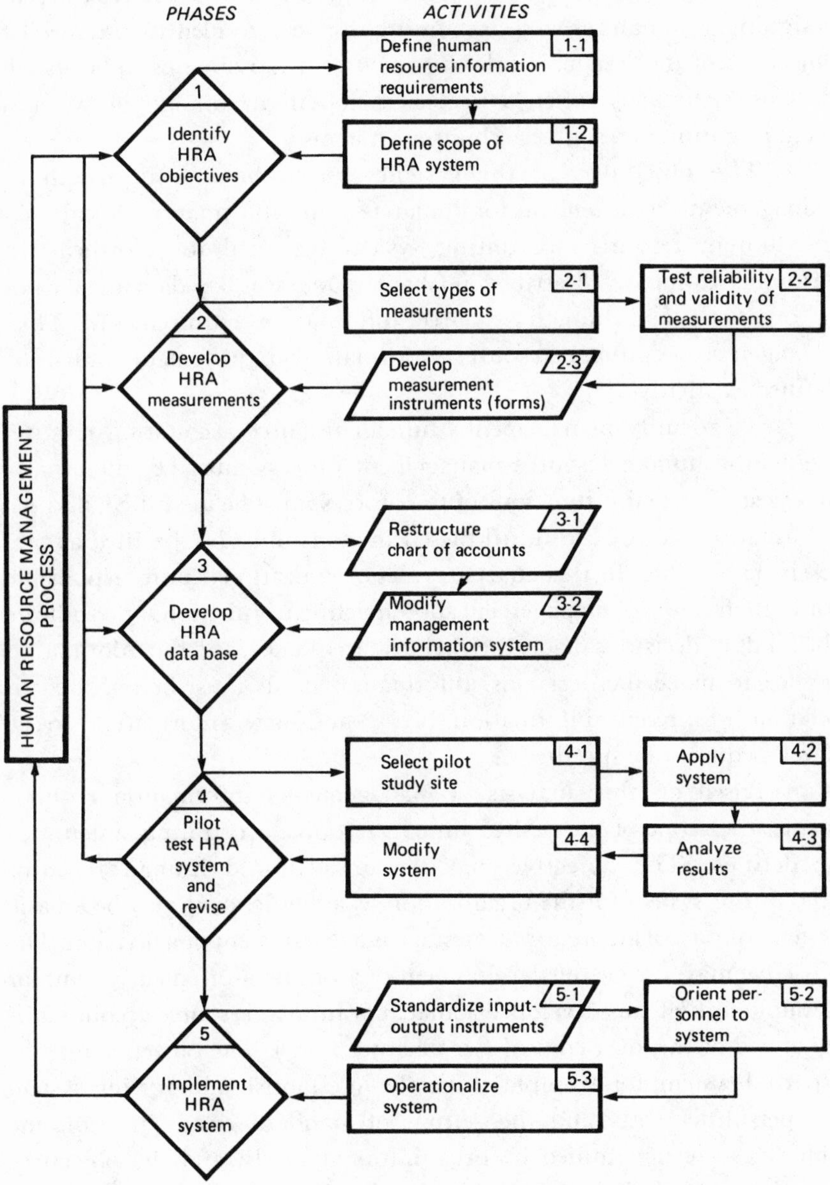

develop a data base for the system, (4) test the system and revise it if necessary, and (5) implement the system in the organization. Each of these phases is described below.

Identify Human Resource Accounting Objectives. The first step in designing a human resource accounting system is to identify the specific objectives of the system. While this may seem too obvious to be stated, it is, unfortunately, often a neglected step in the design of systems, including human resource accounting systems.

The objectives of the system should be an outgrowth of management's requirements for human resource information. Recall that the human resource accounting system designed for Northeastern Insurance Company (described in Chapter One) was based on an analysis of organizational human resource information requirements. Thus management's human resource information requirements must be defined explicitly.

To identify management's human resource accounting requirements, the human resource management process must be studied and analyzed. The major functions of the process must be identified, and the information required to fulfill these functions must be specified as precisely as possible. In this analysis, each organizational unit responsible for human resource management should define its functions and indicate the kinds of decisions made, their relative frequency, and the information needed to make the decisions. Information needs must be analyzed in relation to present information flows, and new information to be developed must be specified.

Based on this analysis of management's information requirements, the scope of the desired human resource accounting system can be defined. The objective may be an advanced human resource accounting system for the organization as a whole, or it may be a basic system for part of an organization such as a department or a division. The objective may also be the development of a problem-oriented system; for example, AT&T has developed a system of human resource accountability aimed at turnover control (see Chapter Four). The objective may be a partial system; for example, it may be to establish a budgeting system for personnel costs and the setting of standard costs. In sum, the objectives are determined by organizational needs, and the objectives must be stated explicitly. The objective should not be merely "to develop a human resource accounting system."

Develop Human Resource Accounting Measurements. The second step in the design of a system is to develop human resource accounting measurements. First the human resource accounting measurements desired should be selected. The system may include either a single measurement or a set of measurements; it may include monetary or nonmonetary measurements (or both); and it may include measurements of cost and value.

Once the measurements have been selected, their validity and reliability must be tested, which typically involves special research studies. It would not be sound to base a system on untested measurements. Once the measurements have demonstrated satisfactory reliability and validity, they can be translated into forms to be used in the system.

Develop Human Resource Accounting Data Base. The next step in designing a human resource accounting system is to develop the data base. The data base is simply the source of inputs required for human resource accounting, including cost data, time sheets, psychological measurements, and the like.

One problem in developing the data base is the need to restructure the company's chart of accounts; the accounting systems of many organizations simply do not classify personnel related costs separately. Typically they are buried in more general classifications such as "administrative expenses." The accounts should be organized in relation to responsibility centers. In the R. O. Mason Manufacturing Company, for example, there are three responsibility centers in the human resources department: recruitment, training, and employee relations. The chart of accounts includes a summary account for each responsibility center and subaccounts to provide adequate detail on costs incurred in each center, as shown in Table 11-2.

In addition to restructuring the chart of accounts, other aspects of the organization's information system must be modified. The information must be adapted to collect various types of nonfinancial data required for human resource accounting. For example, the administration of employee attitude surveys may become a standard data collection routine. Similarly, the human resource planning process may generate probabilistic estimates of employee mobility, which are necessary for measuring human resource value. These data must become part of the formal management information system.

Test the System and Revise. Once objectives have been defined, measurements developed, and a data base constructed, the next step is to

Table 11-2

R. O. MASON MANUFACTURING COMPANY
PARTIAL LIST OF PERSONNEL COST ACCOUNTS
BY RESPONSIBILITY CENTER

Number	*Name*	*Number*	*Name*
7000	Recruitment	8006	Training materials
7001	Salaries	8007	Equipment rental
7002	Payroll taxes	8008	Depreciation
7003	Employee benefits	8009	Consulting fees
7004	Travel-personnel	9000	Employee relations
7005	Testing	9001	Salaries
7006	Advertising	9002	Payroll taxes
7007	Travel-interviewees	9003	Employee benefits
7008	Agency fees	9004	Supplies
7010	Other costs	9005	Turnover Control Project
8000	Training	9006	Evaluation project
8001	Salaries-trainers	9010	Other costs
8002	Payroll taxes		
8003	Employee benefits		
8004	Salaries-trainees		
8005	Living expenses		

test the system. The purpose is to experiment with the system and eliminate its weaknesses prior to fully implementing it.

The site for this pilot study ought to be selected very carefully. It should promise a high likelihood that it will be feasible to operationalize the system. The site should also be controllable; that is, there should be a minimum number of extraneous problems to present "noise" in the pilot study and possibly contaminate its results. It is essential to obtain the cooperation of management at the pilot site, which means that management must understand and perhaps even participate in the system's design.

Once the system has been applied, the designer can obtain feedback on its performance. Weaknesses can be identified, especially the emergence of unintended counterproductive behavior. The system should then be analyzed for its utility, efficiency, and cost and modified if necessary.

Implement the System. The final step involves the actual implementation of the system. In this phase, the input and output documents must be standardized, and instructions for administration of the system must be issued. A key step involves the orientation of personnel to the new system. Its purposes, uses, and methods should be explained.

Modify the System. In time it may become necessary to modify the system, either because limitations in the system's design have been observed or because of changes in management's human resource accounting needs. The modifications may involve simple adjustments in the system or an entire recycling through the design and implementation process.

Summary

This chapter has examined the problems of designing and implementing a system of accounting for an organization's human resources. It has presented a taxonomy of human resource accounting systems (Systems I–V) that serves as a model of the full range of human resource accounting capability.

The chapter has also presented a step-by-step approach to the design and implementation of a human resource accounting system. It has described five phases: (1) identify human resource accounting objectives, (2) develop measurements, (3) develop a human resource accounting data base, (4) test the proposed system and revise it if necessary, and (5) implement the system.

The chapter is intended to provide a framework to assist human resource professionals, working together with accounting-information specialists, to design a human resource accounting system appropriate to their organization's needs.

Case 11-1: New York City Bank (A)

New York City Bank is a large bank employing about 30,000 employees. John Q. Hamilton, senior vice-president in charge of human resources, is interested in the possibility of designing a human resource accounting system. He has invited you, as a human resource accounting consultant, to discuss his company's needs and see what kind of system you would propose.

Questions

1. What questions should you plan to ask the senior vice-president? Why?
2. Given your present knowledge of the situation, what level of system capability do you feel is appropriate for New York City Bank?

Case 11-2: New York City Bank (B)

John Q. Hamilton, a senior vice-president of the New York City Bank, is interested in the possibility of applying human resource accounting in a pilot study in his firm. He is considering focusing a study on the bank's loan officers. The bank currently employs about 3,000 loan officers and recruits between 100 and 250 annually. For the coming year, the bank expects to hire approximately 225 new loan officers.

Starting salary for loan officers is approximately $16,000; the expected salary progression is shown in Table 11-3. Turnover among loan officers during the first few years of employment is relatively high. At New York City Bank, a turnover rate of about 20 percent per year is experienced. In discussing the cost of loan officer turnover, Hamilton said:

Table 11-3

EXPECTED SALARY PROGRESSION

(First Five Years)

Year	*Loan Officers Mean Salary*
1	$16,000
2	18,500
3	21,000
4	23,500
5	26,000

> If we lose a loan officer before he has been with the bank two years, we lose a great deal. I feel that the breakeven point is somewhere between the second and third year, although I don't know that for sure. It seems to me that if

we lose a loan officer before then, we've cost the bank a lot of money.

Hamilton also thought that turnover was controllable: "I can control turnover through salary increases and in other ways. But I want to know what it's worth to me to do so."

Questions

1. What is the expected cost of turnover (ignoring recruiting and training costs) to New York City Bank for the next five-year period?
2. What might Hamilton do to reduce turnover? What would the net savings (cost) to the bank be from your proposal?

Case 11-3: Telephone Components Manufacturing Corp.

Telephone Components Manufacturing Corp. (TCMC) is the manufacturing and supply unit of a large telecommunications corporation. The principal function of TCMC is to manufacture various apparatus, equipment, cable, and wire. The company's plants are located in various parts of the country.

In 1971, the company was planning for the development of a new plant. Plans included developing the plant's personnel subsystem, which was to have a human resource accounting capability. To develop human resource accounting at the plant, a study team prepared a roster of variables involved in the acquisition, maintenance, and utilization of personnel, as shown in Table 11-4.

Questions

1. Using the information shown in Table 11-4, prepare a chart of human resource accounts for the proposed plant.
2. Are there any variables you would add to those shown in Table 11-4?

Table 11-4

HUMAN RESOURCE ACCOUNTING

Identification of Variables for Acquisition, Maintenance and Utilization of Personnel

I. *Position Planning**

A. Job Description

1. Compose initial job description.
2. Update job description.

B. Job Evaluation

1. Conduct initial job evaluation.
2. Update job evaluation.

C. Approval of Job Requisition

II. *Acquisition**

A. Recruiting

1. Public relations costs
2. Advertising
   a. Media (papers, magazines, radio, special booklets)
   b. Search firms
   c. Professional conventions
3. Recruiters' interviewing
   a. Preparations for visit
   b. Contacts (telephone, letter, etc.)
   c. Maintaining relationships with colleges and universities
4. Interviews
   a. Standardized forms
   b. Location contact
   c. Location processing—review of applicants
5. Recruiters' training
   a. Recruiter workshop
   b. Human resource accounting costs (recruiters); learning, maintaining and organizational costs
   c. Administrative—recruiter conference for college development program

B. Final Selection

1. Plant visit
   a. Recruiter's costs
   b. Plant personnel interview time
2. Testing
   a. Administrative costs
   b. Validation costs
3. Administrative reports
   a. Internal reports
4. Medical screening—pre-employment physical
5. Reference checking
   a. Verifying biographical information
6. Decision process
   a. Consultation
   b. Contact with salary administration
   c. "Turndowns"
   d. "Over the counter" screening

Table 11-4 (continued)

III. *On Boarding**

A. Processing Forms

B. Briefing on Benefits

1. Yours
2. Theirs

C. Relocation Expenses

1. Househunting trip
2. Moving expenses
3. Transportation department expenses

IV. *Learning**

A. Orientation

1. Formal training–(Corporate Education Center)
2. Informal training–on-the-job training, tutoring

B. Cost of Performance Less Than Criterion Performance

C. Training Programs' Supervisory and Administrative Cuts

D. Supervisor's Orientation and Training Time

E. Supplies and Clerical Costs

F. Training and Program Development

V. *Maintaining**

A. Updating

1. Formal courses
2. Informal courses

B. Overhead (Non-Physical)†

*A percentage of fixed cost is associated with each variable listed. These fixed costs include:

A. Material costs
  1. Travel
  2. Living expenses
  3. Facilities
B. Clerical support costs
C. Salary
D. Time to do a job task
E. Overhead (non-physical)
  1. Blue Cross/Blue Shield
  2. Extraordinary medical expense
  3. Employment compensation
  4. Health insurance
  5. Insurance
  6. Life insurance
  7. Pensions
  8. Savings plan
  9. Social Security
  10. Tuition refund
  11. Unemployment insurance
  12. Vacation

†Overhead can be broken into two specific corporate costs: (1) investment for each employee, and (2) administration of the various plans.

Case 11-4: Global Bank

Global Bank is a large bank with headquarters in New York City. For the past three years, Global Bank has instituted cost-avoidance and cost-reduction programs.

In 1970, as part of its overall cost-reduction program, Global's executive vice-president ordered all departments to reduce their budgets by 10 percent. In 1971 and 1972, the departments were budgeted at the approved 1970 levels. Departmental work loads, it is recognized, have increased during the past three years.

Herbert H. Muhler, Global's executive vice-president in charge of operations, has recently become concerned about possible adverse effects of the cost-reduction program. He is especially concerned about employee morale. He has asked the vice-president in charge of employee relations to consider how the bank can find out the cost, if any, of decreased morale.

Question

You are a personnel specialist, and you have been asked by the vice-president in charge of employee relations to recommend an approach to this program. Prepare a memo outlining your suggestions.

TWELVE

Applications for Improving Management, Training, and Personnel Decisions

Apart from the range of uses described throughout this book, the technology of human resource accounting has begun to be applied in a variety of ways by human resource professionals and other senior managers in organizations. This chapter shows three major ways in which human resource accounting can be used in making management decisions.

The first application involves the use of human resource accounting in cost/benefit analyses. In particular, it focuses on the process of deciding whether to acquire corporate aircraft rather than use commercial transportation as well as on the cost justification of this decision to government agencies. The role of human resource accounting in this decision is to measure the value of executive time, if any, saved by using corporate rather than commercial aircraft. The second application involves the use of cost accounting information in making personnel layoff decisions. This application shows how human resource professionals can assist management in making optimal layoff decisions. The final application deals with the use of human resource accounting to evaluate the return on investment in management development programs.

Cost/Benefit Analyses

This section deals with the application of human resource accounting in making cost/benefit decisions and analyses. As an example of this class of application, we shall focus on the role of information in deciding among alternative courses of action such as the acquisition of corporate aircraft versus the use of commercial aircraft. This application is of widespread concern to many U.S. organizations.

As the context of this application, we shall examine an actual situation faced by a company. The name of the organization has been disguised and the numbers involved have been changed to preserve the company's confidentiality. The basic aspects of the situation actually occurred, however, and illustrate the type of analysis required as well as the role of human resource accounting information in that analysis.

Greenfield Aviation owns and operates corporate aircraft that they use when commercial travel is unavailable or inconvenient. In general, the direct costs of operating these aircraft exceed the airfare required for commercial travel. Management believed this cost was justified by the increase in executive productivity (time saved) realized with the use of corporate aircraft. Management's judgment, then, was based on the value of human resources, but they knew no way of testing that judgment.

Since Greenfield Aviation is a government contractor, they ultimately had to justify their decision to the U.S. government office with which they were under contract. The government wanted the commensurate advantage, if any, to be quantified. The purpose of this study, then, was to determine the commensurate advantage, if any, of using corporate aircraft over the commercial alternatives.

Overview of the Model. This problem was approached as an economic cost/benefit analysis. An attempt was made to quantify all direct and opportunity costs associated with corporate and commercial travel. The first step in this process was to develop a model for making this type of decision.

The model has two components: direct costs and the opportunity costs of executive time wasted. These components are described briefly here and outlined in Table 12-1.

The *direct costs* refer to the operating costs of the corporate aircraft and the commercial airfares. These are the direct costs most readily available and the easiest to quantify. The cost of the corporate aircraft was questioned primarily because of the clear differentials in the direct costs. These costs, however, represent only a portion of the relevant costs

Table 12-1

DIFFERENTIAL COST ANALYSIS OF USE OF CORPORATE VS. COMMERCIAL AIRCRAFT

Costs	*Corporate Aircraft*	*Commercial Aircraft*	*Differential Costs*
Direct costs	Operating costs	Commercial airfare	______
Opportunity cost of executive time			
Preflight ground transportation	______	______	______
Differential in-flight productivity	______	______	______
Transfer time	______	______	______
Postflight ground transportation	______	______	______
Differential postflight productivity	______	______	______
Total cost	______	______	______

in making the comparison between corporate and commercial aircraft.

As for the *opportunity cost of wasted time,* in this study it was determined that five types of productive time are saved by using the corporate jet over the commercial alternative:

1. Preflight ground time wasted: Employees find that they must leave their homes significantly earlier to make a commercial flight than they do to make a corporate flight—because of traffic, parking, baggage handling, and delays. Moreover, many of the corporate flights leave during, or immediately after, the business day. These flights may effectively have no preflight ground time because they leave directly from work.
2. In-flight productivity: Studies indicate that productivity is greatly hampered while in flight due to noise and other discomforts. Since corporate aircraft are configured differently in order to be quieter and more conducive to work, in-flight time tends to be more productive. The productivity levels are also likely to depend on whether it is a day or night flight, as people are less productive at night. Finally, there may be more flight time on a commercial jet because it may make stops that the corporate jet can avoid.

3. Transfer time: The commercial flights sometimes require plane changes and associated ground time in addition to the actual flight times. In contrast, corporate aircraft take primarily direct routes. This time is likely to be spent in airports or on planes and represents additional lost productivity.
4. Postflight ground time wasted: This element is similar to the preflight ground time—that is, the corporate plane may land closer to the destination and waste less time. Furthermore, there may be fewer delays in parking, baggage handling, and customs (if the flight is overseas).
5. Differential postflight productivity: Research suggests that the effects of jet lag may be felt up to five days after arriving at the destination. There are also a number of studies indicating that flight environments and departure times can reduce the effects of jet lag. It is reasonable, then, to suppose that during the three to five days following a flight across several time zones there may be substantial savings due to reduced jet lag.

Implementation of the Model. This section considers how each component of the model was measured. This stage involved developing the formulas and seeking information to measure or approximate its variables.

We begin with the *direct flight costs.* For the corporate aircraft, the operating costs represent the direct costs and could be taken from company records. This information had previously been accepted by both Greenfield and the U.S. government. If the corporate aircraft were not available, however, the direct costs were determined by the commercial airfares multiplied by the number of employee flights.

The *opportunity cost of time wasted* is based on the time and productivity differentials between corporate and commercial travel. These hours are valued at rates based on three methods: average compensation of the passengers, average compensation plus an overhead allocation, and compensation plus overhead plus a reasonable rate of return. These conceptualizations of value give a range for what the wasted time was worth to Greenfield if they had used corporate or commercial transportation.

To obtain the compensation information required, it was necessary to draw a random sample of passengers from the flight logs of each plane. Greenfield Aviation provided the compensation data for that sample of employees. The averages were considered to be representative of the value of the passengers' time.

Much of the difficulty in measuring the opportunity cost of wasted time rests in determining the *amount* of time wasted. The following calculations were used to estimate the five types of time wasted:

1. Preflight ground time: The preflight ground time may be expressed as follows (see Table 12-2 for the variable key):

$$T_{bf} = G_{bf} \times N_p \times F$$

where T_{bf} = total ground time (hours) before flight
G_{bf} = average ground time (hours) per person before flight
N_p = average number of people per flight
F = average number of flights

The ground times are expected to be different when comparing the use of corporate aircraft to commercial aircraft.

2. In-flight time wasted: The amount of in-flight time wasted is a function of whether the flights are during the day or night as well as the environment on the plane. The in-flight time wasted may be expressed as follows:

$$T_{if} = H_{if}\, D \times (1 - P_{df}) + (1 - D)\,(1 - P_{nf})$$

where T_{if} = total in-flight time wasted
H_{if} = total in-flight passenger hours
D = percentage of flight hours that are day flights
P_{df} = productivity level achieved on day flights
P_{nf} = productivity level achieved on night flights

This formula essentially determines how many passenger hours are during the day and how many are at night. These figures are then multiplied by the expected productivity losses (day or night) to calculate the total number of hours lost.

3. Transfer time wasted: Transfer time applies, for the most part, to commercial travel. Similar to in-flight productivity, the transfer productivity depends on whether the transfer is during the day or at night. Total transfer time wasted may be expressed as follows:

Table 12-2

VARIABLE KEY

Symbol	*Description*	*Source*
C_f	Average commercial airfare per flight	OAG manual
D	Percentage of flight hours that are during the day	Flight logs (corporate), OAG (commercial)
F	Number of flights	Flight logs (corporate jet), management's judgment (commercial)
G_{af}	Average ground time (hours) per person after flight	Survey, management's judgment
G_{bf}	Average ground time (hours) per person before flight	Survey, management's judgment
H_d	Average hours per work day	Survey, employees
H_{if}	Total in-flight passenger hours	Flight log (corporate jet), OAG, management's judgment
H_{tr}	Total passenger transfer hours	OAG, management's judgment
N_p	Average number of people per flight	Flight log
P_{d1}	Productivity level first day after arrival	Literature search, survey employees
P_{d2}	Productivity level second day after arrival	Literature search, survey employees
P_{d3}	Productivity level third day after arrival	Literature search, survey employees
P_{df}	Productivity achieved on day flights	Literature search, survey employees
P_{dt}	Productivity achieved during day transfers	Literature search, survey employees
P_{nf}	Productivity achieved on night flights	Literature search, survey employees
P_{nt}	Productivity achieved during night transfers	Literature search, survey employees
T_{af}	Total ground time (hours) after flight	Dependent variable
T_{bf}	Total ground time (hours) before flight	Dependent variable
T_{if}	Total in-flight time (hours) wasted	Dependent variable
T_{pf}	Total time (hours) wasted from postflight productivity loss	Dependent variable
T_{tr}	Total transfer time (hours) wasted	Dependent variable

$$T_{tr} = H_{tr}[D \times (1 - P_{dt}) + (1 - D)(1 - P_{nt})]$$

where T_{tr} = total passenger transfer hours wasted
H_{tr} = total passenger transfer hours
P_{dt} = productivity level achieved during day transfers
P_{nt} = productivity level achieved during night transfers

Similar to the formula for in-flight time wasted, this formula calculates the number of transfer hours that are during the day and those that are at night. These figures are then multiplied by the percentage of that time which is nonproductive or wasted (1 = productivity factor) to determine the total transfer hours wasted.

4. Postflight ground time wasted: This component is almost the same as preflight ground time wasted. It is expressed as follows:

$$T_{af} = G_{af} \times N_p \times F$$

where T_{af} = total ground time (hours) wasted after flight
G_{af} = average ground time (hours) wasted after flight.

Essentially it is the total number of person flights times the average ground time per person per flight.

5. Postflight productivity loss: The amount of time lost in the days following the arrival may be expressed as follows:

$$T_{pf} = [(1 - P_{d1}) + (1 - P_{d2}) + (1 - P_{d3})] \times N_p \times F \times H_d$$

where T_{pf} = total postflight hours wasted
H_d = average hours per work day
P_{d1} = level of productivity achieved on first day after arrival
P_{d2} = level of productivity achieved on second day after arrival
P_{d3} = level of productivity achieved on third day after arrival

This formula reflects that it takes about three days after a major flight to get back to 100 percent of expected productivity. The average hours per day are multiplied by the percentage of that time which is expected to be nonproductive for that day. This is time wasted due to travel in the days after the trip. This time is relevant only for business trips that cross many time zones.

Application of the Model. This section discusses the application of the model to the cost/benefit analysis between corporate and commercial aircraft at Greenfield Aviation. The economic costs (including opportunity costs) for operating these planes are compared to the economic costs of the commercial alternative. The values for all the independent variables in Table 12-2 are shown in Table 12-3.

Table 12-3

VARIABLE VALUES

Symbol	*Description*	*Corporate*	*Commercial*
C_f	Average commercial airfare per flight		$200
D	Percentage of flight hours that are during the day	0.85	0.75
F	Number of flights	185	185
G_{af}	Average ground time (hours) per person after flight	0.25	1.00
G_{bf}	Average ground time (hours) per person before flight	0.25	1.00
H_d	Average hours per work day	8.50	8.50
H_{if}	Total in-flight passenger hours	10,360	14,245
H_{tr}	Total passenger transfer hours		3,885
N_p	Average number of people per flight	14	14
P_{d1}	Productivity level first day after arrival	0.80	0.70
P_{d2}	Productivity level second day after arrival	0.90	0.85
P_{d3}	Productivity level third day after arrival	1.00	0.95
P_{df}	Productivity achieved on day flights	0.75	0.25
P_{dt}	Productivity achieved during day transfers		0.10
P_{nf}	Productivity achieved on night flights	0	0.05
P_{nt}	Productivity level achieved during night transfers		0

The *direct costs* for the corporate jet were taken from company records and totaled $2,000,000. The direct costs for commercial travel are based on the commercial fares multiplied by the number of passenger flights, or $1,036,000 (5,180 passenger flights multiplied by $200 fare per flight).

The first step in measuring the *opportunity cost of time wasted* is to determine the average value of a passenger's time. The research team drew a random sample of passengers from the flight logs, and Greenfield's management determined the compensation and overhead associated with each (Table 12-4). The cost of this wasted time has been calculated in Table 12-5 under all three conceptualizations of value.

Table 12-4

AMOUNT OF TIME WASTED

Preflight ground (hours) wasted
Formula: $T_{bf} = G_{bf} \times N_p \times F$
Corporate: 648 = 0.25 X 14 X 185
Commercial: 2,590 = 1.0 X 14 X 185

In-flight time (hours) wasted
Formula: $T_{if} = H_{if} [D \times (1 - P_{df}) + (1 - D)(1 - P_{nf})]$
Corporate: 3,756 = 10,360[0.85 X (0.25) + (0.15)(1)]
Commercial: 11,063 = 14,245[0.75 X (0.75) + (0.25)(0.95)]

Transfer time (hours) wasted
Formula: $T_{tr} = H_{tr}[D \times (1 - P_{dt}) + (1 - D)(1 - P_{nt})]$
Corporate: No plane changes necessary
Commercial: 1,263 = 3,885[0.75 X (0.1) + (0.25)(1)]

Postflight ground time (hours) wasted
Formula: $T_{af} = G_{af} \times N_p \times F$
Corporate: 648 = 0.25 X 14 X 185
Commercial: 2,590 = 1.0 X 14 X 185

Postflight productivity loss (hours) due to jet lag
Formula: $T_{pf} = [(1 - P_{d1}) + (1 - P_{d2}) + (1 - P_{d3})] \times Np \times F \times H_d$
Corporate: 6,605 = [(0.20) + (0.10) + (0.0)] X 14 X 185 X 8.5
Commercial: 11,008 = [(0.30) + (0.15) + (0.05)] X 14 X 185 X 8.5

The final step in applying the model involved looking at both the direct and opportunity costs. Because the most realistic valuation is the "reasonable return" method, these numbers are presented in Table 12-6.

Conclusion. While the results presented in Table 12-6 are not conclusive, they suggest that corporate aircraft are actually cheaper. In the long run, factors such as morale may broaden the gap between the corporate and commercial alternatives. It is clear, however, that the opportunity cost of time is a major component in making the decision to use corporate aircraft or the commercial alternatives.

Layoff Decisions

This section describes how accounting for human resource costs can assist in making layoff decisions. An example is used to clarify the difference between how traditional layoff decisions are made and how these decisions are made when human resource cost information is used

Table 12-5

COST OF TIME WASTED

Type of Time	Number of Hours		Compensation-Based* Cost of Wasted Time		Compensation & Overhead† Cost of Wasted Time		Reasonable Return‡ Cost of Wasted Time	
	Corporate	Commercial	Corporate	Commercial	Corporate	Commercial	Corporate	Commercial
Preflight ground time	648	2,590	$ 16,200	$ 64,750	$ 32,400	$ 129,500	$ 38,880	$ 155,400
In-flight time	3,756	11,063	93,900	276,575	187,800	553,150	225,360	663,780
Transfer time	—	1,263		31,575		63,150		75,780
Postflight ground time	648	2,590	16,200	64,750	32,400	129,500	38,880	155,400
Postflight productivity loss	6,605	11,008	165,125	275,200	330,250	550,400	396,300	660,480
Total opportunity cost of time wasted			$291,425	$712,850	$582,850	$1,425,700	$699,420	$1,710,840

*Compensation-based value includes only the hourly compensation as an indicator of value. This conservative measure comes to $25 per hour.

†Compensation plus overhead based value includes an overhead allocation to better approximate the full costs. This valuation indicates that $50 per hour is the value of the average passenger's time.

‡When we add a "reasonable rate of return" to this valuation it most closely approximates a billing rate and serves as a better surrogate value. This measure comes to $60 per hour.

Table 12-6

DIFFERENTIAL COST ANALYSIS OF USE OF CORPORATE VS. COMMERCIAL AIRCRAFT

Costs	*Corporate Aircraft*	*Commercial Aircraft*	*Advantage of Corporate over Commercial Aircraft: Differential Costs*
Direct costs	$2,000,000	$1,036,000	$(964,000)
Opportunity cost of executive time			
Preflight ground transportation	38,880	155,400	116,520
Differential in-flight productivity	225,360	663,780	438,420
Transfer time		75,780	75,780
Postflight ground transportation	38,880	155,400	116,520
Differential postflight productivity	396,300	660,480	264,180
Total cost	$2,699,420	$2,746,840	$ 47,420

in the analysis. We shall see that the calculation of human resource costs related to layoff decisions can result in more rational decision making.

Description of the Problem. Electrotech Corporation was formed in 1978 to develop and manufacture home entertainment products. The main products of this company were video cassette games and video cassette game players.

The firm's founder and president, Keith Jones, anticipated a growing market for home video games due to increasing popularity of video arcades among children and young adults. Since the home market for such products seemed relatively untapped, both video game players and cassettes were designed to meet this need.

The firm was apparently successful in defining a market need and in designing products to meet it, since the company grew very rapidly. From 1978 to 1982, Electrotech's sales increased from $2 million to more than $20 million and the number of employees increased from under 50 to nearly 200. A great deal of the firm's success could be attributed to the skill and creativity of its employees. Their ingenuity combined with their ability to deal with the intricate details of production was highly valued by the firm.

In 1983, Electrotech began to experience declining sales. It appeared that the market for home video games had become saturated. Sales for 1983 were forecast at $18 million. This prediction concerned the company's president since operating costs were also projected to be higher—clearly the company would show a decreased profit for the year if something were not done. The president decided that the company would have to tighten its belt if market conditions did not improve.

In June 1983, conditions had not improved for the year and Keith Jones decided that the company should consider a temporary layoff of some of its employees as a way to cut costs and improve the profit picture. A permanent layoff seemed impractical since the company would soon begin manufacturing a new product line that would require the services of those laid off. This production was scheduled to begin in approximately sixteen weeks. Therefore the layoff period would last no longer than sixteen weeks.

To obtain the information necessary to make a decision regarding the length of the layoff, the president asked the company's controller to estimate the savings from a layoff of some of the work force for four, eight, twelve, and sixteen weeks. In estimating these savings, the controller could have used one of two methods. These methods and their potential outcomes are described in the following paragraphs.

The Traditional Method in Layoff Decisions. Layoff decisions are traditionally based on a consideration of payroll savings. This procedure usually consists of:

1. Selecting the portion of the work force to be laid off
2. Estimating the average salary of these employees
3. Selecting the period of time the layoff will last

The period of time and the percentage of the work force may be allowed to vary so that the company can determine the best alternative.

In the case of Electrotech, the president decided that 140 employees would be laid off. The average weekly salary of these employees was $320. The president asked the controller to determine savings from four-, eight-, twelve-, and sixteen-week layoffs. Using this information, the controller made the estimates presented in Table 12-7.

Based on the information provided in Table 12-7, the president of the firm and top management could select the layoff period that would result in the savings needed to make the bottom line look better for the year. In the case of Electrotech, the president decided that an eight-week

Table 12-7

ESTIMATES OF PAYROLL SAVINGS

Layoff Period (Weeks)	*Employees Laid Off*	*Average Salary*	*Payroll Savings*
4	140	$320	$179,200
8	140	$320	$358,400
12	140	$320	$537,500
16	140	$320	$716,800

layoff, resulting in a savings of $358,400, would significantly improve the company's profit picture for the year.

Using Human Resource Cost Information in Layoff Decisions. This approach to making layoff decisions involves a cost/benefit analysis. In this analysis, both payroll savings and human resource costs are considered. These costs include the cost of rehiring laid-off employees, the cost of replacing employees who do not return after the layoff, and the costs associated with declining morale among employees who are not laid off.

The *cost of rehiring* may be defined as the costs associated with decreased productivity upon the employee's return to the firm. This calculation assumes that it will take a period of time, following the layoff, for the employee to begin working at his or her standard level of performance. One way that this cost can be estimated is by asking supervisors to complete a productivity graph on which they can plot a typical returning employee's level of productivity over time compared to standard. An example of such a graph is given in Figure 12-1.

In this example, the rehired employee is performing at approximately 50 percent of his or her standard performance prior to the layoff on the first day of reentry into the firm. It takes approximately eight working days for the employee to reach his or her standard performance level again. As long as performance remains below standard, there is a cost to the organization in terms of lost productivity.

The *cost of replacing workers* who do not return is equal to the cost of recruiting, selecting, and training new employees to fill the vacated positions. The method for calculating these costs was discussed in Chapter Three.

Figure 12-1

EXAMPLE OF A PRODUCTIVITY GRAPH

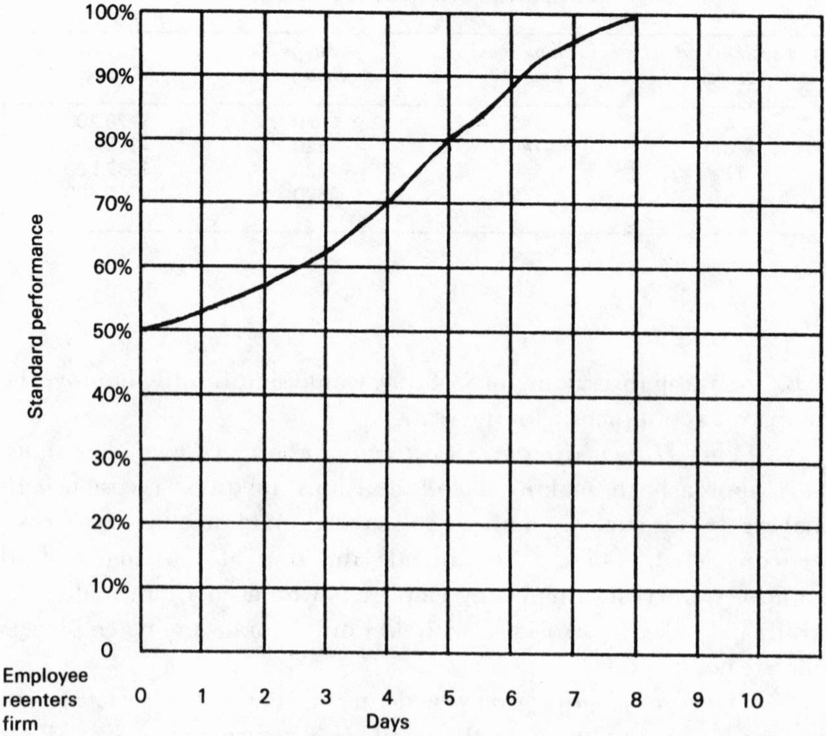

The *cost of decreasing morale* is difficult to measure. In the case of layoffs, it is assumed that employees who are not laid off will be psychologically affected by the situation in the firm. There are at least two possible ways to measure the costs associated with decreased morale. The first method assumes that decreased morale will result in decreased productivity. The cost associated with this decreased productivity can be estimated by asking supervisors to complete a productivity graph. The second method assumes that the decreased morale will lead to increased turnover. This method consists of periodically taking morale surveys and comparing the levels of morale found in the surveys with annual turnover. A drop in morale resulting from a layoff could then be related to a certain percentage of increase in turnover. For example, it might be found that a decline of 10 points in morale results in a 5 percent increase in turnover for the year. Costs of decreased morale, in this case, would be the costs of replacing the differential number of personnel who quit as a result of decreased morale.

To use this method of analyzing layoff decisions, the following steps are performed:

1. Estimate the percentage of employees expected to return after the layoff period. If more than one layoff period is being considered, estimate the percentage of employees who will return after each period. Estimates should be made in terms of "optimistic," "realistic," and "pessimistic" conditions.
2. Estimate the cost of rehiring an employee as described above. Multiply this amount by the number of employees expected to return to produce the total rehiring cost.
3. Calculate the replacement cost per employee who does not return. Methods for calculating replacement cost per employee were described in Chapter Three. To produce the total replacement cost, multiply this amount by the total number of employees not expected to return.
4. Estimate the cost of decreased morale by using one of the two methods described above. A decision may also be made not to consider this cost component. When this is the case, the layoff cost estimates will be conservative.
5. Add the three costs calculated in steps 2 to 4 to produce the total cost of the layoff.
6. Estimate the probabilities of the optimistic, realistic, and pessimistic conditions occurring. For each layoff period, multiply the total layoff cost in each condition by its respective probability. Sum these figures to produce the expected cost of the layoff period.
7. Calculate the estimated payroll savings by multiplying the total number of employees laid off by their average weekly salary. Then multiply this number by the total number of weeks in the layoff period.
8. Subtract the estimated cost of layoff from the estimated payroll savings to obtain the net benefit/cost to the company of making a particular layoff decision.

Using the steps described above, the controller of Electrotech Corporation performed the following analysis:

1. The percentage of employees expected to return after each layoff period and for each condition is presented in Table 12-8.

Table 12-8

PERCENTAGE OF EMPLOYEES EXPECTED TO RETURN
For Optimistic, Realistic, and Pessimistic Conditions

Layoff Period (Weeks)	*Optimistic*	*Realistic*	*Pessimistic*
4	95%	80%	65%
8	90%	75%	60%
12	85%	70%	55%
16	80%	65%	50%

Table 12-9

COST OF REHIRING EMPLOYEES
For Optimistic, Realistic, and Pessimistic Conditions of Each Layoff Period

Cost Elements	*Optimistic*	*Realistic*	*Pessimistic*
4-Week Layoff			
Estimated % employees rehired	95% (133)	80% (112)	65% (91)
Total rehiring costs	$42,560	$35,860	$29,120
8-Week Layoff			
Estimated % employees rehired	90% (126)	75% (105)	60% (84)
Total rehiring costs	$40,320	$33,600	$26,880
12-Week Layoff			
Estimated % employees rehired	85% (119)	70% (98)	55% (77)
Total rehiring costs	$38,080	$31,360	$24,640
16-Week Layoff			
Estimated % employees rehired	80% (112)	65% (91)	50% (70)
Total rehiring costs	$35,840	$29,120	$22,400

2. The cost due to lost productivity was obtained by asking supervisors who had previous experience with layoff rehires to plot the expected productivity of these employees immediately following rehire. An example of such a productivity graph was presented in Figure 12-1. From the graphs obtained from supervisors, it was estimated that the cost per employee rehired would be one week's salary, or $320. The total costs of rehiring for each layoff period and each condition are

presented in Table 12-9. These costs assume that 140 employees (7 percent of the work force) are laid off.

3. Using the procedure described in Chapter Three, the controller calculated the replacement cost of a position holder as follows:

Recruitment costs	$400
Selection costs	$200
Training costs	$10,000
Total replacement cost	$10,600

Table 12-10 presents replacement cost estimates for the work force lost for each of the layoff periods and each of the conditions.

4. The cost of decreased morale among employees not laid off was estimated by using a productivity graph. Supervisors who had experience with layoffs were asked to estimate the decline in productivity experienced among those not laid off using the graph.

Table 12-10

REPLACEMENT COST OF WORK FORCE LOST
For Optimistic, Realistic, and Pessimistic Conditions of Each Layoff Period

Cost Elements	*Optimistic*	*Realistic*	*Pessimistic*
4-Week Layoff			
Estimated % employees not rehired	5% (7)	20% (28)	35% (49)
Total replacement cost	$74,200	$296,800	$519,400
8-Week Layoff			
Estimated % employees not rehired	10% (14)	25% (35)	40% (56)
Total replacement cost	$148,400	$371,000	$593,600
12-Week Layoff			
Estimated % employees not rehired	15% (21)	30% (42)	45% (63)
Total replacement cost	$222,600	$445,200	$667,800
16-Week Layoff			
Estimated % employees not rehired	20% (28)	35% (49)	50% (70)
Total replacement cost	$296,800	$519,400	$742,000

Table 12-11

TOTAL COST OF LAYOFF
For Optimistic, Realistic, and Pessimistic Conditions of Each Layoff Period

Cost Elements	*Optimistic*	*Realistic*	*Pessimistic*
4-Week Layoff			
Total rehiring cost	$42,560	$35,840	$29,120
Total replacement cost	$74,200	$296,800	$519,400
Cost of decreased morale	$52,520	$52,520	$52,520
Total cost of layoff	$176,280	$385,160	$601,040
8-Week Layoff			
Total rehiring cost	$40,320	$33,600	$26,880
Total replacement cost	$148,400	$371,000	$593,600
Cost of decreased morale	$52,520	$52,520	$52,520
Total cost of layoff	$241,240	$457,120	$673,000
12-Week Layoff			
Total rehiring cost	$38,080	$31,360	$24,640
Total replacement cost	$222,600	$445,200	$667,800
Cost of decreased morale	$52,520	$52,520	$52,520
Total cost of layoff	$317,200	$529,080	$744,960
16-Week Layoff			
Total rehiring cost	$35,840	$29,120	$22,400
Total replacement cost	$296,800	$519,400	$742,000
Cost of decreased morale	$52,520	$52,520	$52,520
Total cost of layoff	$385,160	$601,040	$816,920

The cost of decreased morale was estimated to be a half day's wages per employee remaining after the layoff. Assuming that there are 2,000 employees at Electrotech and that 140 are laid off, this means that there is a cost of $59,520 attributed to decreased morale in each of the layoff periods and each of the conditions (1,860 × $32).

5. Using the information provided in the four steps described above, the controller was able to estimate the total cost of layoff for each of the time periods and each of the conditions. This information is presented in Table 12-11.
6. The controller estimated that there was a 10 percent, 80 percent, and 10 percent chance of the optimistic, realistic, and pessimistic conditions occurring, respectively. These probabilities were used to calculate the expected cost of layoff. The calculations are presented in Table 12-12.
7. The controller estimated the payroll savings from layoff by multiplying the total number of employees laid off (140) by their average weekly salary ($320). This product was then multiplied by the total number of weeks in the layoff period in question. Table 12-13 presents the total estimated payroll savings.
8. The final step in estimating the savings from layoff is to compare the estimated costs with the payroll savings for each period of layoff. This comparison is presented in Table 12-14.

Using this method of analyzing the layoff decision, a layoff of eight weeks or less will actually cost the firm more than it will save. This analysis suggests that the firm will receive the greatest cost savings from a layoff of twelve weeks or more.

Comparing the Two Methods. A comparison of the results obtained from using the two methods for analysis of a layoff decision suggests that in the absence of human resource cost information, the decision can be costly to the firm. In order to make a completely rational decision, it is necessary for the firm to perform a human resource accounting cost analysis as outlined here. In this way, the firm can determine the true economic savings from its layoff decisions and avoid a decision that ignores a hidden cost of lost human resources.

Evaluating Management Development Programs

This section examines another application of human resource accounting. It presents a case study of how accounting for human

Table 12-12

CALCULATION OF EXPECTED COST OF LAYOFF

Layoff Period (Weeks)	*Cost**	*Prob.*	*Cost*	*Prob.*	*Cost*	*Prob.*	*Expected Cost*
4	$176	10%	$385	80%	$601	10%	$385,160
8	$241	10%	$457	80%	$673	10%	$457,120
12	$371	10%	$529	80%	$744	10%	$529,000
16	$385	10%	$601	80%	$816	10%	$601,040

*In thousands.

Table 12-13

TOTAL ESTIMATED PAYROLL SAVINGS FROM LAYOFF OF 7% OF WORK FORCE

Period of Layoff (Weeks)	*Payroll Savings*
4	$179,200
8	$358,400
12	$537,600
16	$716,800

Table 12-14

COMPARISON OF COSTS AND BENEFITS OF LAYOFF DECISION

Period of Layoff (Weeks)	*Estimated Payroll Savings*	*Estimated Cost of Layoff*	*Net Benefit (Cost)*
4	$179,200	$385,160	$(205,960)
8	$358,400	$457,120	$(98,720)
12	$537,600	$529,080	$8,520
16	$716,800	$601,040	$115,760

resource value can be used to evaluate management development and training programs.

Management development programs are intended to help personnel gain the skills necessary to be successful managers. Development of managerial skills increases the potential of employees to provide services to the organization and, in turn, increases their value to the organization by increasing their productivity, promotability, and transferability. Human resource accounting provides a way to assess the increased value contributed by management development. It also provides a method of calculating whether the change in value results in a positive return on investment in management development.

Problem Statement. Omicron, a medium-sized high-tech firm, encourages present and potential managers to enroll in university-sponsored training programs. The company provides a small stipend for those who choose to attend, but the individual must schedule the courses so that they do not conflict with work hours. Although only about half of all managers had traditionally attended these programs, the company believes that those who attend are better prepared for the responsibilities of the managerial role. The company also believes that these programs increase the effectiveness of its managers and hence their productivity. These beliefs are based, in part, on the opinions of supervisors, peers, and instructors.

Recently the new president, Kevin Hartman, has begun to question the worth of these management development programs. Hartman has suggested that, in terms of management potential, there is no difference between those who participate in these courses and those who do not. He has also suggested that if this is the case, the programs are costing the firm more than the benefits derived.

The director of human resources, John Walker, does not agree. He believes that the programs should continue, although he cannot quantify their value to the firm. Walker has heard about human resource accounting and, in fact, has recently hired a consultant who is familiar with this field. He has asked the consultant to perform a study assessing the effects of participation in management development programs on the person's value to the firm. The analysis performed by this consultant, based on the principles discussed in Chapter Seven, is described in the following paragraphs.

Identification of Service States. The first step in using the model for valuation of human resources is to identify the service states of

Figure 12-2

CAREER LADDER OF AN ENGINEER

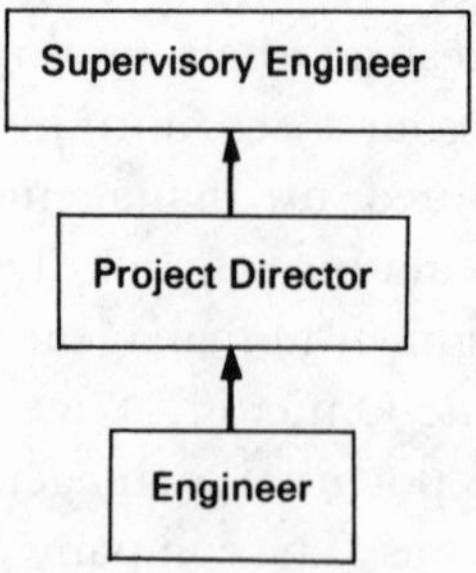

interest. The career ladder of interest at this company is presented in Figure 12-2.

Based on this career ladder, the service states of interest were identified as:

1. Supervisory engineer
2. Project director
3. Engineer
4. Exit state

"Engineer" was identified as the position of interest—that is, the organization was interested in how participation in a management development program affected the value of a person currently occupying the position of engineer.

Determination of Service State Values. The consultant next needed to identify the values of each service state. Since the company billed its personnel on contracts, the consultant calculated the service state values by multiplying the billing rates and expected chargeable hours for each service state classification, as discussed in Chapter Seven. The service state values derived from this procedure are presented in Table 12-15.

Table 12-15

SERVICE STATE VALUES FOR ENGINEER CAREER LADDER

Service State	*Value*
Exit	$0
Engineer	$27,000
Project director	$33,000
Engineer supervisor	$40,000

Calculation of Transition Matrices. The consultant was able to obtain information on the types of state-to-state transitions made by 200 employees for a period of ten years. The consultant was also able to separate those individuals who had completed a management development program from those who had not, since this company made it a policy of noting such participation in its personnel files. One hundred employees in the sample had participated in such programs and one hundred employees had not.

From this information, the consultant was able to construct two transition matrices: one for those who did not participate in management development programs and one for those who did. These matrices are presented in Tables 12-16 and 12-17, respectively.

A comparison of these two matrices suggests that participation in a management development program increases the likelihood of being promoted. An examination of the engineer and project director service states within the two matrices reveals that the probability of promotion to the next service state increases by approximately 10 to 15 percent with participation in a management development program. Moreover, probability of exit decreases by approximately 5 percent with participation. This finding suggests that participation in these programs may not only increase the probability of promotion but may also increase the probability of individuals remaining with the firm. Both changes in the matrix affect the value of individuals to the firm.

Determination of a Discount Rate. The firm has determined that its relevant cost of capital is 10 percent. The consultant has decided to use this as the appropriate discount rate in the model.

Table 12-16

TRANSITION MATRIX FOR NONPARTICIPANTS IN MANAGEMENT DEVELOPMENT PROGRAM

	Year T + 1			
Year T	*Supervisory Engineer*	*Project Director*	*Engineer*	*Exit*
Supervisory engineer	60%	0	0	40%
Project director	35%	35%	0	25%
Engineer	0	25%	50%	25%
Exit	0	0	0	100%

Table 12-17

TRANSITION MATRIX FOR NONPARTICIPANTS IN MANAGEMENT DEVELOPMENT PROGRAM

	Year T + 1			
Year T	*Supervisory Engineer*	*Project Director*	*Engineer*	*Exit*
Supervisory engineer	65%	0	0	35%
Project director	45%	35%	0	20%
Engineer	0	40%	40%	20%
Exit	0	0	0	100%

Calculation of Expected Realizable Value. Using the information obtained from steps 2 to 4, the consultant was able to calculate and compare the expected values of an engineer who participates in a management development program with the value of an engineer who does not participate. These figures, calculated using a ten-year valuation period, are as follows:

Participant: $93,541
Nonparticipant: $80,931

A comparison of these figures suggests that participation in a management development program actually increases the value of individuals to the firm. This increased value results from the increased probability of promotion combined with a decreasing probability of exit.

Since management development programs are intended to give individuals the skills needed to be more productive, service state values would be expected to increase if the program is successful. In the present analysis, changes in service state values were not considered because it was difficult to use a measurement method that would allow the consultant to observe these changes. In the present analysis, service state values were held constant.

Summary

These results suggest that the management development programs attended by individuals in this company were effective at increasing their value to the firm. The company should therefore continue to promote these programs as a way of increasing the effectiveness of their managers. The results also suggest that human resource accounting can make an important contribution to the evaluation of programs intended to increase the value of individuals to the firm.

THIRTEEN

Developing an Integrated System

At the current stage of the field's development, there have been few attempts to establish integrated, on-line systems of human resource accounting. An integrated system of human resource accounting would possess the capability of measuring and accounting for both the replacement cost and the economic value of human resources.

This chapter describes a case study of the development of an integrated human resource accounting system. This system has been established at Touche Ross & Co., one of the "Big Eight" international CPA firms, on a pilot basis.

Project Background

Origins of the Project. During late 1983, the accounting and auditing group of Touche Ross & Co. undertook a strategic planning exercise for the group's future development. As part of this process, the group looked at future trends in the economy and concluded that there was a continuing, major transformation from a manufacturing-based to a services-based economy. The planning group recognized that the hallmark of the emerging economy was human capital or human assets, just as the hallmark of the former economic structure had been physical capital such as plant, equipment, and inventories. The planning group

Note: This chapter was jointly authored by Eric G. Flamholtz and D. Gerald Searfoss, partner and director of accounting standards, Touche Ross & Co., with the assistance of Russell Coff.

also recognized that present accounting systems were geared to the older economic structure and did not provide much information about a company's cost and value of people.

In analyzing the implications of this trend, the group recognized that organizations would increasingly need information about their human resources and concluded that present accounting information systems did not address this emerging need adequately. The planning group was aware of the field of human resource accounting. In fact, one of the offices of the firm in Canada had experimented with its development nearly fourteen years earlier (see Chapter Four). They concluded that although human resource accounting had not taken root as a field during its previous period of development (see the Preface), it would reemerge as a result of current trends in the economy.

The planning group was also aware of the work on human resource accounting that had been done by the author, and contacted me to discuss the current state of research and applications as well as the feasibility of developing human resource accounting at Touche Ross. During the winter of 1984, I made a series of visits to Touche Ross to make presentations on human resource accounting to the firm's partners. In June 1984, the firm decided to undertake a pilot project in human resource accounting.

This project was initially to involve two of the firm's offices and was intended to develop pilot systems of human resource accounting in both offices. The goals were to experiment with the feasibility of developing an integrated human resource accounting system and to help the firm "get on the HRA learning curve." The basic idea was that if the project's results were promising, the firm would then expand the scope of its involvement and move toward the development of a human resource accounting system on a firm-wide basis.

Reasons for Interest. There were a variety of reasons for the firm's interest in developing human resource accounting. First, Touche Ross recognized that it is a human capital intensive enterprise, and yet present accounting information systems did not supply all the different kinds of information that might be useful in managing its human resources—including information about the cost of people recruited, hired, and trained by the firm, the replacement cost of the firm's people, and their economic value to the firm. As a result of the firm's own planning process as well as my presentations, senior management was aware that there were a variety of possible uses of human resource accounting information. Many of these potential applications have been described in previous chapters of this book, especially Chapters One, Two, and Twelve.

Among the issues the firm thought might be of particular interest were the cost of replacing staff members, the value or replacement cost of human capital that was "exported" from one office to another, and information to facilitate "make versus buy" personnel decisions. We now turn to the nature of these issues.

On the national level, Touche Ross hoped to identify offices that exported human resources. Such an office could then be used to determine the replacement cost that would be incurred by the office that had lost out when someone transferred. Those offices could also be compared to others to determine what they do right in developing their human resources. Perhaps they could export their methods as well as their people. On the office level, there was a range of decisions for which human resource accounting could provide useful information. For example, such a system would aid in handling make versus buy decisions. It could also identify characteristics in recruits that seem to predict success. Moreover, management hoped to use human resource accounting to plan and budget their recruiting efforts.

Finally, Touche Ross thought they might be able to develop human resource accounting as a service they could provide to their clients. They realized that their clients faced many of the same human resource management issues as they did and, as such, had a need for human resource accounting. Furthermore, many clients were in a position to acquire service-oriented firms. In these cases, human resource accounting could be used to value the human assets and isolate that value from goodwill (as discussed in Chapter Ten). When used for tax purposes, this process could result in a significant cash savings for companies. The uses of the system actually developed are described later in the chapter.

Research Site. Touche Ross selected an office as the site for the first pilot study. The office was chosen because of its size and its reputation as one recognized "to be good at human resource management." Management believed it would be advisable to get on the learning curve with a well-organized office. The office was medium-sized with approximately 175 professionals.

The original intent was to focus only on the audit department in the office. After the director of tax operations expressed an interest in participating in the study, however, the tax department was also included. Both departments had a six-position career ladder from entry level to partner, as shown in Table 13-1.

The audit department recruited people with undergraduate degrees, while the tax department hired only those with law degrees. For this reason, the investments in people of those two departments were expected to be significantly different.

Table 13-1

CAREER LADDERS AT RESEARCH SITE

Audit Department	*Tax Department*
Partner	Partner
Manager	Manager
Supervisor	Supervisor
Senior	Senior 3 (3 years of experience)
Semisenior	Senior 2 (2 years of experience)
Staff accountant	Senior 1 (1 year of experience)

One goal of the study was to use the process of developing the human resource accounting system to provide information about issues of concern to the local office's management. The office's management wished to determine whether turnover was excessive or at an appropriate level. They cited two positions as being subject to potentially high turnover rates: the audit senior and the tax supervisor. These positions were identified as the critical focus for measuring the replacement cost in this office.

Scope, Limitations, and Goals

The project began as a limited experimental application of human resource accounting. Initially the goals were as follows:

1. To measure the replacement cost of an audit senior and a tax supervisor (the critical positions)
2. To use the stochastic rewards valuation model (see Chapter Seven) to measure the economic value of one person on each job level
3. To begin developing a computer-based support system utilizing human resource accounting information for management decisions

As the project progressed, management became interested in expanding the scope to include other positions for the determination of replacement cost and other types of analysis. Perhaps the most important addition was the development of the *full-cost approach* to measuring replacement cost, which is explained in the following section.

Description of the System

The integrated human resource accounting system that Touche Ross developed had three interrelated but distinct components: human resource mobility probabilities, replacement cost measurement, and human resource value measurement.

Human Resource Mobility. Human resource mobility refers to the movement of people through an organizational hierarchy. In the context of human resource accounting, we consider human resource mobility to be a stochastic or probabilistic process, as discussed in Chapter Seven. This means that, on the average, if we have an audit senior in one year (year T), there is some probability that he or she will make the transition to supervisor in the following year (year $T + 1$). Moreover, there is some probability that this person will remain a senior and some probability that he or she will exit the firm. These probabilities were measured in the pilot office, using historical data, by methods described in Chapter Seven.

The output of the process of measuring these probabilities is a set of transition matrices. The transition matrices are a building block for several types of analyses that are the key to human resource management. They provide vital inputs into recruitment planning, replacement cost measurement, turnover analysis, and human resource value measurement. These applications are discussed later in greater detail under "The System's Output and Uses."

Replacement Cost Measurement. As noted above, management was interested in what it costs to replace an audit senior and a tax supervisor (the critical levels). The replacement cost measurement of the pilot system was therefore limited to these positions.

The cost to replace a person has four elements that must be measured: recruitment, selection, development, and separation (as discussed in Chapter Five). Replacement cost includes both direct costs, such as formal training, and indirect costs such as the opportunity costs of on-the-job training.

Marginal Versus Full Replacement Cost. In previous chapters the concept of the replacement cost has been operationally defined as follows:

1. The cost to recruit *one* person at the entry level
2. Plus the cost to select *one* person at the entry level
3. Plus the cost to develop *one* person at each intermediate level
4. Plus the separation cost for *one* person at the critical level

In brief, this is the cost of replacing an individual at a given position level with a person that we assume will remain in the organization throughout the developmental period. We shall refer to this construct of replacement cost as *marginal replacement cost* because it assumes that one person must be recruited, selected, developed, and separated when a person at the critical level leaves the firm.

In fact, it may be necessary to recruit and select several individuals for each person that actually reaches a target position for replacement (audit senior or tax supervisor in this case). This also means that more than one person may have to be developed at each level. Finally, some staff attrition must be incurred on the intermediate levels (below audit senior or tax supervisor) to replace an individual on the critical level. When attrition factors are taken into account in measuring replacement cost, it is referred to as the *full replacement cost.** The full replacement cost of a person may be expressed (operationally defined) as follows:

1. The cost to recruit one person multiplied by the number of new hires needed to gain one person at the critical level
2. Plus the cost to select one person multiplied by the number of new hires needed to gain one person at the critical level
3. Plus the cost to develop one person at each intermediate level multiplied by the number of people that must be developed on that level to gain one person at the critical level
4. Plus the cost to separate one person on each intermediate level multiplied by the number of people that must separate on that level to gain one person at the critical level

*We are indebted to Russell Coff, a research assistant on this project, who first saw the need to distinguish between two different types of human resource replacement cost, which we have now labeled *marginal* and *full* human resource replacement cost.

The full replacement cost of human resources can be measured in an integrated human resource accounting system. The number of people that must be recruited, selected, developed, and separated (on each level) can be calculated from the transition matrix.

Human Resource Value Measurement. This study utilized the stochastic rewards valuation model, described in Chapter Seven, to value the firm's staff professionals. In this case, the service states used in the model correspond to the job levels within the firm. This study determined the net present value of the average person at each job level (in each department).

In brief, drawing on the model, we must measure the following variables in order to determine a person's value to the firm:

1. Service state values: In an average year, what is the contribution to net income by a person on each job level (staff accountant to partner)? What is the value of one year's service at each job level?
2. Expected service life: This variable is used to determine the length of the valuation period.
3. Mobility probabilities: This variable is used to forecast the probabilities that the staff accountant (or any other person) will occupy each position in future years. It is derived by using the transition matrix method described in Chapter Seven.
4. Discount rate: The discount rate is used to discount future expected income streams to arrive at the net present value.

The service state values and the mobility probabilities are used to determine *expected* income streams. The transition matrices take into account the probabilities that a person will occupy each position in future years, and the income streams are essentially an expected value. For a staff accountant there may be a 0.2 probability of being a supervisor and a 0.05 probability of being a manager five years from now. These probabilities are then multiplied by the service state values to determine the expected income streams (discussed in Chapter Seven).

Developing the System

This section discusses the steps that were taken to develop the system described previously:

1. A research team, headed by myself and D. G. Searfoss (representing Touche Ross), was formed.
2. The research team met with the management in an office of Touche Ross to discuss the purpose and goals of the system.
3. The office selected a manager who would function as project coordinator in their office.
4. That manager began coordination of the data collection process. The mobility data were compiled in dBASE III (a data base management system produced by Ashton-Tate). The replacement cost data collection worksheets, similar to those shown in Appendix 4-1, were completed by the managers and partners. The service state values were calculated by the administration and internal accounting staff.
5. My staff and I performed the data analysis and developed system software. As Touche Ross gathered the necessary information, the software to process the data was developed. This software included:

   - Programs in dBASE III to calculate the transition matrices
   - A replacement cost data processing program to analyze the data collection worksheets
   - A human resource value program to execute the stochastic rewards valuation model
   - A management analysis and decision support system for recruitment planning

   As the data became available, calculations were made to arrive at the outputs discussed in the next section.
6. The outputs were reported to management, and they determined how they wanted to modify the system to suit their needs.

The System's Output and Uses

The system's output comprised four types of information: recruitment planning, replacement cost, turnover analysis, and human resource value. It should be noted that all numbers included in this section are for illustrative purposes only; the actual numbers have been disguised to preserve their confidentiality for the firm.

Recruitment Planning. Recruitment planning involves the forecasting of human resource needs and recruiting to meet those needs. Prior to this study, Touche Ross used a planning heuristic to make recruitment planning decisions. They did not formally take into account the expected attrition on each job level, the firm's anticipated growth, or the length of time it takes to reach the critical levels. Human resource accounting has allowed office management to adopt a more analytical approach to recruitment planning.

Recruitment planning depends a great deal on the mobility probabilities that are given in the transition matrices (shown in Tables 13-2 and 13-3). Table 13-2 shows, for example, that an audit senior during year *T* (in the first year) has a 35 percent chance of promotion to supervisor, a 40 percent chance of remaining a senior, and a 25 percent chance of exiting the firm in the following year. These transition matrices may be used to determine how many people must be hired at entry level to gain one person at any given higher level. The recruitment planning model may be expressed as follows:

$$\text{New hires} = (C_r + C_g)\, H_c \qquad (1)$$

where C_r = number of people on critical level that are expected to leave position in next year (and hence must be replaced)

C_g = number of additional people that will be needed on critical level to reflect firm's rate of growth

H_c = number of new hires needed on entry level to gain one person on critical level (see Appendix 13-1)

C_r and C_g, as defined above, may be calculated using the following formulas:

$$C_r = C_p[P(E) + P(P)] \qquad (2)$$

where C_p = number of equivalent people in critical position in previous year (year *T*)

$P(E)$ = probability of exit from critical position as taken from transition matrix

$P(P)$ = probability of promotion from critical position as taken from transition matrix

$$C_g = C_p(1 + G)^Y - C_p \qquad (3)$$

Table 13-2

TRANSITION MATRIX FOR AUDIT DEPARTMENT

Personnel Classification in Year T	*Personnel Classification in Year T + 1*						
	Partner	*Manager*	*Supervisor*	*Senior*	*Semi*	*Accountant*	*Exit*
Partner	0.90						0.10
Manager	0.15	0.75					0.10
Supervisor		0.30	0.50				0.20
Senior			0 35	0.40			0.25
Semisenior				0.60	0.20		0.20
Staff accountant					0.90		0.10
Exit							1.00

Table 13-3

TRANSITION MATRIX FOR TAX DEPARTMENT

Personnel Classification in Year T	*Personnel Classification in Year T + 1*						
	Partner	*Manager*	*Supervisor*	*Senior*	*Semi*	*Accountant*	*Exit*
Partner	0.90						0.10
Manager	0.20	0.60					0.20
Supervisor		0.30	0.40				0.30
Senior 3			0 75				0.25
Senior 2				0.75			0.25
Senior 1					0.75		0.25
Exit							1.00

where G = firm's anticipated rate of growth
Y = number of years required for new hire to reach critical position

The model may be demonstrated in the following example:

1. There are twenty audit seniors (equivalent people) in year T.
2. The transition matrix predicts that, of these twenty, five (on the average) will leave the firm and seven will be promoted. Twelve seniors, then, will have to be replaced ($C_r = 12$).
3. Since it takes about three years to reach the senior level, the firm will need more than twenty seniors by then to accommodate for growth. If we assume a 10 percent rate of growth, three years from now (year $T + 3$) the firm will need twenty-seven seniors, or seven more than the current level ($C_g = 7$).
4. In essence we are recruiting in hopes of gaining nineteen seniors (twelve replaced plus seven to maintain growth). If two new hires are needed for each desired senior ($H_c = 2$), we must plan to hire thirty-eight (2×19) staff accountants.

Management can now perform the recruitment planning function on the basis of factual data and assumptions where previously they had to use a less analytical approach.

Replacement Cost. Management had no measure of what it cost to replace a person in the critical positions (audit senior and tax supervisor). In particular, they lacked information on the opportunity costs associated with inefficiencies or on-the-job training. Without this information, it may be very difficult to evaluate whether turnover is a problem (that is, whether it is cost effective to do anything about it).

The replacement costs for the critical positions are shown in Tables 13-4 and 13-5. These tables show both the marginal and the full replacement costs of these people and the investments the firm has made in them. The differential costs, shown in the second column, are the costs to recruit, select, develop, and separate on each level. For example, it costs $3,133 to develop a semisenior into a senior. This, in effect, is the differential training cost between a semisenior and a senior.

The investment in a person is the replacement cost less the separation costs of the critical position. The investment may be examined for both the marginal and the full replacement costs. The marginal

Table 13-4

REPLACEMENT COST SUMMARY FOR AN AUDIT SENIOR ACCOUNTANT

Cost Element	*Differential Cost*	*Marginal Cost*	*No. of People*	*Full Cost*
Recruitment cost	$ 925.64	$ 925.64	2.00	$ 1,851.28
Selection cost	580.05	580.05	2.00	1,160.10
Development costs—audit staff accountant	4,503.49	4,503.49	2.00	9,006.98
Development costs—audit semisenior accountant	3,132.80	3,132.80	1.80	5,639.04
Development costs—audit senior accountant	2,507.96	2,507.96	1.00	2,507.96
Separation costs—audit staff accountant	2,001.15	0	0.20	400.23
Separation costs—audit semisenior accountant	3,021.20	0	0.80	2,416.96
Separation costs—audit senior accountant	3,553.59	3,553.59	1.00	3,553.59
Total replacement cost*		15,000.00		27,000.00
Investment in an audit senior accountant*		12,000.00		23,000.00

*Figures are rounded to the nearest thousand.

Table 13-5

REPLACEMENT COST SUMMARY FOR A TAX SENIOR SUPERVISOR

Cost Element	*Differential Cost*	*Marginal Cost*	*No. of People*	*Full Cost*
Recruitment cost	$2,877.65	$ 2,877.65	2.50	$ 7,194.12
Selection cost	488.60	488.60	2.50	1,221.50
Development costs—senior 1	5,301.10	5,301.10	2.50	13,252.75
Development costs—senior 2	3,569.05	3,569.05	1.90	6,781.20
Development costs—senior 3	4,490.17	4,490.17	1.40	6,296.24
Development costs—tax supervisor	4,760.40	4,760.40	1.00	4,760.40
Separation costs—senior 1	3,031.80	0	0.60	1,819.08
Separation costs—senior 2	3,838.16	0	0.50	1,919.08
Separation costs—senior 3	4,644.52	0	0.40	1,857.81
Separation costs—tax supervisor	5,385.49	5,385.49	1.00	5,385.49
Total replacement cost*		27,000.00		50,000.00
Investment in a tax supervisor*		21,000.00		45,000.00

*Figures are rounded to the nearest thousand.

investment represents a direct investment in a person's development; the full investment includes investments that had to be made in other people who exited the firm prior to reaching the critical position. These are investments the firm must make to find people who can work in the critical position.

The fourth column indicates the number of people that must be recruited, selected, developed, and separated on each job level to gain one person in the critical position. This number may be calculated from the transition matrix in a similar fashion to the calculation of H_C in the recruitment planning formula (see Appendix 13-1).

Turnover Analysis. As mentioned earlier, management did not previously have a measure of the cost of turnover to the firm. Turnover in the audit senior position amounts to about five people each year (20 × 0.25). Examination of the replacement cost for an audit senior indicates that this costs around $135,000 per year (5 × $27,000). If management could develop a policy to reduce turnover from 25 percent to 20 percent, and if it cost less than $27,000 annually to implement, it would clearly be cost effective. In general, every good senior who leaves the firm represents a cost of $27,000.

There are three basic policies that may reduce turnover: Hire better people on the entry level; weed out those who are incompatible earlier; or take measures to get people to stay longer. Management at Touche Ross believed that, on the whole, turnover was not a problem in the critical positions. They felt that if they were to reduce turnover in the firm, it would have to be through better screening of new hires. Management opted to do a personnel advancement analysis and determine where the best hires come from. This analysis is accomplished by analyzing the mobility patterns (transition matrices) for different recruiting sources. This type of analysis is described in the next section, "Anticipated Uses for the System."

Human Resource Value. The human resource valuation component of the system utilizes the stochastic rewards valuation model (described in Chapter Seven) with the service states corresponding directly to the career ladder. It should be noted at the outset that the measurement of value is very complex, and there are major theoretical issues that must be resolved before the methods described here can be meaningfully applied at Touche Ross or any other firm. Accordingly, this section is presented primarily for illustrative purposes.

The research team determined that there were two conceptualizations of value that would be useful to the firm. One dictates that revenue be allocated to the service states by billable hours generated at each job level. The second allocates revenue based on productive hours generated (total hours worked) at each job level; these hours are then weighted by the billing rate. The first allocation is termed the *billable allocation* while the second is the *productive allocation.*

The billable allocation examines value only in terms of the direct ability to bring in revenue. This is the method that has been used most often, intuitively, by management. It was realized, however, that nearly half of a partner's time is nonbillable. Clearly this time has some value to the firm. The productive allocation considers such administrative time to be *equally* valuable as billable time because these hours represent services provided within the firm. Even if all of a person's time may be provided as chargeable to clients, it would still be necessary to direct some of the time to internal work for their own firm. In such a case the person would allocate his or her own time so that the time spent internally is equally valuable as the time that is chargeable. If, for example, chargeable time were more valuable than internal and administrative time, conceptually people would alter their time allocation to include more chargeable hours until all time is of equal value. The service state values, calculated under both assumptions, are presented in Tables 13-6 and 13-7.

The service state values under the billable allocation seem fairly constant because the lower positions generate a great deal of billable time at a relatively low rate. The higher positions generate fewer billable hours but at a somewhat higher rate. When managerial and administrative time is included as valuable time under the productive allocation, the higher job levels show the expected increase in value.

The expected values for one person at each job level are given in Tables 13-8 and 13-9. Note the comparison, once again, between the values calculated under the billable and productive assumptions.

At this stage of the system's development, the major use of the value component is to raise a variety of issues concerning the value of people to the firm. Additional research is required before this component of the system can be fully developed.

Anticipated Uses for the System

As the system was developed and implemented, management began to see potential uses they had not anticipated. Specifically, there

Table 13-6

SERVICE STATE VALUES
FOR AUDIT DEPARTMENT

Service State (Job Level)	*Billable Allocation*	*Productive Allocation*
Partner	$24,000	$48,000
Manager	25,000	36,000
Supervisor	17,000	27,000
Senior	21,000	14,000
Semisenior	19,000	7,000
Accountant	15,000	3,000

NOTE: The service state values for any given level represent the (undiscounted) value of one year's service at that level.

Table 13-7

SERVICE STATE VALUES
FOR TAX DEPARTMENT

Service State (Job Level)	*Billable Allocation*	*Productive Allocation*
Partner	$27,000	$52,000
Manager	34,000	50,000
Supervisor	25,000	31,000
Senior*	15,000	16,000

NOTE: The service state values for any given level represent the (undiscounted) value of one year's service at that level.

*Senior 1, senior 2, and senior 3 have been combined for valuation purposes.

were four uses for human resource accounting that management hoped to implement in the future: personnel advancement analysis, make versus buy analysis, human resource budgeting, and client applications of human resource accounting. These applications are described below.

Personnel Advancement Analysis. This application involves determining transition matrices for different subgroups within the firm. With this analysis management hoped to determine characteristics evident in those who excel within the organization and in those who do poorly. For example, do people who graduate with honors really do better at Touche Ross?

Table 13-8

HUMAN RESOURCE VALUATION OF AUDIT DEPARTMENT

Service State (Job Level)	*Billable Allocation Net Present Value of One Person at This Job Level*	*Productive Allocation Net Present Value of One Person at This Job Level*
Partner	$30,000	$198,000
Manager	50,000	143,000
Supervisor	70,000	111,000
Senior	48,000	67,000
Semisenior	50,000	56,000
Accountant	55,000	28,000

NOTE: The value of a given job level takes into account probabilities that a person will make it to partner (and so forth) in future years. The value of each year's service is taken from Table 12-5 and weighted by the probability that the person will occupy that state. These estimated income flows are then discounted to calculate the net present value.

Table 13-9

HUMAN RESOURCE VALUATION OF TAX DEPARTMENT

Service State (Job Level)	*Billable Allocation Net Present Value of One Person at This Job Level*	*Productive Allocation Net Present Value of One Person at This Job Level*
Partner	$59,000	$200,000
Manager	80,000	151,000
Supervisor	75,000	72,000
Senior	68,000	54,000

NOTE: The value of a given job level takes into account probabilities that a person will make it to partner (and so forth) in future years. The value of each year's service is taken from Table 12-5 and weighted by the probability that the person will occupy that state. These estimated income flows are then discounted to calculate the net present value.

Two uses for this information became immediately apparent to management. First, they could use the analysis to determine what characteristics they should examine in recruits. If there is a way to identify the superstars early, it would be very helpful and it could reduce turnover costs as described previously. The second use would be to evaluate the advancement of selected groups within the firm.

Make Versus Buy Analysis. From time to time the firm brings in experienced professionals. Management wished to analyze whether this policy is cost effective as compared to bringing people in at the entry level and "growing" them. This issue has two aspects that must be explored: cost differentials between the two career paths and quality differentials between them.

The cost differentials can be measured in much the same manner as replacement cost. Recruitment (executive search), selection, and development costs must be measured for experienced hires. Separation costs are presumably identical for the two career paths.

Quality differentials may be measured in terms of upward mobility. This can be determined by calculating a transition matrix for experienced hires. How many experienced seniors are required to gain a partner versus how many "home-grown" seniors are required to gain a partner? The unique aspect of the full replacement cost is that it includes *both* factors. We may then find that it costs less to replace a partner from one source than from another. That source, then, is the most cost effective even when we consider the quality of the people on both paths.

Human Resource Budgeting. It is possible to use human resource accounting to aid in the budgeting of development and recruitment costs. We can use the transition matrix to determine the numbers of people on each level that will have to be recruited and developed. We can then use the differential costs to plan a budget.

Client Applications. Management has discovered a number of situations in which they feel they could offer human resource accounting as a service to their clients:

When a client is faced with a recessionary economy, is it more cost effective to lay people off or to retain them until the economy improves?

When a client closes down an operation, is it cost effective to relocate personnel or should they be laid off?

A number of clients are in a position to acquire service-related firms. Will the allocation of goodwill to human assets represent a substantial cash savings?

For sports teams (and other businesses where people are the key assets), human resource accounting may be used to estimate the value of players. What, then, is the appropriate amount to invest and amortize?

Summary

The system developed in this office of Touche Ross & Co. represents the state of the art for human resource accounting at this time. The system they implemented was the first step toward an integrated human resource accounting system. The scope of the project was expanded as it became apparent that the system could provide a great deal of information. With each step of the project, new opportunities were exposed. Although the system developed was based on a pilot study and still requires refinement and extensions, it represents a significant advance in the field of human resource accounting.

Appendix 13-1: Calculation of H_c and Number of People to Be Developed

The calculation of the number of new hires needed to gain one person on the critical level is based on further analysis of the transition matrix. Consider the following example using the transition matrix in Table 13-2:

1. If we hire ten staff accountants, we would expect nine of them to become semiseniors in the next year while the tenth exits the firm.
2. Of these nine semiseniors, 60 percent (or about five) will make it to the senior level in the following year.
3. In this example, then, five out of ten new hires made it to the critical position. For each senior we hope to gain, we must hire two staff accountants on the average ($H_C = 2$).

The calculation of the number of people that must be recruited, selected, developed, and separated is similar to the calculation of H_C above. For recruitment, selection, and development at the entry level, we use H_C for the number of people. It is assumed that each new hire had to be recruited, selected, and developed to function at entry level. We must then follow a similar process to that described above in order to determine the number of people that must be developed at the intermediate positions. For example:

1. Of the two staff accountants hired, we expect 1.8 (on the average) to make it to the semisenior level (90 percent). Hence 1.8 people must be trained to be semiseniors.
2. Of these 1.8 people, only one (60 percent) will make it to the senior position to be trained.

The number of people that must be separated on each level may be derived from the preceding numbers as follows:

1. If only 1.8 of the two staff accountants make it to the semisenior position, 0.2 (on the average) exit the firm prior to reaching semisenior.
2. Similarly, 0.8 of the semiseniors are not expected to reach the senior level (1.8 - 1.0).

For further discussion of transition matrices, see Chapter Seven.

Annotated Bibliography of Selected Resources on Human Resource Accounting

Alexander, M. O. "Investments in People." *Canadian Chartered Accountant,* July 1971, pp. 38–45. This paper advances the notion that present accounting techniques are deficient in failing to provide information on human investments. An application of a human resource management system involving a public accounting firm is given. Other applications in manufacturing and government are reviewed. Finally, proposals for how the concepts of human resource accounting might be developed for society at large are discussed.

Auerbach, L. A., and Sadan, S. "A Stochastic Model for Human Resources Valuation." *California Management Review,* Summer 1974, pp. 24–31. This paper proposes a stochastic model for valuation of human resources that synthesizes the contributions of Lev Schwartz and Eric Flamholtz. The model includes consideration of the uncertain environment and is thought by the authors to satisfy the criteria of easy and direct measurability for external reporting.

Baker, G. M. N. "The Feasibility and Utility of Human Resource Accounting." *California Management Review,* Summer 1974, pp. 17–23. This paper represents a critical assessment of the usefulness of human resource accounting for both external and internal reporting purposes. The potential for profit manipulation is advanced as a negative aspect for such accounting systems. A final conclusion is that research should be directed toward determining the limitations of human resource information.

Basset, G. A. "Employee Turnover Measurement and Human Resource Accounting." *Human Resource Management,* Autumn 1972, pp. 21-30. This article is an attempt to integrate human resource accounting and turnover measurement and costing. The definition, description, and measurement of employee turnover constitute the major emphasis of the paper. Finally, the author concludes that turnover measurement and human resource accounting are inseparable concepts.

Brummet, R. L. "Accounting for Human Resources." *New York Certified Public Accountant,* July 1970, pp. 547-555. This article suggests that the role of accounting should be expanded to include assessments of human resources within organizations and within society. It is hypothesized that such action would induce managers to give more serious consideration to human resource investment decisions. Among other things, the article advocates an interdisciplinary approach to the problem.

Brummet, R. L. "Accounting for Human Resources." *Journal of Accountancy,* December 1970, pp. 62-66. This article illustrates the importance of human resources in society and within organizations. It comments on current deficiencies in dealing effectively with human resources and also discusses potential financial measurement settings involving human resources. Finally, this article reviews past research and future prospects.

Brummet, R. L., Flamholtz, E. G., and Pyle, W. C. "Human Resource Measurement: A Challenge for Accountants." *Accounting Review,* April 1968, pp. 217-224. This article represents one of the earliest works in the area of human resource measurement. The authors analyze prior accounting deficiencies—namely, the treatment of employee costs as expenses rather than assets. Various methodologies for human resource valuation are introduced, and the authors conclude that human resource accounting is primarily useful as a managerial tool.

Brummet, R. L., Flamholtz, E. G., and Pyle, W. C. "Human Resource Accounting: A Tool to Increase Managerial Effectiveness." *Management Accounting,* August 1969, pp. 12–15. This article emphasizes the role of human resource accounting as a tool for increasing managerial effectiveness in the acquisition, development, allocation, maintenance, and utilization of its human resources. R. G. Barry Corporation is presented as an actual application of the technique. Human resource accounting is seen not to be expressly designed for use in external financial reporting, but rather to aid in the process of deciding among alternative investments in human resources and evaluating their maintenance and utilization.

Brummet, R. L., Flamholtz, E. G., and Pyle, W. C. "Accounting for Human Resources." *Michigan Business Review,* March 1968, pp. 20–25. This article assesses the potential impact that human resource accounting can have on the scientific approach to management. Human resource accounting is defined as "the process of identifying, measuring, and communicating information about human resources to facilitate effective management within an organization." The paper emphasizes that managers currently lack the necessary tools for effectively evaluating alternative human resource investments or for optimizing the allocation of human resources. Human resource accounting is proposed to satisfy this void. Finally, a brief description of relevant research is presented.

Caplan, E. H., and Landekich, S. *Human Resource Accounting: Past, Present and Future.* New York: National Association of Accountants, 1974. This monograph deals with human resource accounting and includes case studies of the R. G. Barry Corporation and Lester Witte & Co.

Conrads, M. *Human Resource Accounting.* Wiesbaden, West Germany: Betriebswirtschaftlicher Verlag Gabler, 1976. This is a monograph written in German dealing with human resource accounting.

Cooper, A. A., and Parker, J. E., Jr. "Human Resource Accounting: An Examination." *Cost and Management,* January–February 1973, pp. 21–26. This article conducts a theoretical investigation as a basis for determining the "proper" accounting treatment for human resources in audited financial statements. The article assesses whether human resources fit the various definitions of an asset, describes alternative valuation techniques, and concludes that accountants can value human resources at their historical cost or not at all. Finally, human resource accounting information is proposed as supplementary information to audited financial statements.

Deangelo, L. E. "Unrecorded Human Assets and the 'Hold Up' Problem." *Journal of Accounting Research,* Spring 1982, pp. 272-274. This brief article is a reply to Dittman, Juris, and Revsine's paper (1976), in which specific training is differentiated from general training which may add to a company's unrecorded human assets in some rare instances. Deangelo argues that the total costs of specific training constitute a lower upper-bound limit on the value of unrecorded human assets to employers than proposed by Dittman, Juris, and Revsine (1976). The author makes the point that specific training provides employees with the opportunity to extract higher future wages from the training employer. Employees who receive specific training are more difficult to replace and can, therefore, demand higher wages.

Dermer, J., and Siegal, J. P. "The Role of Behavioral Measures in Accounting for Human Resources." *Accounting Review,* January 1974, pp. 88-97. This article discusses behavioral variables and relationships that are the indirect determinants of human resource value. Using MBA students participating in a business game and a related questionnaire, the authors find little support for the existence of a causal relationship between the behavioral state of a human organization and its performance. (This evidence is contrary to proposals by Likert.) Finally, potentially dysfunctional goal displacement is hypothesized if behavioral information is provided.

Dittman, D. A., Juris, H. A., and Revsine, L. "On the Existence of Unrecorded Human Assets: An Economic Perspective." *Journal of Accounting Research,* Spring 1976, pp. 49-65. The authors state that human resource accounting information has been increasingly recognized as input to legal compliance decisions, personnel planning, and the valuation of human assets for external reporting. It is argued that the existing literature has concentrated on specific issues related to the measurement of human assets and has neglected an exploration of the basic economic and accounting assumptions underlying unrecorded human assets. The purpose of this article is to examine this economic foundation.

Dittman, D. A., Juris, H. A., and Revsine, L. "Unrecorded Human Assets: A Survey of Accounting Firms' Training Programs." *Accounting Review,* October 1980, pp. 640–648. The purpose of this study is to apply the authors' concept of training—ranging from general to specific—to data on employee training collected from the training directors of the Big Eight public accounting firms. The degree of specificity of the training provided was rated on a 7-point scale by the training directors. Data were collected by using a structured interview form. Training courses were grouped by homogeneity of content.

Dobbins, R., and Trussel, P. "The Valuation of Human Resources." *Management Decision,* May-June, 1975, pp. 155–169. This article gives background of research in human resource accounting, presents an analysis of various valuation methods, and considers the implications of human resource financial reporting for the personnel function. Specifically, the significant effect on annual accounts is demonstrated in an application of human resource valuation to a professional soccer league. Finally, the article concludes that the philosophy of human resource valuation enhances the status of the personnel function and acknowledges the importance of training and development for the firm's future.

Doty, J. H. "Human Capital Budgeting: Maximizing Returns on Training Investment." *Industrial Engineering,* March-April, 1965, pp. 139–145. This article presents a treatment of both theoretical and applied "human capital budgeting." It presents a method to derive the rate of return on dollars invested in a job training program for allocating training dollars between competing programs in a manner that maximizes investment in programs promising the highest return on capital. This tool is regarded as important in view of rising costs for training programs.

Eggers, H. C. "The Evaluation of Human Assets." *Management Accounting,* November 1971, pp. 28–30. This article fixes the blame for improper recruiting, training, and development of employees on insufficient information systems that fail to quantify these valuable resources. The author presents both advantages and difficulties in constructing an information system with the capacity to capture such information, but he nevertheless concludes that the effort is worthwhile and should be facilitated by instituting a participatory evaluation process. The participants should include superiors, peers, and subordinates.

Elias, N. S. "The Effects of Human Asset Statements on the Investment Decision: An Experiment." *Empirical Research in Accounting: Selected Studies,* 1972, pp. 215-233. This study represents an experiment to determine whether the common stock investment decision would be made differently with the addition of human resource information. The experiment involves sending questionnaires to individuals with varying levels of sophistication in accounting concepts. The author finds that human resource information does influence investment decisions, although the strength of the relationship is unclear.

Flamholtz, E. G. "The Theory and Measurement of an Individual's Value to an Organization." Unpublished Ph.D dissertation, University of Michigan, 1969. This dissertation is an exploratory study concerned with the problem of measuring an individual's value to an organization. The study's objectives are to formulate a theory of individual value in organizations, to present a model of the valuation of individuals, and to validate a proposed measure of an individual's value to an organization. Replacement cost is proposed and validated as a surrogate measure of individual value. Finally, the author notes that replacement cost cannot provide a meaningful measure of the total value of the human organization since it is validated only on the ordinal level and thus cannot be summed.

Flamholtz, E. G. "A Model for Human Resource Valuation: A Stochastic Process with Service Rewards." *Accounting Review,* April 1971, pp. 253-267. This article examines the measurement of an individual's value to formal organizations and presents a normative model for the economic valuation of individuals. The model assumes that individuals possess the capacity to move through a set of mutually exclusive organizational roles or "service states" during a time interval that can be measured probabilistically. Rewards accrue as the system makes transitions from one state to another over time and can be measured in dollars.

Flamholtz, E. G. "Should Your Organization Attempt to Value Its Human Resources?" *California Management Review,* Winter 1971, pp. 40–45. This article answers three questions pertaining to human resource accounting and gives guidelines for whether a particular firm should develop human resource measures. The questions are: What is management's need for measures of human value? What research is developing such measures? And what are the measures' managerial implications? Finally, the author encourages practitioners to experiment with human resource accounting concepts to validate the proposed approach.

Flamholtz, E. G. "On the Use of the Economic Concept of Human Capital in Financial Statements: A Comment." *Accounting Review,* January 1972, pp. 148–152. This paper presents criticisms of "On the Use of Human Capital in Financial Statements" by Lev and Schwartz There are three major criticisms. First, the notion of human capital treats a person's value intrinsically rather than in conjunction with the organizational role occupied. Second, the Lev and Schwartz model fails to consider the possibility of the individual leaving the organization. And third, the model fails to consider sufficient details concerning organizational reality to permit its usefulness as an aid to decision makers.

Flamholtz, E. G. "Human Resource Accounting: A Review of Theory and Research." *Academy of Management Proceedings,* August 1972, pp. 174–177. This paper represents a comprehensive review (through 1972) of theory and research in human resource accounting. The author defines human resource accounting as "the process of identifying, measuring, and communicating information about human resources to decision makers." The paper gives objectives of research, discusses human resource value theory, offers applications of the theory, and assesses the cognitive and behavioral impact of human resource accounting.

Flamholtz, E. G. "Toward a Theory of Human Resource Value in Formal Organizations." *Accounting Review,* October 1972, pp. 666–678. This paper formulates a model of the nature and determinants of a person's value to an organization. The model represents a first step toward the development of a theory of human resource value. The determinants of a person's value to an organization are the individual's conditional value (comprising productivity, transferability, and promotability) and the probability that the individual will maintain membership in the organization. Organizational determinants of conditional value are also integrated into the model and constitute both the role and the rewards.

Flamholtz, E. G. "Assessing the Validity of a Theory of Human Resource Value: A Field Study." *Empirical Research in Accounting: Selected Studies,* 1972, pp. 241-266. This paper attempts to evaluate the validity of certain hypothesized determinants of human resource value. The study concerns a public accounting firm in a large city and examines how determinants (conditional value, probability of maintaining service life, organizational role, and others) are validated and new determinants are identified (attitudes, traits, and the individual's manager).

Flamholtz, E. G., and Holmes, S. "Sherlock Holmes' Last Case: A Reply to Ronen." *Empirical Research in Accounting: Selected Studies,* 1972, pp. 277-282. This paper represents a reply to J. Ronen's comments regarding a previous paper by Flamholtz entitled "Assessing the Validity of a Theory of Human Resource Value: A Field Study." The paper attempts to vitiate Ronen's criticisms, both those involving methodology and those involving research objectives.

Flamholtz, E. G. "Human Resource Accounting: Its Role in Management Planning and Control." *Economisch en Sociaal Tidschrift,* February 1972, pp. 3-21. This paper introduces the topic of human resource accounting, identifies its role in the management of people in organizations, and describes methods of measuring human resource cost and value. Human resource accounting is viewed as serving a dual purpose: It is a way of thinking about managing human resources based on the notion that people are valuable organizational resources, and it is a system, based on an assessment of cost and value, of providing management with the requisite information to manage human resources effectively and efficiently.

Flamholtz, E. G. "Human Resource Accounting: Measuring Positional Replacement Costs." *Human Resource Management,* Spring 1973, pp. 8-16. This paper focuses on measuring the cost of replacing individuals occupying specified organizational positions. A normative model for the measurement of "positional replacement costs" is developed that includes acquisition costs, separation costs, and learning costs. The model is applied to a medium-sized insurance company, and the results indicate potential applications and implications for management theory and practice (for example, positional replacement cost measures can play a significant role in budgeting personnel requirements), as well as for accounting (for example, positional replacement cost information should be communicated to management for use in decision making).

Flamholtz, E. G. "An Analytical Model for Human Resource Valuation: A Technique for Analysis of Changes in Human Resource Value and Their Role in Human Resource Management." *AIDS Proceedings*, November 1975, pp. 196–198. This paper translates the stochastic rewards valuation model (developed by Flamholtz) into analytical terms. It also presents a method for the analysis of changes in human resource value for a given time period into their underlying causal components. A mathematical model is constructed to break "expected realizable value," the end-result measure of a person's value to an organization, into "expected conditional value" and "the probability that the person will maintain organizational membership."

Flamholtz, E. G. "The Metaphysics of Human Resource Accounting and Its Implications for Managerial Accounting." *Accounting Forum*, December 1975, pp. 51-61. This article deals with the fundamental principles (metaphysics) of human resource accounting and their implications for managerial accounting. Human resource accounting is seen not merely as a set of procedures for assigning numerals to the cost and value of people as organizational resources; rather, it implies a way of thinking about the management of human resources as well. The paper identifies three ideas that, taken together, comprise the basic thesis of human resource accounting: the notion that people are valuable organizational resources, the belief that people are valuable organizational resources is a function of the way in which they are managed, and the premise that information in the form of measurements of human resource costs and value is essential to the proper management of human resources. Finally, quantitative measures are hypothesized to exert stronger influence than qualitative measures.

Flamholtz, E. G. "Accounting for Human Resource Cost and Value." Paper presented to the Ausschuss für Wirtschaffliche Verwaltung Seminar: Das Human Kapital der Unternehmen, Bonn, September 17–19, 1974. This paper presents an introduction to human resource accounting as a managerial tool. It deals with basic questions of concern to management: What is human resource accounting? What is its role in managing people? How can we account for human resources? And what are the various types of human resource accounting systems and in which organizational situation is each appropriate? Finally, a case study involving a CPA firm is presented to illustrate the practical benefits and difficulties involved in accounting for human resources.

Flamholtz, E. G. "Assessing the Validity of Selected Surrogate Measures of Human Resource Value—A Field Study." *Personnel Review,* Summer 1975, pp. 37-50. This article describes a field study conducted to determine the convergent and discriminant validity of three possible measures of a person's value to an organization: replacement cost, compensation, and a performance measure. Criterion validation was the principal methodology applied to the research site (a branch of a medium-sized insurance company). The findings indicate that positional and realizable replacement cost and compensation are valid measures of individual value. Further, replacement cost is found to be more effective for salespeople, while compensation is a better measure for claims personnel.

Flamholtz, E. G. "The Role of Human Resource Accounting in Social Accounting." In M. Dierkes and R. A. Bauer (eds.), *Corporate Social Accounting*. New York: Praeger, 1973. This paper examines the role of human resource accounting within the framework of corporate social responsibility and social accounting. It reviews the research and suggests how this research might be useful to business organizations in meeting their social responsibilities. Two aspects of human resource accounting are presented as being relevant to corporate social accounting: It provides a paradigm enabling managers to better conceptualize the management of people in business organizations, and it provides a measurement method that assists in decision making.

Flamholtz, E. G. "The Impact of Human Resource Valuation on Management Decisions: A Laboratory Experiment." *Accounting, Organizations and Society,* February 1976, pp. 153-166. This paper reports a laboratory experiment designed to determine whether human resource value numbers, which are the output of a proposed method of human resource valuation, influence a selected human resource management decision—the allocation (job assignment or staffing) decision. Human resource value numbers are hypothesized to influence decisions per se as well as the decision maker's set, the criteria used in making decisions. The results indicate that nonmonetary human resource value numbers may influence decisions. However, it could not be established that monetary human resource value numbers make a difference in decisions. The results also indicate that human resource value measures, as well as the numbers per se, may influence the decision maker's set and criteria used in decision making.

Flamholtz, E. G., and Lundy, T. "Human Resource Accounting for CPA Firms." *The CPA,* October 1975, pp. 45–51. This article describes a system for the periodic measurement and reporting of the value of people in a professional organization. The system is an application of the theoretical model developed previously by Flamholtz (a stochastic process with service rewards). Numerous examples of individual values within the firm are illustrated. Finally, the authors express their belief that such a system should be of interest to service firms in addition to CPA firms.

Flamholtz, E. G., Oliver, J. B., and Teague, R. "Subjective Information Valuation and Decision Making." Paper presented at Western Regional AAA Meeting, Tempe, Arizona, May 1976. This paper examines the nature and potential significance of the hypothesized process of subjective information valuation. It discusses the concept of subjective information valuation and examines its implications for decision making and for the design of information systems. It also reports a laboratory experiment designed as an exploratory study to learn about the existence, determinants, and effects of subjective information valuations in a decision context. The experiment involved a human resource management problem. The findings indicate that subjective information valuation exists and managers should be aware of its existence. Moreover, information systems should be broadened to include information presently considered "too subjective."

Flamholtz, E. G. "Human Resource Accounting." In S. Davidson and R. L. Weil (eds.), *Handbook of Cost Accounting.* New York: McGraw-Hill, 1978. This chapter presents a model for measuring the costs of human resources and describes application of the model in studies prior to 1978.

Frantzreb, R. B., Landon, L. L. T., and Lundberg, D. P. "The Valuation of Human Resources." *Business Horizons,* June 1974, pp. 73-79. This article examines two fundamental issues in human resource accounting: the usefulness of human resource information and the selection of a valuation model. It briefly reviews theory and formulates a valuation model (inspired by the economic value model) that was tested experimentally at the Bank of America. The discounted present value of future salaries was used as the basis of the model. The problem situation involved whether, through turnover, the bank was losing its most valuable people or those who were somewhere in between. The authors conclude that the basic use of their system is evaluation of changes in the human resource base. Finally, human resource accounting is seen as a way to view the human resource management process.

Freidman, A., and Lev, B. "A Surrogate Measure for the Firm's Investment in Human Capital." *Journal of Accounting Research,* Autumn 1974, pp. 235-250. This article suggests an approach for the measurement of the firm's investment in human resources. The investment is measured by discounting the stream of cost savings resulting from the firm's specific personnel policies (the differences between a firm's actual wage structure and the average wages prevailing in the relevant labor markets). This method is advanced as an improvement over current external financial reporting practices in that employee training and development costs will not be recorded and therefore reported on a cash basis. Finally, management will be better able to evaluate the efficiency of human resource programs.

Gambling, T. E. "A System Dynamics Approach to HRA." *Accounting Review,* July 1974, pp. 538-546. This article draws attention to the dynamic implications of the current concern for human resource accounting. "Conventional" theories are criticized because the author believes they do not capture the multidimensional flows that occur dynamically within an organization. Finally, the appendix applies a system dynamics simulation (via the DYNAMO program) of Flamholtz's model and is thought to be a better method of capturing the relevant variables involved in accounting for human resources.

Gilbert, M. H. "The Asset Value of the Human Organization." *Management Accounting,* July 1970, pp. 25–28. This article advocates human resource accounting for external financial reporting purposes. The author reviews many of the valuation models—including capitalization of salary, acquisition costs, start-up costs, replacement costs, competitive bidding, economic value, present value, goodwill, and the behavioral variables method. The author questions the effect that human resource accounting would have on employees since society has generally been averse to the concept of people as organizational assets. Finally, the article concludes that human resource accounting will enhance the accuracy of return on investments and hence lead to a more efficient allocation of resources within the economy.

Glautier, M. W. E., and Underdown, B. "Problems and Prospects of Accounting for Human Assets." *Management Accounting* (U.K.), March 1973, pp. 98–102. This article assesses the evolution of human resource accounting from a broad historical perspective. Human resource accounting is viewed as an effort to quantify one more aspect of organizational life. The author regards the present lack of quantifiable human resource information as a serious handicap to both management and investors. The various valuation models are, in turn, examined. Finally, problems associated with human resource accounting are explored—such as the fact that human capital cannot be bought or owned, that the service potential of labor does not extend beyond the current year, and that the firm's human capital value may not be equal to the portion of the firm's income contributed by the labor force.

Hekimian, J. C., and Jones, C. H. "Put People on Your Balance Sheet." *Harvard Business Review,* January-February 1967, pp. 105–113. This article strongly advocates quantitative measures of a firm's human resources to aid in management decisions. The authors review various valuation modes including original cost, replacement cost, and opportunity cost. In accordance with the latter mode, the paper proposes that competitive bidding for employees between investment centers be used as a basis of human resource valuation. Benefits of competitive bidding include more optimal allocation of personnel and a quantitative base for planning, evaluating, and developing the human assets of the firm. Finally, a case is presented that demonstrates how the competitive bidding process might be operationalized.

Hendricks, J. "Human Resource Accounting and Stock Investment Decisions." *Accounting Review,* April 1967, pp. 292-305. This paper represents an empirical study to examine the impact of human resource accounting information on stock investment decisions. The study utilizes MBA students in a large midwestern university and involves their analyzing financial statements with and without human resource information. The subjects were then instructed to make an investment decision based on their analysis. The study finds that stock investment decisions are affected by the addition of human resource accounting information, that selected background and variables do not affect the user's decisions, and that openness of belief system is correlated with the effect of human resource accounting information on the user.

Jaggi, B., and Lau, H. "Toward a Model for Human Resource Valuation." *Accounting Review,* May 1974, pp. 33-36. This paper focuses on developing a theoretically sound model for human resource valuation. The authors critically examine previous models developed by Lev and Schwartz (economic value) and Flamholtz (stochastic process with service rewards) and identify certain factors believed to be omitted from these models. Specifically, Lev and Schwartz's model is said to ignore the variables of career movements of employees within the firm and the possibility of leaving before their retirement or death. The authors believe the Flamholtz model to be a great improvement over Lev and Schwartz's but regard it as too costly to implement. They therefore develop a new model, based on the actuarial concept of homogeneous group and markovian analysis, which is advocated as meeting their criticisms. Instead of attempting to value employees individually, this model uses a group basis as an alternative approach.

Jauch, R., and Skigen, M. "Human Resource Accounting: A Critical Evaluation." *Management Accounting,* May 1974, pp. 33-36. This article takes the position that human resources, by their very nature, cannot be termed assets and therefore should not be capitalized and placed on the statement of financial position for external financial reporting purposes. The authors present criticisms of the various proposed valuation models, both monetary and nonmonetary, and conclude that although human resource accounting has theoretical benefits for financial reporting, its practical applications are extremely confined. The article does not contemplate the utility of human resource accounting information for internal management needs.

Lau, A. H., and Lau, H. "Some Proposed Approaches for Writing Off Capitalized Human Resource Assets." *Journal of Accounting Research,* Spring 1978, pp. 80–102. This paper discusses several procedures pertaining to two different methods for human resource depreciation that are economically and statistically justifiable. One uses expected values and is considered appropriate for intraorganizational and managerial use; the other is suggested for external reporting using a probabilistic and more conservative approach. The authors conclude that human resource capitalization is statistically meaningful only if the employees are treated in large homogeneous groups.

Lev, B., and Schwartz, A. "On the Use of the Economic Concept of Human Capital in Financial Statements." *Accounting Review,* January 1971, pp. 103–112. This article takes the position that financial statements should include the measurement of human assets. The authors note that although accountants have been reluctant to do so, economists have long considered the value of human capital in explaining and predicting economic growth. The paper is organized into six parts. Part I introduces the subject. Part II discusses the concept of human capital and its measurement. (The measurement model is developed by discounting the present value of the employee's future earnings.) Part III extends the concept to the level of the firm. Part IV elaborates on implications for decision makers from human capital reporting. Part V discusses conceptual accounting problems involved when putting human capital values in financial statements. Part VI provides concluding remarks. An appendix offers a hypothetical example of the measurement of human capital for a firm.

Lev, B., and Schwartz, A. "On the Use of the Economic Concept of Human Capital in Financial Statements: A Reply." *Accounting Review,* January 1972, pp. 153–154. This article represents a response to Flamholtz's criticisms of a previous article by the two authors. The authors state that their concept of human capital does account for the organizational role occupied by the employee. They note, moreover, that career movements of employees and turnover were deliberately omitted from the earlier article due to its introductory nature. Given the absence of well-defined investor decision models, the authors did not define those investor decisions for which human capital information is useful. Finally, the authors agree with Flamholtz that at this stage of its development, human resource accounting has a range of solutions.

Likert, R. "Human Organizational Measurements: Key to Financial Success." *Michigan Business Review,* May 1971, pp. 1-5. This article criticizes current accounting for providing after-the-fact measurements and advances the proposition that measuring certain lead-time data of an organization can identify problems in advance of their occurrence. The author further advocates the Michigan school's findings concerning leadership behavior (that is, leaders who demonstrate sensitivity to subordinate concerns will increase their group's productivity). This system of management ("System 4"), when combined with planning-programming budgeting, is felt to be a powerful management tool for the operations of the firm.

Likert, R., and Bowers, D. G. "Improving the Accuracy of P/L Reports by Estimating the Change in Dollar Value of the Human Organization." *Michigan Business Review,* March 1973, pp. 15-24. This paper takes exception to the practice of computing profit and loss without explicit consideration of changes in the value of the human organization. It proposes a method that attempts to alleviate this deficiency by computing estimates, in dollars, of the changes in value of the productive capability of the human organization. The paper identifies a multitude of human organizational dimensions (such as leadership) that are measured at the end of each reporting period. These "scores" are standardized, and changes between periods are computed. Correlation analysis between dimensional and performance variables and conversion to dollar terms completes the process.

Likert, R., and Pyle, W. C. "A Human Organizational Measurement Approach." *Financial Analysts Journal,* January-February 1971, pp. 75-84. This paper advances the position that current financial statements are in error due to their neglect in accounting for changes in the stock of human resources. Two approaches to human resource accounting are offered. First, the net worth of the human organization may be defined as the present discounted value of contributions employees make over their service life less the costs incurred for acquisition, training, and the like. Second, the opportunity cost of using human resources in a certain manner should be evaluated to determine whether they are being used properly. Finally, the paper proposes that historical cost measurements be modified to make them more reflective of current value (for example, data may be adjusted for changes in the expected tenure of employees).

Likert, R., Bowers, D. G., and Norman, R. M. "How to Increase a Firm's Lead Time in Recognizing and Dealing with Problems of Managing Its Human Organization." *Michigan Business Review,* January 1969, pp. 12-17. This article interprets recent experimental results that tend to negate the proposed leadership style (employee-centered) advanced by researchers at the University of Michigan. These results have indicated that, in many cases, poor employee attitudes were associated with high productivity. The results are contrary to those of earlier experiments. The authors contend that the time dimension is responsible for the unexpected results, and they describe a comprehensive, five-year research project designed to investigate the effect of the leadership style on human organizational variables. Preliminary results indicate that sufficient lead time should be incorporated into the analysis when correlating productivity with leadership style.

Marques, E. *La Comptabilite des resources humaines.* Suresnes, France: Editions hommes et techniques, 1974. This is a monograph dealing with human resource accounting in French.

Mirvis, P. H., and Lawler, E. E. "Measuring the Financial Impact of Employee Attitudes." *Journal of Applied Psychology,* February 1977, pp. 1-8. This article presents a new approach for attaching behavioral costs to attitudes, based on data from 160 tellers in a midwestern bank. Attitudes were measured through an employee survey; behavioral measures were based on company records. Behavioral costs per employee were assigned through cost accounting techniques. Attitudes were correlated with future behavior, and the behavioral changes associated with attitudinal shifts were estimated using these relationships. New behavioral costs per employee were computed. The results show an expected direct-cost saving of $17,664 in absenteeism, turnover, and performance from a 0.5 standard deviation increase in job satisfaction; savings associated with enhanced job involvement and motivation are also reported. A critical analysis of the approach is presented, and its usefulness to organizations is discussed.

Mirvis, P. H., and Macy, B. A. "Human Resource Accounting: A Measurement Perspective." *Academy of Management Review,* April 1976, pp. 74–83. This paper argues that human resource accounting has a distinct position within the framework of social responsibility and social accounting. Human resource accounting is evaluated as a potential organizational measurement tool. Specifically, asset and cost models are examined in terms of reliability, validity, and usefulness. Beyond this evaluative perspective, examples are presented of a costing approach that may circumvent some of the cited measurement problems.

Schmidt, H. (ed.). *Humanvermögenscrechnung.* Berlin, West Germany: Walter de Gruyter, 1982. This book is a collection of papers in German on different aspects of human resource accounting that were presented at a conference in Bonn, West Germany, in 1975.

Tomassini, L. A. "Human Resource Accounting and Managerial Decision Behavior: An Experimental Study." Unpublished Ph.D. dissertation, University of California, Los Angeles, 1974. This dissertation represents a first attempt to assess the effects of human resource accounting on management decision making. The study has two objectives: to determine the difference in decision process and choice caused when human resource accounting data were added to conventional accounting information and to explore certain attitudinal issues considered critical to the ultimate fate of human resource accounting. Some 130 accounting students were asked to analyze information and make a decision for each of two personnel-oriented cases. Survey questionnaires were administered to a subset of the experimental group. Several conclusions were reached: Human resource accounting data can affect managerial decisions, both at the choice and process levels; use of such data leads decision makers to consider their human resources more carefully; and users have an intuitive need for the data that human resource accounting provides.

Woodruff, R. L. "Human Resource Accounting." *Canadian Chartered Accountant,* September 1970, pp. 2–7. This paper describes the justification, background, and implementation of a human resource accounting system at the R. G. Barry Corporation. It is believed to be the first application of human resource accounting. The system is described in detail, and its effect on corporate management is presented. Specifically, human resource accounting has developed a heightened awareness among managers of the economic importance of people. Development programs are viewed differently as capital items rather than as expenses, and the statement of operations is thought to be more accurate with the inclusion of human resource accounting information. Finally, an example of the R. G. Barry balance sheet is given that includes human resource accounting data.

Wright, R. "Managing Man as a Capital Asset." *Personnel Journal,* April 1970, pp. 290-298. This article analyzes and interprets certain implications for management from capitalizing human resources—for example, the impact of the change on managerial accounting and, in turn, on managing the human asset. The author sees a multitude of benefits to be derived from human resource accounting—the most important is that when personnel problems occur, an employee will receive treatment as a valuable resource rather than merely an operating expense. Finally, human resource accounting is not seen to be dehumanizing but rather should restore each individual's personality in a complex organization.

Notes

Preface

[1]For a discussion of the nature of this transformation, see, for example, Alvin Toffler, *The Third Wave* (New York: Bantam Books, 1980). See also James Cook, "The Molting of America," *Forbes,* November 22, 1982, pp. 161–167.

[2]American Accounting Association Committee of Accounting for Human Resources, Report of the Committee on Human Resource Accounting, *The Accounting Review Supplement to Vol. XLVIII,* 1973.

[3]Theodore Schultz, "Investment in Human Capital," *American Economic Review,* March 1961, p. 3.

[4]B. F. Kiker, "The Historical Roots of the Concept of Human Capital," *Journal of Political Economy,* October 1968, pp. 481–499.

[5]George S. Odiorne, *Personnel Policy: Issues and Practices* (Columbus, Ohio: Merrill, 1963); Rensis Likert, *New Patterns of Management* (New York: McGraw-Hill, 1961).

[6]Rensis Likert, *The Human Organization: Its Management and Value* (New York: McGraw-Hill, 1967).

[7]D. R. Scott, *Theory of Accounts,* vol. 1 (New York: Holt, Rinehart and Winston, 1925), p. 258.

[8]William A. Paton, *Accounting Theory* (Chicago: Accounting Studies Press, 1962), pp. 486–487.

[9]Uniroyal, Inc. *75th Annual Report—1966,* p. 10.

Chapter One

[1]R. Lee Brummet, Eric G. Flamholtz, and William C. Pyle, "Human Resource Accounting: A Tool to Increase Managerial Effectiveness," *Management Accounting,* August 1969, p. 12.

[2]Eric G. Flamholtz, "The Impact of Human Resource Valuation on Management Decisions: A Laboratory Experiment," *Accounting, Organizations and Society,* February 1976, pp. 153-166.

[3]R. W. Fleming, "State Proposed U-M Budget Would Pose Quality Dilemma," *University of Michigan Today,* Spring 1971, p. 1.

[4]"Budget Request Urged Top Priority for Salaries," *University of Michigan Today,* Spring 1971, p. 2.

Chapter Two

[1]Quoted from Archibald Bowman, "Reporting on the Corporate Investment," *Journal of Accountancy,* May 1938, p. 399, by permission of *Journal of Accountancy.*

[2]Alfred P. Sloan, *My Years with General Motors* (New York: MacFadden-Bartell Corp., 1965), p. 140.

[3]Committee to Prepare a Statement of Basic Accounting Theory, *A Statement of Basic Accounting Theory* (Evanston, Ill.: American Accounting Association, 1966), p. 35.

[4]*A Statement of Basic Accounting Theory,* pp. 35-36.

[5]See, for example, G. E. Newell, "Should Humans Be Reported as Assets?", *Management Accounting,* December 1972, pp. 13-16.

[6]William A. Paton, *Accounting Theory* (New York: Ronald Press, 1922), pp. 486-487.

[7]In *The Nature of Capital and Income,* Fisher defined a property right: "A property right is the right to the chance of attaining some or all of the future services of one or more articles of wealth." He saw the term *property rights* as being synonymous with *assets* or resources. From Irving Fisher, *The Nature of Capital and Income* (London: Macmillan, 1927), p. 22.

[8]Arthur Andersen & Co., *Objectives of Financial Statements for Business Enterprises* (n.p.: Arthur Andersen & Co., 1972), p. 79.

[9]Arthur Andersen & Co., *Objectives.*

[10]Milwaukee Braves, Inc., 1963 Annual Report.

[11]The Flying Tiger Line, Inc., 1969 Annual Report, p. vii.

Chapter Three

[1]"Human Resources Worth?—1.7 Billion," *University of Michigan Today,* Spring 1971, p. 2.

Chapter Four

[1]The problems of accounting for human assets in corporate annual reports are examined in Chapter Two.

[2]For the full history and description of the R. G. Barry system, see reference in the Annotated Bibliography, Robert L. Woodruff, "Human Resource Accounting," *Canadian Chartered Accountant,* September 1970, pp. 2-7.

[3]R. G. Barry Corporation 1971 Annual Report, p. 17.

[4]Woodruff, "Human Resource Accounting," p. 2.

[5]Gordon Zacks, "Objectives of Human Resource Accounting at the R. G. Barry Corporation," in R. Lee Brummet and others (eds.), *Human Resource Accounting: Development and Implementation in Industry* (Ann Arbor: Foundation for Research on Human Behavior, 1969), p. 68.

[6]Woodruff, "Human Resource Accounting," p. 2.

[7]Zacks, "Objectives," pp. 67–68.

[8]Zacks, "Objectives," p. 69.

[9]Robert L. Woodruff, Jr., "What Price People?", *Personnel Administrator,* January–February 1969, p. 18. Reprinted by permission of the American Society for Personnel Administration.

[10]William C. Pyle, "Monitoring Human Resources 'On Line'," *Michigan Business Review,* July 1970, pp. 19–32.

[11]R. Lee Brummet, Eric G. Flamholtz, and William C. Pyle, "Human Resource Measurement: A Challenge for Accountants," *Accounting Review,* April 1968, p. 224.

[12]Woodruff, "What Price People?", p. 19.

[13]Woodruff, "What Price People?", p. 20.

[14]These forms, together with related instructions, can be found in Robert L. Woodruff and Robert Whitman, "The Behavioral Aspects of Accounting Data for Performance Evaluation at R. G. Barry Corporation (with special reference to Human Resource Accounting)," in Thomas J. Burns (ed.), *The Behavioral Aspects of Accounting Data for Performance Evaluation* (Columbus: College of Administrative Science, Ohio State University, 1970), pp. 23–34. Selected forms can also be found in Robert L. Woodruff, "Development of a Human Resource Accounting System at the R. G. Barry Corporation," in Brummet and others (eds.), *Human Resource Accounting,* pp. 73–84.

[15]Woodruff, "Human Resource Accounting," p. 5.

[16]Pyle, "Monitoring Human Resources," pp. 26–27.

[17]Michael O. Alexander, "Investments in People," *Canadian Chartered Accountant,* July 1971, p. 40.

[18]Alexander, "Investments in People," p. 40.

[19]Alexander, "Investments in People," p. 40.

[20]Alexander, "Investments in People," p. 41.

[21]Alexander, "Investments in People," p. 41.

[22]Alexander, "Investments in People," p. 42.

[23]Parts of this section draw upon Eric G. Flamholtz, "Human Resource Accounting: Measuring Positional Replacement Cost," *Human Resource Management,* Spring 1973, pp. 8–16. Reprinted by permission of the Division of Management Education, Graduate School of Business Administration, University of Michigan.

Chapter Five

[1]This section draws upon Eric G. Flamholtz and Richard A. Kaumeyer, "Human Resource Replacement Cost and Personnel Decisions: A Field Study," *Human Resource Planning,* Vol. 3, No. 3, 1980, pp. 111–138.

[2]This section draws upon Eric G. Flamholtz and George G. Geis, "The Development and Implementation of a Replacement Cost Model for Measuring

Human Capital: A Field Study," *Personnel Review,* Vol. 13, No. 2, 1984, pp. 25-35.

Chapter Six

[1]The discussion of the model of determinants of an individual's value draws upon Eric G. Flamholtz, "Toward a Theory of Human Resource Value in Formal Organizations," *Accounting Review,* October 1972, pp. 666-678, by permission of *Accounting Review.*

[2]The following sources are useful background reading for a complete understanding of the model of a group's value discussed in a subsequent section of this chapter: Rensis Likert, *The Human Organization: Its Management and Value* (New York: McGraw-Hill, 1967), especially chap. 8; and Rensis Likert and David G. Bowers, "Organizational Theory and Human Resource Accounting," *American Psychologist,* June 1969, pp. 585-592.

[3]Ludwig Von Mises, *Human Action* (New Haven: Yale University Press, 1963), p. 121.

[4]Irving Fisher, *The Nature of Capital and Income* (London: Macmillan, 1927), p. 189.

[5]This notion of value is attributable to Irving Fisher; see *Nature of Capital and Income,* pp. 188, 202.

[6]Floyd C. Mann, "Toward an Understanding of the Leadership Role in Formal Organization," in Robert Dubin and others (eds.), *Leadership and Productivity* (San Francisco: Chandler, 1965), as cited in David G. Bowers and Stanley E. Seashore, "Predicting Organizational Effectiveness with a Four-Factor Theory of Leadership," *Administrative Science Quarterly,* September 1966, p. 245.

[7]Elizabeth Duffy, *Activation and Behavior* (New York: Wiley, 1962), as cited in William E. Scott, Jr., "Activation Theory and Task Design," *Organization Behavior and Human Performance,* September 1966, p. 11.

[8]Daniel Katz and Robert L. Kahn, *The Social Psychology of Organizations* (New York: Wiley, 1966), p. 50.

[9]Scott, "Activation Theory," pp. 3-30. For a discussion of the mechanisms through which the dimensions of tasks interact with the characteristics of individuals to influence role performance, see J. Richard Hackman, "Nature of the Task as a Determiner of Job Behavior," *Personnel Psychology,* Winter 1969, pp. 435-444.

[10]Daniel Katz, "The Motivational Basis of Organizational Behavior," *Behavioral Science,* April 1964, p. 137.

[11]Basil S. Georgopoulos, Gerald M. Mahoney, and Nyle W. Jones, Jr., "A Path-Goal Approach to Productivity," *Journal of Applied Psychology,* 41, 1957, pp. 345-353.

[12]Ian C. Ross and Alvin Zander, "Need Satisfactions and Employee Performance," *Personnel Psychology,* Autumn 1957, pp. 327, 338.

[13]Glenn P. Fournet, M. K. Distefano, Jr., and Margaret W. Pryer, "Job Satisfaction: Issues and Problems," *Personnel Psychology,* Summer 1966, p. 176.

[14]Arthur H. Brayfield and Walter H. Crockett, "Employee Attitudes and Employee Performance," *Psychological Bulletin,* September 1955, pp. 416, 421.

[15]This argument is supported by the conclusion of Schwab and Cummings, who reviewed the various theories of the relation between performance and satisfaction. They stated that: "We are frankly pessimistic about

the value of additional satisfaction-performance theorizing at this time. The theoretically inclined might do better to work on a theory of satisfaction or a theory of performance. Such concepts are clearly complex enough to justify their own theories." See Donald P. Schwab and Larry L. Cummings, "Theories of Performance and Satisfaction: A Review," *Industrial Relations,* October 1970, p. 420.

[16]Indeed, Porter and Lawler have developed a model of the relationship between managerial attitudes and performance in which there is circularity in the relationship between performance and satisfaction. See Lyman W. Porter and Edward E. Lawler III, *Managerial Attitudes and Performance* (Homewood, Ill.: Richard D. Irwin, 1968), especially chaps. 2 and 8.

[17]Rensis Likert and David G. Bowers, "Improving the Accuracy of P/L Reports by Estimating the Change in Dollar Value of the Human Organization," *Michigan Business Review,* March 1973, pp. 15-24.

[18]For a discussion of this research, see Rensis Likert's classic book, *New Patterns of Management* (New York: McGraw-Hill, 1961).

[19]Likert and Bowers, "Improving the Accuracy of P/L Reports," p. 17. Reprinted by permission of *Michigan Business Review* and the authors.

[20]Bowers and Seashore, "Predicting Organizational Effectiveness," pp. 238-263.

[21]James C. Taylor and David G. Bowers, *Survey of Organizations* (Ann Arbor: University of Michigan, 1972), p. 83.

[22]Taylor and Bowers, *Survey of Organizations,* p. 84.

[23]Likert, *The Human Organization,* chap. 8.

[24]Likert, *The Human Organization,* chap. 2.

Chapter Seven

[1]Ronald A. Howard, *Dynamic Programming and Markov Processes* (Cambridge: M.I.T. Press, 1960), p. 3.

[2]For an earlier version of this model, see Eric G. Flamholtz, "A Model for Human Resource Valuation: A Stochastic Process with Service Rewards," *Accounting Review,* April 1971, pp. 253-267.

[3]This section draws upon Eric G. Flamholtz, "A Model for Human Resource Valuation: A Stochastic Process with Service Rewards," *Accounting Review,* April 1971, pp. 253-267, by permission of *Accounting Review.*

[4]For evidence of the feasibility of measuring the cost incurred in acquiring human resources, see R. Lee Brummet, William C. Pyle, and Eric G. Flamholtz, "Human Resource Accounting in Industry," *Personnel Administration,* July-August 1969, pp. 34-46. See also Chapters Two and Three of this book.

[5]Raymond J. Chambers, *Towards a General Theory of Accounting* (Melbourne: Australian Society of Accountants, 1963), p. 29.

[6]James C. Hekimian and Curtis H. Jones, "Put People on Your Balance Sheet," *Harvard Business Review,* January-February 1967, p. 108.

[7]Roger H. Hermanson, *Accounting for Human Assets,* Occasional Paper no. 14 (East Lansing: Bureau of Business and Economic Research, Michigan State University, 1964), pp. 15-17.

[8]Baruch Lev and Aba Schwartz, "On the Use of the Economic Concept of Human Capital in Financial Statements," *Accounting Review,* January 1971, pp. 103-112.

[9]Hekimian and Jones, "People on Your Balance Sheet," p. 108.

[10]Brummet, Flamholtz, and Pyle, "Human Resource Measurement: A Challenge for Accountants," pp. 222-223.

[11]Hermanson, *Accounting for Human Assets,* pp. 7-11.

[12]Hermanson, *Accounting for Human Assets,* p. 9.

[13]Likert and Bowers, "Improving the Accuracy of P/L Reports," p. 21. Reprinted by permission of *Michigan Business Review* and the authors.

[14]Likert and Bowers, "Improving the Accuracy of P/L Reports," p. 21.

[15]Sloan, *My Years with General Motors,* p. 326.

[16]Likert, *The Human Organization,* p. 103.

[17]Likert, *The Human Organization,* p. 103.

[18]Hermanson, *Accounting for Human Assets,* p. 9.

[19]Hermanson, *Accounting for Human Assets,* p. 17.

[20]Lev and Schwartz, "On the Use of the Economic Concept of Human Capital," p. 105.

[21]Lev and Schwartz, "On the Use of the Economic Concept of Human Capital," p. 105.

[22]Lev and Schwartz, "On the Use of the Economic Concept of Human Capital," p. 106. Expression (2) in this summary corresponds to Expression (4) in Lev and Schwartz.

[23]Lev and Schwartz, "On the Use of the Economic Concept of Human Capital," p. 106. Expression (3) in this summary corresponds to Expression (5) in Lev and Schwartz.

Chapter Eight

[1]Committee to Prepare a Statement of Basic Accounting Theory, *A Statement of Basic Accounting Theory,* pp. 12-13.

[2]For a discussion of the subjective expected utility concept, see Ward Edwards, "Utility, Subjective Probability, Their Interaction, and Variance Preferences," *Journal of Conflict Resolution,* Vol. 6, No. 1, 1962, pp. 42-51.

[3]See, for example, Eugene Galanter, "The Direct Measurement of Utility and Subjective Probability," *American Journal of Psychology,* March 1962, pp. 208-220.

[4]Galanter, "Direct Measurement," pp. 208-220.

[5]See James C. Taylor and David G. Bowers, *The Survey of Organizations: A Machine-Scored Standardized Questionnaire Instrument* (Ann Arbor: Institute for Social Research, University of Michigan, 1972). Copyright 1967, 1968, 1969, 1970, 1972 by the University of Michigan.

[6]William Evan, "A Systems Model of Organizational Climate," in T. Tagiuri and G. Litwin (eds.), *Organizational Climate* (Cambridge, Mass.: Harvard University Press, 1968), p. 110.

[7]Taylor and Bowers, *Survey of Organizations,* p. 63.

[8]Taylor and Bowers, *Survey of Organizations,* pp. 70-74.

[9]Taylor and Bowers, *Survey of Organizations,* p. 73.

[10]Taylor and Bowers, *Survey of Organizations,* chap. 9.

Chapter Nine

[1]Abraham H. Maslow, *Eupsychian Management* (Homewood, Ill.: Richard D. Irwin, 1965), p. 1.

[2]Maslow, *Eupsychian Management,* p. 1.

[3]Maslow, *Eupsychian Management,* p. 217.

[4]For a discussion of transfer pricing, see Gordon Schillinglaw, *Cost Accounting: Analysis and Control,* 3rd ed. (Homewood, Ill.: Richard D. Irwin, 1972), pp. 593–609.

[5]Robert N. Anthony, "Notes on Transfer Prices," in Robert M. Anthony, John Dearden, and Richard F. Vancil (eds.), *Management Control Systems* (Homewood, Ill.: Richard D. Irwin, 1965), p. 259.

[6]Anthony, Dearden, and Vancil, "Financial Performance Centers; Transfer Pricing," in *Management Control Systems,* p. 249.

Chapter Ten

[1]Frederick S. Hillier and Gerald G. Lieberman, *Introduction to Operations Research* (San Francisco: Holden-Day, 1980).

Index